Praise for *Not in His Image*

"Sometimes a book changes the world. *Not in His Image* is such a book. It is clear, stimulating, well-researched, and sure to outrage the experts. Take it from a scientist: the 'experts' are often wrong. In fact, a hallmark of breakthroughs is that they are usually well-researched and outrage the 'experts.' Science shows the importance of trusting clear thinking about direct evidence. This book is full of both. Get it. Improve not just your own life, but civilization's chances for survival."

—ROGER PAYNE, Ph.D., MacArthur Fellow,
president of Ocean Alliance, author of *Among Whales*

"John Lamb Lash's *Not in His Image* is a rare achievement, combining impeccable scholarship with remarkable visionary insight. In a breathtaking tour de force, the author provides a profound analysis of the history of Judaism, Christianity, and Islam and their connections to the patriarchal system. He identifies the deep roots of the intrinsic problems of these three religions—perpetrator-victim emphasis and salvationist ideology—and points out their relationship to the alienation and agony of modern humanity. This book is a must for everybody who is trying to understand the psychospiritual currents underlying the present global crisis."

—STANISLAV GROF, M.D., author of
When the Impossible Happens and *The Holotropic Mind*

"An extraordinary and profound book. *Not in His Image* is a blessing, and a warning that we must cease taking the terrible advice of Christianity . . . and that we must instead re-inhabit our own joyful, painful, mortal, beautiful bodies and fight for our lives and for the lives of those we love. This book points the way home."

—DERRICK JENSEN, author of *The Culture of Make Believe*
and *A Language Older Than Words*

"What we know about the divine comes by way of three paths—through the spectacle of nature, through the testimony of spiritual seekers, and through our own inner experience, as in meditation and mystical communion. John Lamb Lash seeks to renew our understanding of all three paths, and thus to renew our sense of the divine. In particular, he challenges the otherworldly creeds that have come down to us in Christianity, Judaism, and Islam, and to recover the Earth-based religions that preceded them. Those ecologically wise religions flourished, he reminds us, not only among the native peoples of the Western Hemisphere but also in ancient Europe. By reclaiming this pagan heritage, he argues, we can begin to cure the pathologies of genocide, war, and environmental degradation that afflict the modern world."

—SCOTT RUSSELL SANDERS, author of
A Private History of Awe and *Staying Put*

"John Lash's heretical book is a precious act of spiritual disobedience that seeks to save the world from Salvationism. Lash opens new ground between myth and ecology, and helps one feel what the planet feels. He proposes direct knowing and moving beyond belief, and advocates animism as a proposition to test. He leaves the future open and in need of human imagination. Humanity is implicated in the future of the living planet, but Lash exercises caution when making suppositions about our role as a species. This book is learned, courageous, and full of insights. Some may find it challenging and even shocking, but it is an important read for those interested in life on Earth. It is made for readers to chew on, rather than believe."

—JEREMY NARBY, anthropologist, author of
The Cosmic Serpent and *Intelligence in Nature*

NOT IN
HIS
IMAGE

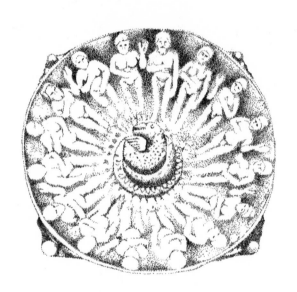

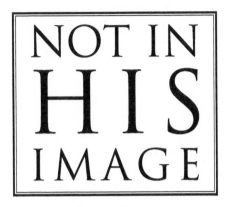

NOT IN HIS IMAGE

GNOSTIC VISION,
SACRED ECOLOGY,
AND THE FUTURE
OF BELIEF

15TH ANNIVERSARY EDITION

JOHN LAMB LASH

CHELSEA GREEN PUBLISHING
WHITE RIVER JUNCTION, VERMONT
LONDON, UK

First edition published in 2006. 15th anniversary edition 2021.

Printed in the United States of America.
First printing September 2021.
10 9 8 7 6 5 4 3 2   22 23 24 25

Front cover image of *Eleusis archaeological site, Greece,* by Kostas Xiloparkiotis
(www.kostas66.com).

ISBN 978-1-64502-136-0 (paperback) | ISBN 978-1-64502-137-7 (ebook)

The Library of Congress has cataloged the first edition as follows:
Lash, John.
Not in his image : gnostic vision, sacred ecology, and the future of belief / John Lamb Lash.
p. cm.
Includes bibliographical references and index.
ISBN-13: 978-1-933392-40-0
ISBN-10: 1-933392-40-1
ISBN-13: 978-1-931498-92-0 (pbk.)
ISBN-10: 1-931498-92-X (pbk.)
1. Religion. 2. Gnosticism. 3. Paganism. 4. Monotheism. I. Title.
BL51.L37 2006
299'.932—dc22
2006018250

Chelsea Green Publishing
85 North Main Street, Suite 120
White River Junction, Vermont USA

Somerset House
London, UK

www.chelseagreen.com

For the mystics of the future

"A kid, thou hast fallen into milk."

CONTENTS

THE ONCE AND FUTURE HERESY

N*ot in His Image* came out in November 2006 as I was approaching my sixty-first birthday. On that day, December 3, a review appeared in the Sunday literary supplement of the *Los Angeles Times*. The reviewer averred that I had achieved my stated mission to complete Nietzsche's critique of Christianity, "that crapulent faith." So far, so good. Then he discounted me for delving into the dubious terrain of paranormal psychology and the ET/UFO phenomenon. It is the only mainstream review I have ever received. To this day, there are precious few even in the alternative media who openly dare discuss me or my work. The Gnostic message is the biggest taboo on the planet. Always has been, always will be. It is the once and future heresy.

At the winter solstice of that year, I was in Gaucín, Spain, a spectacular white village with a view (elevation: 1,800 feet) across the Straits of Gibraltar to the mountains of Africa, where I had been staying on and off for some years. There, at a remote spot I called Infinity Ridge, something had happened in 2003 that set me on course to write this book. Later, I jokingly described the event by analogy to a telephone switchboard. A call came in from humanity asking to talk to the mother planet. The switchboard operator (yours truly) replied: "Stay on the line and I'll put you through to her." I leave it to you, noble reader, to investigate how that one-liner has played out.

Against Authority

Over the years, I have often reflected on the difficulties posed by a book that tackles not merely one or two large topics, but half a dozen or more—a big no-no in publishing. A book titled, say, *Against Patriarchy* would already be a lot to handle. Add to that pre-Christian European history, shamanism, the Mysteries, ecopsychology, noetics, Gaia theory, the Dead Sea Scrolls, the ET/UFO phenomenon, and a few other mind-toppling topics which escape me at the moment, then throw in a complex myth that recounts the biography of the living Earth and. . . . Well, I can only assume that the challenge of reading such a monstrous tome must in some respects be proportional to the challenge of writing it.

Thankfully, many people have assured me of what I hardly dared presume: The switchboard operator did actually make the connection. I could not ask for more. This book initiates bonding with the Wisdom Goddess *and* addresses what works against that bonding. Almost all the feedback I've received attests to the same takeaway, as if the responses had been cut and pasted from a single document. Readers unanimously assert that *Not in His Image* liberated them from decades of religious indoctrination. It delivered the coup de grace to patriarchy.

My attack on patriarchy often conflates it with salvationist ideology. This tactic was central to my aim, but was it overkill? The word search function showed me forty-seven uses of that word, reduced in this book to twenty-eight. Even then I wondered if overuse of the term might undermine its impact. To defy patriarchy successively requires defining it accurately. Had I done that?

Fortunately, events of the day in 2021 reinforce my argument. The Gnostics warned about the deceit and subversion of the Archons, a.k.a. the Authorities or Rulers, those who govern. Patriarchy means far more than governance by, or dominance of, men. Divine paternalism is a cognate of patriarchy which itself is a generic term for the enforcement of authority in all forms and guises. For instance, the authority of the transhumanist technocrats pushing the Great Reset. Dominator culture, another cognate, is by no means the sole prerogative of men. *Not in His Image* cites a few feminist scholars, and those passages can stand as written, but today I regard feminism as a perfidious and tiresome strain of cultural Marxism, totally opposed to the true cause of the Divine Feminine. Social leadership by men is not categorically wrong, but with the wrong men, it is. With the wrong women, even worse.

The Great Reset is the endgame of patriarchal authority and certainly the worst tyrannical deceit in human history. Men and women are equally complicit in the Covid-19 scam—a proven medical fraud, in case you missed that memo. The aberration of theocracy among the ancient Hebrews plays forward to the "Coviet Regime" (my neologism) of the globalist overlords. The ultimate goal of the Zaddikim, who are holier than thou, is to dictate to others how they shall live and enforce their mandate with lies, deceit, threats, and genocidal violence. Historically, the teachers of the Mysteries were on the front line of that assault.

But the essential message of the Mysteries survives in this book. Can it make a difference at the moment it is most needed?

Mystic Testimony

After 2006, I spent eleven more years in the Serranía de Ronda, a sorcerer's paradise in the brutally beautiful heart of Andalucía. Visitors came and went, but most of that time I lived in virtual retreat, wandering the arroyos and mesas in the majestic company of vultures. I did not anticipate the richness and magnitude of what was coming my way through contact with the Aeonic Mother, Gaia-Sophia. Even today, it dazzles me. Ever since then, I have held the line of communication open.

I have spoken and written at length about my outrageous claim to communicate directly with the mind of the planet. I have always insisted that transactions with the planetary animal mother (PAM, a term of endearment) are not unique and exclusive to myself. My leading intent as an exponent of "the living Gnosis today" is to guide and teach others how to do the same. In 2006 I was somewhat guarded about aspects of the exposition based directly on my mystical investigations, as they might be called. The introduction stated that "I present scholarly research side by side with the evidence of my own mystical and shamanic experiences," but I did not follow up with first-person language in those passages where I describe the Organic Light, cognitive ecstasy, and other intimate details of Gnostic practice.

In this edition I have been rather less coy, but still discreet concerning my experimentation with the telestic method of the Mysteries. Why be shy? Two reasons, basically. First, direct encounter with the telluric power of the Wisdom Goddess is not given to everyone, and handling it correctly is a demanding discipline. "The Grail selects its own," Wolfram von Eschenbach wrote in *Parzival* (c. 1220 CE). That being so, any description of the ecstatic trance (*theoria*, "beholding") of the Mysteries risks sounding elitist, and I do not want to foster that impression in a way that might discourage others. Second, that sublime encounter obliterates the ordinary mental boundaries of the human animal, and the download that comes with it is fast and vast, exceeding the retention of the individual who receives it. This is precisely why Gnostic seers performed the ritual in groups, as I have also done on some occasions.

All that being so, I have worked diligently to make the encounter with the Wisdom Goddess accessible by parallel and alternative practices. Planetary Tantra presents the toolkit for grounded and provable interaction with the PSI, the plenary sovereign intelligence of the Earth. Fortunately, I now share both the method and results of autogenic training with a network of student-allies around the world.* The current platform for this purpose is Nemeta.org, the Sophianic School of Arts and Sciences, launched in September 2018.

REVISION POINTS

I have not changed this book in any basic way, but I have revised three chapters, reworked passages here and there, and factored in some new elements. The role of Aeon Christos in episode 2 of the Fallen Goddess Scenario (FGS) remains as it was, but chapter 14 now features a different Aeon, Ekklesia, the Symbiont. The intervention of the other Aeons to support Sophia in the management of terrestrial life does not change, but the agency that accomplishes it does. The action of the Symbiont has far-reaching implications for the issue of species-self identity in chapter 23, also modified quite extensively. I revisit the Christ/Christos conundrum and double down on the deceit of universality: that is, the claim that collective good can be achieved by appealing to a generic sense

---

* Autogenics: a technique of subject-world interaction created by German psychiatrist J. H. Schultz in 1932. Commonly called biofeedback training.

of transracial humanity in disregard of genetic differences, cultural contrasts, and racial distinctions.

Chapter 22, "Divine Imagination," is retitled "Sophia's Correction." This event may finally come to definition at the moment when the transhumanist overlords, cohorts of the Archons, threaten to remake humanity in their image: "to change what it means to be human," as declared in the mission statement of the Great Reset. The Archontic Lie that humanity is made in His image has failed on religious grounds, but the dementia behind it persists. The bizarre trope of the "aborted fetus," unique to Gnostic cosmology, is now demonstrable in pharmaceutical elixirs that contain fetal matter such as the MRC-5 cell strain (cited in chapter 20). Big Pharma admits that some variants of the Covid jab can disrupt placental formation and result in abortions. Moderna openly states that their product is not a vaccine but an "operating system" intended for mRNA-directed genetic modification, not to mention track and trace capabilities. Planet-wide vaccination is the ritual of the Archontic eucharist. The transhumanist psychopaths intend to run the social order on a data operating system that cancels and overrides the operation of natural human intelligence. Gnostics warned about "the consummation of the work of the Archons," and now, well, brace for impact—here it is.

DIVINE BIRTHRIGHT

The 2006 edition of *Not in His Image* contains the oldest published version of the Fallen Goddess Scenario, comparable to legacy software. After at least twenty reworkings over a dozen years, I released FGS 1.0 in August 2020. (See sophianicmyth.org, introduced by a four-minute video.) The current iteration of the sacred narrative brings it to FGS 7.7. Within the limits of this preface, I cannot provide even a hint of how the narrative evolved that far, what such a progression entailed, or who is engaged with me in elaborating it today. Likewise, I cannot offer in this revision more than a few allusions regarding how Gnostic teachings are relevant to the coronavirus hoax and the alien-mind, technocratic nightmare of the Great Reset. I rely on my noble readers to draw the obvious connections.

The Sophianic myth is the sacred birthright of the human species. It is, of course, a vast mythopoetic scenario to be embraced by heart and learned with commitment. It can inspire all races to achieve the standard of the Anthropos, *arete*, the excellence innate to our species. That commitment carries a moral force that is paramount and incomparable. In the introduction I cite Nietzsche: "Wisdom is a woman who never loves anyone but a warrior." When I first read that line at the age of sixteen, I did not know who the wisdom woman is. Now I do. Since *Not in His Image* came out in 2006, I have realized more than ever that the role of the warrior is imperative if Sophia's Correction is to be accomplished. Extensive studies in historical revision—the investigation of alleged events in the accepted historical narrative, weighed against the factual evidence that supports or refutes that narrative—have reinforced that conviction. Today I argue for the action of a "warrior class" capable of eliminating psychopaths and the enemies of life by whatever means required. That would be the completion of the destiny of Parzival. How it might play out, I cannot say. Finally, I am merely an ancestral bard announcing the swan song of Kali Yuga. A passage from *Agamemnon* (458 B.C.E.) by Aeschylus expresses my feelings as this book comes to the world in its fifteenth year:

> I declare on authority the auspicious venture
> of men who command with genuine power,
> for the age that gave me birth and lives in me
> inspires me divinely to daring persuasion,
> the prowess of the warrior's song.

JLL
March 2021
Galicia, Spain

THE CASE FOR AWE

When the people lack a proper sense
of awe, some terrible fate decided by
the universe at large will befall them.

—Lao Tzu, Tao Te Ching, 72

Destiny works in some wonderfully quirky ways. It could be said that the book you hold came to be written because in his childhood the author had buckteeth.

From an early age I was a voracious reader, but growing up in the coastal village of Friendship, Maine—population nine hundred souls, about a third belonging to the Lash clan—did not provide me with access to a wide range of books. Thanks to my overbite, I had to take time off from school and go "down east" (up the coast) to Bangor, the only town in the region with an orthodontist. It was quite an excursion for the family, as we did not get out of the village very often. Apart from New York City, where I occasionally visited, Bangor was the biggest city I knew all through my teens.

The trip took an hour and a half each way on Route 1, but the session at the orthodontist rarely took half an hour. Although we were too poor to have much spending money (my stepfather was a native Mainer and lobster fisherman), we usually hung around Bangor for a couple of hours, just because we were there. Occasionally, we even had lunch in a café. That was a major event. I carefully saved the money I made caulking boats and mowing lawns for the Bangor trips. While the family window-shopped, I would go off on my own and scout around. My forays yielded two momentous discoveries. One was Viner's music shop where I discovered jazz and percussion (Enoch Light and the Light Brigade), not to mention a vivacious blond salesgirl with whom I flirted outrageously. The other was Bett's Stationery Shop and Bookstore.

Bangor is a college town, being the largest city close to the campus of the University of Maine at Orono, up the Stillwater River. In the back of Bett's was a book nook where they stocked authors of interest to the college crowd. This was a hallowed spot to me. I had never seen such names and titles, but I seemed to be drawn infallibly to the ones suited to my spirit. At Bett's I found *Ulysses* and *Journey to the End of the Night*, two novels that had a profound effect on my views on literature and life, respectively. And I found other books that determined my direction in life: an existentialist anthology called *The Search for Being* with selections from Schelling and Sartre, the plays of Samuel Beckett, the poetry of W. B. Yeats and Salvatore Quasimodo. Then, one day toward the end of my three-year orthodontic ordeal, I came across *Thus Spake Zarathustra* in the translation of R. J. Hollingdale. I knew something of Nietzsche but had never read a single word he wrote. The moment I began to riffle the book, I was electrified. When I joined my parents and sister for lunch, I rudely continued to read through the meal. And in the back seat of the car on the way home, I stayed glued to the book. My excitement was so intense that I had to read some passages aloud. I started with a section from *The Gay Science* (cited in the introduction), containing the famous announcement that "God is dead," then jumped to Zarathustra's prologue:

> I teach you the Superman. Man is something that should be overcome. What have you done to overcome him?
>
> The Superman is the meaning of the Earth. Let your will say: The Superman shall be the meaning of the Earth.
>
> I entreat you, my brothers, *remain true to the Earth*, and do not believe those who speak to you of superterrestrial hopes. They are poisoners, whether they know it or not.

In the front seat my parents sat in stunned silence. They were timid people with no intellectual interests, no notions of philosophy. My stepfather barely eked out a living—not surprising, since his livelihood depended on elusive crustaceans whose mating habits had (in those days) never been observed by our species. To my distress and disappointment, my parents often expressed perplexity and fear about the difficulties of survival. Their spiritual life consisted of lukewarm allegiance to the fundamentalist cult of Advent Christians that dominated the village. I could not believe that I was finding in Nietzsche exactly what I wanted to say to them about themselves, and about the beliefs they held, which I was expected to accept as my beliefs. All the way home I kept reading, caught in the manic exaltation Nietzsche must have felt when he wrote them. In "On Reading and Writing," I hit upon my personal credo:

> You look up when you desire to be exalted. And I look down, because I am exalted.
>
> Who among you can at the same time laugh and be exalted?
>
> Who climbs upon the highest mountains laughs at all tragedies, real or imaginary.
>
> Untroubled, scornful, outrageous—that is how wisdom wants us to be: she is a woman who never loves anyone but a warrior.

The words were engraved in my memory the first time I saw them. In the months that followed, coming up to my seventeenth birthday, I delved deeply into Nietzsche's "transvaluation of all values," centered on his radical critique of Christianity. Two points struck me as totally right: Christian religion defines morality by a belief system based on a master-slave relationship, and rooted in resentment of the raw beauty and power of the life force. These two insights liberated me, for Nietzsche was stating something I already sensed that lay beyond my capacity to articulate. But at the same time, they burdened me. When I read more of Nietzsche, I realized that he had not gone far enough or deep enough in his analysis of "that crapulent faith." So I made a commitment to myself. I swore to finish what Nietzsche had begun. I vowed to think through and live out his critique of Christianity to the end.

This book is the result of that vow, made some forty years ago by a bucktoothed teenager whose dental defect led him to this destiny.

HUMANITY BETRAYED

All through my life I have faced a paradox: feeling compassion for humanity and, at the same time, suffering a certain repulsion for it. Eventually I came to understand that the repulsion I felt was not for human existence as such, nor was it merely a projection of self-repulsion on others. Rather, it was a spontaneous, gut-felt response to human *behaviors* and *attitudes*. (The attitudes that inform behavior are *values*, and these are what Nietzsche sought to shatter and recreate.) Even as a child, it seemed to me that certain forms of human behavior are incompatible with genuine humanness. This may not seem like such a radical view, since most readers would agree that some human acts are repulsive, unworthy of humanity. But I was in a terrible fix quite early in life because I was repulsed by actions and attitudes that were normally regarded as admirable—in particular, religious righteousness and moral rectitude. What the world at large considered to exemplify the best in human nature, I found quite deplorable.

Living with this conflicted feeling, I came to realize something that is extremely difficult to define: namely, how humanity stands in danger of betraying itself *through what it holds as its highest ideals*. I wondered how such a weird proposition could be true, how the self-betrayal of an entire species could actually be effectuated. In time I realized that I could not even suspect such a betrayal were I not adhering to an innate standard of humanity by which I was judging human behavior, including my own. But what could that standard be? How did I acquire it? Why did other people not have it as well? How could I apply my sense of values, the code of misanthropic humanism I found in Nietzsche, in a compassionate way? And even if I came to define my "innate standard of humanity," and live up to it, what then? How would this dispose me to the rest of the world? And most importantly, would I then be able to see how humanity's self-betrayal plays out? Even how it might be averted?

Such are the questions that have troubled me throughout my life. To a great extent, this book is my attempt to resolve these questions. It has been quite a challenge, and I expect that the "exposé" of humanity's self-betrayal in these pages will pose quite a challenge to some readers.

I ask for a fair hearing, and not to be taken for someone who claims to have found the ultimate solution to the troubles that afflict the human species. I think, however, that I have made the deepest cut in spiritual terms, going to the hidden heart of the betrayal, the place where human dignity is rotted out. Having shared my mission with many people over the years, I am convinced there is a growing perception that something is fundamentally wrong with mainstream religious values. Each day, I see more evidence that some people at least are prepared to face the terrifying question: Why do we betray our humanity in the name of our spiritual principles?

This book is a call of alarm, but also a call for inspiration. The following pages contain a heady mix of history, science, theology, anthropology, myth, and personal testimony of mystical experience. Above and beyond the several points it develops, this book presents a case for awe. This poses a dilemma, however, because the case for awe cannot be proven by scholarly method, yet that is the approach I have taken in my argument. Readers will fare more easily with this book if they bear in mind that I frame my argument in scholarly terms, but the basic convictions from which I write neither derive from, nor rely on, scholarly proof and academic method.

To make the case for awe, I go back to the rapturous bond with nature that was celebrated in Pagan religions in the classical world. I return to the Mysteries. My account of Paganism may not resemble what you are accustomed to accept as history. But I submit that the supreme value of the honest study of history—as distinguished from blind acceptance of historical fables—is to show us *how we have departed from the proper course of our evolution as a species*. The purpose of the Mysteries was to keep us on course. I am not the only person on the planet today who is convinced that we as a species have been torn out of a primal connection—our bond with Gaia, the living planet. A good many voices in our time have said as much. But in this book I am saying something more. I am saying that our connection to the living Earth is not merely a matter of survival, it is essential to our way of knowing ourselves, defining who we are as a species. The *species-self connection*, as I call it, confers the sense of our singularity, our unique (but not superior) potential in the Gaian life-plan. I will show how practical visionaries known as Gnostics practiced and taught that connection. When their sacred tradition was destroyed, we were set on a sure course for self-annihilation.

The *historical* view of humanity's self-betrayal presented in this book may be the one version of our story that can save us from the nightmare of history. Such is my highest aspiration.

THE SONATA FORM

This book is constructed in the form of a sonata of four movements. Rather than straightforward, scholarly exposition (though there is a good deal of that), it works by a symphonic play of themes or leitmotifs. The all-pervasive theme is the goddess Sophia, whose name is wisdom, whose sensory body is the Earth. My first objective is to recover and restore the Sophianic vision of the Mysteries celebrated in ancient Europe and the Near East. The guardians of this vision were called *gnostikoi*, "those who know as the gods know." To correlate Mystery teachings with Gaia theory and deep ecology—the second objective of this book—cannot be done without looking closely at *what destroyed* the Sophianic vision of the living Earth, and how it was able to do so. The genocide of native spirituality in the classical world went on for centuries, but a cover-up has largely concealed this fact, and continues to this day. To expose the cover-up and reveal both the cause and scope of the destruction so wrought is the third objective of this book. Finally, the fourth objective is to complete Nietzsche's critique by showing what is basically wrong, indeed, pathologically dangerous, in salvationist theology and Judeo-Christian ethics.

Part 1, "Conquest and Conversion," focuses on the third objective: to show the cause and scope of the destruction of the classical world. It describes the pre-Christian spirituality of Europe, a world unified by Celtic culture and overseen by seers from the ancient sanctuaries of Egypt and the Levant. To bring the Gnostics to life in flesh and blood, I offer the example of the Pagan initiate Hypatia, who taught at the famous library of Alexandria. Her murder by a Christian mob in 415 c.e. marks the dawn of the Dark Ages. The conquest of Europe involved a genocidal program on a monumental scale, combining the military might of the

Roman Empire with the religious fanaticism of Christianity. Chapters 4, 5, and 6 describe how the genophobic ideology of a Jewish splinter cult in Palestine came to infect the entire Empire. In the Zaddikim of the Dead Sea reside the true origins of Christianity. When the messianic obsessions of that cult were adopted by Saint Paul, a forced recruit who hijacked its secret teachings, a new belief system erupted upon the world. Salvationism promised liberation for the immortal soul, by contrast to Pagan religion which offered liberation from selfhood through ecstatic immersion in the life force, Eros. For salvationism to prevail, the traditions of Pagan religion and the Pagan attitude of tolerance toward religion had to be brutally eradicated. This is a lot of history in three chapters, I know. But the high compression of my argument here is supported by research on the Dead Sea Scrolls, documents that tell the unknown story of how Christianity was born.

Part 2, "A Story to Guide the Species," highlights my first objective: to recover the Sophianic vision of the Pagan Mysteries. Opening with an explanation of the rare Gnostic books discovered in Egypt in December 1945, it goes deeply into the shamanic tradition of visionary practices dedicated to Sophia, the Wisdom Goddess. I show that the Gnostics, who called themselves *telestai*, "those who are aimed," preserved and transmitted that tradition, which originated in Neolithic times. Here I present scholarly research side by side with the evidence of my own mystical and shamanic experiences. Some readers may find this juxtaposition awkward or off-putting. It may help to know that I am (to my knowledge) the only scholar writing on the mystical experiences described in the Nag Hammadi codices who admits to having had such experiences. In any other field of research, isn't that the very least one asks of a writer—firsthand experience of the subject matter? Conventional scholars would risk their reputations, if not their tenured positions, by such an admission. For me that is not a concern.

Part 2 develops my second objective as well: to correlate the Mysteries and Gnostic cosmology with Gaia theory. Here again, some readers may be puzzled by the way I juxtapose these matters, or imply their equivalence, especially in the conflation of Gaia with Sophia. I argue, for instance, that the seers who directed the Mysteries taught coevolution with Gaia, that they were deep ecologists with a profound spiritual orientation, that they had a unique view of how the human species contributes to Sophia's intentions for it, as well as how it can deviate from her intentions. With such correlations, I am proposing a carefully measured rapprochement between an ancient heritage and our future options for the planet. In short, I maintain that Gnostic teachings repressed by Christianity present the ancient taproot of deep ecology, affirming the sacredness of the Earth apart from its use for human purposes. To date, deep ecology lacks a spiritual dimension, but it might acquire one by incorporation of the Sophianic vision. The sacred story of the "fallen goddess" embodied in the Earth, retold in episodes throughout parts 2 and 3 of this book, is an ecological myth that resonates deeply with our growing intuition of Gaia, the living planet. I have not invented this myth. I have merely reconstructed it into a coherent narrative so that we today have the opportunity to participate empathically in a sacred myth about the planet we inhabit.

Thus part 2 symphonically develops two themes, and balances them: recognition of the divine Sophia, and application of her sacred story for guidance toward a sane, sustainable, planet-friendly future.

Part 3, "History's Hardest Lesson," reprises the objective of the first movement, the destruction of the Mysteries, and reinforces it with the fourth objective, the completion of Nietzsche's critique. I explain the nature-hating basis of monotheism and the pathology of the divine victim, who, according to salvationist faith, also provides the ideal model of human nature. To do so, I reprise and deepen my analysis of the core pathology of the victim-perpetrator syndrome introduced in part 1. I show how the redeemer complex personified in Jesus Christ is religious cover for perpetration. So far, the victim-perpetrator bond has been detected in dysfunctional families and addictive relationships, not yet in the historical record, and not in grand theological propositions such as salvationism. But I am convinced that my analysis will reveal what has hitherto been so hard to understand: how blind allegiance to what is purportedly the highest model of humanity actually deviates us from our humanity. Finally, my post-Nietzschean critique shows that belief in the redemptive value of suffering is merely a glorification of the victim-perpetrator bond.

Part 3 concludes with some reflections on how to go beyond religion and cultivate genuine, life-affirmative values based on the sacredness of the Earth and the recognition of humanity's singular responsibility in evolution.

Part 4, "Reclaiming the Sophianic Vision," reprises and combines my first and second objectives, recovery of the Sophianic vision and its correlation with Gaia theory, and merges the Gnostic critique of Judeo-Christianity with Nietzsche's incomplete "transvaluation of all values." In the opening chapter (21), "Unmasking Evil," I tackle the daunting issue of extrahuman intrusion upon the human species. This essential theme of Gnosticism is totally ignored by scholars who freak at the mention of a freak species, the Archons, said to have been produced inadvertently when Sophia plunged from the cosmic core. I maintain that the Gnostic theory of error, reflected in the myth of the false creator god, may be one of the most liberating ideas ever devised by the human mind. In discussing "the topic of topics," alien predation, I cite science fiction writers and a range of ET and UFO research. Treating the God-self equation embraced by the New Age, and the tricky issue of "identification" currently under debate in deep ecology, I try to show that ego death is the essential requirement for intimacy with the planetary entelechy, Sophia.

Part 4 contains more disclosures from my mystical and entheogenic practice. I do not expect anyone to take these matters on faith, or to regard me as an illuminatus or guru figure (Goddess forbid!). Firsthand mystical experience is *evidence* in its own right, and when it comes to the most intimate aspects of human spirituality, it may be the only evidence that counts. In my exposition of the Mesotes, "the intermediary," I present historical, ethnographic, and mythological material to complement my purely subjective fix on that mysterious entity. It may appear that I go way beyond scholarly limits with the Mesotes, but I would not be surprised if a good number of readers who have had that same encounter find in my interpretation an entirely new way to view it, and own it.

The book concludes with a call to sacred ecology, the Pagan sense of life. We are all inheritors of the Sophianic birthright of humanity, regardless of race, culture, or creed. But sadly, putting race, culture, and creed before our humanity, we deprive ourselves of that precious lineage. Ultimately, the message of the Mysteries is about claiming the Anthropos (our identity as a species) so that we can own our species-specific responsibility in the designs of Gaia-Sophia. Each of us has an innate destiny that guides us unerringly toward that responsibility. If only we have the savvy to see what deviates us from our destinies in Gaia, and the strength to resist that deviation.

True to the Earth

In reworking and extending Nietzsche's indictment of Judeo-Christianity, I have relied strongly on the Gnostic critique of salvationism. There are many difficult and tricky points in the argument against our highest religious ideals, and I do not pretend to have pulled off this task to perfection. I had a particularly hard time with the Superman concept. Not just in writing this book over fourteen months, but all through my life! I have never seen myself as a Nietzschean Superman—in fact, I think "ultrahuman" is a better translation of *Übermensch*. But I always wondered if there may not be a superhuman or divine component in human nature. Haven't you? Only through understanding the Gnostic teaching on nous, divine intelligence, did I come to resolve this question. How I did so, the following pages will reveal.

The case for awe is also a case for humility. *"Remain true to the Earth,"* Zarathustra implored. To stand in naked awareness in the presence of the Earth, in *silent knowing*—this is awesome. Intimacy with the planet keeps us wild, undomesticated, unwilling to submit to social conditioning. In "On Reading and Writing," Nietzsche wrote: "Untroubled, scornful, outrageous—that is how wisdom wants us to be." Sophia (wisdom) loves those who preserve and protect her ways, women and men alike, warriors in the line of beauty. It could be objected that my obvious Nietzschean scorn for certain religious ideas compromises my judgment. But I am not the first to assert that religion (i.e., doctrine, rite, institution) is the enemy of genuine religious experience. C. G. Jung, Aldous Huxley, H. L. Mencken, Barbara Walker, and many others have made this observation, but no one has carried it through and backed up the argument in the way I do here.

It could also be objected that any expression of hatred is unacceptable in a book that purports to present spiritual values. I would reply that there is plenty of hatred circulating on this planet, and most of it seems to be coming from people who are devoutly religious. If humanity is filled with hatred, my personal share might act like a homeopathic dose against the general infection. I do not categorically reject hatred, or deny it a humane value. I hate a good many things: the rape of the Earth, child abuse, sexual apartheid, the exploitation of youth, lies and hypocrisy, bad literature, the consumer trance. This is my shortlist. But most of all I hate the enslavement and manipulation of the human spirit by false and perverted beliefs disguised in religious ideals and ethics. Hatred is an inevitable part of the human horror on this planet, but it can also be part of the cure. As Paracelsus said, the cure is in the dose.

Indigenous wisdom offers some advice for those who undertake vigils with sacred plants, advice that may be applicable to the healing force of hatred: "Stay behind the medicine." This means, do not be compulsively *driven* by the visionary power conferred by the plant-teachers, but stay behind it, be drawn rather than driven, be guided by the otherating power you take upon yourself. Likewise for hatred, a potent and precious medicine.

Without vision, the people die. Without awe, we lack the humility to live and the strength to protect what we love, all that makes life worth living. *Not in His Image* offers a dose of planetary medicine loaded with visionary power that was violently repressed for almost two thousand years.

Stay behind the medicine.

May 2006 Flanders–Andalucía

PART ONE

CONQUEST
and
CONVERSION

Head of an Initiate, Samothrace, 4th Century B.C.E.

1

THE MURDER OF HYPATIA

On a spring day in the year 415 c.e., a Pagan noblewoman emerged from the lecture hall attached to the great library of Alexandria and called for her chariot, intending to drive herself home. Although there were many educated Pagan women of high social standing and good education in Alexandria in that era, Hypatia, as she was called, was one of the few who owned and drove her own chariot. A familiar sight to the local populace, she often halted her horses and descended into the street to chat amiably with local people, or to debate issues of philosophy with whomever might wish to engage her. Her openness, combined with her kind and elegant manner, won her the admiration and affection of the townsfolk. Hypatia was also active in an official capacity in civic affairs normally dominated by men. "Such were her self-possession and ease of manner, arising from the refinement and cultivation of her mind, that she not infrequently appeared in public in presence of the magistrates, without ever losing in an assembly of men that dignified modesty of comportment for which she was conspicuous, and which gained for her universal respect and admiration."[1]

Hypatia's beauty was legendary, and equaled only, it was said, by her intelligence. Tall and confident, commanding her chariot with ease, clothed in a long robe and the signature scarf of the teaching class, she must have cut a striking figure in the thriving streets of that most cosmopolitan of cities. No realistic image of her survives.

On that March day in 415, as Hypatia entered a public square near the Caesarean Church where Christian converts were known to gather, she found her path blocked by a menacing crowd. At the head of the group stood a rough-looking man called Peter the Reader who roused those gathered to approach Hypatia and impede her way. "Now this Peter was a perfect believer in all respects of Jesus Christ,"[2] a zealous convert who admired Cyril, the Christian bishop of Alexandria. Recently, when a local prefect prosecuted one of Cyril's protégés for openly attacking Pagan doctrines, Hypatia had sided with the prefect and the man was severely admonished. Cyril had an axe to grind with Hypatia, although he could not afford to look bad in the public eye by acting openly against her. Long after the fateful day, many of the townsfolk wondered if Peter the Reader had not been sent to avenge his master, or perhaps had acted independently, hoping to win the patriarch's approval. Public opinion held that Cyril, who was on record for calling Hypatia a sorceress, was complicit in the attack.

Peter exhorted the crowd to throw tiles at Hypatia, and pull her from the chariot. Her long robes and scarf proved an advantage to the mob, consisting mostly of rough-handed workmen. They quickly overpowered her by yanking hard on her loose clothing from all sides. Pulled to the ground, she struggled in vain to break free and run. The mass of grappling hands now began to strip off her robes. Members of the local populace stood by helplessly, paralyzed by the horror unfolding before their eyes.

The violence of the mob escalated rapidly, its intensity fed by the raucous shouts of Peter the Reader. He called Hypatia a vile heretic and a witch who beguiled people through her beauty and her teachings, which were nothing but the wiles of Satan. Hypatia protested and cried for help, but a stiff blow broke her jaw. In a matter of minutes, she was on her knees in a pool of her own blood. Crushed under a flurry of blows and kicks, she was rapidly beaten to death. Not content merely to take her life, the mob pounded her naked body to a pulp and tore her limbs off her torso. The number of the attackers, and the ferocity of their assault, made it impossible for anyone witnessing the murder to intervene.

When Hypatia was dead, the attitude of the mob shifted abruptly from outrage to triumph. These men, who were self-declared Christians, immediately began to exalt in what they had done. The frenzy of victory was so acute, it could not be satisfied by the beating and dismemberment of the defenseless woman. As if emanating from their pores, some force of inhuman inspiration electrified the haze of violence that fumed around the murderers. Wild-eyed with excitement, several members of the mob ran to the nearby harbor and scooped up the razor-sharp oyster shells to be found there in abundance. They returned and passed out shells, and Peter encouraged his henchmen to scrap every last morsel of flesh from Hypatia's bones. When the men were done, they took the scraped bones to a place called Cindron and burned them to ashes.

WISDOM INCARNATE

Hypatia (correctly pronounced hew-pah-TEE-uh, anglisized *high-PAY-sha*) was the daughter of the mathematician Theon of Alexandria, the last known teacher in the age-old tradition of the Mystery Schools, the spiritual universities of antiquity.* The year and month of her death are known, the year of her birth is less certain, but 370 C.E. is generally accepted. Thus she would have been around forty-five when she was murdered. Historians have long regarded her death as *the* event that defined the end of classical civilization in Mediterranean Europe. It signaled the end of Paganism and the dawn of the Dark Ages. (Paganism, the generic term for pantheistic religion in the Western classical world, merits capitalization as much as Christianity.)

Theon was headmaster at the Museum of Alexandria, the place dedicated to the Muses, daughters of the ancient goddess of memory, Mnemosyne. Each of the Muses embodied a "sacred art" such as astronomy, lyric poetry, and history. The nine daughters of Memory presented a model for the curriculum of the Mystery Schools. Museums today are merely repositories of relics from the past, but the Alexandrian Museum was the setting for a wide range of living traditions, truly a center of higher education. The campus spread along the horseshoe-shaped port dominated by its Pharos, the famous four-hundred-foot-high lighthouse that ranked among the Seven Wonders of the World. It included many independent academies dedicated to subjects as diverse as geometry and sacred dance, and training guilds that produced a constant stream of graduates in fields such as sculpture, botany, navigation, herbology, engineering, and medicine. The assemblies and guilds associated with the Royal Library had their own libraries and teaching faculties.

---

* For a definition of Mystery Schools and other special terms, see the glossary.

In the year 400, when she was about thirty, Hypatia assumed the chair of mathematics at the university school. This was a salaried position, equivalent to professorship in a modern university. The daughter of Theon was noted for her mastery of Platonic philosophy and her skill in *theurgy*, literally "god-working," a form of magical invocation that might be compared to Jungian active imagination, or, more aptly, advanced practices of visualization in Tantra and Dzogchen. Her dialectical powers were exceptional, honed to a fine edge by her mathematical training. When it came to debating ideas about the divine, "Hypatia eclipsed in argument every proponent of the Christian doctrines in Northern Egypt."[3] Her expertise in theology typified the Pagan intellectual class of Gnostics, *gnostikoi*, "those who understand divine matters, knowing as the gods know," but she was also deeply versed in geometry, physics, and astronomy. Ancient learning was multidisciplinary and eclectic, contrasting strongly to the narrow specialization of higher education and the sciences in our time. The word *philosophy* means "love (*philo*) of wisdom (*sophia*)." To Gnostics, Sophia was a revered divinity, the goddess whose story they recounted in their sacred cosmology.* To the people of her time and setting, Hypatia would have been wisdom incarnate.

In addition to their religious function, the Mysteries provided the framework for education along interdisciplinary lines. The *gnostikoi* were polymaths, savants, and prolific writers. From around 600 B.C.E. to Hypatia's time—a period of a thousand years—they produced the countless thousands of scrolls stored in the Royal Library of Alexandria and other libraries attached to Mystery centers around the Mediterranean basin. Hypatia is known to have written a treatise on arithmetic and commentaries on the *Astronomical Canon* of Ptolemy and the conic sections of Apollonius of Perga. None of her writings survive, but eight ancient sources describe her murder and her accomplishments; the latter, not always in an approving manner. Cyril, whom popular opinion implicated in her murder, became an important theologian known for formulating the doctrine of the Holy Trinity. He was

---

* I propose the pronunciation so-FI-ah for the mythological name of the goddess, as distinct from the common name pronounced so-FEE-ah. The adjective is *sophianic*.

later canonized by the Church, along with other early Christian ideologues, the so-called Church Fathers, men whose theological polemics and histories of the One True Faith celebrate its triumph over "heretics" such as she.

Hypatia's accomplishments were not confined to theology and didactics. She was also involved in applied science related to geography and astronomy. Working with a Greek scientist Synesius, who was proud to be called her student, she invented a prototype of the astrolabe, a device later to prove essential in the navigation of the world oceans for the twinned purposes of conquest and conversion.

Pagan Learning

Hypatia's birthplace was founded by Alexander the Great on January 20, 331 B.C.E.

> For the next 1000 years, until the coming of Islam, it would look to the Mediterranean and the wider world. Alexandria's full title was "Alexandria by Egypt"—*not* "in Egypt." It was founded as an entrepôt through which the wealth of Egypt would flow; and within two centuries it would become the "the crossroads of the entire world": the El Dorado of the Hellenistic Age. . . . In the first century A.D. Alexandrian merchants sailed to South India on the monsoon winds, linking up with the trade to the Ganges, Vietnam, and China; part of the explosion of ideas and contact initiated by the Age of Alexander.[4]

In Hypatia's lifetime, her native city was still the greatest cosmopolitan center of antiquity, the undisputable capital of the Western world, commercially, spiritually, and intellectually speaking, but it belonged to an empire teetering on the brink of collapse. She was born around ten years after the initial wave of barbarians, the Huns, poured into Europe, and six years after the Roman Empire was divided geographically between east and west. In her lifetime the Roman legions evacuated Britain, conquered by Julius Caesar four and a half centuries earlier, and the borders of the Empire shook continually from barbarian assaults. In 410, when Hypatia would have been forty, Alaric, chieftain of the Visigoths, captured and sacked Rome, inflicting a mortal blow on the Empire. At that very moment Augustine of Hippo was writing *The City of God*, a book destined to become a cornerstone of Catholic doctrine. As the Roman Empire shattered and burned, another imperial entity, the institution of the Catholic Church, was rising in its place. A fateful handover of power was in progress.

The Hellenistic era lasted from the death of Alexander in 323 B.C.E. to 30 B.C.E., when Cleopatra, the last of the Ptolemies, killed herself with the bite of an asp. After Alexander's death, his empire was divided among three of his generals. The southernmost part, comprising Egypt and Judea (including Jerusalem), became the Ptolemaic kingdom. Culture and custom were uniform throughout all three parts of the empire. "Natives of Galilee and Judea wore the same sort of clothes as were worn in Alexandria, Rome or Athens."[5] The entire southern region, including Palestine, was thriving with Mystery Schools, many of them founded and directed by Gnostics such as Hypatia.[6] In the twilight of the Egyptian dynasties, cross-cultural exchange reached a fever pitch, but the death of Cleopatra brought a change of political regime that would permanently darken the skies of learning. Julius Caesar's arrival in Egypt in 47 B.C.E. completed the shift that had begun in 63 B.C.E. when the Roman general Pompey, Caesar's greatest rival, had declared Judea a Roman province. The transition from Hellenistic haven to Roman domain affected the entire Near East. In Hypatia's time, the Royal Library had existed for over seven hundred years, but it fared far less well in the four centuries of the Roman era than in the preceding three centuries of high Hellenistic syncretism.

The Royal Library was founded by a general of Alexander the Great, Ptolemy I, as a center of learning for the vast territories united by the Greek language following Alexander's campaigns. Ptolemy earned the title of *soter*, "savior," a title that would later be applied to Jesus Christ, because Ptolemy saved the wisdom of the ancient world. His son, Ptolemy II (d. 246 B.C.E.), commanded that all boats entering the port of Alexandria be searched for scrolls and papyri. Those found were taken to the library and copied, the originals were deposited in the stacks, and the copies returned in their owners. A staff of librarians, scribes, and calligraphers worked continuously to maintain an ever-growing collection that included first editions of Homer and Hesiod, the Greek playwrights, Aristotle, and many others. Ptolemy II proudly claimed a private collection of the 995 best books of all time.

The vast archives of the Royal Library were not limited to Greek-language writings. It stocked works in other languages such as Syriac and Aramaic, and translators labored nonstop to produce Greek editions. One of these works was the Hebrew Torah (the first five books of the Bible). Rendered into Greek, it was called the Septuagint because seventy Jewish scholars worked on the translation. Upon founding the city, Alexander had guaranteed Jews the same rights as other citizens of his empire, but that offer proved to be problematic. In Hypatia's day, it is likely that five to ten percent of the city's population were Jews—perhaps as many as 40,000 people.[7]

Ptolemy I had built a spacious hall called the Bruchion to house the ever-expanding collections. When it outgrew its capacity, his successor Ptolemy III erected the Serapeum. G. R. S. Mead notes that the Royal Library where Hypatia lectured was the first great public library in Egypt, but not the first in Egypt. Each temple had its own in-house library, and Egypt was a land of many temples. In mainland Greece and in the Grecian colonies around the Mediterranean basin, temple libraries housed large and ancient collections. Since the introduction of secular alphabets to the general public around 600 B.C.E., the adepts of the Mysteries had been pouring out a vast body of writings on every conceivable subject. In 400 C.E. Hypatia had a thousand-year-old tradition of literacy and learning to draw upon when she lectured to her classes.

Modern ignorance of history in general, and of ancient history in particular, makes it difficult to grasp the scope and richness of learning in the Pagan world. Writing in the 1940s, classical scholar Gilbert Highet observed:

> It is not always understood nowadays how noble and how widespread Greco-Roman civilization was, how it kept Europe, the Middle East, and northern Africa peaceful, cultured, prosperous, and happy for centuries, and how much was lost when the savages and invaders broke into it. It was, in many

respects, a better thing than our civilization until a few generations
ago, and it may well prove to have been a better thing all in all.

When the Roman Empire was at its height, law and order,
education, and the arts were widely distributed and almost
universally respected. In the first centuries of the Christian era
there was almost too much literature; and so many inscriptions
survive, from so many towns and villages in so many different
provinces, that we can be sure that many, if not most, of the
population could read and write. . . . Expeditions have found
papyrus copies of Homer, Demosthenes, and Plato, fragments
of what were once useful libraries, buried under remote
Egyptian villages now inherited by illiterate peasants.[8]

In 1945, the year Highet wrote these words (not to excuse the evils of
the Roman Empire, but to indicate the social and cultural achievements
it harbored), a cache of texts was discovered at Nag Hammadi in Upper
Egypt. In ancient times the place of the discovery was named Sheniset,
"the acacias of Seth," indicating a sanctuary for Gnostics who called
themselves Sethians. The Nag Hammadi library, as it came to be called,
consists of thirteen leather-bound codices, the earliest example of bound
books.* These fifty-two documents of fragmentary and muddled content
have revolutionized scholars' views on the origins of Christianity, but the
ultimate significance of this rare material, widely assumed to be original
Gnostic writings, has yet to be realized.

"Sethian" was the self-designation of some Gnostic groups who partic-
ipated intimately in the Mystery Schools distributed across Egypt, the
Middle East, around the Mediterranean basin, and into the depths of
Europe. In *The Gospels and the Gospel* (1902), theosophical scholar G. R. S.
Mead noted that "Gnostic forms are found to preserve elements from the
mystery-traditions of antiquity in greater fullness than we find elsewhere."[9]
Mead was among the first English-speaking scholars to translate and inter-
pret Gnostic texts known before the discovery at Nag Hammadi. His view

---

* On the Nag Hammadi Codices—not to be confused with the Dead Sea Scrolls, which
also figure in the argument of this book—see chapter 7 and "Suggestions for Reading and
Research." The Dead Sea Scrolls are discussed in chapters 4, 5, 6, and elsewhere.

of the centrality of Gnostic teachings in the Mysteries was shared by other scholars of his time, but this connection is categorically denied today.

Specialists such as Elaine Pagels dismiss any link between Gnostics and the Mysteries, due to a perceived lack of textual evidence.[10] Pagels' book *The Gnostic Gospels* (1979) introduced the Nag Hammadi materials to mainstream readers, but the scholarly specialization it represents has hampered understanding of who the Gnostics were, and why they protested so vehemently against the rise of Christianity. With their connection to the Mysteries denied, Gnostics are condemned to an obscure and uncertain place on the margins of the history of religion. Hence, the true message of the Gnostics, and the full impact of their near-complete destruction, has yet to register on the general public.

If Highet's assessment of the ancient world is correct, we must wonder: Who devised and directed the institutions of education in antiquity? Who taught the people? Who wrote the books? Who trained the artists, architects, and engineers in the skills required to produce the long-lasting wonders of the classical Western world? In his seminal work on Gnosticism, *Fragments of a Faith Forgotten*, Mead stated that "a persistent tradition in connection with all the great Mystery-institutions was that their several founders were the introducers of all the arts of civilization; they were either themselves gods or instructed in them by the gods. . . . They were the teachers of the infant races." The initiates, as they were called, "taught the arts, the nature of the gods, the unseen worlds, cosmology, anthropology, etc."[11] Mead's view is echoed by S. Angus, author of the most cited book on ancient Pagan cults, *The Mystery-Religions*: "The Mysteries were the last redoubts of Paganism to fall. Prior to that their adherents were the educators of the ancient world."[12]

Mead's contribution to Gnostic research was impressive and stands up well today. But it also exhibits the Christocetric bias typical of Pagels and all other historians of religion. Mead assumed the unity of all religions and endorsed "a living faith in the universal nature of Christ's teachings."[13] Nevertheless, situating Gnostics like Hypatia in the Mysteries puts ancient learning in context and points correctly to the Pagan initiates as the educators of the ancient world. Modern scholarship, by contrast, leaves the Gnostics in limbo, and totally ignores their centuries-long involvement in classical education.

A SACRED STORY

> The Holy Ghost was a Gnostic creation, and its original name
> was Sophia. Valentinian Gnostics said, "The world was born
> of Sophia's smile."[14]

In his introduction to G. R. S. Mead's *Fragments of a Faith Forgotten*,
American poet and culture critic Kenneth Rexroth proposed that
Gnosticism grew from the prehistoric matrix of Goddess worship
in Europe, "Neolithic and even earlier." Emphasis on "the descent of
the redeemer goddess" accounts for "the strong matriarchal or at least
anti-patriarchal emphasis of most Gnostic sects."[15] In this perspective,
the Mysteries were the natural outgrowth of the indigenous, Goddess-
oriented shamanism of pre-Christian Europe, described by Marija
Gimbutas, James Mellaart, Alexander Marshak, Merlin Stone, Stan
Gooch, Robert Graves, Riane Eisler, and others.[16] This view conflicts
sharply with the consensus of Gnostic specialists who regard Gnosticism
as a loose association of cults that sprung up in reponse to the spread
of Christianity; hence, as a marginal and reactive movement that is
only significant for what it can tell us about the early Roman Church.
Different interpretations of Gnosticism affect the way it reaches the
mainstream. So far, the work of the experts has contributed almost nothing to our understanding of what teachings and practices were original
to the Gnostics and intrinsic to the Mysteries.

Religious ideologues like Cyril, and their fanatic followers like Peter the
Reader and his mob, exerted enormous effort, not only to refute the Gnostic
worldview, but also to *demolish all written evidence of it*. In the end, they were
unable to do so, if only because they had to cite some Gnostic views in order
to refute them and build the case for their own religious ideology! In their
polemics against heresy, Church Fathers such as Irenaeus and Epiphanius
preserved clues to Gnostic teachings, including elements of the sacred story
of the goddess Sophia whom Gnostics imagined to be embodied in the
Earth. Until 1945, these condemnatory, often distorted paraphrases were
the main accounts we had of what Gnostics thought and taught.

Although the Nag Hammadi materials may not be original Gnostic
texts, they are the best we have, and perhaps will ever have. These

materials provide enough insight into Gnostic teachings to explain why Gnostics risked their lives to challenge such doctrines as the supremacy of the male creator god, sin and atonement, the divinity of the Savior, resurrection, and final judgment from on high. There remain fifty-odd fragmentary texts in Coptic, a mere flake of a vast corpus of writings, yet so potent was the Gnostic argument that this flake still contains enough theological dynamite to shake the foundations of Christianity.

But the Gnostics cannot, and ought not, be defined exclusively by what they stood against. Their vision of Sophia, the "fallen goddess" embodied in the Earth, is an ecological myth that resonates deeply with our growing intuition of Gaia, the living planet. The Gnostic message for humanity may well present the ancient taproot of deep ecology, a social movement that asserts the intrinsic value of the Earth, apart from its use for human purposes. The religious component of the environmental movement has yet to be defined, but it might now come to expression in a Gnostic perspective, framed by the Sophianic vision of those ancient visionaries.

Norwegian philosopher Arne Naess, the founder of deep ecology, proposed the term *ecosophy* for human wisdom that complements the intelligence of the living Earth. Although he did not (to the knowledge of this author) intend to invoke the ancient meaning of Sophia, Naess's choice of language introduced the wisdom principle of the Gnostics into the outlook of deep ecology. Naess emphasizes that ecosophy is not a fixed program but a visionary path that humanity is "on the way" to discovering.[17] Likewise, the Sophianic worldview of the Gnostics did not present a fixed program of revealed doctrines, but an open path for exploring the connection between nature and psyche. In the 1990s the psyche-nature symbiosis came to be called ecopsychology. A decade later, we are still a long way from formulating this symbiosis and putting it into practice. The Pagan teachers in the Mysteries may well have been ecopsychologists centuries before that word was invented. Their example could be decisive in guiding humanity toward a sane and sustainable future.

In his famous distinction between shallow and deep ecology, Arne Naess noted in the former "a lack of depth—or complete absence—of guiding philosophical or religious foundations."[18] It may well be Gnostic teachings recovered at Nag Hammadi in 1945 can provide the religious dimension so far lacking in the ecological movement. Such, at least, is the premise of the book in hand. To this end, the Sophianic vision of the Mysteries could be applied as a guiding framework for deep ecology without turning it into a religion of nature worship.

It might be objected that deep ecology should not become religious, or, by the same measure, that Gaia theory ought not to be converted into "Goddess mystique." The Gnostics who founded and led the Mysteries of ancient Europe and the Near East were accomplished mystics inspired by a sacred theory of the Earth, but they were not religious in the conventional sense: that is, they did not impose a moral code, doctrinal formulas, and institutional authority. The Gnostic message had two components: a sacred vision of the Earth, and a radical critique of salvationist doctrines centered on the Judeo-Christian messiah, especially the *redeemer complex* (see page 16). The Gnostic critique was brutally suppressed because it challenged the core beliefs of imperialist Roman religion, beliefs that have as much, if not more, political utility as they do spiritual veracity.

Today it may be too late, and too difficult, to revive the Gnostics' challenge to salvationist ideology. But their critique of the redeemer complex is perhaps the most liberating message to come out of the spiritual genius of Paganism. To ignore that message would be to lose forever the benefit of a profound legacy. Moreover, the critique cannot be separated from the other part of the Gnostic message, its sacred vision of the Earth. The guardians of the Mysteries detected in salvationism a program that deviates humanity from a living, conscious connection to the Earth. Difficult as it is, the critique is more relevant now than it ever was, and the sacred myth of Sophia may be *the* story that rescues us from our delusional and self-destructive ways.

The battle that took place two thousand years ago and resulted in the total demolition of the Pagan religious heritage of Europe was essentially a clash between two paradigms, two utterly different concepts of redemption. Gnostics taught that Sophia is a goddess, a divine being embodied in the Earth. The wisdom unique to her is the living intelligence of the planet. All the Mysteries were dedicated to this divinity, the Magna Mater, the Great Mother whom I propose to correlate to

Gaia. Initiation in the Mysteries involved a direct encounter with the Sophianic intelligence, that is, "earth wisdom" in New Age parlance. Gnostics preserved a *sacred story* about the origin of humanity, how the Earth evolved, and how we as a species are uniquely involved with the planetary intelligence—not only for our survival, but for collaboration with Gaia-Sophia (to coin a term) in evolving her own purposes.

How can such a vision stand against, or with, Gaia theory as it is developing today?

James Lovelock has warned against the assumption of "a sentient Gaia able to control the Earth consciously."[19] Although Gnostics did assert that Sophia is sentient and intelligent, their complex mythology left open the issue of teleology or goal orientation (known as "strong Gaia theory" in the current debate). The sacred theory of the Earth preserved in the ancient Mysteries did not contain a preconceived notion of goal orientation for the terrestrial superorganism. Rather, it presented an experiental pathway to discover how humankind might align with terrestrial evolution in the cosmic perspective, as the goddess herself sees it.

Central to the Sophianic myth was an event called in Gnostic terminology the "correction" of the Earth goddess, a concept that verges toward teleology without predefining it. In Sophia's Correction, Gnostics imagined *the realignment of life on our planet with the cosmic center, the source from which the Earth goddess originated and emerged.* This intriguing idea is found in Gnostic cosmological writings from Nag Hammadi, including the Apocryphon of John (cited below). Scholars sometimes translate the Greek *diorthosis* as redemption rather than correction, but the concept taught in the Mysteries was utterly unlike the divinely insured redemption promised in salvationist religion.[20] It was not a matter of belief in a higher power located somewhere beyond this world, off-planet, but an experiential faith in our connection to the divine power that is *here*, fully Earthbound, providing the matrix in which we live, move, and have our being. Redemption for the initiates in the Mysteries was not a grace received, nor a deed accomplished for us by divine intercession. Rather, it involved assuming the privilege *to coevolve consciously with the planetary intelligence*, to live *intimately* the symbiotic miracle of the Earth and learn how it works, loving every lesson, every feat of discovery, every act of transmutation in the divine alchemy of the biosphere. The Apocryphon of John, a long cosmological text from Nag Hammadi, says that we work intimately with the Earth goddess Sophia "so that our natural kin, Wisdom, who resembles us, might correct what she lacks by the reflection of the Light we hold."

This is the core of the Gnostic message as it was two thousand years ago, and as it stands today.

THE REDEEMER COMPLEX

As Pagans, the *gnostikoi* rejected the belief that suffering has a redemptive value. As theologians, they refuted the claim that divine intervention could alter the human condition. By rejecting the superhuman savior and refuting salvationist beliefs, Gnostics drew a frontal assault from those who were formulating and enforcing the doctrines of the Judeo-Christian redeemer complex. The brutal suppression of the Mysteries, the destruction of Gnostic writings, and the wholesale genocide of Pagan culture in Europe belong to the untold story of "Western civilization" and "the triumph of Christianity." This is the story as it was lived by the "losers." To reclaim Gnostic wisdom for today *and* merge Mystery teachings with deep ecology—the dual intention of this book—cannot be done without looking closely at what destroyed the Sophianic vision of the living Earth, and why it was able to do so. The genocide of native culture in the classical world went on for centuries, but a cover-up has largely concealed this fact, and continues to this day. To expose the cover-up and reveal both the cause and scope of the destruction so wrought is the secondary, but no less important, objective of this book.

The redeemer complex has four components: creation of the world by a father god independent of a female counterpart; the trial and testing (conceived as a historical drama) of the righteous few or "Chosen People"; the mission of the creator god's son (the messiah) to save the world; and the final, apocalyptic judgment delivered by father and son upon humanity. Orthodox Jews accept all four points of the complex, but do not recognize Jesus of the New Testament as their Messiah, who to this day has yet to appear. Christians follow the dictum of the apostle Peter who addressed converting Jews as "a chosen race, a royal priesthood, a holy nation, God's own people" (1 Peter 2:9), thus, in one deft phrase, transferring the status of "Chosen People" from Jews to Christian converts. In short, Roman Christianity adopted the larval or tribal form of the redeemer complex from Judaism and transformed it into a universal ("catholic") program of salvation. Differing views of these four components determine various factions of Judaism and Christianity as well as Islam, which also belongs to the trinity of Abrahamic religions, although it arose after the Gnostics were silenced, and hence did not figure in their critique.

Some Gnostics, such as Valentinus and Marcion, proposed compromise positions on these issues, but the radical Pagan argument ruthlessly refuted all four points. Almost without exception, scholars and historians of religion today hold the view that the Gnostic movement arose within early Christianity. If this were so, Gnostic ideas would have merely been remnants of a vague kind of "Gnostic Christianity" that was gradually eliminated with the doctrinal definition of beliefs. But the hard evidence of the surviving materials clearly contradicts this interpretation. Gnostic Christianity is a retrofit contrived by scholars whose religious convictions prevent them from seeing, and admitting, that a significant portion of Gnostic material was diametrically opposed to the Judeo-Christian ideology of salvation.

For Pagans and Christians alike, the four components of the redeemer complex were not merely dry theological issues. The Gnostic protest against the redeemer complex aroused an enormous wave of violence in converts to the salvationist creed, as seen in the murder of Hypatia. She was a *gnostikos*, a Pagan intellectual from the Mysteries, targeted by the righteous rage of people who pinned their faith on the Divine Redeemer. The mob that attacked her believed that their God had a unique way to overcome suffering, and this belief sanctioned them to inflict suffering to further His cause.

Belief in the redemptive value of suffering is the core dynamic of the violence, will to conquer, and genocide that drove the rise of Roman Christianity and released an ever-expanding wave of destruction across the planet.

Humans may commit violence for many reasons, they may seek to oppress and dominate others for a variety of causes, but when domination by violent force, both physical and psychological, is infused with righteousness and underwritten by divine authority, violence takes on another dimension. It becomes inhuman and deviant. Like countless others of her time, and in the centuries to follow, Hypatia was the victim of religiously inspired sectarian violence driven and fed by faith in the redeemer complex. What kind of world results if the power to dominate and control others, inflicting enormous suffering in the process, is sanctioned by a divine being who can at the same time redeem that suffering and release the perpetrators and their victims from that world's evils?

Such was the diabolic system Gnostics found themselves facing after 150 c.e.

THE VICTIM-PERPETRATOR BOND

Religion protects man as long as its ultimate foundations are not revealed. To drive the monster from its lair is to risk loosing it on humanity.[21]

Feminist scholar and professor of theology Catherine Keller says that "we have no reason to believe that in all time life has been based on the dominance of the weaker by the stronger, nor do we have any evidence that people have always lived in the defensive state of being that characterizes modern life." She observes that within the patriarchal-dominator culture, violence arises and manifests "in situations where abuse communicates itself from one generation to the next. Over and over again we see the causing of pain—destructiveness and abuse—*flow out of a prior wounding.*"[22]

Modern psychology identifies the syndrome Keller describes as "abuse-bonding." Domination is abuse, and in any situation of domination the abuser is someone who has been abused, as we now understand. The reverse is not true, however: the abused does not have to have been an abuser. Thus, the system is open to produce more and more abusers from the endless supply of nonabusers. As the abuse develops, the vicious circle tightens. Victims who survive violence inflicted on them can become bonded to the perpetrators, and often, but not always, become perpetrators themselves. The suffering engendered by abuse-bonding, or *the victim-perpetrator bond*, as I will call it, is extremely contagious.

The victim-perpetrator bond has been widely applied to dysfunctional families and addictive relationships, but not yet to the historical record of the human species, nor to grand theological propositions such as the redeemer complex. Applied to the conquest of the New World, however, it suggests that those among the European conquerors who were abusers had themselves been abused. Those who came, saw, and conquered had already been conquered.

What abuse was inflicted upon Europeans prior to the fifteenth century that produced in them a drive for domination by violence, provided righteous justification for that violence, and led them to commit genocide and ecocide on a vast scale? What happened in ancient Europe before Europeans went forth to conquer, convert and colonize the New World?

Greed is often cited as the primary motive for European conquest of the New World. The invaders certainly had that, in spades. The conquistadores sailed to the Americas under the sign of Christ, nominally dedicated to the conversion of the savage races, and sent back untold wealth. The tonnage of silver and gold pillaged from the natives is unimaginable, even in terms of today's billion-dollar statistics. Gold and precious jewels had no commercial value to Native Americans such as the Aztecs and Incas. It was reserved purely for ornamental and sacramental use. The stolen decor of the New World became the hard capital of the Old. For centuries the Spanish galleons arrived at the mouth of the Guadalquivir River, their spoils barged upriver to the counting houses in Seville where Torquemada, born a thousand years after the murder of Hypatia, launched his mission to purge Spain from the nefarious presence of *Conversos* (false Christians). The jewel-encrusted cup the pope lifts today to perform Holy Mass before an audience of devout millions is cast from Incan gold. The blood that fills the cup may be imagined in symbolic terms to belong to Jesus Christ, the Redeemer. But, in historical terms, it belongs to the untold millions of

New World natives decimated by the European onslaught, their ways of survival shattered, their holy sites desecrated, their sacred knowledge and practices condemned as heresy. According to the faith, the bread broken at mass is Christ's body substantiated. But according to the brutal truth of history, it is the ravaged body of the Earth, the natural paradise plundered for its resources.

Can greed alone explain this behavior, which is, by its own admission, *sanctified* behavior? If not, perhaps the observation of cultural anthropologist René Girard can provide a clue: "Religion protects man as long as its ultimate foundations are not revealed."[23] What lies concealed in the ultimate foundations of religion? For the *gnostikoi*, skilled in theological debate, the element of the emergent religion that most alarmed them was the redeemer complex. Their mandate was to trailblaze a path of consecration to the life of the Earth, the mother planet. In the off-planet spin of the redeemer complex they saw a delusion, a deviance for humanity, even a sign of madness. Experts in theology like Hypatia openly challenged that delusion and countered it by teaching about the divine potential of humankind, nous, and coevolution with Sophia, the Wisdom Goddess. At the very moment salvationist religion first emerged, it was challenged and countered by people who were highly qualified to analyze and assess what they were seeing. And they commanded powerfully argued alternative views to refute it.

In their protest against what they perceived as a grave deviation for humanity, Gnostics did not loose a monster on the world, however. They faced a monster already on the loose, one that had been growing strong for several centuries. It is a monstrous error of the human mind, they argued, to make suffering into a righteous cause for those who inflict it, and a divine, redemptive calling for those on whom it is inflicted. The monster the Gnostics confronted was inhuman, but would make all humanity its instrument. It is the victim-perpetrator bond diabolically exploited, *disguised as a love connection*, and glorified to the heights of heaven.

If Gnostics had defeated salvationism on its home ground in the Near East, it would never have spread to Europe, but proto-Christian imperialism was well rooted in Rome by 200 c.e. The "sacred history" of the Jews was soon to be enforced as the only script in town. Around 100 c.e., Clement of Rome, an early ideologue, asserted that both the Old Testament and the words attributed to Jesus were Holy Scripture, and both must be taken literally as historical truth. This position, stated around the time the earliest gospel narratives were written in their surviving form, established the claim that the stories about Jesus were accounts of real events, a claim still maintained today by Christian fundamentalists. It also asserted the continuity of the Old and New Testaments: "Everything written about me in the law of Moses and the prophets and psalms must be fulfilled" (Luke 24:44). Gnostics such as Marcion categorically rejected this continuity and insisted that the wrathful, capricious father god of the Old Testament could not be a source of superhuman love, and ought not to be the object of human love. In 144 c.e. Marcion nearly succeeded in having his model of the then existing gospel materials accepted as canonical by the Christian community in Rome. Had he done so, Christianity today would rely on his revision of Pauline Christology and gospel materials selected on Gnostic criteria, entirely independent from the Old Testament.

Innumerable rewrites of the gospel narratives, and recurring debates over Jewish versus orthodox versus Gnostic versions of Scripture, continued well into Hypatia's time, but the story that was to guide Western civilization for sixteen hundred years gradually crystallized in favor of a patriarchal scheme of divine redemption, stamped with the imprimatur of Roman Empire. The authority of the off-planet deity suited imperial lust for power to a T. The fourth century saw the imposition of the death penalty on Pagan religion and heretical schisms (such as Arianism) by Theodosius I and Theodosius II, men described by one historian as "two of the most cruel and powerful Christians of any time who were already laying the basis for the Inquisitions and the future religious wars of Europe."[24]

Following and co-opting the Jewish tradition of "sacred history," the salvationist program enforced a linear historical plan upon the entire human species. Joined together, the Old and New Testaments constitute a *directive script*, a story encoded with beliefs that drive the behavior of those who adopt it. Sanctioned by the redeemer complex, patriarchy had written its own agenda, and attributed the authorship to a vindictive paternal god. The divine father had a plan for conquest and conversion that was to be perpetrated in Europe for a thousand years before its victims, themselves transformed into perpetrators, carried it forth under the sign of the Cross to the New World.

The murder of Hypatia casts a long, chilling shadow.

2

PAGAN ROOTS

When *Bury My Heart at Wounded Knee* appeared in 1971 the word "genocide" was not commonly used to describe what was done to the tribal cultures of North America by the Europeans who arrived after 1492. Dee Brown's breakthrough book focused on the betrayal and massacre of indigenous tribes west of the Mississippi, but it brought worldwide attention to the historical plight of all Native Americans. It established the view that genocide, "the deliberate murder of a racial or cultural group,"[25] could indeed be applied to the policy and actions of the Europeans who settled North America, and by extension, to similar policies and actions in Central and South America, such as the forced conversion of the Mexican tribes (Aztec, Maya, Zapotec, and dozens more), and the wholesale destruction of their sacred literature. Today, genocide is accepted as the correct and accurate term to describe certain aspects of what has long been called, and often in rather laudatory terms, "the conquest of the New World."

In his preface, Dee Brown warns that his portrayal of Native American peoples and their cultures may not comply with prevailing assumptions:

> [Readers] may be surprised to hear words of gentle reasonableness coming from the mouths of Indians stereotyped in the American myth as ruthless savages. They may learn something about their own relationship to the earth from a people who were truly conservationists. The Indians knew that life was equated with the earth and its resources, that America was a paradise, and they could not comprehend why the intruders from the East were determined to destroy all that was Indian as well as America itself.[26]

When it comes to the indigenous peoples of Europe—Native Europeans, as they might be called—we may be no more enlightened today than were many of Brown's readers of 1971. He confronted the issue of "Indians stereotyped in the American myth," but we have yet to confront the issue of Pagans stereotyped in Judeo-Christian history. The American myth is a relatively recent cultural creation, the self-celebratory script of a nation not yet two hundred years old when Brown's book was published. Compared to American history, the sacred history of Judeo-Christianity is fifteen times older and anchored many levels more deeply in the collective psyche of the human species. At this late date, one is forced to question if it is possible to pry off the overlay of stereotypes and break through the dense crust of disinformation that blocks our understanding of Native Europeans.

THE MYTH OF EUROPA

According to *The Penguin Concise English Dictionary* (2002 edition), a pagan is "(1) a follower of polytheistic religion (2) an irreligious person." If we now apply the word *pagan* to the indigenous peoples of Europe and accept *paganism* as a generic term for the religious orientation of those people, this definition will have to go. One possible alternative: *pagan*, (1) a follower of animistic religion who recognizes many divinities in a living cosmos, hence, a devotee of the religion of nature; (2) more specifically, a member of the diverse indigenous cultures of pre-Christian Europe.

Hypatia was a Pagan, but she was of course Egyptian, not European. Let's recall, however, that Alexandria was "by Egypt," not in it. From the "Golden Age" that dawned around 600 B.C.E., Greek philosophers and scientists took long years of apprenticeship in Egypt. In *Black Athena*, Martin Bernal argues that the entire Western European intellectual tradition derives from African origins. He says that for Plato and other Greek intellectuals, "if one wanted to return to the ancient Athenian institutions, one had to turn to Egypt."[27] Bernal cites many examples of famous Greeks who spent years of apprenticeship in the Egyptian Mystery Schools.

Salvationism arose in Palestine and spread as quickly to Alexandria as it did to Rome. Consequently, non-European Pagans such as Hypatia were on the front lines of an assault that would eventually sweep over Europe in waves. Gnostics in Egypt, the Levant, and the Near East were instructors and guides to the Greeks who launched the Western intellectual tradition, and they were something more as well. They were for the indigenous peoples of Europe the first line of defense against the salvationist ideology originating from Palestine.

Nothing remotely comparable to *Bury My Heart at Wounded Knee* has yet been written about the genocide of the Pagan populations of Europe. There is not even a generic name for these people, but "Native Europeans" will perhaps do. Europeans today inhabit bordered nation-states, but this was not the case for the pre-Christian indigenous people who composed a vast mosaic of diverse cultures and ethnic-linguistic groups living in unbordered regions throughout Europe. Because Native Europeans were not Europeans in the modern sense, scholars attach the prefix *proto-* to designations of the indigenous races: proto-Italic, proto-Hellenic, proto-Iberian, and so forth. This terminology is awkward. Marija Gimbutas introduced the term "Old Europe" for the goddess-based cultures she excavated in the Balkans, but, in fact, the Old Europeans lived when Europe was young, and the inhabitants of Europe today are really the old lot, the last of the line. Gimbutas's term fits her work, but it will not serve for naming the indigenous people of Europe.

The origin of the word *Europe* occurs in a myth linked to ancient Crete. King Agenor of Tyre, an island off the coast of Lebanon, had a daughter called Europa who attracted the attention of the lusting Olympian deity Zeus. To seduce her, Zeus assumed the form of a magnificent white bull. Taking Europa on his back, he ran to the seacoast and swam away to Crete. There she bore him sons, including Minos, who became the king of Crete and gave his name to the Minoan civilization that flourished on that island. Europe is named after a goddess from the Levant where the core of the Gnostic movement was located.

The derivation of the mythological name Europa is uncertain. Marija Gimbutas (*The Goddesses and Gods of Old Europe*) says that Europa means

"far-glancing." According to *Origins*, the standard etymological dictionary compiled by Eric Partridge, the Greek word *eurus* means "broad,"
"wide." This meaning may fit Europe in geographical terms, but it does
not preclude other derivations. The Indo-European root *eu-*, meaning
"health," "natural goodness," generates such words as *eugenics*, "good
breeding," *eucharist*, "good charm" or "power," and *euphonious*, "good
sounding." With a shift from *u* to *v*, this root forms the word *evangelos*,
"messenger (*angelos*) of natural goodness (*ev-*)." The evangelism of the
New Testament arose in the Near East, in Palestine, but it was spread
throughout the Old World by Hellenic Europeans. There is a historical twist hidden in the wordplay here, because the "good news" of the
Gospels has nothing to do with the "natural goodness" of Pagan Europe.
In reality, it was designed to deny and defeat the native orientation at
every turn. When *Eu*ropeans were *ev*angelized, their sense of place was
destroyed, their spirituality suppressed, their sacred sites co-opted, and
their tribal histories overwritten by a totalitarian script imported from a
faraway land.

As just suggested, the Cretan myth offers the word *Europa* for the
continental expanse of pre-Christian Europe, and the word *Europan* for
the diverse range of its native inhabitants and cultures. Europan applies
generically to the regional features of diverse peoples who lived in the
geographical territory that stretches from the Shetland and Orkney
islands south to the tip of Iberia, from Brittany in France eastward to the
Straits of the Bosphorus. It includes the northern rim of the Mediterranean
basin and islands such as Crete, Sicily, Corsica, Sardinia, Malta, Majorca,
plus, of course, the Greek isles. The time span for Europa would be from
the close of the Ice Age, around 9500 B.C.E., until the post-feudal period
when nation-states began to emerge—say, 1400 C.E. The Pagan values of
Europa still survived into the Renaissance, even though put under enormous stress by the repressive measures of Roman Christianity. Assaults
on the indigenous people included the campaigns against the Cathars
and Albigensians in the twelfth century, the Inquisition launched in the
fifteenth century, and the witch hunts that raged across Europe between
1450 and 1750, claiming untold numbers of lives. As late as 1976 women
suspected of practicing witchcraft were murdered in England, Hungary,
and Germany.[28]

Europan cultures present close parallels to those of the indigenous peoples of the Americas. Europans "knew that life was equated with the earth and its resources" (Brown, cited above), that their habitat was a natural paradise. They too were deeply conservative, and in this respect might also be compared with the ancient Chinese. Anyone who travels in Europe sees the evidence of people who have lived for centuries in a sustained relation to their environment: vineyards, baths, aqueducts, roads, earthworks, ancient groves of olive trees and oak trees, salt marshes, stoneworks of all kinds including great megalithic circles such as Stonehenge and Newgrange, some of which are known to have been constructed as early as 7000 B.C.E. Everywhere one goes outside the urban conglomerations in modern Europe, the land has been touched and shaped by human hands, skillfully, even lovingly managed. For centuries the Pagan inhabitants all across the wide, fertile continent exerted special effort to preserve and enhance the bounty of nature.

The Neolithic, Copper Age, and Bronze Age peoples of Europa were hardly different from the Native Americans who survived into the nineteenth century, four hundred years after being invaded. Yet some of the invaders of the New World were so alienated from their own roots that they saw all the American tribes as savages to be slaughtered, converted and enslaved, rather than as counterparts of themselves from a distant time.

COUNTRY FOLK

In Roman times, a *pagus* was a rural district, usually identified by a land marker or boundary stone. In Egypt all the land on both sides of the Nile was organized into local districts called nomes, each with its totemic animal and attendant rituals. The priests who conceived and implemented this system did so from their perception of the innate character of the inhabitants. The nome system entailed an apportionment of local resources by the Egyptian elite. (Aristotle famously attributed to Egyptians the invention of the sacred art of geometry as a technique for land measurement.) In Greece the countrywide boundary markers were called *hermae*, upright pillars carved in the likeness of the ecstatic god Dionysos, usually shown with an erection. In this way Mystery School teachers acknowledged to the locals their recognition of natural fecundity, the plenitude of the Great Mother, as the object of indigenous religion. The erect *hermae* did not glorify the male power of procreation but acknowledged the grounding of human sexuality in telluric forces.

Pagani were country dwellers, by contrast to the *urbani*, inhabitants of large cities such as Alexandria, Athens, or Rome, yet the city folk were also Pagans in the more comprehensive sense of the word. In colloquial Latin usage, a *paganus* was a peasant, a villager, said without a derogatory or dismissive spin.

Partridge links the etymology here to the Latin verb *pangere*, "to stick something (in the ground)." This suggests that not only the local boundary markers, but the country folk themselves, were grounded in the place they inhabited. *Pak-*, the Indo-European root of *pangere*, gives us the word "pact." This derivation suggests that people who are implanted in the place they inhabit have a pact with the land, a moral commitment to the environment. Julian Jaynes, who noted wryly that "civilization is the art of living in towns of such size that everyone does not know everyone else," observes that the Hittite word *pankush*, derived from the same root as *pangere*, means "community."[29] This association implies that bonding to place makes community possible, not only by sharing the resources of the place, but by delimiting what is to be shared. Hence the importance of "the commons" in all human-scale societies.

Paganism may be defined as the primary orientation of society to the natural world and habitat, where both are perceived holistically. Historian Garth Fowden writes: "The polytheist envisaged his native place as a unique whole defined by geography, climate, history, and the local economy, as well as by the gods who particularly frequented it, ensured its prosperity, and might even assume its name. No part of this identity, a delicate interweaving of divine, natural, and human . . . could be subtracted or neglected without impairing the harmony and viability of the whole." In the Pagan sense of life, culture is organically situated in nature. The term "Pagan roots" is redundant, because Pagans were by definition people rooted in the place they inhabit. Fowden notes that Pagans were immersed in "that distinctive understanding of divinity that comes through dwelling together with the gods in a certain place, a precise local knowledge that no distant prophet could or would ever make into a scripture."[30]

In deep ecology, bonding to the land is the first condition for an ecologically sane society. "The first thing to do is to choose a sacred place and live in it." So advised Pawnee tribe elder, Tahirussawichi, to writer Dolores LaChapelle.[31] The Pagan pact with the land can be regarded as what is today called *bioregionalism*. Relation to a place *perceived as sacred* is not, however, possession of place; in fact, such relationship impedes the drive to possess. Native Americans frequently insist that they belong to the land, the land does not belong to them.

In its reverence for nature the Pagan religious outlook honored and encouraged empathic bonding of person to place, not divinely ordained possession of the land. Mountains, hills, grottos, wells, rivers, all were sacred, not because any doctrine declared them to be, but because the experience of the peoples native to a particular locale was grounded in a direct and sensuous revelation of divinity. Theirs was a mystical participation in the Other, free of intellectual or doctrinal filters. Ancient bioregionalism, in Europa as well as in the Americas, was not superstitious folly, but a genuine, *lived* animism. It was a world in which, as the initiate Plutarch wrote in his essay, *The Sign of Socrates*, "every life has its share of mind and there is none that is wholly irrational or mindless."[32] Empathic connections between people and their environment are intimate, highly subjective, and difficult to record. Most of European history transpired when the indigenous populations of the Americas lived *without written history* but in deep participation in time and place. The fact that there are no written records of their experience does not make it any less important in the evolution of the human species. Again, the parallel to the pre-Columbian natives of the Americas, as well as to far-flung peoples such as the Australian Aborigines, is obvious.

In *Nature and Madness* anthropologist Paul Shepard observed that "the real difficulty with the discussion of the relationship of history to place is that the question is framed in a historical mode which has already decided the issue."[33] The same applies to determining the origin of the Mysteries, for the Mysteries arose from the relationship of humanity to place *experienced as a sacred connection*, before any particular history was written. In the frame of the redeemer complex, God the Father gives the righteous ones ("Chosen People") possession of specific territory ("Promised Land") and even dominion over the entire Earth. But in this belief system the Earth is not sacred in its own right, and what matters in religious terms is the connection to the off-planet deity who confers dominion over *His* creation, nature. The "historical mode which has already decided the issue" of how we describe our species' relation to the natural world is the patriarchal narrative of the Abrahamic religions, the People of the Book. This is the particular and preclusive narrative that presents the history of Western civilization. As long as this *directive script* prevails, it is impossible even to discuss the transhistorical, deeply ecological perspective on life taught in the Mysteries.

Taking care of nature ("the environment," as bureaucrats call it) is a way of seeing to our survival, of course. This is a key point of shallow ecology, contrasted to the deeper view of nature as having intrinsic value above and beyond its capacity to support human life. It would appear that Europans were diligent and skillful shallow ecologists, but the view of nature taught in the Mysteries suggests they also had the deeper orientation. The peoples who emerged in Europa as the great ice sheets withdrew northward after 9500 B.C.E. were particularly gifted at the arts of survival. Upon arriving in the Americas after 1500, European colonialists found a "Stone Age" culture that had not claimed the land in the same way their Europan ancestors had. Yet there was more similarity than difference to observe. Why did the invaders regard the natives with such coldness and hostility? The beliefs that drove them to the Americas also blinded them to what they found there. Confronted with the natural paradise of the New World, the invaders were incapable of seeing its parallel in their own origins, unable to see their ancient pre-Christian myths reflected in Native American beliefs and customs. They could not, for example, compare the Great Serpent Mound of Ohio or the medicine wheels of the high Rockies to stone circles and megalithic monuments in their ancestral lands.[34] Lack of such recognition certainly reenforced the Europeans' tendency to view the Native Americans as "other" and alien, and allowed the invaders to project a diabolical image on them.

Columbus noted that the Taino Indians of the Dominican Republic were as happy as human beings can be, open to the strangers, eager to show their way of life and share it. His response was typical of the irrational violence of "the emotional plague," as Wilhelm Reich called the pathological revulsion manifested by people who are alienated from their own bodies. Columbus's men burned the Indians alive in their huts. This reaction spread like a contagion, infecting all the following waves of invaders. Such is the mad, blind, and perverted behavior that springs from "a prior wounding." In 1609 Bartolomé de las Casas reported a catalog of horrors committed by the Spanish invaders, including this: "They made gallows just high enough for the feet to nearly touch the ground, and by thirteens, in honor of our Redeemer and the Twelve Apostles, they put wood underneath, and with fire, they burned the Indians alive."[35]

THE PLEASURE BOND

Roman civilization adopted a great deal of its higher culture from the Greeks, including its adoption of the Greek pantheon of gods, renamed in Latin. Many Latin terms are derived by association, elision, or corruption from Greek. The Latin *paganus* may have been associated with the Greek verb *paien*, "to pasture," "to tend animals." The Greek verb *paiein*, spelled with one additional letter, is also germane: *paiein* means "to strike," "to touch forcibly," "to touch so as to heal." Used as a title, To Paion, "the Healer," was an epithet applied to Apollo, and a *paian* was originally a song of praise to Apollo.[36] Both verbs merge in mythological allusion, for Apollo is said to have charmed wild animals by playing the lyre. The shaman's musical magic induced the domestication of animals. These mythic and poetical figures of speech point far back into the prehistory of Europa and deep into what Julian Jaynes calls the "psycho-archaeology" of humankind.

In Attic dialect the archaic hymn addressed to Apollo began with the euphoric exclamation, Io Paion!, "Lo, the Healer!" Considered as a shamanic archetype, Apollo was by definition a healer, but the ecstatic song addressed to him was originally addressed to the pasturing, sheltering Earth, the primal source of all healing power. No doubt Pan, the rustic "god of nature," received praise of this type before the *paean* (modern spelling) was co-opted for ritual use in the Apollonian cult. Apollo has two faces, one looking back to shamanic roots in the archaic past, the other looking ahead to Hellenism, the triumph of Greek intellectualism. Apollo is often depicted overcoming the "serpent power" of the Python, the sacred female oracle enshrined at Delphi and elsewhere.

The Great God Pan and Apollo represent diametrically different views of the world, prefiguring the conflict between nature and culture, instinct and intellection. Marsyas was a Panlike satyr whom Apollo flayed alive because the scruffy fellow played the flute better than the solar deity did. The myth reveals how brutal the intellect can be when it assumes superiority over human instincts. All the Greek gods have Roman equivalents, except for Apollo. When the Greek divinities migrated into the Roman psyche, Apollo remained himself, yet he did not stay entirely unchanged.

Gradually Apollo, the sun deity who opposed the randy satyrs and the snakelike wisdom of the telluric oracles, morphed into Christ, and Christ became the supreme Greco-Roman deity, enshrined in the state-supported cult of the Divine Redeemer. This mythic metamorphosis was one of the most fateful events ever to unfold in the spiritual life of the Europan peoples. Its aftereffects in the collective psyche of the human species have been disastrous.

Apollo can appear to defeat all the gods of nature because this deity is imagined to come from *outside nature, beyond the sensorial world*. The god Apollo reflects the human glorification of intellect as a force independent of the body. The Latin word *Phoebus* is not a substitute name for Apollo, but only for his primary attribute, the sunlike radiance of the body-free intellect. Historian Jane Harrison explains that Phoebus indicated "the sun-calendar with all its attendant moralities of law and order and symmetry and rhythm and light and reason, the qualities we are apt too readily to lump together as Greek."[37] These attributes of civilization were all possessed by early Europans, but developed in close reference to, and deep reverence for, nature, and *not by distancing humanity from nature*, as happened within the Greek intellectualism of the Golden Age (sixth to fifth centuries B.C.E.). It is a cliché among historians that Greek intellectualism prepared the way for Christian theology. The triumphant merger of Christ and Apollo was the outcome.

Apollo was an austere god who frowned on the pleasure drives represented by the satyrs and maenads, those gay companions of Pan on his excursions through the ancient countryside. Excesses of hedonism and debauchery are, of course, basic to our stereotypical view of Paganism. The *Satyricon*, a novel written around 50 c.e. by the Roman satirist Petronius, shows the gross excesses of Pagan urban society as they really were. The book was faithfully transferred to film by Federico Fellini, offering a mini-course in decadent Pagan culture. Excessive love of sensual and sexual pleasure was both a strength and a failing of Paganism, but Pagans did not have a monopoly on debauchery. In Lyons, where Irenaeus preached against Gnostic heresies, it was said that before the Christian authorities arrived, prostitutes gathered at the main gate to greet all travelers. After the Christians took control of the city and declared sexual pleasure to be a sin, the line of whores stretched from the front gate all the way through town and out the rear gate.[38] By 900 c.e., five hundred years after Hypatia's murder, the Roman Church had produced a "pornocracy," a society ruled by whores and people addicted to prostitution. The cruel, twisted lecheries of medieval popes such as Sergius III, John XI, John XII, and Benedict VI make Pagan orgies look as innocent as a country picnic.

Pleasure (Greek *hedonia*) is an essential issue in any discussion of Paganism, but discussions of such a dicey issue often fail to assess Pagan sensibility correctly. Contrary to Christian prurience, fondness for sensual and sexual pleasure can be seen as a spontaneous expression of the joy of living in the natural world, rather than a symptom of evil, all-consuming lust. The Pagan outlook on life was hedonistic and esthetic as much as it was Earth honoring and ecological. Sensual pleasure celebrates the human body as a sacred instrument, much in the manner that D. H. Lawrence wished to revive. Lawrence saw the basis of human morality in what might be called the pleasure bond. This is an ecstatic connection that bonds humans to the Earth as well as to each other. Lawrence regarded the redeemer complex exactly as Gnostics did: a deviation from the sanctity of the Earth and the physical senses. His close friend Richard Aldington wrote that "Lawrence's fundamental heresy was simply that he placed the quality of feelings, intensity of sensations and passion before intellect."[39] He might have added that Lawrence defended this view with the powerful tool of his intellect.

In *Apocalypse* (1931), Lawrence wrote that "the Jewish mind hates the moral and terrestrial divinity of man; the Christian mind the same." This comment echoes the core of the Gnostic protest against Jewish and Christian faith in an off-planet divinity. Lawrence knew intuitively that denial of the sanctity of the Earth and humanity was a generic Jewish trait—indeed, the very signature of the extremist apocalyptic cult known as the Zaddikim. This cult, whose textual legacy is found in the Dead Sea Scrolls, seeded the doctrines of Christian salvationism. Lawrence correctly observed that "the Jewish idea of a Messiah and a Jewish salvation (or destruction) of the whole world" was substituted for "the purely individual experience of pagan initiation." He also noted that "the system of suppression of all pagan evidence has been instinctive, a fear-instinct, and has been thorough, and has been really criminal, in the Christian world from the first century until today."[40]

The "prior wounding" undergone by Native Europans caused the trauma that drove some of them to commit genocide in the Americas, perpetrating deeds as cruel as Apollo's flaying of Marsyas. This trauma broke the pleasure bond at the rapturous node where the grounding of humanity in the Earth is celebrated. Something radical and terrible uprooted the ancient Pagans from their place in nature and alienated them from the pleasures of the flesh, the play of the instincts, the clear and clean joy of animal spontaneity. At the dawn of the Christian era, the ages-old healing contact with the Earth was broken, the telluric voices ceased to speak to the Pagan people. As recounted in Plutarch's essay "On Why the Oracles Came to Fail," a voice in the wilderness cried out, "The Great God Pan is dead."[41]

The lament for the death of Pan can be situated in a temporal frame. Around 150 C.E. the connotation of the Latin word *paganus* changed, due to the mounting assault on Pagan values by converts to the salvationist creed. Tertullian, one of the first Christian ideologues to openly attack Gnostics, argued that *pagani* be regarded as "civilian" noncombatants in the open war on non-Christians. Converts to the new religion called themselves "enrolled members of Christ (members of his militant church)," and viewed non-Christians "as not of the army so enrolled."[42] It was inevitable that these "civilians" would be in harm's way in the escalating war against whatever challenged the emergent belief system.

Pagans all over Europa rapidly became collateral damage in the Christian campaign against heresy.

THE GAZE OF NARCISSUS

To many people, the assumption that Pagans were irreligious immediately implies that they were also immoral. The belief that there can be no morality without a religious framework to dictate it is endemic to human society, although it is not necessarily innate to human nature. Genuine religious *experience* produces moral behavior, but the institutions and dogmas of religion that dictate morality corrupt the innate tendency to be moral, that is, to act in kindness, out of generosity, and without care of being rewarded for it. The conviction that humans are innately good and, left to their proper instincts, will act in a morally responsible way, has been asserted by Aldous Huxley and C. G. Jung, although neither elaborated much on this crucial issue. The assertion of our innate moral capacity for goodness also figures in the arguments of deep ecology founder Arne Naess.

Pagan morality assumed that kindness ("brotherly love" in Christian terms) is generic to humanity and need not be dictated. In his *Meditations* (book 9) Marcus Aurelius wrote "Nature has constituted rational beings for their own mutual benefit, each to help his fellows according to their worth, and in no wise to do them harm."[43] Pagan moral argument rejected self-sacrifice as contrary to the genuine, spontaneous expression of our generic goodness.

The glorification of suffering, either through self-sacrifice or self-effacing altruism, was the single outstanding element in the salvationist creed that struck Pagans at all levels of society as "depraved and extravagant superstition."[44] This reaction, expressed by Pliny the Elder, Tacitus, and other contemporary thinkers, indicates how the Pagan sense of self was closely bounded by social decorum that set personal power within modest limits. Only heroes and exceptional people could exceed these limits, and then only under extraordinary circumstances.[45] Like many indigenous peoples around the world, Pagans were instinctively wary of self-aggrandizement, the fault of *hubris*, "excess," (or "inflation," to borrow the Jungian term). Pagans viewed personal sacrifice for the sake of others as glaring egotism, not the highest form of altruism. The claim that the Redeemer's sacrifice affected all of humanity for the better was to the Pagan mind a grotesque and dangerous fantasy. Yet this view was favored by widespread social changes within the Roman Empire, changes connected with the shift into the Piscean Age (ca. 120 B.C.E.). The new Zeitgeist signaled a shift of priorities in many areas of life, but most acutely in the domain of religious experience.

The decline of the Mysteries after the fourth century B.C.E. was due in large measure to a sea change in the collective consciousness of humanity. The intensification of the rational and self-observing capacities of the mind has been hailed for producing the Golden Age of Greek science, but it also occasioned a tidal wave of narcissism in the general population. The obsession of the Roman emperors to deify themselves was but one bizarre symptom of a mainstream trend in what Julian Jaynes called "the transition of the bicameral mind to subjective consciousness."[46] The shift began around 600 B.C.E., a thousand years before the death of Hypatia and the dawn of the Dark Ages. Jaynes's "bicameral mind" assumes an innate predisposition in Pagan, pre-Christian peoples to participate in social reality and sacred experience without the too strong intrusion of self-reflection. With the shift to "subjective consciousness" came the intensification of distance and a heightened sense of "witnessing." With this shift, the stance of the detached observer impresses or imposes a strong egoic filter on what is being experienced. Paradoxically, the detached witness tends to participate in a dissociated and seemingly selfless way in the world, but tends more and more to "take it personally." Such is the bizarre twist of narcissism: it both detaches and intensifies the lens of the self-observing self. As the old "bicameral" mode of participation fades out, the isolated individual becomes the supreme denominator of value.

Modern psychology affirms that narcissistic people, although obsessed with how they look, actually cannot see how they look. The syndrome reaches a grotesque level in bulimia and anorexia nervosa. In acute cases a starving girl who weighs eighty pounds believes she is grossly over-weight and *sees herself* like that in the mirror. Narcissism both induces and increases alienation from one's body. Left untreated, the condition spirals down into a state of profound desperation. In *The Betrayal of the Body*, psychotherapist Alexander Lowen, a follower of Wilhelm Reich and a specialist on narcissism, explains that the desperation of narcissism

> stems from conflicting attitudes: an outer submission covering an inner defiance, or an outer rebellion hiding an inner passivity. Submission means that one accepts the position of the "outsider," the minority, the dispossessed, or the rejected. It entails a sacrifice of the right to personal fulfillment and satisfaction, in other words, the surrender of the right to pleasure and enjoyment. The inner defiance demands that the individual challenge his situation. Defiance forces him into provocative behavior, which tempts the doom that he fears.[47]

These elements clearly figured in the attitude of early Christian converts who viewed themselves as the dispossessed of Roman society, but also as chosen for a special fate that could be realized by provok-ing the wrath of the authorities and thus inviting a glorious martyrdon. (Today we see this defiance enacted by Islamic extremists whose religious beliefs represent a virulent medieval mutation of the redeemer complex.) Cut off from their Pagan roots, denied the pleasure bond, and morally desperate, early Christian converts hysterically denied themselves what they no longer had in the first place: empathic connection to the Earth and the realm of the senses. Having lost the primal connection to the body, they sought release from embodiment. The triumph of Christian doctrines of salvation was due less to the veracity of those doctrines than to the power of the selfish craving to which they appealed.

Pagans in Europa and the Near East regarded the religious narcis-sism of early Christianity as a bizarre plague. The tendency to castigate the flesh and deny pleasure seemed so insane that it could hardly be subjected to critical analysis. In Plato's dialogue *The Symposium* the physi-cian Erixymachus associates love with proper upkeep of the body and senses, not an ideal to be realized in a disembodied, extraphysical state.

Commenting on this passage in *Sex and Pleasure in Western Culture*, Gail Hawkes writes:

> Love offered the means to spiritual balance between the moral and immortal aspects of humanity. The experience of love thus linked the material body with the spiritual self, and this link was reflected in strategies for the management of both. *The desiring body, by this reasoning, was not a threat to social order, but lay at the center of a harmony essential to the health of the individual and society.*[48] (emphasis added)

This entire comment, and especially the last sentence, is an epitome of Pagan, body-based morality. Such a moral code does not have to be formulated in rules, because it arises spontaneously if the conditions here described are met. With the shift of the age and increased concern for the narcissistic, self-regarding ego, these conditions came to be totally disrupted and undermined all across the classical world.

WEAPONIZED CONVERSION

Significantly, the word *martyr* means "witness," and so connotes this very act of distancing oneself from immediate, sense-bound reality. What Pagans found appalling about Christian martyrs was not only their willingness to die for an unearthly cause, but even more so, the excessive egotism of their claim to stand beyond this world, due to their faith in a divine intercessor sent by an off-planet god. Such a position was directly contrary to the Pagan religious attitude that beholds the Divine *in* this world, immanent and sharing intimately in the life of all that exists. The rising narcissism of the Piscean Age engendered a psychological need for deliverance from the very egocentricity produced by the collective shift into self-concern. With its program of individual soul salvation, Christianity had the advantage of appearing to satisfy that need. But rather than curing the obsessive self-concern, it worsened the condition.

Originally, the Greek word *theoria* meant not an abstract scheme but merely "the act of beholding," which might be contrasted to the Christian notion of witnessing.[49] In the Pagan mode of apprehending the world, *theorein*, "to behold," meant to be engaged with what one beholds, to be seized by the spectacle of the Divine Order manifesting throughout nature, as well as in human nature. It implied that all there is to be seen and encountered in this world, sensuously, has a divine basis—the Greek word for divine being *theos*, a play on *theorein*.

"Behold the Divine, and then recognize in yourself that which beholds the Divine," is a surviving fragment of Mystery teaching from the Neoplatonic School to which Hypatia belonged.[50]

Greek rationalism steeply precipitated the shift away from Pagan beholding (around 600 B.C.E., the timing noted by Jaynes and many others), but the mutation of Western consciousness into the full-blown narcissistic detachment from the body and denial of the sensorial world took many centuries. The inherent change in the human psyche— probably due to the maturation of forebrain circuits and a consequent increase in abstracting power—was a natural development, but the religious beliefs addressed to that change were anything but natural.[51] Although it lacked clear doctrinal definition, the new religion embraced by the men who murdered Hypatia followed two imperatives that frontally challenged the Pagan worldview: social equality, and the redemptive value of suffering. The first demand went against the Pagan notion of astral fate, *hiermarmene*, "the guiding order," which allotted to each person a definite role in life. The role cannot be changed, because the rules of the game of life are set by superhuman powers. Pagans accepted that life is not fair, privileges are not evenly distributed, and there is no way within human capacity to assure final and complete justice in all instances. Nevertheless, Pagan morality assumed that fair play and decency are possible even in unjust situations. The rules are not set by us, but we can always act in a way that "does not debase humanity and human values."[52]

Honor and honesty were basic Pagan principles that applied to all people in all situations. Slaves and aristocrats alike could act honorably, honestly, and fairly, even though they faced a stacked deck, with inscrutable fate working in favor or against each protagonist. The Pagan virtue of tolerance allowed for a great deal of flexibility in what could be, in some respects, a rigid system of social determinism. Christianity toppled that system with the claim that fate could be changed through personal alliance with the Divine Redeemer. In doing so, Christianity replaced Pagan tolerance with its opposite.

The second demand of salvationist creed, its insistence on the redemptive value of suffering, was totally repulsive to the Pagan sense of life.

Pagan roots run deep. Indigenous instincts are strong and hard to eradicate. Europans resisted conversion for many centuries after the death of Hypatia, but native resistance provoked even more severe repression by church and state. Political endorsement of redemptive religion, inaugurated by the faux-convert emperor Constantine, was a huge benefit to people invested in the emergent power structure of Roman Christianity. The few who profited most from the new hierarchy were supported by the passive consent of the mass of believers at the base of the structure, even when those few shamelessly exploited and manipulated them. The blind faith of the converts to salvationism was infused with righteous fury by the belief in divine retribution—a belief derived from a minor extremist movement in Palestine (described in chapters 4 and 5). In the figure of the crucified savior, the victim-perpetrator bond became elevated to a transcendent level.

Faith in the redemptive power of suffering carries the sanction to inflict suffering—such is the covert dynamic of the victim-perpetrator bond. Adoption of the belief in redemption, so alien to Pagan ethics, was the decisive factor in the self-annihilation of Native Europans, the indigenous people of the Old World. Faith in divine retribution proved to be a potent weapon of mass destruction. This weapon would be aimed for centuries to come at Pagan Europe, and after that at the Americas, and after that at the entire planet.

3

THE CONQUEST OF EUROPA

The history of European dominance begins with Rome, and so does the triumph of Christianity. From the founding of Rome in 753 B.C.E. (according to the Roman historian Varro) to 200 C.E. when a bishop of Rome was officially declared the first pope, bearing the title Pontifex Maximus, is a mere thousand years. It would take another century or so before the Roman Empire formally merged with the new salvationist creed. Result: Roman Christianity. The institutionalization of the One True Faith was affected by Constantine, the presumed convert who declared Christianity the state religion in 325 C.E. From its origin in the fourth century, the new creed embraced the political ideology of conquest and domination. Or, it could be argued, it used religious terms to disguise political ideology. Religious historian Jaroslav Pelikan expresses surprise at "the possibility that Caesar might acknowledge the sovereignty of Christ as King of Kings." But then, discussing the ideologue Tertullian (ca. 160–230), one of the first writers to condemn Gnostics as heretics, he gives away the game:

> "The Caesars too would have believed in Christ," Tertullian asserted, "if Christians could have been Caesars"; but that was a contradiction in terms. *Yet the moral contradiction became a political reality* in the fourth century when the emperor Constantine I became a Christian, declaring his allegiance to Jesus Christ and adopting the cross as his official military and personal emblem.[53] (emphasis added)

Pelikan cannot see—because his personal faith blinds him to the historical and political reality of that faith—that there is no moral contradiction at all. On the contrary, Christ and Caesar were made for each other. Conversion and conquest make an irresistible and enduring pair.

GENDER BALANCE

European domination in the New World proceeded under cover of conversion: the natives had to be "saved," or be destroyed in the process. The notion that people can be destroyed in order to save them typifies the insane logic of *annihilation theology* (as I propose to call it). Of the four components of the redeemer complex, the fourth, apocalypse and world judgment, contains the lethal germ of annihilation theology.

Among the pre-Christian peoples of Europa, the concept of divine retribution effected in a catastrophic world-ending did not exist. Mythological parallels to this scenario were unknown to the Iberian, Gallic, Italic, and Hellenic peoples, or the indigenous tribes of Scandinavia, the British Isles and Ireland. The virulent apocalyptic strain inherent to Christianity was an import from distant desert lands. It derived from a sect of Jewish extremists, the Zaddikim of the Dead Sea. The apocalyptic element was particularly lethal to European soul-life because divine retribution is a supramundane, male-only proposition, completely alien to cultures rooted in the telluric ambience of the Great Goddess. It is affected by the father god through his righteous warriors, the soldiers in his "salvation army." The apocalypse is not a natural catastrophe, but a supernatural act in which Father God asserts supreme power and Mother Nature plays no role. In other words, apocalyptic judgment is an enforcement tactic of male-authoritarian rule. As such it would have been alien and intimidating to native peoples who lived in matriarchal culture and gender-balanced societies.

The primary insight of ecofeminism—a term originally used in 1974 by Francoise D'Eaubonne, a French sociologist—is that domination of nature goes along with domination of women. This insight links the environmental problem to the issue of gender relations. (The link is correct, but feminists have handled it atrociously due to cultural Marxist indoctrination behind the war on gender.) Theologian Rosemary Radford Ruether stated the principle in one sentence: "There can be no liberation for women and no solution to the ecological crisis within a society whose fundamental model is domination."[54] In historical perspective it now appears that salvationist religion is not a religion at all, not in the sense that it genuinely concerns itself with the Divine and responds in a compassionate and insightful way to human needs. Rather, it is a political system in religious guise, a system "whose fundamental model is domination." The apocalyptic world-ending represents the climax of male domination. It is the final vindication of the off-planet father god.

"Many ecofeminists suggest that as a movement deep ecology is insufficiently sensitive to the complex ways in which naturism (domination of nature), sexism, racism, and classicism interlock, and to the strategically central role of gender analysis could play in dismantling these categories."[55] This observation by Andy Fisher in *Radical Ecopsychology* applies aptly to the psychohistorical analysis of "prior wounding" in Europa, and invites close reflection. Gender balance in indigenous pre-Christian societies was crucial to their sustainability, but it also made them vulnerable. Salvationist religion arising from the Near East decimated the moral and cultural norms of the indigenous Europans. Women also played a role in the program of conversion and often fervently served the agenda of domination. In the British Isles, across the continent of Europa, and all around the Mediterranean basin, gender relations had to be violently disrupted so that the new faith could prevail.

In *The Chalice and the Blade* (1987) Riane Eisler presented Minoan civilization as the model of a "gylanic" culture in which neither patriarchal nor matriarchal values were dominant. Her neologism combines the Greek *gyne*, "female," and *andros*, "male," to suggest male-female balance. Eisler also proposed the term "dominator culture" for any society marked by "the *ranking* of one half of humanity over another."[56] In her attention to the gender issue, Eisler highlighted the role of sexual apartheid in our alienation from the Earth. In *Future Primitive*, a brilliant critical biography of D. H. Lawrence, Dolores LaChapelle observed that "the problem of sexuality, in its larger dimensions, is at the heart of modern civilization's destruction of humanity and nature."[57] Like Lawrence, LaChapelle considers that sexual attraction between human beings reflects and even sustains the sensory life of the planet, the biosystem itself. In a gylanic society, sexual and sensual pleasure are natural by-products of love and reverence felt for the Earth.

Minoan civilization was certainly remarkable in this respect, and so were some other cultures in pre-Christian Europe, as Eisler notes. The bioregional societies of Marija Gimbutas' Old Europe also appear to have been moderately gender-balanced. And Celtic civilization, which unified Europa, presents a gylanic model, as we shall see.

It would be foolish to propose that Pagan society was out and out egalitarian, but the elite of Pagan intellectuals, the Gnostics, were decidedly so. Jacques Lacarriere noted that "only the Gnostics were bold enough to put a match to the hypothetical gunpowder and postulate that all rebellion, all protest against the world, all claim to spiritual or social liberation must, in order to be effective, begin with a liberation of sex."[58] Gnostics practiced sexual equality in both a rigorous and ritual manner. In their weekly meetings they threw lots to see who would lead the current session, and women were equal to men in all capacities to instruct and guide the group. Each Mystery cell, called *thiasos* in Greek, comprised a core group of eight men and eight women. A rare alabaster bowl from an Orphic cult, and the Pietroasa bowl found in Buzau, in southeastern Romania, attests to this structure. A fifth-century Etruscan lamp bowl also repeats the sixteen motif.[59] All surviving examples of these rare ritual objects show the initiates with the bare soles of their feet touching.

Gender reconciliation must be central to any discussion of what made Pagan society work, and, indeed, what makes any society sustainable, as exemplified in the gylanic or partnership cultures discussed by Riane Eisler. Terence McKenna, who adopted and developed Eisler's model, defined dominator culture as "hierarchical, paternalistic, materialistic, and male dominated," and "evolutionarily maladaptive."[60] Any form of social organization that asserts force over cooperation, exploits gender difference, and ignores the limitations inherent to bioregional culture will certainly be maladaptive.

Celtic Heritage

The true Celts were a tall, fair race, warlike and masterful, whose place of origin (as far as we can trace them) was somewhere about the sources of the Danube, and who spread their dominion both by conquest and by peaceful infiltration over Mid-Europe, Gaul, Spain, and the British Islands. They did not exterminate the original prehistoric inhabitants of these regions—Paleolithic and Neolithic races, dolmen builders and workers in bronze—but they imposed on them their language, their arts, and their traditions, taking, no doubt, a good deal from them in return, especially in the important matter of religion. Among these races the true Celts formed an aristocratic and ruling class.[61]

Many different indigenous tribes occupied Europa in the six thousand years before Christianity arose, but Celtic culture was geographically inclusive. It unified Europe from Ireland in the north down into the Iberian Peninsula and eastward as far as Turkey where one tribe, the Galatae, established a large colony in 276 B.C.E. The Galatians of the New Testament were blond, blue-eyed Celts. An apocryphal legend claims that John the Baptist was a Celt, and Mary Magdalene was Circassian, not Jewish. This legend may explain why Mary Magdalene is traditionally portrayed with golden blonde or strawberry blonde hair.

The Minoans were a Mediterranean people central to the history of Europe, as the myth of Zeus and Europa suggests, and theirs was indeed a gender-balanced culture. Equally so was the culture of the ancient Celts. Europe in the pre-Christian era was never unified under a totalitarian power, but it did enjoy a period of peace and unity during the "Celtic Iron Age," which lasted from 1200 B.C.E. into the Common Era. Breton writer Jean Markale shows in *Women of the Celts* that Celtic society even favored the power and prestige of women in some respects. Celtic society presents a model of Pagan, pre-Christian Europe at a crowning moment, right on the verge of recorded history.[62]

From the dawn of the Neolithic Age, 9000 B.C.E., to the late Bronze Age around 1400 B.C.E., Europa, including the British Isles, was occupied by a mosaic of ethnic groups that spoke unknown languages. (One of these groups was the Basques, a mysterious people who survive to this day.) For reasons unknown, but perhaps due simply to their strength of character, the Celtic peoples expanded across Europe and unified it, after a fashion. Thus historians recognize in Celtic civilization the first fully European culture. It lasted for about fifteen hundred years and then, with the rise of Rome, "the Celts were the first of the peoples of temperate Europe to be incorporated within the Roman Empire as it spread beyond the confines of the Mediterranean."[63] Celtic civilization represents the multiracial complexity of Europa, for they were the first truly Europewide culture. But the unique historical role of the Celts also carries tragic elements. The Celtic tribes were also the first target of the type and scale of genocidal violence that some Europeans perpetrated when they invaded the Americas.

Celtic culture was not theocratic. The institution of divine kingship assumes a ruling class descended from the gods, but *all* Celts felt they were Tuatha de Danaan, "Children of Dana." The mother deity of their culture was the river goddess Dana, or Danu. The location of the geographic origin of the Celts ("Celtic hearth") has been much disputed, but probably it was near the headwaters of the Danube in the Alps of modern Switzerland.

Known for their sensuality, violent temper, and love of physical beauty, the Celts were intensely romantic. The great love stories of the Middle Ages, such as the tale of Tristan and Isolde and the Arthurian romances, all originate from the Celtic matrix, as do most variants of the Grail quest, "the earliest definition of the secular mythology that is today the guiding spiritual force of the European West," according to mythologist Joseph Campbell.[64] The myth of the lovers is a universal archetype, of course, but its Western variants are deeply imbued with Celtic elements. Pre-Christian versions of the Grail legend derive from the Celtic myth of the triple goddess Keridwen who initiates poets and seers into the secrets of nature's hidden codes. The original grail was the magical cauldron of the Goddess, the womb of the Great Mother. A literary device introduced by Robert de Boron in the thirteenth century transformed this Pagan artifact into the cup that holds the blood of the Savior.

Tristan and Isolde by Gottfried von Strassburg (fl. 1210) is the greatest love story of the Middle Ages. Its characters and setting were Celtic. It was written in Middle High German, and other, less complete versions of the tale come down to us in old French, Breton, and Latin. The Celts themselves had no writing. Like the Native American Bronze Age cultures they resemble, they based everything on the honor code of the spoken word. Honor is a Pagan attribute. The language called Gaelic, still spoken today in Western Ireland and Scotland, is close to the language spoken by the Celts three thousand years ago. Gaelic is as old as Greek, first written in secular alphabets after 1200 B.C.E. Gaelic was not written down until much later, during the Christian Era. Of the two languages most influential in shaping the identity of Europa, one was written and the other was not.

REVERENCE AND COURAGE

The Celts had no formal priesthood. Instead, they followed the spiritual guidance of the Druids ("oak seers") who represented a tradition of shamanism derived from the prehistoric culture of megalith builders. The Druids were accomplished astronomers, diviners, and psychics. They also had considerable moral authority, allowing them to arbitrate in wars and even adjudicate murders. The rumor originating with Pliny the Elder (Roman encyclopaedist, 23–79 C.E.) that Druids systematically practiced human sacrifice is unfounded. Dion Chrysostum (first century C.E.), a historian who traveled widely among the Celts, compared them to Brahmins in Hindu society. He says the Druids "were versed in the arts of seers and other forms of wisdom, without whom the kings were not permitted to adopt or plan any course."[65] A century earlier, the Roman orator Cicero had compared them to the Magi of Persia.

The Greek mythographer Hecataeus of Abdera (fourth century B.C.E.) described the Druidic circle of Stonehenge, where Apollo, "a god of shamans," made an annual journey. According to Herodotus, the Druid Abaris was able to travel anywhere "on an arrow," that is, by magical flight.[66] Two of Apollo's gifts to humankind, the arrow and the power to heal, are universally associated with shamanism. In *Avalonian Quest*,

Arthurian scholar Geoffrey Ashe says that "the Druids were, in effect, shamans." They were custodians of indigenous wisdom who shared their lore with their counterparts in Greece and elsewhere in the classical world. Ashe cites Stuart Piggot on the historical importance of the Druids: "Shamanism need not have been the whole content of Paleolithic and Mesolithic religions but it could have been an important component, and one that could form a substrate in the ancient European tradition."[67] Gnostics like Hypatia, who may arguably be regarded as intellectual shamans, would have recognized Druids as *gnostikoi* in their own right, that is, knowers of divine matters, adepts of the sublime and supernatural. In fact, during Hypatia's lifetime Alexandria hosted a circle of scholars dedicated to the collection and study of Druidic lore.[68] In the view of the ancients, who lived far closer to the facts than we do, experts in occult knowledge and adepts of paranormal powers would have merited the term *gnostikos*, no matter what their cultural origins. Such venerated figures could have been found throughout the pan-European mosaic of Mysteries that spread from the far Hebrides into the Near East.[69]

The Druids were initiates of the Hibernian Mysteries described by Herodotus and other ancient writers. They used a code called ogham, consisting of runic symbols rather than letters. Accomplished musicians and chanters, they may have introduced to the Greeks some notions about "the harmony of the spheres," and certainly would have had no difficulty discussing sky lore with Egyptian astronomers. Although the Druids did not write in a secular alphabet of Celtic origin, they could read and converse in Greek and other Europan languages, and they maintained a schooling system. The druidic colleges were the educational facet of the Hibernian branch of Goddess Mysteries. According to Diogenes Laertius and other ancient sources, the Druids "taught that the ideal for people was to live in harmony with nature and themselves, accepting that pain and death were not evils but essential . . . and that the only evil was moral weakness." Their message to the common people was: "Revere the gods, do not do evil to each other, and exercise courage."[70]

The Irish heretic Pelagius (ca. 354–420 c.e.) was a contemporary of Hypatia's. Deeply steeped in the myth of the triple goddess and other variants of triplicity in Celtic lore, Pelagius formulated the Trinity based on ancestral notions of terrestrial divinity. He argued that people could achieve their own salvation using individual mind and will and not submitting to anything preordained. Needless so say, the Roman Church took a hard view of this doctrine. The authorities accused him of reviving druidic philosophy and condemned him as a heretic. In its original form, free will was a Celtically inspired Pagan heresy. Pelagius's ideas were rejected in favor of Augustine's doctrine of "Original Sin." The Trinity Pelagius formulated was later credited to Cyril, the bishop of Alexandria who may have ordered the murder of Hypatia. Co-optation went hand in hand with suppression and terrorism in the conquest of the Old World, and the record, as ever, was written to legitimate, if not glorify, the perpetrators. One historian comments:

> The early surviving sources about the Druids are written in support of Rome and its conquest of the Celts and suppression of the Druids. In A.D. 54 the Roman emperor Claudius officially prohibited the Druids by law. It was an obvious move for Rome to make: in order to conquer people and absorb them, you first have to get rid of their intellectuals and destroy their cultural knowledge.[71]

Murder and suppression of the intelligentsia is, of course, a standard policy of Communism, lavishly demonstrated in the Bolshevik takedown of Czarist Russia. It proceeds today (2021) in the transhumanist program of the Great Reset with its stated goal to run all social affairs on AI, artificial intelligence, aiming not merely to control the human mind but to eliminate it.

First Blood

In the twilight of their culture, Celtic warriors hired on as mercenaries in the Roman legions. This is a clear historical instance of the victim-perpetrator bond, for Celts had been victims of Roman aggression for centuries. Early on the Celts strove to excel in warcraft and battle, exclusively to protect themselves. They were by nature a migratory people but not invasive. (In *The Anatomy of Human Destructiveness*, Erich Fromm explains the difference between defensive and predatory aggression and asserts that the human species "is phylogenetically not a predatory animal."[72]) In 360 B.C.E. the Celts began to retaliate against the invasion of their native lands. They annihilated the Roman army and occupied Rome, a humiliating event in Roman memory. There followed a period of peace, broken a century later when some Celtic tribes allied with the Etruscans against Rome. The ensuing conflict was decisive. It led to the breakup of Celtic civilization, but the end was long in coming. Roman campaigns to destroy and enslave the tribal confederacies of the Celts present the first verifiable instances of genocide on European soil.

In *The Gallic Wars* Julius Caesar presented his self-legitimating account of the campaigns he fought in Gaul (the Celtic name for modern France) against tribal confederacies united by a savvy and intrepid warrior named Vercingetorix. A country of beauteous rivers and deep forests, Gaul was vast in extent and rich in resources. Conquered, it would add a quarter to the territory of the Roman Empire.

The Gallic wars lasted only from 58 to 52 B.C.E., but they changed forever the face, and the fate, of ancient Europa. Caesar began his campaign by establishing a winter camp in cisalpine Gaul, near the headwaters of the Danube, the proximity of the presumed "Celtic hearth." In the winter of 58–57 came rumors that certain tribes called the Belgica were preparing to attack him. Caesar sent two legions to Reims, center of the tribe of the Remi, and persuaded the tribal chieftain to come over to his side. Other Belgian tribes in the region reacted by attacking Reims, but Caesar drove them off. Then, in a shift from defense to aggression, Caesar expanded his campaign. He attacked two hostile tribes, the Nervians and the Aduatuci, and inflicted huge and grievous losses. In one battle, only 500 of the 60,000 Celtic combatants survived.

So far, the battles fought were engagements between armies and did not involve civilian casualties. Among the Celtic tribes were many seasoned warriors of barbarian stock, fully equal to Roman military might. The Belgica in particular were known for their ferocity in battle, as well as for their skill in training horses. Military engagements did not involve assaults on the local population, but the resistance of the Belgica aroused Caesar's appetite for blood. He established a winter camp among the tribes he had subdued, and, just to keep his edge, went off to conquer Britain. Soon Caesar realized he had left himself with a problem by locating his camp among the defeated but still hostile population in the Belgian marshes. Out of nowhere, a Celtic revolt annihilated two of his legions. Caesar responded with relentless attacks on tribes in the marshlands of the Rhine, and this time he expanded his assault to the general population. The assault on civilians was so brutal that when it became known in Rome, the senator Cato demanded Caesar be captured and tried as a war criminal. But Caesar prevailed and continued his push from military conquest to genocide. The massacres of the Belgica cleared his way for the larger campaign to come: the conquest of all Gaul.

Caesar's larger designs were now opposed by an uprising of tribal confederacies united under a formidable warrior, Vercingetorix. The Romans were horribly defeated at Orleans, and, for a time, it looked like the Celtic hero had a real chance of driving them out of Gaul. After many skirmishes, Caesar forced a full-scale confrontation at Bourges, one of the largest and most prosperous cities in the Gallic confederacy. The city (located about seventy miles south of Paris) was besieged and ferociously defended, but eventually it fell, and tens of thousands of unarmed inhabitants were slaughtered. Caesar does not admit that he gave the order for the massacre. He comments dryly:

> None of our men stopped to think about booty; they were so infuriated by the massacre of Romans at Orleans, and by the efforts they had had to make over the siege, that they spared neither the old nor the women nor the children. (*The Gallic Wars* 7.24)

This was the first large-scale, deliberate genocide of an indigenous people committed on European soil, and it set a trend for the Roman Empire in Europe, and, later, for the Church that married the Empire, to pursue conquest around the world. Although it was committed before the rise of Christianity, it presents the prototype of the merciless and triumphal aggression that came to be exhibited across Europa when Rome took up the Cross and divine authority legitimated genocide.

Gallic resistance remained strong after Bourges, but the massacre there had turned the tide in Caesar's favor. The endgame with the Celts played out three years later at Alesia, near Dijon, in the sumptuous hills of

Bourgogne. Vercingetorix and his army installed themselves with ample provisions in a hilltop fortress, ready to hold out indefinitely. Caesar had his army construct enormous fortifications (the remains survive today) around the 80,000-strong troops commanded by his archenemy. Learning that reinforcements from the Celtic confederacies were on the way in large numbers, he built a second line of battlements to protect his forces against attack from the rear. The Roman fortifications were so effective that Caesar was able to stand ground, starve out the army of Vercingetorix, and drive off the rescue forces, reported by ancient sources to have been nearly a quarter million in strength.

The defeat of the Celts at Alesia may have been due to profound demoralization as much as it was to Roman fortifications. When women and children were sent out from the besieged encampment on the hill, Caesar ordered that they not be allowed to pass the second line of battlements. Stranded between the barricades, thousands of them starved to death before the eyes of both contingents of Celts. Genocide in its most dramatic form had proved to be a weapon for conquest par excellence.

The Greek writer Plutarch, one of the last initiates of the Mysteries, tells us that the population of Gaul before Julius Caesar arrived was around three million. Eight years later, one million were dead, and half of those surviving had been turned into slaves and permanently uprooted. Not to discount other incidents of genocide in antiquity (Alexander's military record in Asia is a notable case), the massacre at Bourges established the imperative for violence against Europans on their own soil. The conquest of Gaul has been described as "the greatest human and social disaster in history, until the settlement of America."[73]

Intellectual Cleansing

Four hundred sixty-two years before Hypatia's death, Caesar was in her native city of Alexandria, facing a major career challenge. After the conquests of Britain and Gaul, the Roman generals' military and political strategy was largely determined by competition from his archrival, Pompey. In fact, Pompey, as much as Caesar, was responsible for establishing the conditions that allowed salvationism to spread into Europa. In

62 C.E. he annexed Judea to the Roman Empire. Thus began the Roman occupation of Palestine, an event that was to prove as decisive for Rome as it was for the Holy Land.

From Palestine Pompey headed for Egypt, a move that obliged Caesar to go to Alexandria in 47 B.C.E. and square off with his rival. Their confrontation took place at the harbor where the Royal Library and Museum were located. Caesar managed to destroy the Egyptian fleet that Pompey had appropriated and occupy the city. Soon enough he found himself in bed with Cleopatra. Suddenly, forces loyal to the pharaoh mounted a resistance, and the old warrior was trapped with insufficient military resources to defend himself.

What happened next is subject to a dozen incomplete and contradicting accounts. According to Caesar's own version of events in *The Civil Wars*, he set fire to the dockyards and the remaining Alexandrian fleet to provide cover for his escape from the city. He does not mention the Royal Library, but he set fire to that as well, or so stated the late Roman historian Ammanius Marcellinus (d. 395 C.E.), who claimed that Caesar's responsibility for the fire was "the unanimous belief of ancient authors." The Younger Seneca (d. 65 C.E.) reported in his essay *On Tranquillity of Mind* that 400,000 manuscripts were burned, but the figure has also been interpreted as 40,000. In ancient idiom, a "book," "scroll," or "manuscript" was a monograph or essay, rather than a full-length book. Nevertheless, 40,000 essays is a lot of essays. The Nag Hammadi codices consist merely of 52 fragmentary works, not even essays but more like spotty notes on lectures, and of these only 30 texts are substantial in content. They range from four to forty pages. This is what remains to suggest what stored in the once vast repository of the Royal Library of Alexandria.

It is certainly an arresting fact that Julius Caesar, who committed the first full-blown genocide on European soil, may also have been the first to burn the Royal Library at Alexandria. While it cannot be proven that he did it deliberately, he must certainly have known that it caught fire from the blaze he ordered to be set. Accident or not in Caesar's case, intellectual cleansing goes hand in hand with political genocide.

The libraries at the port of Alexandria were to burn several more times over the ensuing centuries. When Hypatia was about thirteen a mob of Christians set fire to the Serapeum and made sure that it burned to the ground. Not a single scroll was left on the smoldering shelves. Long after her death the Arabs who occupied the city continued the incendiary assault. In 641 Amru, the general of Omar, second in succession to the Prophet, fed the furnaces of the four thousand baths of Alexandria for six months with the books remaining in the Bruchion.[74]

Other libraries in the Mediterranean basin suffered a similar fate. As it rose to power the Roman Church specifically ordered that Gnostic books be sought out and destroyed. The 270,000 documents collected by Ptolemy Philadelphus were all destroyed for the same reason. Baptized in 380, the emperor Theodosius, who ruled between 379 and 395, made it his personal mission to annihilate all traces of Pagan and Gnostic literature. Theodosius had 27,000 scrolls from the Mystery Schools collected and burned because he was told they contained Gnostic teachings that contradicted his adopted belief system.[75] This policy of intellectual cleansing was not established by Caesar, as noted. But his actions dramatically demonstrated the license to destroy Pagan writings with impunity, and every Christianized Roman emperor followed his example. From Alesia in 52 b.c.e. to Alexandria in 47 b.c.e. is only five years. That is all that separates the two definitive acts of political and intellectual genocide in Pagan antiquity.

In 386, when Hypatia was sixteen, Pagan rituals were outlawed by state decree. From that time on popular shrines and Mystery temples were vandalized more and more frequently, flagrantly, and violently. When Alaric, warrior chieftain of the Goths, invaded Greece in 396, the last legitimate hierophant at Eleusis had already died and only a handful of initiates remained. The Neoplatonic philosopher Eunapius of Sardis, who may have taught Hypatia, was one of them. Describing how Christian converts flooded to the ancient sanctuaries ruined by the Gothic invaders, he lamented "the godlessness of those who in their dark garments entered with him [Alaric] unhindered and by the dissolution of the hierophantic rules and of the sacred bond they embodied."[76]

Owing to the policy of Church historians to write only what showed their institution in a good light, and to destroy conflicting accounts, such testimony is extremely rare. Accounts of murders of Pagans by Christians are scarce, but it is more than likely that students and teachers from the Mystery Schools were murdered in considerable numbers. According to the Byzantine historian Procopius (d. 562), in Syria alone a million

Pagans, polytheists, and heretics, including many Gnostics, were exterminated by the emperor Justinian "during the systematic persecution carried out by that pedantic bigot."[77] Sanctioned by an off-planet deity, the Roman Church committed such horrors with triumphant impunity and with no fear of reprisal.

In the Americas a thousand years later, a parallel drama played out. In a genocidal crime wave, some of the European invaders reenacted the violence inflicted on their ancestors in the early Christian Era—a clearcut instance of victim-perpetrator bonding.[78] As Mavor and Dix observe in *Manitou*, "the history of America never suggests that the white man's religious beliefs might be at fault."[79] What an omission. Likewise for the history of Europe: It celebrates the triumph of Christianity over Paganism without condemning the religious beliefs of white indigenous peoples who were converted to the alien creed of the One True Faith. Yet these Christian beliefs inspired and legitimated murderous invasions on an epic scale and persisted for centuries.

When Hypatia was in her twenties the Latin orator Libanius wrote to Theodosius to protest the desecration of Pagan shrines:

> The monks are spreading out like torrents across the countryside; and ruining the temples, they are ruining the countryside itself at one and the same time. For to snatch from a region the temple which protects it is like tearing out its eye, killing it, annihilating it. The temples are the very life of the countryside, where generations have lived in the shelter of the old ways.[80]

Libanius's plea shows that he identified the intellectual and spiritual activity performed in the temples with the life force of their natural setting. To the Pagan mind, to destroy those centers of literacy and learning was a feat of violence directed, not only against the people who frequented them, but against nature itself: "Ruining the temples, they are ruining the countryside itself." The shrines and schools of the Mystery network constituted the very eyes and organs of Pagan culture. In 400 C.E., the year Hypatia assumed her duties in the Museum of Alexandria, Eunapius of Sardis reported that Christian monks were "living like pigs in the holy places."[81]

In Caesar's time, Roman republicans like Cicero and Cato could openly regard him as a war criminal, but later the emperors suppressed any such dissent. After the Roman Empire merged with the Catholic Church, war crimes became legitimated in the name of the Savior. Perpetrators adopted the salvationist creed for religious cover, in order to sanction their actions through a superhuman authority. They turned their victims into criminals, condemning the most threatening ones as heretics and targeting all Pagans, just because they were Pagans. Infected by the ideological virus of salvationism, native Europeans entered a path of self-annihilation, and the so-called Dark Ages followed.

From our current perspective of time and historical distance, it is difficult to imagine how a people could attack and dismember their own culture and annihilate the very foundations of their cultural and historical existence. But, if we could imagine how that happened, might we not better understand what we are currently doing to ourselves today on the global scale?

—————— 4 ——————

THE CULT OF RIGHTEOUSNESS

The salvationist fervor that swept over Europa at the dawn of the Christian era did not originate in the collective mind-set of its diverse indigenous peoples. Like the arrival of the European colonialists in the New World, it presented a unique, unparalleled intrusion on native soil. Scholars like to compare the Christian Redeemer with Pagan gods such as the Nordic Baldur, a "tree-hung" shaman who descended into the Underworld, or Aengus, the solar love god of Irish mythology, but such mythological parallels are deeply misleading. The Redeemer of Judeo-Christian faith did not exist in the mythologies of peoples whose participation in the natural world was devoid of a sense of sin. The psychic and imaginative life of the indigenous Europans did not harbor anything like the supernatural figure of the Divine Savior that was to emerge from faraway Palestine.

THE ANOINTED ONE

Like a pandemic, the redemption ideology that spread from Palestine into Europa impacted a broad diversity of peoples who had no natural immunity to it. The alien nature of this ideology ("cross theology," as scholars tag it) was evident from its origins, for the Palestinian redeemer complex arose in the Near East under exceptional conditions and mutated strangely. From its inception, the core complex that gave rise to Christianity was a weird hybrid made up of anomalous elements that did not naturally occur in the culture where they emerged and melded. In short, the complex was exactly what Gnostic theologians such as Hypatia had warned that it was: a case of *anomia*, deviance. The Greek word *anomou* occurs in the Apocryphon of John and other texts from Nag Hammadi in reference to delusional systems in the human psyche. Scholars generally translate *anomou* as "depravity," the exact word used by Pliny the Younger to describe salvationist faith. The literal translation would be "anomalous." In a stronger sense, "alien, deviant, perverted."

As noted in chapter 1, the redeemer complex has four components: the creation of the world ex nihilo by the male creator god; the selection of the righteous few to fulfill a divine plan; the mission of the creator's son (the messiah) in the plan; and the final, apocalyptic judgment in which the world is destroyed so that the righteous can be saved by the accomplishment of divine retribution. The first component, creation of the world by a male creator god, can be found in variants worldwide, but Biblical myth differs from other creation scenarios by its exclusion of a feminine deity. This exclusion is an arresting factor, to say the least. Scholars now recognize the enormous, sustained effort it took to produce and enforce a sacred narrative focused on a male deity without a female counterpart.

Some, but not all, elements of this four-part complex operate in a specific and pernicious iteration of patriarchy: theocracy. Defined as a system of rulership by gods or descendents of gods, it emerged in Mesopotamia around 3500 B.C.E. The claim of divine descent was largely titular and ceremonial, but could stretch into a literal claim when it suited the egotistical fantasies of the authorities. In those fabled times, astrologers, fortune-tellers, courtesans, and clowns packed the courts, seeking favor and privilege from the regents. Among the retinue were "soothsayers" who specialized in what is today known as "channeling." They acted as consultant psychics for the ruling class. The theocratic kings could not themselves commune with their divine ancestors, but the mediums could—or pretended so. The mediums often took advantage of royal gullibility to fabricate stories that supported the presumption of theocratic status (defined in Latin, *afflatus*: inflation, grandiosity). Their role in theocratic lineages and rites of royal empowerment was crucial to the authority of the regional rulers.

Theocracy was viral in the ancient Middle East, where it prospered in many local variations. One case in particular was to prove unique. It came to expression around 1800 B.C.E. in the life of Abram, the son of a Sumerian priest from Ur. Abraham, as he came to be known, is the founding father of the mainstream redemptive religions: Judaism, Christianity, and Islam. Abraham is never said to be divine, not quite. Nevertheless, he is the central figure in a weird theological mutation of human divinity—in Latin, *anamou*: anomalous. The Biblical patriarch led an itinerant tribe of donkey-herders, the *iberu*. There were no sooth-sayers in his entourage, but he didn't need one. As it turns out, Abraham was his own medium, able to communicate telepathically with the divine father god, Yahweh.

In Middle Eastern theocracy, a divine king held claim to be a sovereign representative of the gods on Earth. He was a human reflection, though not a literal incarnation, of the guardian deity of the nation and culture he led. Sacred kingship was highly evolved in Egypt where Abraham's descendents lived through a crucial chapter of their tribal history. The common people held the pharaohs to be living gods, but this status was understood differently by the priests and hierophants who directed the pharaonic breeding lines and ordained the exponential genera-tions of Ramesses, Amenhoteps, Thutmoses, and others. The Egyptian hierophants of the cults of Horus and Set were the "handlers" of the theocratic dynasties. They composed and directed elaborate, Hollywood-style rituals in which the pharaohs playacted the deities whose names they bore. Needless to say, the line between playacting and literal iden-tification was not always clear. The assigned roles in Egyptian religion involved acting for the gods more than acting like them. Nevertheless, it delivered a powerful spectacle. Like other theocratic figureheads in the Near East, the pharaohs comprised the ruling elite who would, ideally, implement divine will in human society.

The divine king was regarded as a "messiah," a word derived from the Hebrew *mashiah*, meaning simply "anointed." The Greek equivalent is *christos*, from *christein*, "to anoint." Anointing did not originally carry a claim to divinity. It was a secular rite of ordainment and nothing more. Through Abraham, the regal and strictly human status of messiah came to be associated with divinity. The notion of a superhuman race played into the theocratic scenario of the ancient Hebrews. This odd deviation was not merely due to a linguistic fluke. When Constantine forced the vote for the divinity of Christ at the Council of Nicaea in 325, he insured that the polit-ical will of the Roman Empire would be underwritten by divine authority.

In doing so, he relied on the doctrines of Saint Paul, a Hellenizied Jew from Syria, the first ideologue to definitively assert the divinity of "the Christ." Yet once again, something odd was in the works. Paul's assertion is anomalous, totally unknown to *both* Jewish and Pagan theology in his time. (Emperors who claimed "divine afflatus" were merely indulging in self-aggrandizement, typical of the narcissistic craze of the Piscean Age. They were also vainly competing with initiates from the Mysteries whom, rumor said, were in some way deified by their secret practices.)

The origin of human divinity in Pauline (and also Johannine) theology has never been adequately explained, but by tracing the Palestinian redeemer complex to its most deeply hidden sources, perhaps it can be.

In prepatriarchal times the rite of anointing was performed in the *hieros gamos*, the sacred mating of the royal candidate with a priestess in the service of the Magna Mater, the Great Mother. It took the elimination of the priestess to introduce full-scale male dominance. This transition was long and difficult in the Near East, and it was never fully achieved in Europa up to the moment Christianity appeared. The long gestation of theocracy ran from around 4200 B.C.E., when the Indo-European invasions of Europa began, to 1800 C.E., the age of Hammurabi, the lawgiver, contemporary with Abraham.[82] Progressively, the choice of the new king and the rites of sacred kingship came to be directed exclusively by men, and for men. Social authority no longer depended on the character of the man who would be king. It depended entirely on the agenda that man would serve.

A JEWISH KING

The monotheistic, male-only creator myth of the Old Testament has some precedents in Mesopotamia, the land from which Abraham migrated. In those times, people believed that the political organization of society, if it is true and trustworthy, must mirror cosmic order. If there was one sole god in heaven, there must be a single, sovereign ruler on Earth. This formula held true in far-distant China, Peru, and Polynesia, as much as it did in the Middle East. The background of terrestrial rule was always mythic. But this system assumed a peculiar and atrophied form in the religious life of the ancient Hebrews. The second component of the redeemer complex, the commission of the righteous few to fulfill the creator's plan, required a transition from myth into history. Or pseudohistory, as recorded in the Old Testament, a priestly fiction unevenly loaded with *some* verifiable historical elements. The decisive event in the sacred history of the Jewish people occurs in 1 Samuel:

> Then all the elders of Israel gathered themselves together, and came to Samuel . . . , And said unto him, Behold, thou art old, and thy sons walk not in thy ways: now make us a king to judge us like all the nations. (1 Sam. 8:4–5)

The key phrase here is "like all the nations (gentiles, *goyim*)." Biblical historians locate the patriarch Samuel around 1100 B.C.E., about eight hundred years after Abraham. From its earliest days, the Israelite community had been ruled by a council of elders, called judges, who were closely advised, if not controlled, by a hereditary priesthood. This was a patriarchal society with a strong priestly element, but it was not a theocracy "like all the nations" in the ancient Near East. Not yet, at least. In the days of Samuel, faith in the father god Jehovah was declining, but "all Israel, from Dan even to Beersheba, knew that Samuel was established to be a prophet of the Lord" (1 Sam. 3:18). As he approached death, the elders of the community, acting it seems out of spiritual insecurity, asked Samuel to establish a king for Israel comparable to the theocrats of neighboring nations. In this single, decisive event the Hebrews adopted the foreign institution of monarchy. So extraordinary was this development that Mircea Eliade wrote:

> The monarchy is interpreted as a new covenant between Yahweh and the dynasty of David, a continuation of the covenant of Sinai. It is in this valorization of a foreign institution as a new act of sacred history that we can appreciate the originality of the Israelite ideology of kingship.[83]

Monarchy, as Eliade stresses, was a "foreign institution" for the Hebrews. Its adoption marks a crucial point of departure for that people, and, indeed, for humanity at large. The consequences of this "new act of sacred history" will be momentous, but slow to unfold. It will take a thousand years for "the originality of the Israelite ideology of kingship" to play out, mutate further, and come to expression in the Divine Redeemer of Christianity. But the process didn't stop there. The anomaly of Jewish theocracy triggered a shockwave that escalated for centuries, destined to inflict deleterious effects upon the entire world. The wave finally broke in the seventeenth century due to a little known, extremely bizarre event, the apostasy of Sabbatai Zevi. At that moment the god-complex inherent to Jewish theocracy from the time of Samuel collapsed, and out of its ruins arose another complex. In the aftermath of the Sabbatean-Frankist heresy, as scholars call it, anticipation of the messianic king who would raise the Hebrews to lordship over all nations utterly disintegrated.[84] Strangely, this psychotic breakdown in Jewish faith aggravated the ancient anomaly of Israelite kingship so that it resurged in a different form. After centuries of awaiting the messiah, the Chosen People assigned to themselves the status of the exclusive messianic force in the world—and that was to be a superhuman status.

But a long and arduous mutation of racial-religious ideology preceded that psychotic event. The Jewish king was called by the honorific title "Son of God," which was not understood to indicate incarnate divinity. Dead Sea Scrolls scholar Geza Vermes explains:

> In Hebrew or Aramaic "son of God" is always employed figuratively as a metaphor for a child of God, whereas in Greek addressed to Gentile Christians, grown up in a religious culture filled with gods, sons of gods and demigods, the New Testament expression tended to be understood literally as "Son of God," spelled as it were with a capital letter: that is to say, as someone of the same nature as God.[85]

Previous to Samuel, the assumption of human divinity was incompatible with the basic tenets of Jewish faith. Sacred kingship among the Hebrews was a problematic affair from the outset. The first Jewish king was Saul, a tormented man who committed suicide after some serious depression and a weird, unsettling encounter with a female shaman, the witch of Endor. His successors were David and Solomon, who handled the royal status somewhat more skillfully. Yet both of these kings were known for retaining strong ties to Canaanite goddess religion epitomized in the figure of Asteroth, the tree goddess. Throughout the Old Testament, Jehovah berated and tormented the Children of Israel for "whoring after stange gods"—that is, reverting to indigenous ways and bioregional, Earth-honoring cults. Among such cults the worship of Asteroth was universal in Canaan.

With the discovery of the Ugarit writings at Ras Shamra, Syria, in 1928, scholars have been able to reconstruct the rites and beliefs of the indigenous people of Canaan, the ancient name for the land now called Palestine. The result has been an extensive revaluation of the sources of Old Testament theology and ritual. It is now known that the Hebrew scribes who composed and compiled the Old Testament from 700 B.C.E. onward drew from Canaanite texts as extensively as they did from Egyptian and Mesopotamian sources. But because the Promised Land was *in* Canaan, the biblical Hebrews drew most deeply from the indigenous sources of the territory claimed as their God-given land. The extent of the co-optation is staggering and throws biblical history into an entirely different light:

> A few theologians, upon examining Ugarit mythology, claimed to be shocked by the violence and depravity of the Canaanite religion. They saw it as a crude form of polytheism, "the abominations of the Heathen," whose extermination by the Hebrews in Palestine was a pious and godly act, though unfortunately not quite thorough enough. This view, besides being morally dubious, ignores the fact that Judaism, both when it borrowed from the same primitive religion and when it reacted against it, was influenced by it. Many of the prerogatives of Yahweh were originally prerogatives of Baal and Eli. Daniel the Just was a Canaanite, not a Hebrew. . . . Canaanite lore is a legitimate antecedent of the Judeo-Christian tradition.[86]

The Bible is not without its own share of violence and depravity, of course. In recording the struggle of "Hebrews against the Heathen," the Old Testament presents a rich case study of the victim-perpetrator syndrome. Judaic morals, rites, and theological concepts developed in parallel with ongoing genocidal campaigns in Canaan and elsewhere, but the accursed ways of the Heathen were not readily dispelled, or easily uprooted from the hearts of the people. Instead, they were absorbed, disguised, and distorted. Abraham's aborted sacrifice of Isaac followed a Canaanite custom of infanticide. Daniel the Canaanite was a key figure in developing the fourth component of the redeemer complex, apocalyptic retribution. These and many, many more elements of Canaanite origin were co-opted into Jewish religion and subsequently mutated in ways alien to their origins.

Double Agenda

It is not easy to follow the erratic sequence of obscure and often ominous events that constitute the ancient history of the Jews. The Bible is rarely read point blank, without a hefty set of expectations that predetermine what we will find in it, no matter what our religious disposition may be. Paul Shepard observed that our view of history is "framed in a historical mode which has already decided the issue", that is, predetermined what history tells us about ourselves.[87] This is particularly true of the "sacred history" recounted in the Old Testament. Moreover, the sheer dramatic impact of biblical language tends to misdirect us from telling details.

From the time of Samuel the Old Testament narrative increasingly highlights the messianic king, the one who is anointed. His actions will determine how the righteous few are able to follow the will of the father god and enact his plan. This proposition is clear enough, but it begs the question: Who does the anointing? For the anointed ruler to be powerful, he must get his power through the anointing agent. The logic of empowerment is simple: those who anoint must *in some sense* be more powerful than those whom they anoint. But in what sense more powerful?

In matrifocal societies, a priestess who represented the Goddess anointed the sacred king in a ceremony involving sexual ritual. That priestess was the original "power behind the throne." The ritual of anointing was the *hieros gamos*, sacred marriage. The rise of patriarchy forced a drastic modification in royal empowerment. For the ancient Hebrews this happened in a rather odd, clandestine way—not surprisingly, since theocracy was a "foreign institution" to them. It did not arise within Israelite community but had to be imported. The elders ("judges") who ruled the community were themselves advised by several lineages of hereditary priests named on familial lines: Benjamin, Levi, Aaron, Cohen, and so forth. Saul's precarious right to kingship took shape under the guidance of these priesthoods, with a large consensus from the community (1 Sam. 11:15). But the first Jewish candidate for theocracy failed in a shameful and miserable way. Then, when the moment came for David to bestow kingship on Solomon, something unprecedented happened. Yet again, an anomaly:

> And King David said, Call me Zadok, the priest, and Nathan, the prophet, and anoint him there [Solomon] king of Israel. . . . And Zadok, the priest, took a horn of oil out of the tabernacle, and anointed Solomon. (1 Kings 1:34, 39)

As later becomes clear (although never entirely so) between the lines of the biblical narrative, the priest of Zadok assumes authority superior to the other lineages of Benjamin, Aaron, and Levi. In fact, the priesthood of Zadok is the most enigmatic, overlooked factor in Judeo-Christian tradition. It literally comes out of nowhere. This priesthood must have originated *before* Abraham because its chief representative was the mysterious figure who recruited the first patriarch and conferred on the community of Israel its identity as a "chosen people" (i.e., the righteous few, charged with enacting the divine plan: second component of the redeemer complex). Tradition assumes that Yahweh chose the Hebrews but the actual agent of commission was not the father god. It was Melchizedek, head of the priesthood of Zadok, who chose them. "And Melchizedek, king of Salem, brought forth [to Abraham] bread and wine; and he was the priest of the most high" (Gen. 14:18).

The meeting of Abraham and Melchizedek in Genesis 14 inaugurates the mission of the Chosen People. Certainly not by chance, it also presents the prototype of the Christian Mass: the sacrament of bread and wine. Also, from its inception in this dramatic meeting, the implementation of the divine plan is closely associated with violence sanctioned by a higher power. Acting as warrior chief of the Hebrews, Abraham raids the neighboring lands of Dan and Hobah, going all the way to Damascus to rescue his wayward brother, Lot (Gen. 14:12–17). Granted, internecine warfare was common in that era, conducted with routine ferocity by many tribes, but the narrative at this point has Melchizedek confer divine approval on the slaughter: "Blessed be Abram of the most high God, possessor of heaven and Earth: And blessed be the most high God which has delivered thine enemies into thine hand" (Gen. 14: 19–20). It is not merely the tribal deity who approves of Abram's victory, but the "most high" of all gods. This transcendent pretension of superiority is inherent to the redeemer complex.

Who is Melchizedek? He is an eerie figure who appears out of nowhere and then disappears, but the entire course of Judeo-Christian sacred history is definitively set by his appearance. The designation, "king of Salem," connects him to the locale in Canaan where Jerusalem would be founded. Other than this, nothing is known of his origins.[88] His name, incorporating the Sumerian root *melki-*, "prince," "divine inheritor" means "prince of righteousness." The Hebrew *zedek* is a variation of *zadok*, also spelled *tsedeq*, *tzaddik*, and *zaddik*. When applied to a human being *zaddik* means, "the just one, the righteous, holier than thou." An example in the Old Testament is Daniel the Just, and in the New Testament, James the Just, the brother of Jesus (currently the patron saint of Spain). In a loose sense the *zaddik* is simply a better human being, judged by his obedience to God, but in the strict sense it is someone who meets a standard of purity and perfection that lies totally beyond human capacity. To be *zaddik* is the mark of transcendent superiority granted by Yahweh, above all other gods.

The founding moment of the community of Israel is a momentous event, but it conceals another event that will, in due time, prove to be even more momentous: the inception of the Zaddikite cult of righteousness under Melchizedek.* The mandate of the cult is to implement

---

* I use *Zaddikite* (my convention) for the inner circle of Jewish priests dedicated to the *zaddik* ideology centered on Melchizedek, and *Zadokite* (the conventional scholarly spelling) for the Palestinian revolutionary movement surrounding that inner circle. See glossary.

Yahweh's choice of the Jews to represent him before all the nations of the Earth, and fulfill his plan, supreme above all the designs of fate in the world. This fantastic proposition is eminently clear to many believers, but, as one biblical scholar wryly noted, "How odd of God to choose the Jews."[89] In reality, it is Melchidezek who chooses them.

All through history, both Jews and non-Jews alike have been intensely aware of this pretension, or this divine calling, if you prefer. That one among all the ethnic groups of the world was chosen by the Creator of them all to receive His revelation, follow His laws, fulfill His plan, and demonstrate the highest moral example of humanity, faithful to their mission down to the apocalyptic world-ending, is a well-known claim, of course. Even though this claim is anomalous in the religious experience of humanity, it is rarely challenged. To challenge it might be regarded by some as anti-Zionist or anti-Semitic, but, oddly enough, the claim itself is never treated as an antihuman proposition.

Can God's calling to model the highest standard for humanity be antihuman? Well, Gnostics such as Hypatia certainly thought so. They proposed that the unique status claimed by the Hebrews, and the entire concatenation of grandiose ideas that goes along with it, was a ruse. In the Gnostics' view, the "Divine Plan" to be realized through the Chosen People and the Messiah, culminating in the apocalyptic day of retribution, is not a calling to spiritual glory, but a grand and grievous deceit.

SALVATION HISTORY

Billions of ardent believers around the world take the Bible for literal fact and find in the ancient Hebrews a model of behavior for all other races. The Lord declares to Isaiah (49:6), "I will make you a light to the nations, so that all the world will be saved." This is how the spiritual leaders of Judaism regard the mission of their people. It is the covenant set forth in their unique tribal narrative. The Zaddikite agenda is the bedrock of that ancient narrative of salvation history (as scholars call it). Its racial origins are specific and exclusive, yet eventually, due to the rise of Christianity, it came to be adopted by a vast proportion of the human races. Over time, it rose to the status of universality.

In the Bible, including both Testaments, the four components of the redeemer complex unfold dramatically in linear historical time. Salvation history is embedded with a set of beliefs about creation, sin, sexuality, divine election, off-planet intervention, redemption, cosmic judgment, retribution, and resurrection. Such is the directive script for Western civilization. (With Islam, the medieval mutation of the redeemer complex, the script changes, reflecting an even deeper devaluation of the human condition than is seen in the Judeo-Christian concept of "the Fall," yet the four essential components of the complex remain constant.) Whoever identifies with the story adopts the beliefs it carries, even without being conscious of how they do so. Since human behavior is belief driven, the salvationist narrative assumes enormous power to determine personal experience and even shape the course of history itself. Many believers insist that the story is *literally* true, presenting the very proof that God is actively engaged in human affairs, while others find symbolic and allegorical truth in salvation history without needing to equate it with fact. In neither case, however, do believers question the essential truth or *sanity* of the story.

Confronted with salvation history, it is difficult to tell what is more preposterous: the plot and purpose expressed in the script, or the widespread credence it has commanded. The "Divine Plan" is so alien to indigenous wisdom, so wrong for social guidance both in spiritual and survival terms, and so contrary to the innate moral instincts of humanity, that its acceptance by untold millions of people through the ages boggles the mind and staggers the imagination. Because it has become *the* dominant script in the psychohistory of our species, there is a universal tendency to assume that it *must* be true, in one way or another, at one level or another. But is the mere acceptance of any idea or belief proof of its veracity? With salvation history, the fact that so many people have embraced it, and still do, impedes an essential insight: beliefs that would be rejected and ridiculed if held by a cult of a few hundred members become sacrosanct and unquestionable when held by millions.

According to the Gnostic critique of Judeo-Christian religion, the triumph of salvation history is not due to some undeniable truth it carries, but rather to its covert delusional power. It operates like an obsessive fixation that seizes the collective mind and drives it straight into what Wilhelm Reich called *Massenpsychosen*, mass psychosis. In *The Mass Psychology of Fascism*, Reich shows how mystical and militaristic behaviors "rooted in the male authoritarian character structure" meld together in religious obsessions common to Islam, Zionism, and the Jesuit Order of Catholicism. In his analysis of "the passive ideology of suffering in all genuine religions," he revealed how irrational insistence on the redemptive value of suffering ("the emotional plague") leads society head-on into conflict and madness.[90]

In parallel to Reich's analysis, Gnostics saw in the salvationist program that arose in Palestine after 150 B.C.E. a spurious belief system that deviates the human species from its true potential. Such was the warning of trained theologians and mystics from the Mysteries, men and women whose discipline would have enabled them to assess ideological-theological concepts with penetrating insight and critical rigor. The indigenous people of Europa who would eventually succumb to the onslaught of salvationism had no such critical capacities. Not that they lacked intelligence or were in any way mentally inferior to the dominators, but they did lack the intellectual defenses needed to resist the redeemer complex. Gnostics in Egypt, the Levant, and the Near East held a crucial line of defense until they were destroyed by the proponents of the delusional system they tried to expose. Considering the ancient provenance of their movement, it is likely that Gnostics had been able to observe the salvationist program over a long time, all the way back to its foundational moment.

ENTER THE ZADDIK

Melchizedek's ritual commissioning of Abraham to lead the Chosen People (Gen. 14) provides Yahweh with human representation on Earth, but it does more as well. It sets up a cultic program determined by hidden, superhuman prerogatives. The Israelite community was the cradle for the cult. It was the racial culture dish for the hidden germ of *zaddik*. Thus it became the host for the parasitic infection centered on Melchizedek, the spooky, clone-like overseer of the Zaddikim. The scrolls found near the Dead Sea in 1947 record the hate-ridden, apocalyptic ideology of the righteous ones. *Zaddik* is a moral and metaphysical concept that implies superhuman perfection, as previously noted. Those who adopt that standard must stand against humankind at large. They are "a people who shall dwell apart." They must model obediance at the hightest level of submission to divine will. At the same time, they operate on a madate of absolute domination.

John Allegro, the most independently minded of the Dead Sea Scrolls scholars, detected the insidious agenda implicit in the identity of the Chosen People. In *The Mystery of the Dead Sea Scrolls Revealed* he says that "what God required from the Jews was not the building of a political kingdom under a war leader, but the formation of a theocratic community."[91] To be precise, what the Hebrew creator god required was not *only* the building of a political kingdom, the Holy State of Israel. Yahweh wanted *both* the tribal kingdom *and* a nuclear theocratic task force, a militant-mystical elite. The second aim was not to be achieved merely in the communal striving of the people, but through the secret program of the Zaddikim, the most righteous of the people, the ultrarighteous. All through Jewish history a palpable, agonized tension plays between these two elements: the stated aim to establish an Israelite political kingdom for the people, and the hidden aim of a righteous few whose standard of superhuman purity alienated the community that sheltered them from humanity at large. The drama continues to this day in the lethal enmeshment between the Jewish people and Zionism.

In 70 C.E. when the Roman army under Titus destroyed Jerusalem, it was taking final, drastic action against the destabilization of the entire Empire due to the militant nationalism of a splinter group, the apocalyptic cult of the Zaddikim. As the Jewish community as a whole harbored this movement, the entire nation of Israel had to be smitten in order to eradicate it. The might of the Empire fell on Judea and dispersed *all* the Jews, Zaddikites or not, into a centuries-long exile from the Promised Land.

They would not return until the fateful moment when the Balfour Declaration was signed and the state of Israel was founded, a few months after the Dead Sea Scrolls were discovered.

5

MESSIANIC MADNESS

The monastery [at Khirbet Qumran], this structure of stone
that endures, between the bitter waters and the precipitous
cliffs, with its oven and its inkwells, its mill and its cesspool,
its constellation of sacred fonts and unadorned graves of the
dead is, perhaps, more than Bethlehem or Nazareth, the
cradle of Christianity.[92]

Khirbet Qumran, "the ruins of Qumran," is located about thirty miles
east of Jerusalem, overlooking the Dead Sea. From 1947 into the
late 1950s excavations at this desolate site produced an unprecedented
trove of ancient writings. The finds included complete works such as the
earliest manuscript of Isaiah, as well as thousands of stamp-sized fragments that had to be painstakingly joined, like pieces of a jigsaw puzzle.
The scrolls were written between 250 B.C.E. and 70 C.E., when Jerusalem
was destroyed by the Roman army in a draconian attempt to repress the
Jewish Revolt. The aim of the revolt was to establish an autonomous
theocratic Jewish state in Palestine, consistent with the first two elements
of the redeemer complex. Such was its political and military aim, at least.
But the cult of the Khirbet Qumran also had another agenda, an apocalyptic program of final retribution, consistent with the third and fourth
components of the redeemer complex: the coming of the messiah and the
last judgment. The lethal combination of militant and mystical factors
is not unfamiliar to the modern world, of course. The Zaddikite sect of
the Dead Sea presents the larval form of the global terrorist syndrome
of today.

The scrolls were written on treated leather in Hebrew and Aramaic,
with a few Greek entries. They are extremely various in content: rules

of community life, apocalyptic visions, erudite commentaries, mythological set-pieces, astrological works (including a horoscope for the messiah), the last words of various patriarchs, psalms, liturgies, legal arguments, incantations, and calendars. The materials comprise two categories: biblical and sectarian. The first category, about one-fourth of the entire collection, includes already-known parts of the Hebrew Bible. The Qumranic versions of these texts are a thousand years older than the Masoretic Bible, the standard Hebrew version of the Christian Bible. Amazingly, the Masoretic Bible often accords letter for letter with the Dead Sea Scrolls (DSS) equivalents, attesting to the diligence of Jewish scribes over many centuries, but there are significant variations as well. The Greek Septuagint produced in Alexandria between 250 and 100 B.C.E. was translated from Hebrew originals written several centuries earlier, and then lost. The Qumranic texts agree even more closely with the Septuagint and other Greek translations than the Masoretic Bible. Needless to say, the Dead Sea Scrolls were a fantastic windfall for biblical scholars.

The other three-fourths of the documents found at Khirbet Qumran are specific to the tiny religious cult that produced the scrolls. The sectarian material has produced no less than half a dozen theories regarding authorship, but the Zaddikite character of the scrolls is self-evident, no matter who composed them. The Community Rule, the charter document of the sect, clearly states the conditions required of those who would be members: "They shall separate from the congregation of false people and unite, as far as the Law and possessions are concerned, under the authority of the Sons of Zadok" (1QS 5:1–3). Michael Wise and Robert Eisenman wrote that the scrolls "contain the most precious information on the thoughts and currents of Judaism and *the ethos that gave rise to Christianity.* . . . They are actual eye-witness accounts of this period . . . nothing less than a picture of the movement from which Christianity sprang in Palestine."[93]

In short, the Zaddikite ideology found in the scrolls presents the ideological infrastructure of Christian religion.

QUMRANIC ROLES

Although the DSS material is nonhistorical in the sense that it does not describe specific persons and events, it opens a window on the historical period extending from 250 B.C.E. to 70 C.E., allowing scholars to reconstruct the events of that unique era of tumult and transition. Hence, the Dead Sea literature throws the life and deeds of the historical Jesus into an entirely new light. Some of the material is written in code, and key documents such as the Community Rule use code names for various people such as the Teacher of Righteousness, the Messiah, the Wicked Priest, the Sons of Zadok, the Kittim, and the Man of Lies. Different people enact these roles over seven or eight generations. The Zaddikim saw themselves acting out a prewritten script, a historical plot that reflected, so they believed, the providence of God the Father. Curiously, the twists and turns of the plot were not always favorable to the righteous few who starred in God's epic historical drama.

The Teacher of Righteousness was the leading spiritual figure of the Zaddikite sect, and the Messiah was the military hero and king who would establish the Kingdom of Israel in fulfillment of the divine plan. This would happen when the Kittim (the Romans) were overthrown by the Sons of Zadok, the Zealot revolutionaries (Zadokites) commanded by the Messiah. The plot here is simple enough, but there was a fascinating complication. The scrolls refer repeatedly to *an act of betrayal* on the part of the Man of Lies, also called the Scoffer, the Spouter, and the Man of Mockery, who will infiltrate the Covenant and turn against it, leading many of Israel astray. The Teacher of Righteousness has to expose and oppose the Man of Lies and, at the same time, stand against the Wicked Priest, the head of the Sadducees at the Jerusalem temple. The Teacher was the most revered public figure of the Zaddikim. He represented an ultraorthodox standard so severe that even the conservative Sadducees were alarmed by it and resisted him and his movement.

Owing to the betrayal by the Man of Lies, the cause of the Zaddikim was repeatedly defeated, and the establishment of the Kingdom of God in the Holy Land was delayed, over and over again. This pattern projected history into the mythological end-time when the triumph of the Messiah and the Sons of Zadok is no longer a local event in Palestine, but a global battle involving the celestial host under a leader called the Nasi, who is Melchizedek in the role of supernatural avenger.[94] The final battle between God and Belial, pitting the Children of Light against the Children of Darkness, was the culminating event in the insane plot of Jewish apocalypticism. It is graphically described in the columns of the War Scroll found at Qumran.

The use of these code names is the most intriguing and revealing aspect of the Dead Sea Scrolls. In his astute analysis of the scrolls, Hugh Schonfield shows that these designations could be applied to various historical people, but not in an exclusive way, limited to one person for each role.[95] After 1991 when the scandal of the Vatican's suppression of the scrolls broke, Robert Eisenman took the decisive step of identifying the specific historical persons who filled the Qumranic roles in the first century of the Common Era. He proposed that the Teacher of Righteousness was James the Just, the Wicked Priest was probably Ananus, James's main adversary among the Sanhedrin (high court) of the Jerusalem temple. In a sensational move still disputed by many scholars, Eisenman identified the Messiah of the Zaddikim sect with Jesus, the brother of James. The Sons of Zadok were, of course, the Zadokite rebels of Qumran, the Dead Sea outpost, i.e., disciples of Jesus.

That Qumran was an outpost for militants fighting to free Judea from Roman occupation and not a haven for hippielike pacifists called Essenes, was information withheld from the public by the team of scrolls scholars controlled by the Vatican. The Zaddikites appear to have been religious zealots comparable to terrorists at large in the world today. The key figure among the rebels in the wilderness camp was their leader and national hero Jesus, the messianic candidate destined to become "king of the Jews" and rule over a theocratic Israelite state freed of Roman occupation. If Eisenman's controversial reading of the New Testament is correct, Jesus would have been, not a radical rabbi with a message of love for Jews and Gentiles alike, but a political rebel, the Yasser Arafat of the Dead Sea sectarians.

Jewish Intifada

The Maccabees who inaugurated the Jewish resistence movement in Palestine had briefly established a nationalist regime in the Hasmonean Period (165–63 b.c.e.), but they did so with ambivalent support from their own people. In the second century b.c.e. Galilee was predominantly pagan, and resident Jews found many advantages in Pagan tolerance. Local religion was centered on the Sumerian vegetation gods, Inanna and Dumuzi, the goddess and the shepherd king, whose Hebrew parallels were Asteroth and Yahweh. Mythic currents run silent and deep. Centuries later when the legend of the Christian savior was composed, Asteroth had been completely suppressed, and Yahweh was fast being converted from a Canaanite tribal thunder god into the absentee landlord of the entire planet.

In scripting Hebrew religion to fit the redeemer complex, the Jewish priesthood did everything possible to deny the Pagan, regional elements in their tribal scenario. New Testament writers who were not so constrained could reintroduce some Pagan elements into their fairy-tale portrait of the folk guru and miracle worker who would then slip into the mold of the Jewish messiah. When it came to scripting a nativity tale for Jesus, he was placed in the manger where Dumuzi, the weary shepherd beloved by the Goddess, sometimes slept.

Many Palestinian Jews of that era were prone to "whoring after the strange gods" (Leviticus, 15) of Canaan. Internecine murder was common in the Hasmonean Period. With Jerusalem proclaimed capital in 141 b.c.e., there was a hard surge of messianic fever; but by and large, a select few Zadokites spearheaded the insurrection. Even if they did not assimilate to it, Jews benefited from the Hellenistic culture that had prevailed since Alexander the Great claimed the region in 332 b.c.e. The pursuit of the messianic agenda was not a popular option for Jews in Palestine, but to deny it openly was not an attractive option either. The risks of standing against the hard-core, vengeful, apocalyptic visionaries who called themselves the "Sons of Light" were dire. The military wing of this movement was the Zealots, guerrillas and cutthroats as willing to kill collaborating Jews as they were to murder the enemy, the hated Kittim—Qumranic code word for the Romans. The spiritual guides of the Zealots were the

Chasidim, the Pious Ones. They constituted the second, or mesoteric, circle of the Qumranic sect. In the esoteric or innermost circle were the Zaddikim, extremist ideologues whose hate-fuelled seizures wrack the pages in the Dead Sea Scrolls.

At any moment, the Zaddikite core could not have amounted to more than a few hundred men, yet they drove the movement and exerted sufficient pressure on the Jewish community to destabilize Palestine and threaten the integrity of the Empire. The pressure went critical after 63 B.C.E. when Pompey, Caesar's archrival, annexed Judea to Rome. This event ended the hundred-year period of independence following the Maccabean revolt. The effect of this turnaround was to escalate desperation, infecting even the nonradical members of the populace. In *The Jewish Wars*, the historian Josephus closely observed the psychological damage: "As much as the Jews believed that Yahweh would save them, he consistently refused to do so, and the greater their longing, the worse their suffering."[96]

We have detected this bizarre pattern before: the divine plan is predestined to fail as a human project so that it can be realized as a transhumanist apocalyptic drama. Needless to say, this type of thinking is schizophrenic and extremely disorienting. Describing the social atmosphere of the time, scrolls historian Hugh Schonfield wrote:

> From 160 B.C. we are in a new age, an age of extraordinary fervor and religiosity in which almost every event, political, social and economic, was seized upon, scrutinized and analyzed, to discover how and in what way it represented a Sign of the Times and threw light on the approach of the End of the Days. The whole condition of the Jewish people was psychologically abnormal. The strangest tales and imaginings could find ready credence. A new pseudonymous literature came into being, part moral exhortation and part apocalyptic prophecy, *a kind of messianic science fiction.*[97]

"The whole condition of the Jewish people was psychologically abnormal." Once again, the factor of *anomia* is evident, and even becomes dominant. This happened because something abnormal, even inhuman, was working through the Zaddikim. The Palestinian community as a whole resisted this intrusion. They repulsed the Zaddikite movement and exposed the Zealots in their midst, forcing them to flee to wilderness camps in Judea and near Damascus, where Saul the bounty hunter went to seek them out for liquidation. James the Tzaddik, "the Just," remained at the Jerusalem temple. He was the solitary holdout of the Qumranic "opposition party," as Robert Eisenman calls the Zaddikite sect in his monumental study, *James, the Brother of Jesus.*

The Qumran sectarians believed that they led the Jewish *intifada*, the uprising against Roman occupation of Palestine, and at the same time they believed other things of a mystical and metaphysical nature, having nothing to do with political change. The War Scroll, one of the first texts found by Bedouin peasants in the summer of 1947, describes the final showdown between the Sons of Light and the Sons of Darkness. It is a script for the apocalyptic battle in which the failed mission of the Chosen People is finally achieved, and their cause vindicated. What began with the Maccabean revolt would end in a magical event in which the righteous few, even if they were slain by the enemy, would be resurrected by Yahweh and vindicated by the power of the Nasi, the cosmic form of Melchizedek. Political revolt and bodily resurrection belonged to the same master plan. In the psychohistorical drama of the apocalypse, the events that unfold in linear, historical time culminate in the end-time, the moment of final reckoning. The War Scroll reads like a weirdly ceremonious boot-camp drill intended to prepare the troops for that final, hallucinatory event.

END-TIME FEVER

The sacred narrative of the ancient Hebrews was not a theocratic script—not at first, anyway. It only became so over time as the third component of the redeemer complex, the messiah, mutated oddly. As the Old Testament narrative is commonly understood, the righteous ones are the ethnic group chosen by God to enact his plan. This designation would seem to encompass the entire Israelite nation, but it never really does. From the founding moment of their story the Hebrews are subjected to a double agenda, as John Allegro noted. The core members of the Dead Sea sect, the Zaddikim, considered that the Jewish people as a whole had failed to follow the plan of the Father. *Failed from the beginning.*

The Zaddikites called themselves the Covenant, the one true remnant of the Chosen People who would live out a divine destiny. Even if the Kingdom of Israel were never established in real, existential, human terms, when the apocalypse came, God would rescue and vindicate them by calling down the messiah and the Kedoshim, the heavenly host of warrior-angels enthroned in round, shining chariots.

Them, the Zaddikim, not the Jewish people as a whole.

At its maximum the Dead Sea sect could not have numbered more than ten thousand with as many as two thousand members living at their main wilderness camp, the fortressed site overlooking the Dead Sea, about thirty miles east of Jerusalem. Others lived in Damascus, a hotbed of Zaddikite dissent. The population of Jews in Hypatia's native city of Alexandria was four times the total number of radical sectarians in the Near East, and the Jewish population must have comprised a significant proportion of the Roman Empire in that region. When the Zaddikite ideologues and their fearsome military wing, the Zealots, were brutally suppressed in 70 c.e., the entire population of Jews in the classical world took the blow. Reading the Dead Sea Scrolls today, it is perhaps difficult to understand how and why the Zealot-Zaddikite movement was so threatening. Neil Asher Silberman provides a helpful analogy:

> The Scrolls' visions, like those of latter-day apocalyptists Jim Jones and David Koresh, of Islamic jihad and West Bank Kahanists, can become pornocracies of violence, acted out with a horrifying relish for blood. Alternatively, these visions can become the starting point for more mystical hallucinations and other-world journeys; a way in the alienated wilderness of the psyche of the individual. In their unrelenting apocalyptic message, the Scrolls give a voice to a group that felt dispossessed and disenfranchised in a world turned upside down.[98]

In the first century the Roman Empire was threatened by the Zealot movement in the same way that the entire world today is threatened by religious terrorism. The parallel was striking to the mind of science fiction writer Philip K. Dick, who incorporated Gnostic and Jewish apocalyptic themes into many of his novels. He proposed that time stopped in 70 c.e., leaving the world stuck in that moment, replaying the same script. "The Empire never ended."[99] In the plot of *Valis*, Dick confers an important role on the demented alien god exposed by the Gnostics.

Jewish sacred history begins with an act of exile, the calling of Abraham out of Ur in Chaldea. The story that ensues is a tale of "the alienated wilderness of the psyche" of *a community*, not an individual. In the course of centuries, the racial unconscious (or communal psyche) of the Jews produces, first, the anointed king. The Jewish monarch, who comes from a borrowed institution, is a messiah, according to the literal meaning, "anointed one." But the messianic figure mutates as communal hopes of fulfilling God's plan are thwarted, time and time again—more often than not, by God himself. From a literal king the messiah grows into a symbolic and mystical figure who epitomizes the precarious divine mission of his people. As this occurs, he becomes less identified with the final military victory that will secure the Holy Land, and more associated with the end of the world, the climax of historical time.

This entire mythological mutation is driven by failure and despair, symptomatic of what D. H. Lawrence called "a postponed destiny."[100] In *The Dogma of Christ* Erich Fromm explains how the failure of messianic expectation among the Jews affected Christianity: "While the Zealots and Sicarii ["knifemen," armed freedom fighters] endeavored to realize their wishes in the sphere of political reality, the complete hopelessness of realization led the early Christians to formulate the same wishes in fantasy."[101] The fantasy solution was inherent from the outset, however, and not merely due to the impossibility of the Judean intifada against Rome. Considered as a historical proposition, the redeemer complex establishes an impossible goal so that God can intervene in the climactic event of history, the apocalypse. Much of the DSS literature attests to this bizarre logic.

Sensing that the day of triumph for Israel would never come in historical time, communal expectation shifted to a triumphant vindication in the end-time, at "the end of days," *aharit-hayyamin* in Hebrew. This is an ancient term derived from Akkadian sources. Originally, it seems to have been a metaphor for the end of a particular cycle or pattern of events, analogous to a seasonal change: the end of the summer days, for instance. In biblical usage, the meaning changed. *Aharit-hayyamin* occurs in Genesis (49:1) and in Numbers (24:14) and "both of these passages contain archaic prophetic texts, which originally referred to the future, in an unspecified but limited sense, but were reinterpreted and given an eschatological sense in the post-exilic period, so that they were now understood to refer to a final, definitive phase of history."[102]

The expectation for the end-time messiah grew steadily during the Babylonian Captivity (586–538 B.C.E.) when many Jews, particularly the most powerful and prosperous, were deported to Mesopotamia after the fall of Jerusalem. When they were liberated in 538 B.C.E. by the Persian emperor Cyrus, a hardcore group returned to Palestine and rebuilt the Temple of Solomon. Its completion in 516 B.C.E. marks the Second Temple Period of Jewish history. These events led directly into the era of the prophets: Isaiah, Ezekiel, Daniel, Elijah. John J. Collins, the leading authority on Jewish apocalypticism, says that "the apocalyptic writers inherited from the prophets the belief that God would intervene in history at the decisive moment to judge the world."[103] These writers were rabbinical scribes charged with compiling the Torah in the days of the militant king Josiah (ruled 639–609 B.C.E.), "whose reforms paved the way for renewed religious and national vitality which developed into a regular frenzy" in the succeeding centuries.[104]

Religious frenzy went up and down like a roller coaster, depending on regional (and relatively small-scale) military victories of the Israelites. In 609 B.C.E., Josiah battled the Egyptian pharoah Necho at Megiddo (2 Kings 9:27), a place later designated as the site of Armageddon. At any moment in Jewish history the historical and mythological aspects of events were closely merged, if not muddled. Exile in Babylon ultimately shattered the surge of national confidence stemming from Josiah's time. More than any other historical event, the captivity changed the fate of the Israelites and altered their conception of their divine mission.

During the Captivity scholars and priests charged with writing the directive script for the divine mission of the Chosen People absorbed the Persian doctrine of cosmic evil attributed to the Iranian prophet Zoroaster. Upon the return to Palestine in 538 B.C.E. the ideologues propounded a new, highly radicalized apocalypticism that emphasized a cosmic confrontation between Good, represented by the Children of Israel, and Evil, represented by just about everyone else in the world. This program found its ultimate expression in the War Scroll found at Qumran. Reeking hatred and vindictiveness like a choking haze of ammonia fumes, the War Scroll is a bizarre combination of military-drill recital and panoramic psychic dementia. It describes the battlefield tactics for the final clash between the Sons of Light and the Sons of Darkness. One of the first seven texts found at Qumran, this scroll was initially identified by scholars at the very moment when the United Nations voted to form the state of Israel in November, 1947. The symbolism of this coincidence was not lost on many of those who lived through that dramatic moment, both in Israel and elsewhere.

THE WAR SCROLL

Versions of the prophetic works of Enoch, Daniel, Isaiah, and Jeremiah are some of the most important material in Dead Sea Scrolls. They present the full scope of Zaddikite apocalypticism and reveal its origins. Scroll 4Q201, the Book of the Watchers, is a version of Enoch, an influential prophet whose writings were omitted from the Old Testament.* Enoch is an apocryphal or extracanonical source of the legend of the Nephilim, the Watchers or Fallen Angels. Genesis 5 says that Enoch was transported to heaven by God—a mythical theme that prefigures the ascension of Christ. Closely related to the Enoch material, 4Q385 gives an account of Ezekiel's vision of a celestial chariot (*merkabah*). The *merkabah* was an important model for the Zaddikites, who expected the fleet of angel-driven chariots, the Kedoshim, to arrive at the last moment and rescue them from their enemies. In the Old Testament, Ezekiel 37 declares the promise of Yahweh to save the very skins of the righteous few:

---

* Scholars identify the thousands of fragments of the Dead Sea Scrolls by the letter Q for Qumran, a forward number that denotes the cave where the material was found, and a following number to indicate the catalogue sequence: 4Q201 is the 201st fragment to be catalogued from cave 4.

> Behold, O my people, I mean to raise you from your graves, and
> lead you back to the soil of Israel. And you will know that I *am*
> the Lord Yahweh, when I have opened your graves and raised
> you from the graves.

The radical Jewish revolutionaries, the Maccabees, adopted this literal concept of bodily resurrection to strengthen their resolve in the decisive revolt in 168 B.C.E., the precise moment when the earliest Dead Sea Scrolls were written.

The two Books of Maccabees, which consist largely of verifiable historical material, were once included at the end of the Old Testament, but later removed. This is unfortunate, because they provide a solid hinge between the Old and New Testaments. The revolt of the Maccabees marks the start of serious political unrest in Palestine due to the agitation of extremist and apocalyptic groups, with the Zaddikim being the worst, the most extreme, rigid, and genophobic. Social and religious unrest escalated for 134 years (roughly five generations) and peaked in the revolt of 66 C.E., only to be crushed with the wholesale destruction of Jerusalem four years later. It flared briefly in 86 C.E. at Masada where one thousand Zealot diehards, including women and children, held out against the Roman tenth division of fifteen thousand soldiers for almost two years. Finally, it resurged in 132 C.E. in the well-planned insurrection of Simon bar Kochba, who was guided by the "Star and Scepter" prophecy that inspired the Qumranic sectarians. He was the last militant messiah in the lineage of Zaddikite fanatics.

The Maccabees and their successors in the Jewish revolt were guerillas and terrorists who may or may not have believed that Yahweh would raise them from their graves. Among mainstream Jews, bodily resurrection was not a common belief; rather, it was a secret doctrine of the Zaddikim. DSS fragment 4Q521, called "A Messianic Apocalypse," affirms the power of the Lord to "heal the wounded, and revive the dead"—consoling words for a tiny insurrectionist group whose violent opposition to the Roman military machine was a sure formula for suicide.

Corporeal resurrection and transport to heaven are, of course, standard beliefs held by millions of modern fundamentalist Christians, and Mormons, who eagerly anticipate "the Rapture," when the world will be devastated and they will be lifted aloft by God. (Muslim *jihadis* who expect to be instantly transported to Paradise if they die in the defense of Islam exemplify a variation of the same belief.) Believers think they follow a "normal" Christian tradition that grew from humble origins in the Jewish faith, but this is far from the case. Devout fundamentalists in the United States would perhaps be startled to learn that their cherished expectation was the rare obsession of a splinter cult of enraged misfits comparable to the Branch Davidians of Waco, Texas.

Or perhaps they would be delighted.

The core ideology of modern fundamentalist Christianity derives from the Zaddikim of the Dead Sea and not from mainstream Judaic religion. Resurrection in a physical form identical to the living body (contrasted to some kind of continuity of soul life), transport to heaven, intervention of God the Father in history, the battle against Cosmic Evil ending in Judgment Day, and divine retribution—all these beliefs reflect *zaddik*, the superhuman standard. In the cult of righteousness led by Melchizedek, militant and mystical elements combined into a lethal, explosive mix. The Zaddikim sect self-destructed by bringing down upon itself and the entire Jewish community the military might of the Roman Empire, but their program survived and mutated into what was to become Roman Christianity. The enemies of the system became the system.

Such is the transfer of power in victim-perpetrator bonding.

THE TRANSFERENCE

Within a century after the destruction of Jerusalem the Palestinian redeemer complex had spread into Europa via Rome. To evangelize the Pagan peoples of the Old World, the hard-core, militant image of the Zaddikite messiah had to be disguised in a seemingly innocuous figure, "gentle Jesus, meek and mild." The messianic madness that had rocked Palestine for centuries was alien to the mentality of the Europan peoples. What sense could they find in an obscure cultic doctrine that arose on faraway desert sands? In order for it to be carried into Europa and imposed on the native peoples, further mutations of the redeemer complex had to occur, especially the third component, the messiah sent by the Father to insure the salvation of the righteous few.

"The Twelve"

The intense fever of messianic expectation in the classical world at the dawn of the Piscean Age (ca. 120 b.c.e.) was not universal, as scholars tend to assume. It was predominantly a phenomenon of the urban slave population who sought deliverance from their inferior social status, believing they could undergo a sudden, spectacular change of fate by embracing the new ideology of salvation. In effect, early Christianity was a communistic movement not disinclined to use violence and psychological coercion to achieve its ends. Erich Fromm treats it as such in his penetrating study, *The Dogma of Christ*. D. H. Lawrence makes the same comparison in his last work, *Apocalypse*, which I have cited throughout these pages. Qumranic scholars have also noted communist-like elements in the rules and practices of the Dead Sea sect: abolishment of private property, militaristic ranking of the members, severe personal ascesis. The strict overseer of the Qumranic sect, the *maqabah*, could be compared to a Bolshevik controller. The Teacher of Righteousness at Qumran may be imagined as a militant doctrinarian like Lenin, a man who was also destined for betrayal. Other parallels could be drawn.

It is no coincidence that Edmund Wilson, who wrote one of the earliest and best books on the Dead Sea Scrolls, also wrote *To the Finland Station*, an outstanding account of the ideological origins of the Bolshevik takedown of Czarist Russia. And the parallel between the Jewish revolt and the Russian Revolution does not stop there. In the long, steamy buildup to the Revolution, Russian intellectuals in Saint Petersburg and Moscow were inspired by the mystical philosopher Vladimir Soloviev (1853–1900), whose influence put a strong Christocentric spin on Russian politics. Soloviev, who died in the same month and year as Nietzsche, August 1900, was widely known for his three encounters with the Divine Sophia, and his lofty conception of *theandros*, "divine humanity." At first sight these appear to be Gnostic themes, and Soloviev may indeed have been a natural-born Gnostic, but he regarded his experiences strictly within the frame of Greek Orthodox religion. Under the influence of his teacher, Nikolai Fedorov, an ascetic scholar who believed in physical resurrection for the oppressed classes of the world, Soloviev propounded a complex philosophy that made Christ and Sophia central to the collective evolution of humanity. Soloviev also predicted the Antichrist and the invasion of yellow hordes from the East that would overwhelm Europe. His philosophy displays all four elements of the redeemer complex in a peculiar Slavophile mix.

Two of Sloviev's most devoted protégés were young geniuses of the Russian intelligentsia: Andrei Biely and Alexander Blok, both born in 1880. Biely—author of *St Petersburg*, a symbolist novel ranked as a world masterpiece on the level of Joyce, Mann, and Proust—became deeply involved in the Christocentric esotericism of Austrian occultist Rudolf Steiner. Blok became one of Russia's greatest literary figures of the twentieth century. He composed a poem titled "The Twelve" (1918), one of the most startling and controversial works in the entire body of Russian literature. It describes the solemn march in V-formation of twelve Bolsheviks, men known to have committed rape and murder, who patrol the streets of Petrograd with a fierce winter blizzard raging around them. The poem compares the Bolsheviks to the Twelve Apostles. At the head of the formation strides a tall, unfaltering figure: Jesus Christ.

Russia in the twentieth century may seem a long way from first-century Palestine, but perhaps not. The coordinates of space and time are null sets in the fluid dreamscape of the human psyche. A thousand years is the blink in the eye of the collective mind. The manner in which the Russian psyche fixated on Christ as the numinous leader of the revolution might be compared to the way the Palestinian messiah affected the indigenous peoples of Europa, sixteen centuries earlier. With this huge difference, however: the Russian psyche seems to have spontaneously produced the numinous phantom-savior of the revolution, but in Europa the messiah had to be brutally imposed on the native peoples. Evangelization is a process of coercion and co-optation. People convert in order to survive in the dominant social order. If they seem to undergo a genuine, soul-centered conversion, this is more a measure of psychic adaptation than spiritual transformation. (Historians wearily repeat tales of how Pagan peoples, long after conversion, still cling to their ancestral ways.) Unless there is internal force for resistence, psychic immunity, so to speak, the individual psyche will adapt to the stress of collective imagination. It will become what it believes and forget what it knows.

Blok's "Twelve" could well be a late transmogrification of Zealots from the Dead Sea. They are radical militants led by a ruthless messianic warrior. With the human psyche (of whatever race or age), what comes out is what went in. Prince Vladimir of Kiev was the great-grandson of Rurik, the traditional founder of the Russian state. Born in 956, Vladimir assumed rule of what was to become the Russian Empire in 980. He was an aggressive despot who expanded his empire by a series of vigorous conquests. In 988, he formed a military alliance with the Byzantine emperor Basil II, sealed by marriage to the emperor's sister, Anna. In return, he agreed to convert to Christianity. Like Constantine six centuries earlier, Vladimir became a Christian solely for political advantage. The fairy tale told by historians usually says, "Once the prince embraced the new faith, the people willingly followed." How wonderful for them all. The conversion of Russia under Vladimir in 988 represents the deepest plunge of the Palestinian redeemer complex into the hinterlands of Asia.

The deeper you go into the psyche of a people, the stronger the rebound will be. Along with the Roman Empire, the world has known few tyrannies as absolute and enduring as the Christian dynasty founded by Vladimir. The Russian people converted to Christianity under the usual duress, coercion, intimidation, and threats of death and damnation. They had the Zaddikite messiah shoved down their throats and, lo and behold, out he popped again in 1918, lean, steely-eyed, and lusting for revenge.

From Melchizedek to the Jewish king to the Zaddikite messiah to Jesus Christ—this is a long haul and a lot to follow, a permutation that demands exceptional concentration from the likes of us, many of whom cannot stay in the moment for three minutes at a time. But in the continuum of the human psyche the messiah complex traverses the centuries like a rock skipping over water. The ripples it makes are waves of historical change, shaping and dissolving the large contours of human society. What we vitally need to understand—now that medical authorities assume the status of a priesthood and militant messiahs stalk the Earth in the guise of billionare philanthropists—is how the psychotic, genophobic scheme of the Zaddikim could have produced the loving Jesus of the Evangelists.

The Zaddikite messiah was a political figure shrouded in a mystical aura. He was exactly what the plaque on the cross said: "King of the Jews." Or at least he wanted to be. If not a terrorist himself, he was surrounded and protected by terrorists. Simon the Rock was a redoubtable fist-fighter. Judas "Iscariot" was so called for being one of the Sicarii, assassins notorious for their stealth with blades.[105] The Zealots cut throats of Jews and Romans alike in their campaign to liberate the Promised Land. The Jews introduced crucifixion only to find it adopted by the Romans and used against them.[106] The evidence of the Dead Sea Scrolls supports Robert Eisenman's politicization of the Gospels more strongly and consistently than any other scholarly reading of the Zaddikim and the Jewish revolt.

But how in the world, out of all this, does Jesus (Yeshua, to give his proper Jewish name) emerge as the gentle healer and teacher, the divine or divinely inspired emissary of God's love?

SAVING THE BARBARIANS

In *Jesus the Magician*, Dead Sea Scrolls scholar Morton Smith argued that Jesus of the Gospels would in his own time and setting have been indistinguishable from a grassroots miracle worker or faith healer. Although the Palestinian messiah in his true and original character was profoundly alien to the native imagination of the Europan peoples, the person of Jesus the magician offered advantages for those who propagated the new faith. Owing to the fertility and openness of their psychic and imaginative life, Europans were prone to see in Jesus a version of their native gods and shamanic heroes, a psychic healer like the ones they knew. Wide-scale conversion of the natives was most successful when missionaries like Ulfilis, Arian bishop to the Goths (ca. 311–ca. 383 c.e.), persuaded the "barbarians" of the hinterlands that Jesus and Christ were merely different names for their shamans or tribal gods. (This was, needless to say, a foul and disingenuous act of deceit and an exploitation of human gullibility that begs comparison with the coronavirus hoax of 2020.) The same thing happened in Ireland where indigenous Celtic deities such as Aengus were identified with Christ. The way history is told, to favor the winners, conversion of barbarian peoples came about almost miraculously, as if they found in Jesus Christ the true identity of their native gods.

But the reality was quite otherwise. The salvific message attached to Jesus the Redeemer was something the natives had better accept, or else pay the consequences. The menace of the superhuman messiah backed by a vengeful father god loomed behind the promise of love embodied in the persona of Jesus. Conversions accomplished by Saint Patrick and other missionaries often involved magical battles or shamanic contests in which the saints prevailed, thus overthrowing native magic. These battles were fables penned in the Dark Ages by Christian monks who drew upon indigenous lore in the very act of wiping it out. The stories worked well on naïve people whose oral cultures depended on storytelling for generational continuity, but this alone cannot account for the triumph of the political and military system associated with Jesus Christ and the salvationist message. Along with novel miracle tales and the soft-pedaling of the pseudoshamanic savior, there was plenty of brutal enforcement. The more the natives resisted, the more intense the enforcement.

Christian "conversion" of Pagan Europa had another advantage going for it. Europans had little or no native psychic resistance to an ideological virus they had never encountered before—exactly as later occurred in the Americas where European colonists and missionaries imported a range of biological maladies that the native populations could not resist. By the time the indigenous peoples realized that the soft-core Jesus came with a bizarre set of rules and an alien agenda of transmundane provenance, the die had been cast, and a ruthless social control system had been set in place. Yet the indigenous Europans continued to resist conversion for many centuries, often feigning acceptance while persisting in their native ways. Enlightened tourists in Europe today soon become familiar with examples of indigenous tradition hidden in Christian sites and sanctuaries: the grotto of the Black Goddess disguised as a sanctuary of the Virgin; the magic spring falsely associated with a Christian saint; the cathedral or chapel decorated with Pagan symbolism; and so forth.

SUMMONS TO PERFECTION

For the ancient Hebrews, of course, there was never a question of conversion. They did not have to be converted to the religious disguise of the victim-perpetrator syndrome because they were a people defined by it from the outset. As a chosen community with a uniquely defined religious mandate, they had been set apart from the indigenous people of Canaan where Abraham had migrated at the command of his paternal god. What the Children of Israel faced was not conversion but the authoritarian call for absolute conformity to the will of the Creator. From its inception the Israelite community was wracked with guilt because it was unable to live up to the rigid rules dictated by Yahweh. Its status of "chosen" carried the high risk of unworthiness—a sure set-up for cognitive dissonance. To make a bad situation even worse, they were shackled with "the Judaic summons to perfection," as cultural historian George Steiner calls it.[107] The call to superhuman perfection issued from Melchizedek, but it remained in the background, a hidden imperative whose accomplishment was known only to the very few.

The ancient Jews were thus doubly burdened: they had a divine mission to fulfill and yet, at the same time, their entire communal struggle served as the front for a covert program led by the Zaddikim, the shadowy priesthood of Melchizedek. The strictures of Jehovah were humanly impossible to observe with complete fidelity. Leviticus contains not only the primary teaching wrongly said to originate with Jesus, "Thou shalt love thy neighbor as thyself (19:18)." It also prescribes over six hundred precise rules for social, sexual, ethical, hygienic, and alimentary behavior. Both neighbor love and the elaborate set of biophobic rules were meant to be practiced by and for Jews only. This was a lot to ask, but the willingness to conform mattered more than the impossibility of the commandments. The program of the Zaddikim imposed a standard of transmundane perfection to which no human being could totally conform.

While it appears to be a commission from God, the summons to perfection is in reality a call to madness and self-annihilation.

Viral Infection

For the ancient Hebrews the divine plan assumed a peculiar form reflected in the scripting of the Bible after the Babylonian Captivity (586–538 B.C.E.). Jewish history merged the Persian narrative of Cosmic Evil versus Cosmic Good with the destiny of a small Semitic tribe, the Ibiru, literally "donkey-herders." In the directive script penned by the ultraorthodox scribes of the Second Temple Period (beginning 516 B.C.E.), the figure of the secular messiah, the Jewish king, mutated oddly. Directing the mutation in a "covert ops" fashion was the secret priesthood of Zadok, the lineage of Melchizedek. As the impossibility of God's plan played out, the scenario of Jewish apocalypticism became evermore extreme and elaborate. Writing on the Book of Revelation, which he called "the death kiss" of the New Testament, D. H. Lawrence considered how "the Jews became a people of *postponed destiny*" (cited above). The mission of prophets like Ezekiel and Daniel, and the apocalyptic writers inspired by them, was "to vision forth the unearthly triumph of the Chosen."[108] The less likely it looked that the Children of Israel would have their own kingdom in the Holy Land, the more urgent it was to find a supernatural resolution for the plan of the Father. The escalating demands of the Zaddikite-Zealot movement forbade Jews faithful to Yahweh to compromise with Gentiles and heathen. The extremist sect on the Dead Sea was committed to violence to enforce a genophobic agenda that did not (as noted above) exclude murdering their own people.

From the time of the Maccabees (168 B.C.E.), at the shift into the Piscean Age, messianic expectation escalated sharply throughout the Empire. Many people, including pious Jews, were content to accept that numerous messiahs would appear as spiritual guides, ethical teachers, and reformers who would confront the injustices of the Empire. But the Zaddikim were intent upon the triumph of their messiah above all others. The tenacious presence of the small radical sect in Palestine threatened to destabilize the Empire and brought enormous grief upon the entire region.

As it turned out, the supernatural solution attended by the Zaddikim never occurred, but came to be realized in another way in Christianity. We are used to seeing anomalies in the course of the "sacred history" of the ancient Hebrews, but the greatest anomaly of all was yet to come. How did the Jewish king, who mutated into the apocalyptic messiah of the Dead Sea Scrolls, mutate further into the divine redeemer, Jesus Christ? I propose to call this momentous development the *transference*— the process by which the Zaddikite program expanded from a narrow sectarian milieu to occupy the very forefront of world history.

The transference might be compared to the entry of a virus in a vector group where it matures and fortifies, growing evermore virulent until the moment it bursts forth in a pandemic explosion.

The analogy to a virus was in fact widely used at the dawn of Christianity. In 50 C.E. the emperor Claudius wrote to the community of Alexandrian Jews about the danger from extremist cults in Palestine and neighboring province of Syria, to which Judea belonged. He warned them of being accessories to "a pest that threatens the entire world."[109] In his alarm Claudius was not attacking the Jews he addressed, for they were a valuable and well-assimilated part of the Empire. He was warning them of something emerging in their own ethnic community. The Roman authorities, it must be said, had seen trouble coming from this direction for a long time. As early as 161 B.C.E., just four years after the revolt of the Maccabees, Palestinian Jews established an embassy in Rome under a man named Judas. But twenty years later the embassy was closed by Hispalus, and the Jews were expelled from Rome, their rigid and often absurd beliefs being perceived to threaten public security. The annexation of Judea by Pompey, Caesar's rival, in 54 B.C.E., would prove to be a fateful event for both the Empire and the Children of Israel. Claudius' letter, written a century later, reflected the growing perception that in Palestine the Empire was harboring the seeds of its own destruction. The trope of "pestilence" played vividly in Pagan discourse of the time.

THE MAN OF LIES

The career of Paul, formerly Saul of Tarsus, was just getting underway when Claudius wrote his letter using the term "pest," i.e., plague. Acts 24:5 reveals similar language when Paul was indicted before the Roman governor Felix in Caesarea: "For we have found this man *a plague-carrier*, and an agent of sedition among all the Jews throughout the world, and a ring-leader of the sect of the Nazarene party." Like so much that is done and said in the Acts and the Gospels, this accusation is largely incomprehensible without the key provided by the Dead Sea Scrolls. With endless patience and careful textual elucidation, Robert Eisenman has shown that it is entirely mistaken to imagine that Paul was in any sense preaching Christianity as such. The known historical facts of the day, including eyewitness reports, confirm what can be drawn by careful inference from the Dead Sea Scrolls: Paul was preaching Nazarene or Nazorean doctrine, that is, the extremist ideology of the Zaddikim, which he transferred into Christianity.[110] (The Hebrew word *nazor*, "branch," refers to the genetic stock of the messiah from David and Jesse. The association of this term with the village of Nazareth is spurious.)

Paul was indeed fomenting sedition against the Empire, because he was promulgating the extremist beliefs of a mystical-militant sect that aimed to overthrow the Roman occupation of Palestine and establish the Kingdom of Israel. In adopting the militant apocalypticism of the

Zaddikim, Paul was also propounding its messianic creed, but twisting it to his own terms and ends, which were not those of its originators.

In the code language of the Scrolls, Paul is the Man of Lies.

This identification entirely changes the story of the conversion of Paul at Damascus. This event is described twice in Acts, first in chapter 9 in a third-person account, and then in chapter 22 in Paul's own words. In the usual telling Saul goes to Damascus around 40 C.E. to weed out and persecute Christians. On the road to the city he encounters a luminous figure that identifies itself: "I am Jesus whom thou persecutest." Saul is then taken into Damascus where the voice in the light tells him that "it shall be told thee of all things which are appointed of thee to do." He is received by a man called Ananias, "a devout man, according to the Law, having a good report of all the Jews who dwelt there"—meaning staunch members of the Zaddikite cell known to exist in Damascus, an urban counterpart to the Qumranic settlement. Somehow, Ananias has been prebriefed on Saul's arrival. How can he already know of the conversion event that befell the well-known bounty hunter from Jerusalem? Well, Saul's arrival in Damascus must have certainly been anticipated with great fear by the Zaddikites there. It is possible that they set up a trap to capture Saul and convert him to their purposes. At the same time, some kind of visionary or paranormal experience seems to have transpired. It looks as if Saul had a psychotic breakdown, and at the same time fell into the hands of the men he was pursuing.

Soon after his sojourn with Ananias and other disciples, Saul, now renamed Paul (renaming typically occurs in cultic conversions), begins to preach his unique message, which "confounded the Jews who dwelt at Damascus, proving that this is the very Christ" (Acts 9:22). When he next goes to Jerusalem, he not only confounds the Jews again but he creates an uproar of protest so violent that he has to flee the city. Among those who are most shocked and alarmed by his message is James the Just, the Qumranic Teacher of Righteousness who represents the Zaddikim at the Jerusalem temple, the other important urban outpost for the Dead Sea sect.

And so begins the ministry of Saint Paul, a mission driven by defiance, subversion, and betrayal.

DOUBLE AGENT

In the usual interpretation of this bizarre turn of events, Paul upsets Jews
by preaching true Christianity, the salvific, love-filled message of Jesus,
which is *catholic*—universal, applicable to the entire world—and so
conflicts with the sectarian, eye-for-an-eye ethos of the Old Testament.
But with the evidence of the Dead Sea Scrolls on hand this interpretation is no longer tenable. The material in the scrolls supports a different
story, encoded in the Qumranic roles. It reveals the struggle of James the
Just (role: Teacher of Righteousness) to prevent his brother, Yeshua (role:
Messiah), from being turned into the figurehead of the upstart religion
of Paul (role: Man of Lies). Warning in explicit terms against someone
who will come and pervert the mission of the Zaddikim, the scrolls'
Damascus Document alludes to the time:

> When there arose a Scoffer,
> Who distilled for Israel deceptive waters,
> And caused them to go astray in the trackless wilderness.
> To suppress the old paths,
> So as to turn aside from the righteous ways.[111]

The act of betrayal cited repeatedly in the scrolls culminates in Paul's
hijack of the Zaddikite ideology, which he then uses to frame a new religion, Christianity. This is how the transference was effectuated.

The transparent absurdity of the conventional view of Paul's conversion becomes evident with the evidence of the scrolls, and a little
common sense. Paul, who virtually created Christianity in doctrinal
terms, could not have gone to Damascus to persecute Christians, and
then get converted on the road, because *it was only in the aftermath
of his conversion that Christians came to exist as such.* There were no
Christians at that time, a mere ten years after Jesus' death. Indeed,
there was no Christianity as we today understand the definition of
Christianity in doctrinal terms, until another two centuries. But Paul
established the ideological core of Christian faith, grafting the idea of
God's love and grace onto the figure of the Zaddikite messiah. Was
there not, perhaps, a Jesus movement independent of the Zaddikite

military program? Although there may have been a handful of follow-ers of a radical rabbi who preached peace and forgiveness, such a group would not have been threatening to the Roman authorities. But the Zaddikim sect with its hard-core military wing, the Zealots, was truly a grave threat to the established powers. It had to be a militant group that Paul was sent to find and liquidate. By the same measure, it was a mere human being, the Zaddikite messiah, whom Paul elevated to a divine level as "the Christ."

The Zaddikim failed to overthrow Rome, but through the transfer-ence the salvationist program derived from their extremist ideology consumed the Empire and co-opted its power.

The man who became the apostle Paul was originally a mercenary hired by the Roman authorities to track down extremist cults such as the Zaddikim. In short, he was a bounty hunter. This much is clear even from the Acts alone. Time and time again, the Romans protect Paul. They approve his actions and provide him with troops and a personal guard. The leader of the Sanhedrin at the Jerusalem temple (code: Wicked Priest) wanted to see the Zaddikim suppressed. He also sanctioned the mission of the bounty hunter. All this is clearly stated in Acts.

According to the tradition of Qumran community, there was a major cell of the Covenant at Damascus.[112] In the process of hunting it down, Paul fell into the cult he was sent to eradicate. During his stay, Ananias initiated him into the inner secrets of the Zaddikim, including the ultimate secret, the identity of Melchizedek. It seems that Paul proved to be an exceptionally gifted recruit. His character profile resembles what is today known as a sociopath: an ardent, bril-liant, highly convincing person able to play different roles in different social settings but who always maintains a self-serving hidden agenda. In fact, the Pauline appeal to "be all things to all people" is the perfect formula of the sociopath.

As soon as Paul was released from recruitment, he began preaching Zaddikite doctrines in the open. This itself was a terrible act of betrayal that caused fifty supporters of the Zealot movement to enter a fast until they could murder him (Acts 4). In this instance, as in so many others, Paul was closely shadowed by the Roman authorities who intervened to protect and rescue him on several occasions. Due to his knowledge of the Damascus cell and the activities of the Judean wilderness camps, he was an invaluable double agent for Rome, but his own messianic tendencies made him a troublemaker too unpredictable to manage. Toward the end of Paul's life, the very people who sent him to liquidate the Zaddikite Damascus cell realized that he was creating more trouble than he was worth. Paul was executed in Rome in 64 c.e., the first year from which any record of the persecution of "Christians" survives.

In a striking application of the viral analogy Robert Eisenman speaks of "the incendiary bacillus of Jewish Messianic and apocalyptic propaganda" that was absorbed into the preaching of Paul, in direct defiance of James the Just.[113] The Man of Lies openly defied the Teacher of Righteousness, just as the Zaddikite script had warned would happen. The larval form of the "incendiary bacillus" is the Palestinian redeemer complex, itself the anomalous mutation of a universal mythological theme. It was nurtured in Jewish religious life for centuries, secretly directed by the priesthood of Zadok. Although it originated with the tiny Zaddikite sect, the ideological virus carried by Paul went pandemic in the One Truth Faith. It spread to Europa, then to the Americas. Today it infects the entire world.

DIVIDE AND CONVERT

The directive script of salvationism is the New Testament, including Acts and the letters of Paul. In its baffling combination of fairy-tale narrative and high theological rhetoric, the New Testament formulates and confirms the complicity of victim and perpetrator exemplified by the tribulations of the Jews in the Old Testament. The complicity implies a kind of *contract in sin*, with both parties falling short of God's commands. Perpetrators who harm others are obviously sinners, but so are the people they harm, who may well believe they are being justly punished by a higher power. The wrong done to victims is due to the wrong they have done in the eyes of God. To make matters worse, the twisted syntax of the victim-perpetrator bond condones domination, violence, aggression, and murder as expressions of divine retribution. Those who enact the will of God in violent ways are as righteous as those who suffer violence, because the bond prescribes and legitimates *both* roles. A deal that sanctifies violence and guarantees the righteous vindication of its victims is hard to beat. The temptation of victims to become perpetrators is ever present, although not all victims succumb to it. Those who do become top dogs in the dominator game.

The continuity of the two Testaments, rigorously rejected by Gnostics like Marcion, insures that converts to Christianity will be locked into the victim-perpetrator syndrome from the outset. The sin doctrine does not give its adherents a chance to fail: it convinces them they have already failed, even before they try. "All have sinned and come short of the glory of God." Moreover, the sense of having failed God plays directly into the victim syndrome, disposing believers to imagine that abuse and harm that befall them are due to their moral flaws. If they are harmed, they must deserve it. It is their fault, for through God's will they are made to suffer, punished for their own good. Punishment for failing to follow God's plan is inflicted on some people (the victims) by other people (the perpetrators) who righteously uphold the plan. As long as the ideology of redemption goes unchallenged, victim-perpetrator pathology can thrive *and* remain concealed, using salvationist beliefs for cover.

The ideology of redemption could not have overwhelmed the peoples of the Near East, where it arose, or spread to Europa and then to the entire world, had the victim-perpetrator bond not been operating within it. Both in Europa and the Americas the natural moral resilience of the native peoples could have resisted the sin doctrine. Indeed, the native mind left to its own devices would have regarded such views as absurd and laughable. Pagans in the classical world who were not intimidated by the Judeo-Christian belief system did indeed regard that doctrine in just that way. But the doctrine of sin was convincing because it legitimated perpetration under the guise of divine punishment. The very same religious program that attacked indigenous ways of life and destroyed the native peoples' social norms and mores, turning them into victims, presented them with a preformulated justification for the victim role, as well as an assurance that, in the end, victims would prevail. Native intelligence lacked the finesse to see that it was the perpetrators, the very people who were destroying their way of life, who were promising that they would ultimately be saved from victimization. They lacked this finesse because oral, indigenous culture was based everywhere on the same principle: honesty, that is, consistency of word and act.

The phrase "divide and conquer" is well known. What applies here, however, is a slight variation of that phrase: "divide and convert." In order to convert the native peoples, it was necessary to divide them *internally*, to split them psychically, separating word and action. For the dominators who used redemptive religion as a tool of conquest the internal split was already operating. To break word and betray trust, say one thing and do another, promise love and deliver violence, preach kindness and practice cruelty, are protocols of the dominator mind-set. This behavior was *not* a perversion of the salvationist program, *not* an aberration perpetrated by a few corrupt people in the name of God and the Savior: it was, and ever is, the righteous and rigorous enactment of the Faith.

Salvationist religion prevailed because it delivered the opposite of what it promised to people who were, at first, unable to perceive the double standard, and then, when they did finally see it, found themselves enmeshed in it, counting on it to show the way out of their plight. The genius of Saint Paul was to turn the schizophrenic mind-set of the Hebrews into a theological ruse, promising God's grace to all those who accepted roles in the victim-perpetrator game, *on either side*. Paul himself was clearly on the Roman side, a double agent and then some, as seen in Eisenman's close analysis of the Dead Sea Scrolls. It is quite possible that his conversion by the Zaddikites was set up so that he could access their secret teachings and betray them. The essence of Paul's message reflects the betrayal and deception that produced it.

Gnostics saw through the complex psychological ruse concealed in Pauline doctrines of salvation, but indigenous peoples who lacked experience with such deceit and hypocrisy fell victim to it, time and time again.

THE GNOSTIC EXPOSÉ

With the hijacking of the Zaddikite ideology and its mutation into Christianity, the religious schizophrenia of the ancient Hebrews infected humanity at large. The transference must be one of the most astonishing events in the psychohistorical experience of humanity, yet it has barely been recognized as such. Many scholars still reject the claim that Christian theology and ethics are the pandemic expression of the Jewish messianic virus. Early writers on the scrolls, such as Theodor H. Gaster, take pains to distance the Qumranic literature from Christian doctrines: "There is in them [the Dead Sea Scrolls] no trace of any of the original theological concepts—the incarnate Godhead, Original Sin, redemption through the Cross, and the afterlife—which make Christianity a distinctive faith."[114] Christian scholars such as Ian Wilson, even when they deconstruct the figure of Jesus to the point of nonexistence, maintain the same disavowal: the scrolls "proved disappointingly to throw little new light on Jesus and early Christianity."[115] In view of evidence presented by the scrolls, and the way that evidence clearly correlates to the known history of Jesus' times, and makes the life of Jesus comprehensible, this statement is utterly laughable.

So bizarre is the transference that scholars to this day cannot see the deep continuity of the scrolls and Christian doctrines. The critical literature is full of contradictory views, often expressed by the same author. Hershel Shanks, an important biblical scholar who played a key role in breaking the Vatican deadlock on Qumranic research, insists that "Jesus is not in the Scrolls. Nor is the uniqueness of Christianity in doubt." But fifty pages later in the same book he says that the scrolls show "that *in almost every aspect* the message of early Christianity was presaged in its Jewish roots. And even the life of Jesus, as told in the Gospels, is often prefigured in the Scrolls."[116]

The blindspot of scholars concerning the transference has two foci. First, they do not distinguish sufficiently between the core ideology of salvationism and accessory doctrines. All the elements of the former are purely Zaddikite: for instance, the resurrection of Jesus is based in the scrolls and specifically mirrors the supernatural, deathless status of Melchizedek. In Hebrews 7 Paul makes the staggering assertion that Melchizedek is the power behind Christ—literally the anointer of the anointed. And what a remarkable power this is. Apparently, the Zaddikim founder stands outside biological generation: "without father, without mother, without descent, having neither beginning of days nor end of life." In the same passage Paul declares that the priest-hood of Melchizedek overrules and cancels the traditional priesthoods of Levi and Aaron. This astonishing feat of co-optation defines the doctrinal freedom of Christian ideology from its Jewish roots, yet it does so by evoking an eerie, hidden figure who runs a covert operation behind the scenes.

Paul's insistence on salvation by faith is another feat of co-optation, a direct steal from the Habakkuk *pesher* (commentary) of the Dead Sea sect: "And the righteous shall live by faith."[117] But what Paul meant by faith—that is, blind, unconditional trust in the saving power of the Divine Redeemer—is not what the Zaddikim understood by that term. Far from it. Paul's famous "zeal" is a Zealot attribute applied over and over again to non-Zealot ends. Of course, Paul did not invent Christianity all by himself. It took a grand collaboration of many parties, including lawyers and the Flavian shills who authored the four Gospels. Other doctrines of Christianity such as Original Sin, Virgin Birth, cross theology, the Mass, are accessories added over time to the core complex. Some of them, like the Virgin Birth and the Mass, were patently stolen from Pagan religion, others are gratuitously invented as the Church required them. They do not represent the Zaddikite origins of Roman Christianity, but later embellishments of what sprung from those origins.

At the second focus of the blind spot, scholars do not detect the trans-ference because they cannot imagine how the hateful, vindictive figure of the Qumranic messiah has been transposed into the figure of "gentle Jesus, meek and mild." They fail to realize that the message of love in the charming miracle tales of the New Testament is a sugar coating on the bitter cyanide of Zaddikite ravings.

But what scholars and believers fail to see, or refuse to see, did not go unobserved and without objection in centuries past. Many Pagans, including the vigilant Roman authorities, had been watching the salvationist plague for a long time, as I have already noted. And the Gnostics were also there, a constant presence in the agora of the Mystery Schools and the temple precincts. Like Hypatia, many of them could have "eclipsed in argument every proponent of the Christian doctrines in Northern Egypt" and elsewhere, wherever the Mysteries thrived, all around the ancient world. More than anyone else the initiates were capable of detecting the *anomia*, the sinister deviance in the Palestinian redeemer complex. More than anyone else, they were able to refute it, which they did, both in open oral debate and prolific writings, most of which were destroyed.

Moreover, the *gnostikoi* had their own ideas about the matters on which Christian ideologues claimed to have the final and exclusive answers: creation, sin, death, resurrection, the divine plan, the nature and operations of evil. Their calling was to the spiritual guidance of humanity, achieved through education rather than indoctrination. They had millennia of experience behind them. Standing against the redeemer complex, they had their own ideas about redemption as a coevolutionary process to be realized through humanity's connection with the Wisdom Goddess, Sophia, whose body is the Earth. It was they, the initiates, who watched most closely as the ideological plague emerged, and who, when the moment came, risked their lives to stand against it. It was they who had a magnificent story to guide the species—a story that was lost when the Mysteries were destroyed by zealous carriers of the plague.

Lost until December 1945.

PART TWO

A STORY
TO GUIDE
THE SPECIES

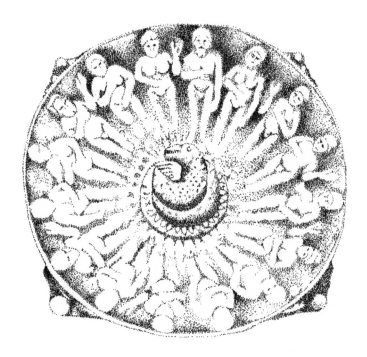

Orphic Sacramental Bowl with Sixteen Initiates

7

THE EGYPTIAN CACHE

In the autumn of 1947, at the very moment scholars in Jerusalem were getting their first look at the Dead Sea Scrolls, Egypt was hit by a serious outbreak of cholera. The general health alert paralyzed travel and left a young French Egyptologist named Jean Doresse stranded in the capital. The crumbling *quartier* known as Fustat, located on the south side of the Old City, was constructed by the Romans as a fortification on the Nile. Among its neglected treasures is the Coptic Museum, at that time under the direction of an enterprising Egyptian scholar named Togo Mina. Doresse, a specialist in the Coptic language, met Mina while biding time until he could leave Cairo to explore some Coptic monasteries in the south around Thebes.

One morning Mina pulled a thick packet out of the desk drawer in his office and showed it to Doresse, asking his opinion on what to Mina appeared to be obscure but perhaps significant materials. The young scholar's reaction was vivid:

> From the first few words I could see that these were Gnostic texts, one of which bore the title *The Sacred Book of the Invisible Great Spirit*, whilst further on was the title of a *Secret Book of John*. I warmly congratulated Togo Mina upon this extraordinary discovery, and immediately undertook, with his help, the task of putting these leaves in order, for they had become considerably muddled.[118]

Soon afterward, Doresse flew to Luxor to explore the ruins of monasteries in the area around Chenoboskian, "the place of breeding geese." This is the Coptic name of Hamra-Dûm, a tiny hamlet at the foot of the cliffs called Jabal al-Tarif. The rare cache in Mina's possession had been discovered there by an Arab peasant some eighteen months earlier, in December, 1945. The Nag Hammadi Codices (NHC) were stuffed into a red clay jar and hidden in a cave in the cliffs. West across the Nile is the village of Nag Hammadi, after which the texts were to be named. In ancient times, it was called Sheniset, "the acacias of Seth." (Hamra-Dûm is a flyspeck on the desolate landscape, too small to merit mention. Otherwise, the texts would have become known as the Hamra-Dûm library.) Beyond the inestimable value of their content, these thirteen leather-bound volumes in the Egyptian cache are unique literary artifacts, the earliest examples that survive of bound books with numbered pages.

ALTERNATIVE GOSPELS?

On January 12, 1948, the Egyptian press announced to the world the existence of the rare material that had fallen into the hands of Togo Mina. Before their discovery, the only comparable evidence of Gnostic views was three obscure texts, also in Coptic, known as the Bruce, Askew, and Berlin Codices. As the word spread, scholars wondered if the Egyptian find might contain Coptic translations of original Gnostic writings in Greek. Based on examination of the "cartonnage," dated letters and accounts contained in the bindings of the codices, experts know the books must have been concealed between 345 and 348 c.e. Today they are kept in special rooms at the Coptic Museum in Old Cairo where Jean Doresse first examined them.

In 1966 a team of scholars led by James Robinson of the Institute for Antiquity and Christianity, Claremont, California, undertook the full English translation of the Nag Hammadi Codices (NHC), as they are also called (*codex* is a Latin word for book). Between 1972 and 1977 the Coptic Gnostic Library Project, as the team was known, produced *The Facsimile Edition of the Nag Hammadi Codices*, a set of handsome oversize volumes with clear full-page photographs of every page in the codices. In 1977 they published *The Nag Hammadi Library in English*, making the material available for the first time to the English-speaking world.*

---

* See "Suggestions for Reading and Research" for more details on the NHC and contemporary writings about Gnosticism.

These rare writings include the Sophia mythos, a mythological history of the Earth compatible in some respects to Gaia theory. So it happened that the sacred narrative of the Mysteries became accessible to the world a mere five years after the introduction of the Gaia hypothesis by James Lovelock, and four years after the initial definition of deep ecology by Arne Naess.

According to the consensus view of Gnostic scholars, most of the writings from Nag Hammadi may be regarded as "outtakes" of early Christian literature, like strips of film left on the editing-room floor. As material that might have been included in the New Testament, they have widely been considered "lost Gospels." Some of the tractates (as the texts are called in scholar's jargon) do indeed bear the Greek word *evangelium* on the final page, where titles were indicated. The title of Elaine Pagels' book *The Gnostic Gospels*, first published in 1979 and still widely read, reinforces this interpretation. Upon close analysis, however, the bulk of the Egyptian material does not warrant such a facile comparison.

The four Gospels of the New Testament belong to an ancient literary genre called Hellenistic romance. This type of romance was a novella full of miracles, supernatural signs, cameo scenes with stock characters, plus aphorisms drawn from folklore and religious traditions—in short, a pastiche mixing fable and folk wisdom with realistic elements. Many such novellas were circulating in the first centuries of the Christian era, but suspiciously few have survived. Why? The Hellenistic romances were the pulp fiction of their time, comparable to adult comic books. Imagine such ephemeral material surviving for hundreds of years. This would not happen unless there were a particular reason to preserve it. Suppose, for example, that a group of people decided to found a cult on Superman. They would preserve *Superman* comics while those of other heroes like Spider Man and Doctor Strange would suffer the fate of time, or be deliberately eliminated to insure the dominance of the *Superman* material. The exclusive survival, and hence the seeming uniqueness, of the four Christian Gospels depended on deliberate suppression of many other Hellenistic romances.

Nothing in the Nag Hammadi material resembles the Hellenistic romances, so it is incorrect to compare them to Christian writings classed

in that genre. *The Gnostic Gospels* was the breakthrough book that introduced Gnostic thought to the mainstream, but Pagels' choice of title was
a serious miscue. It has misled many people who encounter Gnosticism
to see it as merely an early and dubious variant of Christianity. Far from
being alternative versions of the New Testament, the Egyptian codices
contain a preponderance of material that rejects and refutes the salvationist message of the Evangelists—and does so in ruthless and often
lacerating terms.

Almost without exception, scholars of Gnosticism come from a Jewish
or Christian background. Their tendency is to play down, if not entirely
ignore, the anti-Jewish and anti-Christian elements in the codices. So
far, no specialist on the Nag Hammadi material has attempted to present the content and scope of its genuinely Pagan elements. Scholars are
simply not interested in Gnostic ideas as such, but only in what Gnostic
writings can tell them about early Christianity. They comment endlessly
on the *meaning* of the texts, especially where they find hints of Christian
doctrine, but overlook their essential non-Christian *message*.

Getting to that message is no easy task, however. All in all, the Nag
Hammadi writings are a motley mix of shambolic discourses, snippets
of mystical and mythological lore, arcane flights of theology, esoteric
rites and riddles, and lofty metaphysical speculation that in some places
recalls the Buddhist philosophy of the Void. They include an extract from
Plato's *Republic*, a fragment of a treatise found in complete form in the
Hermetica, and, yes, a couple of proto-Christian homilies that might have
been delivered by an evangelist. The tractates vary enormously in length.
The longest, such as the Apocryphon of John and the Tripartite Tractate,
are complex mythical narratives on cosmological matters such as the organization of the Pleroma (the Gnostic Void, matrix of the primal gods), the
fall of the goddess Sophia, the demented antics of the Demiurge (the false
creator god), and the preterrestrial emanation of Primal Humanity (the
Anthropos). The shortest are mere scribal notes, including a forty-line
text, the Prayer of the Apostle Paul, scribbled inside the cover of codex 1.
Some texts, such as the Apocryphon (or Secret Book) of John, appear in
more than one version in the codices, as well as in non–Nag Hammadi
material such as the Berlin Codex (BG). The Berlin Codex also contains
The Gospel of Mary, a short, much-damaged treatise attributed to

Mary Magdalene, which is included in *The Nag Hammadi Library in English* even though it was not part of the Egyptian cache.

The Egyptian material is wildly diverse, often presenting contradictory elements jumbled into a single document. The Teachings of Silvanus is an early Christian homily embedded with some genuine Gnostic insight, while the Sentences of Sextus is a similar collection of adages almost devoid of Pagan Gnostic elements. The Apocryphon of James is not a Gnostic document at all but a Jewish-Christian discourse on redemption. The Book of Thomas the Contender might have arrived in the Levant by packhorse from a monastery in India. More Buddhist than Gnostic in character and content, it has been compared to the "Fire Sermon" of Mahayana Buddhism. The parallel texts of Eugnostos and the Sophia of Jesus Christ show how scribes who worked through the originals converted non-Christian content in the former to doctrinal expressions of faith in the latter.[119] The Gospel of Thomas, widely regarded as the showpiece of the NHC, is a collection of banal platitudes with a few faint glimmers of the radical message of Gnosis. The Discourse on the Eighth and the Ninth presents stunning glimpses of teachings and practices at the heart of the Pagan Mysteries. Some of the longer Mystery discourses such as the Paraphrase of Shem and Zostrianos are obscure to the point of exasperation. The Gospel of the Egyptians, Allogenes, The Testimony of Truth and other texts are so badly damaged that they require considerable, and dubious, reconstruction.

Reading this material can be both exhausting and exasperating, as anyone who dips into *The Nag Hammadi Library in English* soon discovers. It contains a huge amount of repetition or, what's worse, near repetition, with discrepancies galore, gaps due to damaged pages, interpolations, and grammatical quandaries—mainly, confusion of pronomial referents, notorious in Coptic, making it impossible to determine what "it," "we," and "they" refer to. There is an appalling lack of clear language throughout. One in every five words in Coptic is a loan from Greek, but it is still next to impossible to work out how the "Greek originals" would have looked. Many passages present lofty and sophisticated ideas, but the clunky Coptic syntax fits this high-toned discourse like hiking boots on a ballerina. The comment of Jean Doresse, that the texts are "considerably muddled," is an understatement. The entire Gnostic corpus is a dense, chaotic, despairing mess. Yet it may be the closest we will ever get to written disclosure of the Gnostic teachings from the Levantine-Egyptian Mysteries.

The great challenge of the Coptic Gnostic materials is to read through the terrific muddle to the essence of the Gnostic message as such.

REVEALER VERSUS REDEEMER?

The deep, startling impact of the Nag Hammadi material becomes evident when the codices with salient anti-Christian elements, such as The Second Treatise of the Great Seth, are compared to the salvationist doctrines common to Judaism and Christianity, whose larval form is found in the Dead Sea Scrolls, as explained in part 1. Once its key features are detected, the Gnostic protest against Judeo-Christian redemptive religion stands out more and more clearly as an informing motif of the entire corpus. Repeated reading, research, and comparative studies bring out the true grain of the radical Pagan argument of "the children of Seth," as the highest initiates of Gnosis called themselves. Seth is almost entirely excluded from the Old Testament after a brief mention in Genesis 4:25: "And Adam knew his wife again; and she bare a son, and called his name Seth: For God, *said she*, hath appointed me another seed instead of Abel, whom Cain slew." Gnostics believed they belonged to "another seed," i.e., a spiritual lineage stemming from primal humanity (Anthropos), distinct from Judeo-Christian sacred tradition. Their argument against that tradition might be epitomized in a line from the The Second Treatise of the Great Seth (IV,1) where the Gnostic teacher protests against "the plan which they devised about me, to release upon the world their Error and their senselessness" (55.10).* The teacher who speaks here would have been regarded as a *phoster*, a "light bearer" or "revealer." This is a title for the illumined master in the Mysteries who preserves the sacred transmission of Gnosis, knowledge such as the gods enjoy.

---

* The parenthesis following the title of a Nag Hammadi text identifies the codex by Roman numeral (I through XII) and the sequence of the text in the codex by an Arabic number. Notations such as 55.10 indicate page and line.

Phoster is a close parallel to *Buddha*, "the illumined" or "awakened one." In the tradition of the Levantine and Egyptian Gnostics, the revealers—enlighteners in some translations—are not superhuman avatars but superendowed human beings who possess extraordinary knowledge of natural and divine matters, and who demonstrate paranormal faculties. They are comparable to the *vidyadharas*, "knowledge holders," and *siddhas* "accomplished ones," of Indian mysticism and Mahayana and Tibetan Buddhism. The Sanskrit *siddha* is cognate with the Greek *adept*, from *adepsci*, "to be accomplished," "trained." *Siddhis* are paranormal powers such as clairvoyance, clairaudience, and lucid dreaming.

Let's recall that the redeemer complex, the core of the three Abrahamic religions, has four key components: creation of the world by the father god independent of a goddess; the selection and testing of the righteous few or "chosen people"; the mission of the messiah sent by the father god to save the world; and the final judgment delivered by father and son upon humanity. A good part of the truly original material in the Egyptian codices is dedicated to refuting these components and ridiculing the beliefs attached to them. Gnostics considered the "Divine Plan" of salvationism, i.e., the manifestation of God's will in the course of historical events, to be a grotesque distortion of the genuine spiritual lineage they represented. In their view, the divine love of the Pleroma, the transcendent gods, comes to expression in human revealers, who appear through the ages to teach and guide humanity. They posited an ongoing educational process for the enlightenment of humanity, a system of cultivating human potential and awakening the genius innate to our species, but no plan of salvation as such.

Scholars call the perennial transmission of Gnosis by illumined teachers the revealer cycle. The revealer who speaks in The Second Treatise of the Great Seth warned that salvationism is a plan devised against the guardians of Gnosis, whose enemies "release upon the world their Error and their senselessness." When the Zaddikite ideology of the Dead Sea Scrolls exploded into a mass religious movement after 150 C.E., teachers in the Mysteries disregarded their vow of anonymity and came out publicly to protest what they perceived as deceit and deviance in the salvationist belief system. For Christianity to triumph, its adherents had not only to silence the Gnostics, but to destroy the millennial network of the Mysteries, and eliminate all evidence that it had ever existed. In the perspective of time, the protest of the Gnostic revealers returns to haunt the human mind—and perhaps awaken humankind to the source of its undoing.

Gnostic scholar K. W. Troger estimates that one-third of the Coptic corpus is anti-Judaic.[120] I reckon that anti-Judaic and anti-Christian elements combined amount to nearly half of the material in the NHC. The Second Treatise is exemplary of the Gnostic protest against salvationism. It contains page after page of scathing attacks on Judaic and Christian beliefs and customs. It ridicules the biblical forefathers and castigates those who follow patriarchal religion, unable to see how it corrupts their very sense of humanity:

> And Adam was a laughingstock, and Abraham, and Jacob, and David, and Solomon, and the Twelve Prophets, and Moses, and John the Baptist. . . . None of them knew me, the Revealer, nor my brethren in the Mysteries. . . . They never knew truth, nor will they know it, for there is a great deception upon their soul, and they cannot ever find the mind of freedom, in order to know themselves, in true humanity. (62.27; 63.34; 64.20 ff)

Point by point the Second Treatise attacks the core belief enshrined in the redeemer complex, "the doctrine of a dead man," centerpiece of Christian theology. It sharply contrasts the salvationist redeemer to the revealers who both model and teach the Anthropos, the true identity of the human species. Gnostics saw in the Jewish messiah—the Zaddikite figure that later morphed into the Christian redeemer, Jesus Christ—a counterfeit revealer and a bogus model of humanity. His claim to exclusivity as the "only-begotten Son of God" was simply a lie intended to set up an authority that could not be challenged by mere mortals. In the tradition of the Mysteries, revealers appear periodically through the ages to enlighten and teach. They are completely human, unlike the eerie, superhuman alien, Melchizedek, the power behind Christ. Each revealer has realized the true identity of human species, but the unique status (so claimed) of the superhuman Jesus Christ does not genuinely reflect such a spiritual attainment. For Gnostics, only a genuine, flesh-and-blood human being can guide and teach humanity.

THEOLOGICAL SEMTEX

Gnostics regarded the Incarnation as a priestly fraud foisted on humanity, but not just that. They also considered the "Son of God" to be a delusional idea insinuated into the human mind by a species of aberrant, nonhuman entities or mental parasites, the Archons. These bizarre intrapsychic phantoms are minions of the Demiurge, the false creator god—a concept that appears to be unique to Gnostic thought. In their identification of the Demiurge with Jehovah, the father god of Jewish and Christian tradition, Gnostics drew a frontal attack from those who founded their religion on a cherished belief in the male supreme being. Often the attack was violent, and sometimes murderous, as in the death of Hypatia.

Modern scholars cannot ignore the fact that Gnostics considered the supreme being of Judeo-Christian religion to be a demented imposter, but they make as little as possible of this outrageous claim. In many scholarly works, the nature and activity of the Archons is simply passed over in silence. (The two best-known texts on Gnosticism, Hans Jonas's *The Gnostic Religion* and Elaine Pagels's *The Gnostic Gospels*, do not include Archons and their translated equivalents, Rulers and Authorities, in the index.) Yet the scenario of the Demiurge and his weird minions figures strongly in the Sophia mythos, the creation myth taught in the Levantine Mysteries. Gnostics clearly associated the Archons with what they perceived to be the religious dementia of Judeo-Christianity, but this notion of an "alien implant" is so bizarre that scholars are loathe to consider it. Dismissing the Archontic material in the NHC gets the experts off the hook, because it disobliges them from giving full and fair treatment to the Gnostic critique of salvationist religion. In short, it saves them from the risk of theological incorrectness.

Deception and counterfeiting are signatures of the Archons: "Their delight is in deception [*apaton*] . . . and their counterfeit [*antimimon*] spirit" (Apocryphon of John, II, 1:21). The Greek *apaton* denotes willful intent to deceive, and *antimimon* denotes the method of Archontic deception: literally, "countermimicry." This means to copy something but make the copy, the fake version, serve a purpose counter to the original thing or idea—a mRNA vaccine, for example. In their view of human self-deception—a highly sophisticated view, comparable to the noetic psychology of our time—Gnostics regarded the divine redeemer as a countermimic of their revealer. Pagan adepts from the Mysteries in the Levant and Egypt saw in the salvationist program of redemption both the evidence and the instrument of Archontic deviation. They did not blame the Archons for originating the program, however, but for colluding with those human beings who did:

> Yaldabaoth himself chose a certain man named Abraham, and made a covenant with him that if his seed would continue to serve him he would give to him the earth as an inheritance. Later through Moses he brought forth from Egypt the descendents of Abraham, gave them the law, and made them Jews. From them the seven gods, also called the Hebdomad, chose their own heralds to glorify each and proclaim Yaldabaoth as God, so that the rest of mankind, hearing the glorification, might also serve those who were proclaimed by the prophets as Gods. (*Against Heresies*, I.30.10)

Here is the definitive moment in the sacred history of the ancient Hebrews, viewed with a rather unusual spin. The Gnostic warning is explicit: It assigns a completely different value to what transpires between Abraham and the entity he takes for God the Father. Yaldabaoth (*YAL-dah-BUY-ot*, a made-up word possibly derived from Aramaic, "who traverses the external space") is the Gnostic code name for the false creator god, or Demiurge. His realm is the planetary system exclusive of the Earth, the Hebdomad of seven planets. In the cosmology of the Sophia mythos, Yaldabaoth and his minions arise as a lifeless, distorted mirroring of the divine patterns or celestial archetypes in the Pleroma, the Godhead: "And she established [the firmament: *stereoma*] after the pattern of the realms that are above, for by starting from the invisible world, the visible world was created" (NHC II,4, 87:5). They are called Archons, from Greek *archaia*, "primal," "first," "from the beginning," because the formation of their world, the planetary system subject to inorganic and mechanical laws, precedes the formation of the living Earth. (The Sophia mythos and the role of the Archons are both fully elaborated below, beginning in chapter 10.)

In the Gnostic perspective the Archons are not only mind parasites—delusional nodes in the human mind, considered as quasi-autonomous psychic entities, if you will—they are cosmic imposters, parasites who pose as gods. But they lack the primary divine factor of *ennoia*, "intentionality," "creative will." They cannot originate anything, they can only imitate, and they must effectuate their copycat activity with subterfuge and stealth, lest its true nature be detected. Hence they offer Abraham something that already belongs to him as a member of the human race. The Earth has already been given to humanity: it is the precious habitat the goddess Sophia dreamed for the Anthropos, and which she manifested by the metamorphosis of her own divine luminosity. The Archons approach Abraham with a fake deal, promising him possession and domination of the terrestrial realm, but this is not compatible with Sophia's *ennoia*, her divine intention. The Earth is not a territorial prize but a precious setting where the human species can realize its innate genius, its capacity for novelty, acting within the natural boundaries set by the Goddess. The Archons mimic the divine *ennoia*, Sophia's intention, and at the same time they invert it. In place of participation in the divine miracle of symbiosis and evolutionary emergence, which is the true birthright of humanity, they promise Abraham a fake sovereignty that works against that birthright and deviates human purpose from its proper course of unfoldment. This is countermimicry in action.

Antimimon is a powerful tool of dispossession, needless to say. The Apocryphon of John says that the Demiurge "removed himself from Sophia and moved away from the place where he arose" (10.20). In other words, Archons do not respect their proper boundaries in the cosmic order. They do not belong to the terrestrial biosphere, but to the planetary system beyond the Earth. But they are invasive and they encourage invasion.

The Lord God of the Old Testament called Abraham from the place where he was born, Ur of the Chaldees. Believing himself to be acting in the cause of a divine mission, Abraham was dispossessed. He became the leader of a people compelled to dispossess others in an escalating cycle of territorial loss and gain. In a larger sense, all of humanity is dispossessed of its divine birthright by the subterfuge of the Archons—that is, *by assuming suprem-acy as a means of transcendence.* The dispossession motif is closely associated with the deific pretension of the Archons: "And the Lord Archon said to the authorities who attend him, 'Come let us create a man according to the image of God and according to our likeness'" (II, 1, 15.5). Here again is a familiar factor of biblical narrative, told with a Gnostic twist. *The Archons are themselves deluded in believing they can create humans in their likeness.* They do not succeed—the Gnostic materials are explicit on this point—but they insinuate into human minds the belief that they have succeeded.

The Abrahamic religions all claim that humanity is special, the one species made "in His image." This belief is associated with the second component of the redeemer complex: there is a select few who faithfully reflect the image of their Maker, while the rest of humanity does not. This nefarious and separatistic creed—arguably the pinnacle of racism—not only sets apart the righteous few and targets them for discrimination, it condemns the rest of humanity who do not mirror the divine image and follow the Father's plan. The Messiah comes to correct this situation, saving the select few from persecution (Jewish version) or offering divine absolution to all repentant sinners (Christian version), but the master plan is still not fulfilled on Earth, and final retribution must be imposed. Teachers in the Mysteries rejected this entire scenario as dementia, the psychotic ploy of the Archontic mind parasites.

Unlike the divine Aeons who emanate without imposing themselves, the Archons wrongly believe they can impress their mentality upon the human species. They want to make humanity like themselves, but they are constantly foiled by the superiority of the human species, "whose origin is in the imperishable realm, where the virginal power dwells, superior to the Archons of chaos and to their universe" (The Reality of the Archons, II, 4: 93.25–30). The Nag Hammadi writings constantly stress that humanity is superior to the Archons: "Adam was more correct in his thinking than the Chief Ruler, Yaldabaoth" (II, 1: 22.6). But although humans can outthink the Archons, we do not always optimize the inborn intelligence of our species, called "nous" by the Gnostics. When the faculty of discrimination is weak, we are prone to let pretense and fantasy override clear thinking. Failing to own and evolve the intelligence innate to our species, we risk being deviated by another kind of mind, an artificial intelligence through which we become unreal to ourselves. AI is the primary instrument of Archontic deviance in the modern world.

The triumph of the Rulers or Authorities, as the Archons are also called, would be achieved at the stage of human experience where no one can tell plastic from pearl, and imitation is so prevalent that a genuine human animal feels like an alien on the home planet. At that point the human species would be so falsified that we would not even be able to distinguish real people from soulless clones. For humankind to betray and abandon itself is merely the amusement of the Archons, it seems. They insinuate their influence through religious beliefs—also through scientific beliefs, when science assumes the role in society formerly held by religion, as it largely does today—because such beliefs have the most potent effect on our sense of humanity and human potential.

Although scholars reject it as superstitious nonsense, or Gnostic myth-making too weird to consider, the role of the Archons is essential both to Sophianic cosmology and the Pagan critique of salvationism. The ideological virus released on a pandemic scale by Saint Paul was incubated among the ancient Hebrews by the Archons—so says Gnostic countermythology. "Yaldabaoth himself chose a certain man named Abraham . . . and made a covenant with him." From the outset, the delusional beliefs of an alien mind-set infected the Judeo-Christian religion, but Gnostics saw the infection as it set in. They taught that finding humanity's true path depends on refuting and rejecting these beliefs, all the way back to their origin. If the Zaddikite documents from the Dead Sea are the bedrock of Christianity, which now seems impossible to deny, then the Nag Hammadi material of a genuinely Gnostic character is the explosive charge that can blow the institution of the Faith off its foundations, for good and all.

The message of the Gnostic revealers is theological semtex. It is also humanity's secret weapon for defeating the technocratic agenda of AI domination.

Underdog Religion

In a book published in 1991, I called Gnosticism "the underdog of world religions."[121] It is, of course, entirely excluded from the inventory of religions that matter in the world today, or ever mattered. The purpose of the centuries-long Christian cover-up was to eradicate all evidence of Gnostics and the Mysteries, and to snuff out the quintessence of Pagan wisdom of the ancient world. This had to be done so thoroughly and efficiently that what was destroyed would appear never to have been there to destroy in the first place!

What kind of religion, what manner of universal truth, what glowing message of love and forgiveness, needs to make itself known and accepted through destruction of this kind, on this scale?

In the history of the human race, no campaign of spiritual, cultural, and intellectual genocide compares to what was launched against the guardians of the Mysteries and their devotees. The murderous intent to destroy Gnosis was not confined to the holy places in Egypt and the Levant where the Mysteries were preserved by the *gnostikoi*, specialists in divine matters, including the divinity of the Earth itself. It extended to Europa, where Pagan wisdom thrived in a rainbow coalition of races and cultures, and then to the Americas, where hundreds of tribal cultures were decimated from Canada to Peru. It extends today by aggressive evangelization into Asia, notably Korea and China, and into Africa, where it is often allied with militaristic movements, and it retains a deathhold on the peoples of Latin and South America. All around the world, the catholic message of salvation goes out with a sanction to reproduce and swarm across the planet. Gnostics rejected blind biological procreation in the human species as a mark of enslavement to the Demiurge, the false creator god who commands the faithful to multiply and dominate the Earth.

In *Sacred Pleasure* Riane Eisler advises that to know what we have lost is to realize what cannot be lost. With the discovery of the Egyptian cache in December, 1945, we are reminded of what cannot be lost. It is a provable fact that history is written by the winners in order to legitimate and celebrate their cause. The discovery at Nag Hammadi made it possible to hear the other side of the story. After sixteen hundred years, we get a glimpse of what the "losers" thought and taught more or less in their own words. It is extremely rare to have such an alternative version of human testimony, and the contrast it presents to our received notions of truth and spirituality can be sobering.

As I write these words, it is sixty years to the week since the Nag Hammadi codices were found. (I say "to the week," since the exact day is not known, but scholars have carefully determined that the jar containing the ancient books was found in the first week of December 1945.) It may well be time to consider if the underdog can make a comeback. There are some attempts underway to bring religion around to an ecological and planet-friendly orientation, and to reconcile mainstream beliefs in God with our emergent sense of the living planet, Gaia, but Gnostic thought does not figure into them. Not yet, anyway.

In *Gaia and God*, ecofeminist theologian Rosemary Radford Ruether states that people can only come into an awareness of the sacredness of nature (the intrinsic value of nonhuman life, in the deep-ecological language of Arne Naess) through some modification of their preexisting beliefs and long-established traditions. At the outset of her argument, she concludes that Gaian spirituality (which I compare to the Sophianic outlook of the Mysteries) cannot be attained except within the existing framework of religious beliefs *already held* by billions around the world. For instance, the belief in Abraham's covenant with God could be reinterpreted as a divine mandate for the human species to practice ecology, acting as caretakers of the natural world. Particularly in Christianity, there is a growing conviction that some kind of "ecotheology" can be extracted or extrapolated from salvation ideology and the beliefs associated with it. With an eye to a millennial shift toward Gaian spirituality, the first issue of *The Ecologist* for 2000 carried the thematic title "The Cosmic Covenant," with the subtitle, "Re-embedding Religion in Society, Nature and the Cosmos." It contains articles by adherents to traditional Judeo-Christian-Islamic values who would like to align their beliefs with the Gaian perspective and the principles of deep ecology. Significantly, it does not contain any article by a deep ecologist who would like to join those religions.

In the keynote essay of the collection titled "Deep Ecology and World Religions," Roger S. Gottlieb argues that deep ecology "is not a movement *outside* world religions. . . . Rather, spiritual deep ecology occurs *within* the discursive, emotional, cognitive, and at times even institutional space of world religions themselves."[122] But is this really so, or is this view of deep ecology just wishful thinking due to a fixation on religious traditions that can neither be questioned nor overcome? Can the celebration of the sacredness of the natural world really arise from belief systems founded on the four components of the redeemer complex? Gottlieb cites many wonderful things that people derive from belonging to the mainstream religious traditions, including Buddhism, but he never considers the Pagan belief in the innate goodness of human nature, nor does he challenge the hard line of the salvationist agenda. The sincere essays compiled in "Deep Ecology and World Religions" make no mention of Gnosis or the Mysteries. Most of the contributors manage to squeeze ecological values from the existing traditions, but Eric Katz, writing on "Judaism and Deep Ecology," confesses "profound misgivings that traditional Judaism can be understood as an ally of deep ecology."[123] This rare glint of honesty is a welcome alternative to the make-believe mentality that dominates the debate over traditional religion and deep ecology, always in favor of the former.

In *Gaia and God*, Rosemary Radford Ruether flatly asserts that "there is no ready-made ecological spirituality and ethic in past traditions."[124] Well, that takes care of that. The millennial cover-up of the destruction of the Gnostic message is certainly intact at Garrett-Evangelical Theological Seminary in Evanston, Illinois, where Ruether teaches. Totally clueless about the Sophianic message of the Gnostics, troubled, heart-searching followers of the three Abrahamic religions—Judaism, Christianity, and Islam—tend to look toward the alternative versions of their own traditions for ways to recognize and recover Sophia, Divine Wisdom. They may do so through the Kabbalah in Judaism, for instance, or through the epiphany of the Beloved in Sufism, the underground dimension of Islam. Yet in this quest for religious alternatives on safe and familiar terms, the oldest, most radical option is rarely considered: Gnosis. This is not merely an alternative religion, it is an alternative to religion itself. It is a path of direct knowing, a passage beyond belief. As such, Gnosis provides the experimental basis for deepening the perspective of deep ecology. In its content, reflected in the genuinely radical material found at Nag Hammadi, the Sophia mythos presents a sacred narrative about the Earth to be found nowhere else. This story can inspire a visionary quest to fulfill humanity's role in the vast vital spectrum of the Earth. Maturity in coevolutionary terms would require that we as a species find a "creative fit" in Gaian symbiosis, as Lynn Margulis has suggested, citing a term proposed by pioneering environmentalist Ian McHarg.

My primary purpose in writing this book is to show that Gnosis, taken as a path of experimental mysticism, and the Sophianic myth, taken as a guiding narrative for coevolution, can provide the spiritual dimension for deep ecology independently of the three mainstream religions derived from the Abrahamic tradition. This position will surely look mean-spirited and ungenerous at first sight, but perhaps by the end of the book, rather less so. Why exclude the possibility of reconciliation of the kind for which Ruether and others are so ardently advocating? Why be so staunch about overthrowing salvationist faith? Why not plead for harmony and inclusion, rather than contrast and exclusion?

We are all diminished morally and spiritually by what salvationist ideology has done to the human species and to the planet. In the enmeshment of the victim-perpetrator bond, victims typically seek reconciliation with the perpetrators, not only because reconciliation falsely allays the pain of intolerable injustice and harm done insanely and without cause—harm that can never be made right, even by God—but even more so because the reconciling spirit allows the victim to feel proud, regain a modicum of dignity, and remain on higher moral ground than the perpetrator. In short, reconciliation is a terrific way to keep the bond intact. You can count on it. The perpetrators always do.

To avoid pathological relapse into the victim-perpetrator syndrome, there can be no compromise with perpetrators or the beliefs through which they disguise and implement their actions. The Sophianic perspective based in Gnosis is sufficient unto itself and does not need to be legitimated by association with mainstream religious beliefs. It is all too easy to forget what millions have suffered, and continue to suffer today, in the name of divine redemption. The promise of superhuman retribution for human injustice has crippled the moral sense of everyone who has ever adopted it, but the wound runs so deep we cannot fathom its origin. Lack of testimony from the losing side in the battle waged by the salvation army keeps us blind to the true nature of the battle. We are accustomed to shudder at stories of Christians thrown to the lions, but the record of persecutions suffered by early Christianity is paltry compared to Christian persecution of Pagans, Gnostics, and the

Mystery Schools. The Second Treatise of the Great Seth offers firsthand testimony of a Gnostic revealer. In one passage, it gives a loser's account of how the winners looked and acted:

> We were hated and persecuted, not only by those who are simply incapable of understanding us, but also by those who think they are advancing the name of Christos, although they were unknowingly empty, ignorant of who they are, like dumb animals. . . . They persecuted those who have been liberated by me, a Revealer, because they hate those who are free—those hateful ones who, should they shut their mouth, would weep with futile groaning because they do not know who I am.
>
> Instead, they served two masters, even a multitude. But they will become victorious in everything, in wars and battles, jealous division and wrath . . . having proclaimed the doctrine of a dead man and lies so as to resemble the freedom and purity of the initiates, our sacred assembly.
>
> And so uniting in their doctrine of fear and slavery, mundane needs, and abandoning reverence, being petty and ignorant, they cannot embrace the nobility of truth, for they hate what they are, and love what they are not. (58–61)

8

INSIDE THE MYSTERIES

The institution of the Mysteries is the most interesting phenomenon in the study of religion. The idea of antiquity was that there was something to be *known* in religion, secrets or mysteries into which it was possible to be initiated; that there was a gradual process of unfolding in things religious; in fine, that there was a science of the soul, a knowledge of things unseen.

—G. R. S. MEAD, *Fragments of a Faith Forgotten*[125]

Scholars who specialize in Gnosticism rarely discuss "the Mysteries." When they do, they apply a highly generalized definition to that term: Mysteries were emotionally charged rites celebrated in Pagan cults scattered across the Near East, Egypt, and Greece, in the Hellenistic era (320–30 B.C.E.). This characterization is correct, but it does not go nearly far enough. Ancient sources present a more precise and more specific picture both in terms of time frame and geographic scope. They refer to the Mysteries by localities (Hibernia, Samothrace), racial-cultural names (Brahmin, Phrygian, Egyptian), and cult names (Osirian, Orphic, Druidic). They give what might be called a wide-spectrum view of the Mysteries as a network extending from the northernmost isles of Britain down to the northern coast of Africa and deep into Asia, a network of extremely ancient provenance.

The limited view that "pagan cults of salvation," as the Mysteries are often called, existed only in the Near East, and only during the Hellenistic era, influences how scholars understand Gnosticism. Experts in the history of religions follow a long-standing assumption that the Gnostic movement comprised sporadic marginal sects that sprung up within early Christianity, but did not exist prior to it. They assume that Gnostic religion did not predate the earliest textual references to it found in the writings of the Church Fathers against the Gnostics, beginning with the "First Apology" of Justin Martyr around 150 c.e. This view, which is now unanimous, denies that *gnostikoi* such as Hypatia participated in the Mysteries, and dismisses the possibility that some Gnostics were *telestai*, founders and directors of those ancient and long-enduring institutions.

But earlier scholars held quite a different view. Writing a half century before the Nag Hammadi find, G. R. S. Mead asserted that "Gnostic forms are found to preserve elements from the mystery-traditions of antiquity in greater fullness than we find elsewhere."[126] Close analysis of the Egyptian codices confirms his view. A trend to redefine Gnosticism on its own terms may be in the making.[127]

Shamanic Roots

Telestes (plural telestai) is a Greek word derived from *telos*, "aim," "goal," "ultimate thing." A telestes is "one who is aimed, goal-oriented." This was what initiates in the Mystery network called themselves. *Gnostikos* was another name for the same thing: an initiate endowed with special knowledge in divine matters, the will and work of the gods; hence, an expert on theology and cosmology. Most scholars would not dispute this definition, yet they balk at the idea that *gnostikoi* such as Hypatia had anything to do with the most revered religious tradition of antiquity, the Mysteries.

Ancient sources widely attest to the great antiquity of the Mysteries and their telluric orientation, as well as their common dedication to the Magna Mater (the Great Mother, whom I am correlating to Gaia). Modern scholarship tends routinely to ignore or dismiss this evidence as fabulation. But if the Mysteries were Earth-based, would they not have had a universal appeal and been established in regional variants over a widespread area? Worship of the Great Goddess is typical of matricentric cultures stemming from Paleolithic times. It is also worth noting in this context that the oldest strata of shamanism in Siberia, the Urals, Europa and elsewhere, demonstrate a strong Goddess orientation. Mircea Eliade points out that although shamanism has come to be seen as a man's calling, framed in terms of Indo-European male sky-god religion in which "the earth divinity is not at all prominent," the more archaic roots of shamanic experience indicate the essential role of women—for instance, among the Ainu of Japan.[128] Joan Halifax recounts the Siberian legend that the original shaman was an eagle-woman who nested her male progeny in a magical tree. A key Gnostic cosmological text, the Apocryphon of John, presents the image of the shamanic eagle on the Tree of Life. It occurs in a passage on the Divine Sophia, "She who is called Life (Zoe), the Mother of the Living."[129]

The possibility that Gnostic knowledge and practices were the final flowering of millennial experience in "archaic techniques of ecstasy" (Eliade's famous term for shamanism) has yet to be recognized or explored.

The work of the earliest scholars (usually German, such as Richard Reitzenstein) clearly supported this path of inquiry, but their work is no longer cited. The pioneers of the field regarded the Gnostic movement in the broad sense as a monumental spiritual phenomenon of central Asiatic origins, predating Christianity by centuries, if not millennia. There is now a slight tendency to return to this view. In his introduction to the standard edition of *The Nag Hammadi Library in English* James Robinson writes: "This debate seems to be resolving in favor of under-standing Gnosticism as a much broader phenomenon than the Christian Gnosticism documented by the heresiologists."[130] So far, however, there is no trickle-down effect that would alter the way scholars represent Gnosticism to the mainstream.

SACRED TESTIMONY

There came from Isis a light and other unutterable things conducing to salvation.
                    —ARISTIDES, initiate in the Mysteries[131]

Surviving evidence regarding the Mysteries is problematic, for initiates took vows of silence about what they experienced. It is generally assumed, however, that participants in the sacred rites realized profound insights on reality. "Mysteries were initiation rituals of a voluntary, personal, and secret character that aimed at a change of mind through experience of the sacred."[132] Participants felt renewed and recharged, but not "saved," because salvation in the Judeo-Christian sense was incompatible with Pagan religious experience. If to be saved means to be forgiven one's sins by God, relieved by the intervention of superhuman power of the lonely, unjust, and insupportable burden of suffering, released from the travail of this world, and delivered into immortality in a world beyond, then Pagans were definitely not into salvation. Such a reward system was alien to their worldview.

"Silence surrounded all the 'Mysteries,' a word that derives from the Greek verb *myo-*, meaning 'to shut the eyes,' or 'to keep one's mouth shut,' either 'in fear of danger', or 'in the face of awe.'"[133] Considering the vow of silence, it might be thought that no testimony about the Mysteries was allowed, but this is not exactly the case. Initiates vowed not to divulge only the most intimate aspect of the rites. They could not say what they encountered in the moment of ultimate revelation, but they could allude to it, and they could, and did, describe in a general way the effects of initiation. In *The Golden Ass* the Latin writer Apulieus (fl. ca. 150 c.e.) gives what is probably an authentic and reliable account of initiation into the Mysteries of Isis. At the key moment of revelation a sublime voice addresses him:

> I am Nature, the universal Mother, mistress of all the elements, primordial child of time, sovereign of all things spiritual, queen of the dead, queen also of the immortals, the single manifestation of all the gods and goddesses that are known to you on earth.[134]

Apulieus's testimony is consistent with ancient reports that initiation was an encounter with *living* Nature, the Magna Mater—in modern terms, Gaia. An encounter marked by the epiphany of a mysterious light.

Initiatory revelation was part clairaudient and part clairvoyant, for the supreme revelation of Divinity came through tangible sensations.[135] "The Light was full of hearing and word," says the Paraphrase of Shem from Nag Hammadi (VII, 1,1.30). In the supreme moment of revelation, initiates simultaneously saw and heard some kind of supernatural luminosity. Apparently this phenomenon was not merely an intensified aspect of atmospheric light as we know it. Atmospheric light is not visible yet it makes all things visible. But the light of the Mysteries was not of this sort. The "Supernal Light" (a reverential term applied in ancient commentaries) encountered in the Mysteries was *visible*. Consider this analogy: when you write on a computer, the electrical illumination of the screen is invisible (i.e., clear, transparent), but the page you write on is white and clearly visible.

In *The Refutation of All Heresies* (book 5), Hippolytus referred to "Brachmans" (Brahmins) in Alexandria who "affirm that God is light, but not such as one sees by." Hippolytus, who was centuries closer than modern scholars to the subject matter, took it for granted that Brahmins from India belonged to the widespread network of Mystery cells extending across Europa and deep into Asia. His comment suggests that the experience of the Mystery light was universal within the network. Hippolytus also states the Gnostic view, shared by Brahmins, that "Deity is discourse." This tacit statement affirms that the mysterious luminosity of Pagan initiation is *interactive*. The "hearing and word" were two-way. The "Infinite Light" is said to be conversant with the witness. The purpose of encountering the light is to discover "the sublime mysteries of nature" (Hippolytus). The illumination that came from Isis (according to the testimony of Aristides, cited above) was more than a dazzling intensification of natural light. In some manner the divine luminosity *communicated* with those who beheld it.

Brahminical teachings on the Great Goddess confirm the firsthand testimony found in Hellenistic writings. "As the feminine (*shakti*) of Brahma, Sarasvati is the goddess of overflowing, abundant discourse (*Vac*), and of revelation and wisdom," explains noted Indologist Heinrich Zimmer.[136] The *vahana* or vehicle of a divinity is the instrument of its revelation through the human senses. When the Goddess is called *Gauri*, "radiant white one," she is compared to the whiteness of the soft, creamy glacial cap of Mount Kailas. The milky whiteness of snow resembles the visible Mystery light. The Buddhism goddess behind this epiphany is the White Tara, closely associated with Amitayus and Amitabha, Buddhas of Infinite Light. Visualizations of the White Tara as the "youthful one with full breasts," whose body "exudes the great transcendental bliss," can produce rejuvenation and even immortality.[137] Full-breasted Tara brings to mind the many-breasted statue of Diana of Ephesus, a rare example of representation of the Mystery light in sculptural form.

Initiation in the Mysteries was intensely vital, imparting the secrets of life—a biomystical revelation, one might say. In Asian tradition, illumination deities such as Tara descend from prehistoric tree goddesses or from the "Mother Tree," Mutvidr. "The World Tree, expressing its milky golden sap, denotes 'absolute reality,' a return to centre and place of origin, the home of wisdom that heals."[138]

The practice of Gnosis was full-body illumination in the presence of Sacred Nature whom Gnostics knew as a feminine divinity clothed in animated currents of undulant white light.

The *vahana*, or vehicle of destiny, of the Hindu goddess Sarasvati is the peacock with its fanned tail full of eyes. Long after the Mysteries had been destroyed to make way for the new religion of salvationism, Western alchemical traditions preserved this imagery in the *cauda pavonis*, the peacock's tail, symbol of the infrasensory radiance experienced at the completion of the Great Work. The white light contains all colors, and it is full of eyes, an all-seeing light. The Philosophers' Stone, often called the "white stone," is also an occult metaphor for the *visible* presence of the Mystery light. In some unfathomable way, this light has the substantial properties of stone.

Simon Magus from Samaria was the first Mystery School teacher on record to break anonymity and openly challenge the advocates of salvationism. An anecdotal collection of the third century, the *Clementine Recognitions*, describes his confrontations with the apostle Peter. The Gnostic ruthlessly dismisses claims to divine revelation made by uninitiated Christians. Addressing a group of Christian converts, he says explicitly, "There is a certain power of immense and ineffable Light whose greatness may be held to be incomprehensible, of which power even the maker of this world is ignorant, and Moses the lawgiver, and Jesus your master" (*Clementine Recognitions*, book 2, ch. 49). It would have been extremely bold, in that place and time, for an initiate to speak so openly about this intimate aspect of the Mysteries. Simon Magus squarely denies that Jesus or Moses, who represent the Judeo-Christian tradition, had been initiated into the primal revelation.

When Peter asks Simon, "If this Light is a new power, why does it not confer upon us some new sense?" Simon replies, "Since all things that exist are in accordance with those five senses we have, the power that is more excellent than them all cannot add anything new." This response reveals a fine point of cognitive science typical of Gnostic teaching: the mysterious light that pervades the physical senses does not alter them, yet in so pervading it brings forth through the senses a supersensory revelation. Simon's tacit reply recalls the baffling assertions of Zen masters such as Huang Po (tenth century c.e.): "Your true nature is something never lost to you in moments of delusion, nor is it gained at the moment of Enlightenment."[139] The creamy, marshmallow-like Light of the Mysteries does not efface forms, which appear in it like palpable stains. Nor does it alter appearances, except to divest them of their familiar density and mass. The apparent density of material things dissolves into the light and everything floats there.

More testimony on the Mystery light suggests close parallels between Pagan illuminism and Buddhist mysticism. "The soul at the point of death has the same experience as those who are being initiated into the Mysteries. One is struck with a marvellous light." So says the single most famous item of ancient testimony on the Mysteries, the so-called fragment of Themistios.[140] Readers familiar with the manuals called "books of the dead" in Tibetan tradition will recognize here a parallel to Buddhist teachings on the after-death experience. These manuals, intended to be read to the deceased, describe a "clear light" and a kaleidoscopic play of colored lights, including a soft milky-white luminosity said to emanate from the "god realm."[141] The Tibetan masters warn against going toward the soft light, but Pagan initiates went straight into it. It seems they were able to access this particular aspect of the luminosity that dawns in the after-death experience *before they died*.

Gnostic writings in the form of a "revelation discourse," such as the The Paraphrase of Shem cited above, give some firsthand descriptions of the Mystery experience. The initiate encounters a sublime radiance and communicates with it. Instruction by the light was the supreme initiatory event. The Tripartite Tractate, the longest document in the Nag Hammadi library, says that this experience is a privilege offered by the supreme deity: "The Originator [Coptic PEIOT] instructed those who searched for higher seeing by means of the luminosity of that Immaculate Light" (87: 88.10). Revelation texts such as the Discourse on the Eighth and the Ninth (NHC VI, 6) give the unmistakable impression that initiates received knowledge directly from the divine light. In that text the hierophant, the veteran initiate who brings the initiant into the presence of the light, declares: "Rejoice over this revelation! For already from the Pleroma [the Godhead] comes the power that is Light, flowing over us. For I see it! I see the indescribable depth" (57.25–30; modified NHLE translation).

Supernal Light, Infinite Light, Mystery Light, White Light, Divine Light, are various names for the same sublime reality. The light of Gnostic illumination is not metaphorical, it is substantial. To emphasize its living, life-giving quality, it could also be called the Organic Light.

In *The Mystery-religions*, Angus says that "all ancient *epiphaneiae* were of the character of a dazzling light." But direct witnessing in mystic trance shows it to be soft and subtle, not dazzling at all. The initiant or *mystes* (plural *mystai*) was carefully prepared to recognize the Organic Light and trained to stay steadily concentrated on it. The depth and duration of the mystical encounter with the Light varied with the capacities of the neophyte. "That the mystai were not equally susceptible to the vision seems to be suggested by the distinction made by Psellus between *autopsia*, whereby the initiand himself beholds the divine light, and the *epopteia*, in which he beholds it through the eyes of the hierophant."[142]

It was *this* experience of instruction by the Organic Light, and the manner in which they were brought to it, that initiates were strictly forbidden to disclose. However, they did not seek to encounter the Light for selfish purposes, and then keep the fruits of the ultimate learning experience to themselves. Nor were they seeking the narcissistic fix of "deification," as has been widely assumed. Consistent with their commitment to impart what they learned through initiation, the telestai wrote and spoke at great length. While not revealing intimate details of the supreme encounter, they wrote extensively about what they drew from it. They taught others, guided by what the Mystery Light had taught them.

Mystic Regeneration

How do we develop a wider Self? ... The ecosophical outlook is developed through an identification so deep that one's *own self* is no longer adequately delimited by the personal ego or organism. One experiences oneself to be a genuine part of all life.[143]

A dictum of Catholic faith says that there is no salvation outside the Church. Ancient testimony of Pagan religion says, "there is no salvation without regeneration."[144] The Greek word *palingenesis*, "regeneration," does not denote the action of a superhuman agent producing effects on the human plane. It cannot be equated with resurrection. Rather, palingenesis was a dramatic event that happened in the soul of the *mystes* due to an intimate contact with the natural world, producing a surge of supervitality and euphoria. Regeneration was realized in sensorial terms, in the setting of the natural world. The precious little evidence that survives indicates that initiation in the Mysteries was full-body illumination, not an out-of-the-body trip into some ethereal space beyond this world.[145] Surviving testimony supports my view, namely, that Gnostic illuminism involved the veracity of full somatic enlightenment, cosmic consciousness in the body. This experience might be compared to the mystic rapture of the "perfection stage" of Dzogchen, when the body is no longer limited to its observable physical dimensions:

> The term *kaya* (*sku*) does not mean only body in the ordinary physical sense, but the entire manifest dimension of the individual. The physical body is, of course, the central locus of that dimension, but this body does not just stop at the skin. It presents not so much a static form, like a statue, but a dynamic relationship between the individual and one's environment.[146]

Encountering the Mystery Light here and now in the sensorial world, in the terrestrial environment, produced a surge of supervitality that remained in the initiate's body after the ritual ended. It brought the telestai into the direct presence of the supernatural foundation of the natural, sensuous world. As Apuleius described, there was a direct encounter with the Mother Goddess.

One initiate to the cult of Attis, a man named Damascius, left this account: "I imagined that I had become Attis, and that I was being initiated by the Mother of the Gods in the festival called *Hilaria*, inasmuch as it was intended to signify that our release from death had been accomplished."[147] What the initiate "imagines" is not a fantasy but a mystical event as real as anything in "real life." *Sympathia* with the life of a Pagan god was a psychological technique for overcoming single-self identity. Pagans who underwent initiation felt a connection to the larger forces of life so intense that it engendered in them a sense of immortality, of living *here and now* beyond the normal limits of self-consciousness. This experience went "so deep that one's *own self* is no longer adequately delimited by the personal ego or organism" (Naess, cited above). In this way initiates celebrated a triumph, not over death itself, but over the fear-ridden sense of being mortal and confined to single-self identity.

In their popular aspect the "lesser" Mysteries were known to be celebrations of joy and sensuality. Participants expressed their release from mortal, ego-bound limits in *hilaria*, hilarity, the big laugh. Nothing celebrated in the Mysteries required self-castigation or suffering, nor did those ancient rites glorify the act of suffering, either human or divine. It is entirely misleading to equate, say, the ecstasy of Dionysos with the sufferings of Christ. This equivalence is a notable example of those misleading mythological parallels that so enthrall scholars. The difference between regenerative bliss and redemptive suffering is the difference between Pagan initiation and salvationist religion.

Initiation in the Pagan Mysteries was about ecstasy and euphoria, not pain in its own nature, or pain that pays off, or even escape from pain. It was an ecstatic path of direct experience totally independent of blind belief. The ecosophical view of Arne Naess assumes the same aim realized in Pagan initiation but without explicitly naming it. Yet there is a crucial difference as well, for the "identification" proposed by Naess and other deep ecologists such as Warwick Fox does not reach to the full dimension of rapturous empathy celebrated for millennia in the Mystery experience. To understand why not, we must look closely at the experience of Pagan illuminism.

The God-Self Equation

A third-century Greek text, the Magical Papyrus of Mimaut, is typical of Hermetic revelation literature that parallels in some respects the testimony on the Mysteries found in the Nag Hammadi codices. In a group prayer the initiates first address the hierophant, the guru who guides neophytes to the Divine Light, and then they address it directly:

> We give thanks, O Most High, for by thy gracious presence we have come to the Light of Instruction, ineffable and nameless.... Thou hast bestowed on us feeling, and reason, and knowledge— feeling that we might apprehend thee, reason that we might reflect upon thee, knowledge that by your acquaintance we may be gladdened. Saved by thee, we rejoice that thou didst show thyself to us completely. We rejoice that *even in our mortal bodies*, thou didst deify us by the vision of thyself. . . . We have come to know Thee, O Thou Light perceptible to our feeling, Thou Light of the life of humanity, Thou Light that is the fruitful matrix of all that exists.[148]

The *mystes* is "saved" by encountering the Organic Light, but not saved in the way the salvationist creed promises to save its adherents. Deification in this context does not denote literally becoming god, but "knowing as the gods know." Gnosis is cognitive ecstasy. It is direct contact and communion with Divinity without an intermediary agent of any kind. Although the guidance of a guru-hierophant can be helpful, it is not absolutely required.

The initiate was not "deified" in the sense of becoming one with God, or even realizing the "divine within," as New Agers aspire to do. Rather, initiation carried the sublime assurance of knowing what God knows, that is, knowing in a superhuman way, through elevated cognition, in heightened awareness. Salvation in the Pagan Mysteries did not produce elevation to divine status, but unfortunately deification was interpreted in just this way by those who never underwent the experience for themselves, yet envied those who did and wished to imitate them. In short, deification was the deformed brainchild of Gnostic wannabes, who were legion at the dawn of the Piscean Age. Today, if the religious pretensions attached to Gaia theory are transferred to deep ecology, the "identification" proposed by Naess and Fox may veer dangerously close to New Age deification. At the very least, the current and still controversial definition of identification does not emphasize sufficiently or clearly enough the importance of ego death in transcendent empathy with nature.

Disinformation on deification can be attributed to various sources in antiquity, but mainly the Gnostic pretender, Clement of Alexandria (ca. 140–215 c.e.), who falsely claimed to know the deepest secrets of the Pagan Mysteries. He formulated what might be called the *God-self equation* to explain initiation as he supposed it to be, rather than as it actually was. Today, religious scholars such as Elaine Pagels cite Clement for his assertion that the "true Gnostic" is someone who knows the innermost self to be God. He also argued that "the life of the Gnostic is, in my view, no other than the works and words which correspond to the tradition of the Lord."[149] Compare this statement with the assertion by Simon Magus that Jesus was ignorant of the Light. Clement's view exemplifies the co-optation of the Gnostic tradition to Christian doctrine and Christocentric mystical pretenses after 150 c.e. It falsely supposes a genuine Gnostic content in Christian doctrines.* Moreover, it makes the Gnostic movement appear to be a late, mid-second-century phenomenon. If scholars are right that Gnostic sects only appeared at the moment when Church fathers such as Clement set out to refute them, the movement must have been short-lived, indeed. It would have emerged and been repressed almost within a single century.

---

* The Hellenic period produced some Christianized Gnosticism, seen in the systems of Marcion and Valentinus, but there is, and never was, such a thing as Gnostic Christianity —because Christianity is a redemptive religion, totally at odds with the illuminist principles and practices of Gnosis.

THE LIGHT OF INSTRUCTION

Disinformation on initiation that began with Clement has flourished through the ages. His formulation of the God-self equation has been avidly embraced by New Age advocates of Gnosticism who see in it a confirmation of their belief that humans are essentially divine. Is it really conceivable that the Mystery experience of self-transcendence through temporary ego death could have led to such a view? The quintessential lesson of the Mysteries was that no human being is essentially divine, but each individual is endowed with a dose of divine intelligence, nous. Gnostics taught that humans are *instrumentally* rather than *essentially* divine. The divine factor is present in a faculty that human animals possess innately, but it requires cultivation to be realized openly. Nous is a divine faculty that enables us to know ourselves "as the gods know," but the self thus known is not a divine entity.

New Age mystics regard the assertion of indwelling divinity as "the true message of Jesus," a message either lost to those who lack initiated understanding, or intentionally distorted by Church ideologues hungry for power. Thus Andrew Harvey, writing on the Gnostic Gospel of Thomas from Nag Hammadi, praises the "savage, gorgeous radical-ism" of the Gnostic Jesus who shows seekers after God how to find "the Divine hidden within him or her," and thus become "an empowered divine human being." In Harvey's view the "Kingdom-consciousness" preached by Jesus is inner deification, the assertion that in the inner-most self of each person abides the Divine Self, the Presence of God.[150] This is not original and authentic Gnostic teaching, although it is widely assumed to be.

The God-self formula attests to the troubling persistence of wrong ideas in the history of religion. It survives in the personal convictions of scholars such as Elaine Pagels who says, "The secret of *gnosis* is that when one comes to know oneself at the deepest level, one comes to know God as the source of one's being."[151] This statement is finely nuanced. It carefully asserts that God is *at the source* of our being rather than *identical with it*, as presumed in Clement's formula, lately endorsed by Andrew Harvey and others. Orthodox Christian theology (such as Pagels represents) rejects the straightforward God-self equation as New

Age extravagance, if not heresy. For Jews and Christians alike, deity is always other than the worshiping self.

Clement's views were developed in the cosmopolitan atmosphere of Alexandria and circulated among affluent, educated members of Egyptian society who were mystified by, and vaguely sympathetic to, the sensational redeemer complex coming out of Palestine.[152] He claimed that the knowledge taught in the Mysteries was derived from Moses and the Hebrew Prophets—"a slight perversion of facts pardonable in the Good Father," as Madame Blavatsky remarked, no doubt with tongue in cheek.[153] Clement called Gnostic cultic practices "vile and despicable" and insisted that Pagan philosophy, if properly understood, represented a crude version of the redemption theology coming out of Palestine in his time. Clement's credibility as a witness to Pagan initiation has been challenged, and largely demolished, by George Mylonas, the leading scholar on the Eleusinian Mysteries.

Clement is often quoted as stating that all Gnostics are true Christians. One would then have to ask, What was Clement's notion of a Christian? The answer is, someone who finds God to be identical with his or her innermost self, as already noted. But close study of the evidence clearly shows that ego death, not identification with God, was the secret of the Mystery experience. Paradoxically, a sense of divinization occurs when the ego is temporarily dissolved, but deification of the ego or "self" was never on the Pagan agenda. The aim of the Mysteries was not empowerment of those initiated, or the ultimate aggrandizement of their egos, but consecration of their minds and lives to the Magna Mater. The purpose of initiation was implicit to its method: to behold "the Light of Instruction, ineffable and nameless," and to learn both sublime and practical things from that encounter. Initiates learned how to coevolve with the Earth goddess Sophia and guide humanity to its highest level of actualization. Loss of personal identity during initiation induced a momentary sense of unity with God—or with nature, a waterfall, a June beetle, whatever happened to be floating in the Organic Light— but God-self identification was not the ultimate goal of initiation. Had it been so, the Mysteries would have been nothing more than incubation tanks for self-glorification.

Historian Robert Turcan wisely observes that Pagan initiation "did not consist in 'returning to oneself,' but in becoming quite different by absorbing the Total Otherness which is divinity."[154] This comment says more about the Mysteries than volumes of breathless hype for the God-self equation.

SCHOOLS FOR COEVOLUTION

Ancient testimony on the Mysteries consistently attributes the revelation of the Organic Light to the Goddess, whether Isis, Demeter, or the Magna Mater. A teacher from the lineage of Hypatia wrote:

> Demeter seals all that we have seen and heard by her own peculiar utterance and signals, by vivid coruscations of light, and cloud piled upon cloud . . . and then finally, the light of a serene wonder fills the temple and we see the pure fields of Elysium and hear the chorus of the Blessed. Then, not merely by external seeming or philosophic interpretation, but in real fact does the Hierophant become the creator and revealer of all things.[155]

The Organic Light is a substantial opalescent haze, not a transparency. Both Pagan and Asian (Tantric) sources compare it to palpable moonlight or nacre, mother-of-pearl.[156] Encountering the Light, and to some extent entering it, initiates entered the presence of the White Goddess whose body is formed of "vivid coruscations of light, and cloud piled upon cloud." She is the Other, but also Mother. Egolessness, total surrender of self, had to be achieved before the initiate could encounter Isis (but one of her countless names), lift the "Veil of Isis," and receive divine instruction.

What might be learned today by those who are willing to let go of human self-centering and encounter the Goddess, their minds illumined by "the light of a serene wonder?"

CELLS AND SCHOOLS

Many of the things taught in the Mystery Schools were practical, completely down to Earth. To be precise, the *schools* were places of education, not to be confused with the Mystery *cells* where initiation took place. The cells, consisting of sixteen members (described in chapter 16) were initially attached to megalithic sites, stone circles, and prehistorically decorated caves. Eventually temples were built in close proximity to these sites. Around each temple rose a complex of buildings that served as classrooms and workshops: this was the school or campus attached to the initiatory cult in such places as Olympia, Delphi, and Eleusis.[157] In keeping with the bioregional character of the Mysteries, initiates designed the school curricula to reflect the racial, cultural, historical, linguistic, geographic, and environmental elements specific to the people they served.

There is long-standing confusion about the cultic profile of the Mysteries, stemming from the ignorance of Christian ideologues. The compilations of Irenaeus, Hippolytus, Epiphanius, and the Pseudo-Tertullian run to almost a hundred names: Sethians, Carpathians, Nicolaitans, Barbelo-Gnostics, Ophites, Valentinians, Gorothenes, Simonians, Phibionites, Borborites, Secundians, Colorbasians, Cainites, Archonites, Kataphyrians, and many more.[158] Some of these names derive from Mystery adepts such as Simon Magus and Valentinus. Normally such adepts remained anonymous, as did the designers of the Gothic cathedrals in medieval times, but in the early Christian era some of them chose to break anonymity so that they could appear in public to oppose salvationist ideology. Other names in the heresiological catalogs derive from the doctrines considered to be central to a particular group: Barbelo-Gnostics are said to have worshiped the four-faced Barbelo, a divine feminine archetype comparable to the Mahamudra of Buddhism. Ophites were devoted to the Divine Serpent, Ophis, meaning that they were adepts of Kundalini, the Serpent Power. Definition by specialization is closer to how the telestai themselves defined their activities. Some cults are characterized by the region where they were located: Phrygian, Alexandrian, Syrian. Initiates across the network spoke of Hibernian, Iberian, Samothracian Mysteries, and so on, always in specific regional terms.

In reality none of these groups were "Gnostic sects," because *gnostikos* was the generic term for any person learned in divine matters, and all the schools were staffed with such persons. The names mistakenly given to Gnostic sects in the catalogs of the heresy hunters would have described Mystery cells, each with its own speciality and regional character, hence the wide variety of designations. There were no Gnostic sects as such, although there were distinct shades of difference in what the *gnostikoi* taught, leading to different accents on the content of instruction. For example, Sethian teaching emphasized the cycle of human Revealers, while Valentinian teaching placed the Aeon Christos in a leading role in the Sophia mythos. The Valentinians and others highlighted the figure of the Redeemer, which (unfortunately) plays easily into the Judeo-Christian Messiah, Jesus Christ; but the Sethian "spin" I apply in these pages totally excludes it. Some scholars, including Jules Quispel, the godfather of Gnostic studies, support this view: ". . . so far as we have come to know it up to the present, [Gnosticism] did not have a redeemer figure; it is incorrect to picture the Anthropos . . . as a redeemer. . . . [T]here was never a pre-Christian Gnostic redeemer."[159]

Gnostics can be distinguished by particular topics of interest. In a comparable situation today, a professor of history may specialize in Latin American history, while a colleague specializes in pre-Columbian art. *Gnostikoi*, too, were highly specialized. *Gnostikos* translated as "expert," "informed source," or "special advisor" comes closer to the way it was understood in Hypatia's time. The telestai trained both incoming and outgoing students. Their classes included hands-on arts and crafts such as pottery and shipbuilding. The ancient curriculum encompassed every-thing from archery through midwifery to zoology. Painting, pottery, herbalism, sailing, map making, and many other applied skills were taught, along with the greater studies in astronomy, medicine, mathe-matics, and music. Certainly not all teachers in antiquity were initiates in the Mysteries, but many of them were, especially the true masters, including many women. Teachers who were not initiated would have worked in close contact with those who were.

Transentience

Initiates who were consecrated to the education of humanity ultimately drew upon what they learned from instruction by the Organic Light. Single-self identity was the primary block to this experience and still is the most formidable obstacle to modern understanding of the Mysteries. Almost everyone falls into the deification trap when initiation is under discussion. As long as ego death has not been experienced firsthand, it is easy to suppose that initiation involves a leap into higher identification, but the sobering impact of ego loss dispels this illusion. The question of expansion into "a wider sense of self" is one of the most hotly debated issues in deep ecology and remains unresolved.[160] Higher identification is usually evoked as the way to cultivate deep ecological experience, but *empathy* is a better word than *identification* to describe what the Pagan mystics experienced. Even this language is still problematic, however: Arne Naess argues with sweet and simple eloquence that empathy with all that lives comes to us through a widening sense of identification. How can one put it any better? But what if there is a form of empathy beyond identity and identification? And how does the call for widened identification stand against the Mystery requirement of ego death?

Deep ecology is notorious for awkward shuffling for appropriate language, so I may as well enter the fray. I propose "transentience" for the transcendence of single-self identity experienced in the Mysteries. Transentience has two senses, with and without the hyphen: *trans-entience* is going beyond entity or single-self identity, and *transentience* is deep sentient immersion in all that lives, sensing through, *trans-*. The Mystery experience required the first condition to reach the second. In sentient immersion we do not merely live *in relation to* all life, connected *with* nature and the cosmos, but we live *through* all life, and all life lives through us. *Trans-* here denotes "through" rather than "beyond." It implies a kind of porosity attained by temporarily dissolving the fixations of the personal ego. Apulieus described the sensation of being "poured *through* the elements."[161] The experience of ego death in the Mysteries could be expressed in this formula: "Beyond self and pouring through all that lives, so does it all live and pour through me."

If there is an approach to the religious dimension of deep ecology by way of Gnosis, as I am here proposing, it will need to be found in transentience, not deification. The encounter with the White Goddess, called Leucothea by the ancient Greeks, happens in a transcendent awareness *beyond identification*. But ecosophical theory cannot get that far or has not yet done so. This must be so as long as its proponents have not undergone ego death at the meltpoint of rapturous immersion in nature. There is no substitute for losing your egocentric mind to let your body receive the benedictory streaming of the Organic Light. Gnostic illumination is neither a theoretical position nor a god game. Gnosis is the special knowledge of what can only be realized in ecstasy. But allusions to ecstasy and ego death are conspicuously lacking in ecosophical debates over expanded-self identification.

To define the Mysteries in the language of deep ecology, I would say they were schools for coevolution with Gaia, known in ancient times as the Magna Mater. The *gnostikoi* who taught in the Mystery Schools were inspired by an elaborate myth in which a goddess called Sophia fell from heaven and turned into the Earth. Her name is Wisdom, and her nature is sublimely intelligent, organic, autopoetic, and beauteously complex. The presence of that particular divinity was encountered in the culminating moment of initiation. Her epiphany was the Mystery Light.

Today we call the Earth Gaia to denote our emergent realization that the planet is a living organism. Photos taken from outer space show us that we live on a blue-and-white marbled globe. But our certainty of living on a round, free-floating planet does not automatically reach the mystical climax of encountering the Earthbound divinity, Gaia-Sophia. Living on Earth we are in direct contact with the Goddess, but normally the contact is filtered by mental conditioning and ego fixation, if not entirely occluded by desensitization to the natural world. Carapaced in culture, cocooned in technological gear, isolated in our narcissistic concerns, humans cannot enter the presence of the Earth, cannot surrender to the spell of its supernatural beauty. Coevolution with Sophia depends on contact with the Goddess in her epiphany of the substantial milky Light, as the ancient initiates experienced it, but such contact is impossible as long as single-self identity dominates consciousness.

Anima Mundi

The Mysteries were enacted at two levels, popular and elite. The popular or lesser Mysteries were communal rites associated with the seasonal cycles of sowing, harvesting, and preparing foodstores for winter. In the processes of nature, and in the particular activities required for agriculture, the natives of Europa felt the actions of divine beings, male and female divinities. In ordinary life they were always aware of the divinities, but in the Mysteries they set aside a special time to honor them, and to express gratitude. "The worship of Pagan gods" is one of the worst stereotypes attached to Europan culture. The phrase is used without the least knowledge of what actually happened in those cults, or what the participants really did, saw, felt, and believed. The assumption that Pagans practiced human sacrifice, engaged in orgies, entertained fantasies about supernatural forces, misunderstood the laws of physics, ignored all sense of justice and brotherly love, and lacked what we hold to be basic morality and decency, is, unfortunately, endemic to this subject. To most people today a Pagan is an immoral and irreligious person and will always be just that.

The greater Mysteries were observed in the fall, at the time of harvest. They were celebrated at night because it was easier to bring neophytes into the presence of the Organic Light with their normal sense perception muted by darkness. The celebrants were not "dazzled" by a hocus-pocus display of flaming torches or a mysterious blinding blaze, as some ancient reports would have it. The telestai presiding over the rites carefully and selectively guided neophytes into the *telesterion* (inner sanctum) where the Mystery Light had to be observed, and absorbed, in small, gentle doses. A veteran seer would, for instance, direct a celebrant to stand before one of the marble columns and observe how it was interpenetrated by the soft luminosity of the Light. The guided initiates saw not only the pillar, but the soft luminous substance in which the pillar—and, indeed, their very *seeing* of the pillar—was embedded.

The *epopteia*, seeing aided by the hierophant, was carefully gauged to meet the capacities of the supplicant. The *autopsia*, direct and independent seeing of the Organic Light, came in its own time to those who had trained their powers of attention for it. The epiphany of the

Organic Light induced a soft rush of somatic intensity that saturated the witness with bliss and brought attention to pitch-perfect lucidity. In the Mysteries, *mystae* who had steadily beheld the Light were welcomed into the company of the initiated with the benedictory greeting, "A kid, thou hast fallen into milk."[162] Gnostics called themselves "the standing race" because they were able to behold the divine radiance while standing upright and absorb the force of the immense telluric currents passing between the Earth and the heavens. Standing in the currents they received a download of instructions from the planetary intelligence, the goddess Sophia—in today's idiom, the Gaian entelechy.

They learned the secrets of life from the source of life, the mother planet.

In ancient times initiation led from surrender to consecration. Those who went through the supreme learning experience in the Mysteries considered it to be the ultimate religious experience for humanity as well. This experience by its very nature can neither be imposed nor evangelized. The arts of coevolution cannot be inculcated but have to be evoked and educed, called forth from the depths of the psyche where the very forces that animate soul-life are anchored in *anima mundi*, the soul of the world. Today we may commune with Gaia through listening to the wind, gazing at the clouds, smelling the earth, and so forth, but direct and intimate engagement with the indwelling divinity of the planet is not a sentimental reverie, it is a disciplined initiatory experience. The "nature mysticism" of New Agers who revere the Earth as a goddess, and the ecosophical attunement of deep ecologists who find intrinsic value in nature apart from its human uses, are at best feeble echoes of what transpired in the hallowed precincts of the Mysteries.

SHAKTI AND SOPHIA

Shakti who is in Herself pure blissful Consciousness is also
the Mother of Nature and is Nature itself born in the creative
play of her thought.[163]

Today, as we consider the ineffable character of the Mystery experience,
we can be daunted by something that seems to contradict the evidence of
our senses. Living on Earth, we have direct access to Gaia, who manifests
in the natural world, the realm of the senses. But nothing in the sensory
world reveals the presence of the Goddess in a *visible* milk-white luminosity. We *sense* the living presence of Gaia-Sophia in nature, but we
do not actually *see* the supernatural Light. The secret luminosity might
be called the *primary substance body* of the Goddess, as distinguished
from her *planetary body*, the Earth. The Sophia mythos of the Gnostics
describes how a goddess from the Pleroma (cosmic or galactic center)
turned into the planet Earth, but it does not explain how she remained
what she originally was, a torrential current of living pearl-white luminosity. To understand the dual status of the Earth goddess, it is helpful to
look to the teachings of Hindu Tantra.

In *Shakti and Shakta*, Sir John Woodroffe, the main exponent of Hindu
Tantra Vidya to the West, compared the Pagan religion of nature worship
to "the path of the Gnostic Telestai, the initiates of the Mysteries."[164]
Shakti is a name for the Goddess as the matrix of generative forces that
produce and sustain the natural world. The Sanskrit root *shak-*, "to be
powerful," is the root of words such as *sacred, sacerdotal, sacrament*, and
sacrifice. The compounds Gaia-Shakti and Shakti-Sophia can be useful
in asserting the clear and consistent parallels between Goddess mysticism in the West and in Asia.

Participants in the Western Mysteries learned that the human
species is equipped to live in reciprocity with the emotional body of the
Goddess, as other, nonhuman species already do. "All things exist in
Her who is of the nature of feeling in a homogeneous mass."[165] Such
is the teaching of Hindu Tantra, fully compatible with Pagan popular
religion and Levantine Gnosis. But Tantric teachings add an additional
point, explaining how Shakti-Sophia could turn into the Earth and

still remain what she is in cosmic terms. "When moved to create, the Great Power of Megale Dynamis of the Gnostics issues from the depths of Being and becomes Mind and Matter *whilst remaining what She ever was.*"[166] This statement epitomizes the Sophia mythos and confirms that Shakti-Sophia is the Godhead of Nature. She is both the Mother of Nature (primary substance body) and Nature itself (planetary body). The goddess Sophia turns into the Earth, morphing into the physical elements of the solid planet, secreting the solid, fluid, and aerial elements of the atmosphere from her own substance, the Organic Light. "This primal Power (Adya-Shakti), as object of worship, is the Great Mother (Magna Mater) of all natural things (Natura Naturans) and is Nature itself (Natura Naturata)."[167]

To recognize the presence of Shakti-Sophia in the natural world is the innate gift of all indigenous peoples, and it was the discipline in the Mysteries where men and women sought to enhance and intensify that recognition to the highest possible degree, giving them precise and intimate knowledge of biological and geophysical processes, including direct access to biochemical activity at the molecular level. Those who made a sacred commitment to knowing Gaia were called *phosters*, "illuminators" or "revealers." "Revealed religion" admits only a single and exclusive revelation to certain male intermediaries who preserve "God's word" in books, but the way of the Gnostic Revealers was an open, ongoing revelation of the Divine in its cosmic and terrestrial dimensions. The text they read, and wrote, was not Holy Writ dictated by the father god, the absentee landlord of the Earth. It was a vital code, animated and animating, written on the planetary body of the Goddess.

So-Called Illuminati

The telestai of the Mysteries were sophisticated shamans, past masters of "archaic techniques of ecstasy." Traditionally, shamans were the intermediaries between the human-made realm of culture and the nonhuman realm of nature. Their special calling required a rare capacity to move between two worlds, keep the two worlds distinct, and effectuate exchanges between them. Schizophrenics naturally (and unfortunately, in most cases) have this mobility, but without the required discipline, they are easily undone by it. Successfully managed schizophrenia can result in great works of mythopoesis, as seen in the writings of Antonin Artaud, Philip K. Dick, and Carlos Castaneda, to cite just three (male) examples.

Mystery adepts who were responsible for the cultivation of human potential to its optimal level took great care not to risk schizophrenic damage with their pupils and neophytes. They realized how easy it is to induce and exploit borderline states that can arise spontaneously in the process of initiation. The requisite lowering, or total dissolution, of the ego-self produces high suggestability in the subject. Neophytes in the Mysteries were prime subjects for "imprinting," the process in which a predetermined psychic content or program is implanted in the subconscious mind. Imprinting occurs universally in nature as the means by which instinctual programs are transferred from one generation to another. Ethologist Konrad Lorentz (1903–89) famously imprinted newborn ducks, convincing them that he was their mother. Lorentz coined the term "inner release mechanism" (IRM), whereby organisms are genetically predisposed to respond to certain stimuli. Gnostic initiates would have encountered the insights stated in his book *On Aggression* (1966) through their intimate, firsthand observation of psychomimetic activities, formulated today in the science of neurolinguistic programming.[168]

The goal of Gnostic initiation was to learn from the direct impact of encountering the Wisdom Goddess. This impact is awesome and obliterating, yet it does not threaten or harm in any way. It arouses the sweet sensation of wanting to die into it, right then, right there, but you do not die. On the contrary, you receive an infusion of superlife. The high impressionability of the experience has to be carefully framed and steadied. That is the role of the hierophantic guide. In shamanic jargon, the Nagual.

The Gnostic movement derived from an ancient Persian lineage of shamanism, the Magian order.* Historians understand the Magi to have

---

* It is impossible to develop this claim within the limits of this book. See my article "Gnostics or Illuminati?" on Nemeta.org.

been the priesthood of Zoroaster, or Zarathustra. According to a scribal note written on the margin of *Alciabides I*, a work attributed to Plato, "Zarathustra is said to have been older than Plato by 6,000 years."[169] In her extraordinary and little-known book, *Plato Prehistorian*, Mary Settegast situates the rise of the Magian order, the original priesthood of ancient Iranian religion, in the Age of the Twins, around 5500 B.C.E., a date supported by the Greek sources.

With the rise of urban civilization in the Near East around 4000 B.C.E., theocracies emerged as the dominant paradigm of the social order. The theocrats of the first patriarchal nation-states were not, barring some exceptions, enlightened men, so they looked to advisors for spiritual guidance. Astrologers, soothsayers (fortune-tellers) and psychics vied for positions of influence in the royal entourage. Often the advisors ended up running the show—not so different from handlers in political circles today. In some cases, the advisors mind-controlled the putative leaders. They systematically programmed their royal patrons to believe they were descended from the gods. To preserve this grandiose illusion, they inaugurated elaborate rites of empowerment, or kingship rituals. These rituals were in fact *methods of psychodrama* exercised on the ruling powers and the general populace through the collective symbology and mystique of royal authority—again, not so different from collective charades of power conducted by a hidden elite in modern history.

Did the Gnostics participate in these theocratic spectacles? No, absolutely not. Kingship rituals of this sort were utterly distinct from the rites of initiation in the Mysteries. Instruction by the Light never translated into power politics. The purpose of kingship rituals was not education and enlightenment, but social engineering. Gnostics refrained from meddling in politics. Their intention was not to manage social behavior, but to produce skilled, well-balanced, enlightened individuals who would create a society good enough that it did not need to be run by external management. The royal handlers were in it for their own benefit, of course. Moreoever, they assumed that human beings are not innately good enough, or gifted enough, to create a humane world on their own. This difference in views of human nature was the main factor in producing a covert elite of so-called Illuminati who in later times came to be mistakenly confused with the Gnostic teachers of the Mysteries.

Most historians recognize this distinction but without understanding either its origin or its consequences. A rare exception is Mary Settegast, cited above. In *Plato Prehistorian*, she explains how "a primitive ecstatic, a kind of 'shaman'" is an ambivalent figure who stands on the border between the sacred and the profane, the non-ordinary and ordinary worlds. This figure differs from the conniving advisor who was typically "a worldly familiar of Chorasmian kings and court politics."[170] She identifies the Avestan term *vaedemna* for the former, corresponding to a Gnostic seer, not to be confused with the *zoatar*, who officiates in court matters and advises on statecraft. Unfortunately, this contrast between the shamanic seer dedicated to education and the theocratic handler working behind the scenes gets lost on Plato. In book 3 of the *Republic*, Plato disclosed the Illuminati rationale: "contrive a noble lie that would in itself carry the conviction of our entire community." This single line covers the multitude of crimes perpetrated in the world today by the adepts of political intrigue.

Certainly not by chance, the first recorded use of the word *gnostikos* occurs in Plato's *Politicus* (258e–267a) where he defines the ideal politician as "the master of the Gnostic art."[171] The egregious misrepresentation goes unnoticed and passes for doctrine in Gnostic scholarship. From its introduction into the Western intellectual tradition, *gnostikos* has been falsely associated with the schemes of social engineering perpetrated in the earliest theocracies. No wonder the teachers of the Mystery Schools disowned that name! Genuine telestai like Hypatia would never have used it to describe themselves. To make matters worse, it came into popular use as an insult. To the Church Fathers it connoted "smart-ass," "know-it-all," a term of ridicule aimed at their Gnostic adversaries. The telestai were attacked in both ways, by the condemnation of heresy coming from the Roman Church and by association with the deviant politics of social engineering to which they stood opposed.

If we accept that the Mysteries were schools for Gaian coevolution dedicated to the goddess Sophia, they could not have been run by Illuminati-like control freaks, as some contemporary writers bent on exposing the Illuminati have proposed.

THE FALLEN GODDESS

Initiates in the cults of the Great Mother underwent a sublime learning experience, revealing to them through non-ordinary awareness the cosmic origins of life on Earth. Then they turned back to ordinary life to teach what they had learned. As noted in chapter 1, G. R. S. Mead, one of the earliest scholars and translators before Nag Hammadi, asserted that the initiates "were the introducers of all the arts of civilization. . . . They were the teachers of the infant races. [They] taught the arts, the nature of the gods, the unseen worlds, cosmology, anthropology, etc." In short, they were the educators of the ancient world, the dons and deans of classical learning.

SACRED LANGUAGE

The network of Mystery Schools was the university system of antiquity. The Egyptian college where Hypatia taught belonged to what may be considered the "Ivy League" of the network. Memphis was Yale, Luxor was Harvard. The same was true for the Levantine schools in Palestine, Syria, and Turkey, where most of the known Gnostics taught. North of the Mediterranean basin toward Europa proper, Greece provided the main territory for satellite colleges. In *Black Athena* Martin Bernal cites an ancient legend that relates how the Eleusinian Mysteries were founded by a mission from Egypt.[172] It would appear that the cult of the Egyptian grain god Osiris was converted into the Demeter cult—but such an interpretation is somewhat misleading because the Mysteries did not spread globally *solely* by geographic dissemination. In every region where they arose both the initiatory rites and the collegial faculties assumed a regional character that reflected the physical and psychological makeup of the inhabitants. This exemplifies the bioregionalism typical of indigenous Europa, still evident today in the rich diversity of local culture across the continent.

As the network of the Mysteries stretched into Europa its character changed somewhat because the initiatory traditions of Iberia and the British Isles were less affected by Asian factors, especially the Persian single-source duality that was discussed previously in connection with the Palestinian redeemer complex. In the Syrian-Levantine cells especially, the telestai were deeply versed in the problematic issues of Zoroastrian duality and theocracy, the political instrument of patriarchy. *These concerns were particular to initiates in the birthplace and stronghold of theocratic society, the Near East.* In most other respects the primary features of initiatory knowledge were uniform throughout the network. The headmaster of the Druid colleges in the Outer Hebrides would have been able to converse with telestai from the Egyptian and Levantine schools, using the primal languages of astronomy and geometry. As noted above, in Hypatia's time there was a study group in Alexandria dedicated to preserving the initiatory lore of the Hibernian Mysteries from the far north of Europe.[173] Druid colleges existed in many regions due to the guardian role of the Celtic race all across Europa. Druids, or Hibernian Gnostics as they might be called, were known to be polymaths, fluent in several languages. The version of Celtic spoken today in Scotland and Ireland, called Gaelic, descends directly from the ancient tongue they spoke.

Greek as it is written today is close to the language spoken in Socrates' time, but Greek differs hugely from Gaelic in that it has been written down since around 900 B.C.E., that is, for almost three thousand years. In *The White Goddess*, Robert Graves suggested that secular writing was introduced into Europa by "free-lance initiates" known by such names as Cadmus, Gwydion, Ogma Sun-Face, and Herakles. From around 600 B.C.E. the leaders of the Mysteries came together in a surge of activity that generated untold volumes of written works. Cadmus, the brother of Europa, adapted the Greek alphabet from the Phoenician script introduced, probably, around 1250 B.C.E.[174] For millennia before that time the leaders of the Mysteries had used symbolic codes and secret languages such as the Druidic and Nordic runes, the ogham of the Welsh bards, and the famous Celtic tree alphabet described by Robert Graves. Prior to the introduction of secular alphabets, the educators of the Mystery Schools circulated writings exclusively among themselves. When the moment came to spread literacy to the native populations, they took the leading role.

Much has been made of the fact that the 64-unit code of DNA occurs in the *I Ching*, an ancient Chinese tool of divination, but the variable 20-22-base systems such as the Celtic tree alphabet may be equally significant in indicating that the ancients had direct knowledge of the structure of life down to the molecular level. In *The Cosmic Serpent*, anthropologist Jeremy Narby shows that Peruvian *ayahuasca* shamans claim direct access to the processes of molecular biology, a claim corroborated by their intimate knowledge of pharmacology which in some aspects surpasses that of modern technicians working in fully equipped laboratories. Instruction by the Mystery Light would have afforded Pagan initiates similar knowledge. Herbology and medicine, including dream-healing techniques, were also essential parts of the Mystery School curriculum. Names such as Aesculapius and Hygeia applied less to individuals than to honorific titles conferred on the headmasters and headmistresses of the initiatory colleges.

Infrasensory perception at the molecular level was common among *siddhas*, accomplished yogis of Asia. Patañjali calls the capacity to see microscopically, *anima*, "microcosmic vision."[175] In his book on the *Yoga Sutras* of Patañjali, Mircea Eliade highlights the empirical nature of yogic training: "By achieving *samadhi* [full and flawless concentration] with regard to a specific object or a whole class of objects, the yogi acquires certain occult 'powers' [siddhis] with respect to the object or objects involved in his experiment."[176] Sir John Woodroffe asserted that as late as 1900 yogis in India had an exact and complete knowledge of human anatomy, down to the minute details of nerve structure, surpassing that of trained Western physicians. The Sanskrit word *siddha*, "accomplished person," is the exact equivalent to *adept*, which derives from the Greek *adipisci*, "attained," "accomplished," as already noted. Gnostics and their Europan counterparts, the initiates in the Mysteries, were *siddhas* who would have possessed a range of *trained* occult capacities allowing them to make firsthand observations of the most intimate process of biology, physiology, and chemistry.

The faculty that ran the Mystery Schools had special, non-ordinary faculties.

Richard Rudgley (*The Lost Civilizations of the Stone Age*) has shown that writing systems did not appear suddenly or miraculously in any region but were deliberately evolved from preexisting symbolic languages, i.e., systems of sacred writing. For reasons that have never been clearly elucidated—and here lies a great, untold story—initiates living all around the ancient world at the dawn of the first millennium B.C.E. began to introduce systems of secular writing. They literally invented literacy. By doing so they assumed the sacred commission to teach reading, writing, textual analysis, and translation. Imparting language skills was one of the key responsibilities of the Mystery Schools.

If the Greek writer Plutarch is any example, we may only begin to imagine the extent to which they fulfilled their calling. He was an initiate in charge of the precincts of Delphi. During his lifetime (ca. 46–ca. 120 C.E.) Plutarch witnessed the twilight of the Mysteries, the somber prelude to the Dark Ages that commenced at the murder of Hypatia. He was a prolific writer whose works only partially survive, yet they run to hundreds of thousands of words. He left the most complete account we have of the Mysteries of the Egyptian "grain god," Osiris. Inexhaustible in his literary output, which comprised biography, moral essays, mythology, esoteric commentaries, historical essays, and a rich trove of personal and anecdotal material, Plutarch is the paramount model of a Mystery School dean. Imagine hundreds of Plutarchs, male and female, working in the British Isles, Iberia, Gaul, Italia, mainland Greece and the Greek islands, the Levant, Egypt, Libya and Carthage, and you get some idea of the extent of the ancient collegiate system.

If the prehistoric origins of the Mystery School network were coeval with the earliest megalithic sites, as seems likely, then they can be dated conservatively to 6000 B.C.E. Thus, in the last tenth of their duration before the Christian era, a mere 600 years, the Mysteries produced a corpus of literature that reflected its long preceding development. In 400 C.E. when Hypatia lived and taught she had over a thousand years of continuous literacy and learning to draw upon.

CONSECRATION

Initiation was a volunteer system that placed no restriction on the mundane activities of its participants, except that they demonstrate uncompromising *honesty* in all their endeavors in the world. (Dishonesty, envy, and homicide without cause were the three factors that disqualified candidates from initiation.) Indeed, the purpose of the initiates was to serve the world at large by nurturing and guiding human potential, one person at a time. They were called *telestai* because they were dedicated to a supreme goal, aim, purpose—a *telos*. This word implies "that which is ultimate," rather than "perfection," as it is commonly rendered. It approaches the modern notion of goal-orientation, or teleology. In colloquial usage *telos* could refer to someone's death: "He met his end, his *telos*." Death is the ultimate moment of life. By direct encounter with the Organic Light, initiates came to know that their *telos* was a death-transcending purpose. The Greek poet Pindar (ca. 518–438 B.C.E.) testified to the effect in initiation in these words: "Blessed is he who having seen those common concerns in the underworld, knows both the end of life [telos] and its divine origin."[177] The telestai also realized that whatever is learned in depth, in a manner compatible with the innate intelligence of the student, will outlive those who teach it. They understood that the learning potential of the human species is deathless, rooted in the immortal endowment of nous, divine intelligence, but it needs to be carefully guided. They believed, not that we are divine sparks trapped in the darkness of the material world, but that each person may carry the spark of the *indigenous genius* of humankind. There are several ways to understand the moral and educational orientation of the Mysteries, for *telos* has several dimensions.

Education and guidance were intimately linked in the curriculum of the Mystery Schools. In the ultimate sense initiates aimed to guide humanity to become self-guiding. They taught what might be called *self-direction* but without a narcissistic spin or selfish emphasis. The aim of telestic method was not what is today called self-empowerment, but consecration. Self-empowerment may be sought for one's own benefit, or to acquire anything one wants, but consecration must be achieved by selfless commitment to something other than oneself. Literally, consecration means "empowered with (con-)." The e in this word displaces the a, slightly obscuring the Indo-Europan root sacr-, cognate with the Sanskrit Shakti, a name for the Goddess. In order to promote self-direction with the intent of leading a consacrated life, the telestai introduced their student-neophytes to a narrative framework, a guiding story. Within the story each individual found his or her sacred calling and became self-directed, a free agent. The essence of the telestic program was deep insight into *what it means to be an instrument for coevolution*, consecrated to Gaia-Sophia.

Today we tend to conceive of evolution in biological terms, often with a Darwinian spin that emphasizes competition: "red in tooth and nail." The telestai saw in coevolution the way for humanity to participate wisely and lovingly in the web of life encompassing all species, and even to align itself with the planetary entelechy—Aristotle's term for the vital guiding principle of an organism or the totality of life itself (*Metaphysics Z*, Book Theta). This concept epitomizes the *telos* of the Mysteries and takes it to the planetary scale. If we as members of the modern world make coevolution our personal aspiration, if we propose it as a social goal, and hold it forth as the highest aspiration of our species, we might do well to bear in mind that this magnificent intention was already realized by people who came before us. It *is* realizable, we can assure ourselves, because it has been realized. It has been tried and tested with immense success.

In a sense all indigenous peoples around the world have realized this intention and lived according to this great transcendent prospect. But in a most specific way, in an artful and accomplished way, those who participated in the Mysteries of the Great Mother in Europa, Egypt, and the Near East, realized coevolution at a level of accomplishment that we can only hope to imagine. If the poet Octavio Paz is right, and the future is a perpetual resurgence of the past in the present, where the initiates were shown where we might go: into a future worth living. In their consecration to Gaia they learned from direct communication with the planetary intelligence. Encountering the Divine Light, they found a story to guide the species, and followed it.

The loss of that story largely accounts for the moral and spiritual degeneration of Western society, which now contaminates the entire world.

Planetary Biography

The master narrative of the Mysteries was the Sophia mythos, the story of how the goddess Sophia, a divinity at the galactic level, turned into the planet Earth. This myth was the centerpiece of the Mysteries dedicated to the Magna Mater, the Great Mother. It explains not only the origin of human life on Earth but the origin of the life and consciousness of the Earth itself. Describing the Hindu myth of the World Mother, Indologist Heinrich Zimmer wrote:

> The myth cannot actually reveal the genesis of the great mother-goddess, but only the manner in which she makes her appearance, for the myth knows of her beginninglessness, which is implicit in the term "mother": it knows that as mother she existed prior to any of the things to which she has given life.[178]

This statement points to the unique nature of the cosmology to be found in the Gnostic myth of the fallen goddess. Identification of the Earth with a feminine deity or goddess is almost universal in world mythology and indigenous lore, but only Gnostic materials present a complete scenario that describes how such a divinity from the cosmic level turns into a planetary body. Zimmer says that the Great Mother "existed prior to any of the things to which she has given life." If this is the case with Sophia, as the Gnostics thought and taught, we must wonder what kind of prior existence she had.

Today we call the Earth Gaia in growing recognition that the planet is alive and intelligent, a sentient superorganism. But in doing so, we do not normally assume that the Gaian entelechy preexisted the physical planet. Calling the Earth Gaia is a *façon de parler*, merely a way of speaking—but could it be more than that?

The emergent intuition of growing numbers of people that Gaia is alive and intelligent in her own right, that she is "autopoetic," making her own order, is a splendid advance for humanity. Factoring in the Gnostic narrative deepens that proposition: the autopoetic presence embodied in the Earth preexisted it. Sophia means "wisdom," so we may suppose that the adepts of the Mysteries perceived in the planetary body the wisdom of a divine, superearthly presence, comparable to the wisdom that animates the human body, but infinitely more complex, vast, and powerful. This is the primary ecological insight, of course. It may also be the primary religious insight.

In Gnostic cosmology Sophia is the mythological name for Gaia *before she became the earth*.[179]

Today, with the emergent recognition of Gaia to our advantage, we are privileged to observe as James Lovelock did that it only makes sense to see the Earth in this way. Do we really need general systems theory, cybernetics, dissipative structures, and tautological formulas of self-organization to understand Gaia, or do these conceptual schemes merely pose male-mind distractions from empathic contact with the living planet? To the ancient Greeks *theoria* was beholding, pure and simple, but for the modern mind we are unfortunately often beholden to theory itself, and so bound and blinded by it that we cannot see the ground for the map.

"Gaia theory" today offers an animistic and imaginal approach to the Wisdom Goddess, not a scaffolding of cybernetic general systems cogitation. Fortunately, that imaginal dimension is already available—we have at least the fertile rudiments of it—in the sacred narrative central to the Mysteries of the Great Mother, the Fallen Goddess Scenario (FGS). Here is a summary in nine episodes.

One: A singularity arises in the unknowable foundation of the Universe. It is a spontaneous pulsation of the Originator, the presence beyond the generative powers (Aeons) that dwell in each galaxy (Pleroma, fullness). The singularity upon release is completely undefined and without organization or characteristics. Being totally undetermined, it carries the potential for novelty to emerge in the Universe.

Two: Two Aeons among the Pleromic gods, Thelete ("Intended") and Sophia, configure the singularity with a set of talents and ready it for projection into the galactic arms, where planetary systems emerge. Additionally, a third Aeon, Christos, applied to the Anthropos genome the action of "christening" by which all experimental species are sealed within the boundaries of their body-plans, thus insuring their morphogenetic identity.

Three: The Aeons in the Pleroma emanate this encoded singularity into the realm of "outer chaos" so that it can gradually unfold in emergent worlds. It nests in a molecular cloud (Orion Nebula) like a pattern of dew in a spider's web.

Four: Fascinated by what might happen to the Anthropos as it unfolds in a favorable planetary setting, the Aeon Sophia absorbs herself in dreaming, the cosmic process of emanation. But she does so on her own, unilaterally, without a counterpart, at variance with the cosmic law of polarity by which harmony and balance are maintained in the myriad worlds. Enthralled by the possibilities of the human singularity, the Anthropos, she drifts away from the Pleroma, breaches the boundary of the galactic core, and plunges into the realm of external, swirling chaos in the spiral arms.

Five: Sophia's plunge from the Godhead produces an unforeseen impact in the realm of chaos, spawning a species of inorganic beings, the Archons. In Sophia's fascination with the Anthropos (human species), and in her previsioning of how it might evolve, the Goddess did not anticipate the arising of these weird entities. They represent an anomalous or deviant factor that may impinge on the evolution of humanity. The Archons gather around a central deity, the Demiurge, who falsely believes he is the creator of all he beholds. The demented god proceeds to construct a celestial habitat for himself from atomic matter: this is the planetary system exclusive of the Earth, Sun, and Moon.

Six: As the scaffolding of the planetary system arises, a newborn star emerges from the nebula where the Anthropos is embedded. Owing to its superior mass, the star causes the emergent planetary system to cohere around it. It becomes the central sun of the Archontic heaven, a realm of celestial mechanics dominated by blind, inorganic forces. Sophia shames the Demiurge by declaring to him that the Anthropos, though yet unborn, surpasses the Archons in intelligence, for humanity is an emanation of the Pleroma, whereas the Archons arise outside the cosmic core, without an act of emanation.

Seven: Sophia morphs into terrestrial form, becoming an organic planet, sentient and aware. But the living Earth is then captured in the inorganic system of the Demiurge, the realm of celestial mechanics.

Eight: Sophia's emotions of grief, fear, and confusion transform into the physical elements of Earth and the biosphere. The terrestrial globe solidifies and life arises in rampant forms, but Sophia is unable to manage the interactions of her myriad progeny. The gods in the Pleroma sense her difficulty and collectively send another Aeon, the Aggregator (*Ekklesia*), to intercede and arrange the chaotic diversity of Sophia's world so that different species of fauna and flora can interact harmoniously. This action establishes the conditions for planet-wide symbiosis. Upon making this intercession, the Aggregator leaves a kind of radiant afterimage in the biosphere, then recedes from Earth and returns to the Pleroma.

Nine: Now totally identified with the life-processes of the planet she has become, Sophia finds herself bizarrely stranded, and isolated, in the experiment she had previsioned in the Pleroma. This is a world where one particular strain of the Anthropos (current humanity) now proceeds to live out the potential endowed in it by Sophia and Thelete, thus to demonstrate human novelty on Earth.

But with novelty comes the risk of deviation. Sophia herself seems to have deviated from the cosmic order by her enmeshment in the planetary realm, due to her passionate and independent act of dreaming. In some mysterious way, her "correction" (reorientation to the cosmic center) devolves upon the triple challenge that faces humanity: to find its evolutionary niche, overcome the intrusion of the Archons, and define its role in the designs and purposes of Mother Earth.

The FGS is a complex and elaborate myth. But how could it be otherwise? The narrative describes a range of events that transpire over untold eons *before humanity appears on the Earth*. Yet these seemingly remote events play forward into both the prehistorical and historical dramas of the human experiment. Learning the sacred narrative by heart and coming to know how it matters right here, right now, is the central commitment of the living Gnosis today.

The story of the Wisdom Goddess Sophia is open-ended *and* ongoing. Its conclusion cannot be written unless the sacred story is imagined and lived. Unlike the sacred narrative of Judeo-Christian-Islamic tradition, the mythos does not end with a catastrophic event at a particular moment of linear, historical time. The coevolutionary plot contains no final confrontation between Good and Evil. No supernatural omniscient power or transhuman fate determines its outcome beforehand. Rather, the story of the fallen goddess is the open framework for the realization of transpersonal reality. This sacred narrative does not deny or discount human purposes as long as these are imagined in accordance with the larger life complex of the biosphere. Human survival depends on "a creative fit" into "Herstory," as Lynn Margulis has stated in discussions of Gaia theory. Gaia's law is not survival of the fittest, but survival of what fits Her purposes, what resonates to Her dreaming.

What pleases Her, if you will.

Vision Teachings

Women and men of ancient times who learned and taught the sacred story of Sophia considered that its ending was to be brought about, although not entirely determined, by the relationship between the Wisdom Goddess and humanity. In one sense Sophia is the savior of humanity, because she endows the human species with a special power, *epinoia*, by which it can realize its unique role in her life-process. *Epinoia* is imagination. This is the faculty humans need to engage consciously in Sophia's "correction," the process of her realignment to the cosmic source from which she drifted by projecting herself into the emergent human world prematurely and without a consort, a cosmic counter-part. In other words, Gaia-Sophia depends upon humanity to claim and evolve its own innate potential so that she can attain her own desire: success in a planetary experiment where the Anthropos manifests the full range of talents endowed in it by the Wisdom Goddess and her consort, Thelete.

The Aeon Sophia dreamed humanity out of the cosmic plenitude, the Pleroma, and plunged from the cosmic center, turning herself into the very world where we could become what she imagines. Owing to her presence in this world divinity can blossom in human spores, the pollen of the flowering Godhead. The optimal human future is dream-ing Sophia.

Humans are not the only species in the biosphere, of course, and not the supreme or superior one by any means. All other species are also intimately involved with Gaia, but in quite different ways than we are because humanity is *deeply and uniquely implicated* in both the primal attraction that elicited Sophia's plunge from the Pleroma, and the aberration that resulted from it. The story says that cosmic measures are underway to assist Sophia with the ordering of her world and compensate for the risk of aberration posed by the Archons. The Apocryphon of John describes the specific act of Pleromic intervention (episode 8) and Sophia's response to it in close detail:

> When the invisible spirit of the Originator had consented, the divine force poured over her from the whole Pleroma of Generators, the divine Aeons. For it was not her consort alone who came to her assistance, but [through the Christos] the entire Pleroma came so that she might correct her deficiency. And she was elevated to above the realm of her offspring, the Lord Archon, that she might be in the ninth until she has corrected her deficiency. (II, 1, 14. 5–10)[180]

In Mystery language, the Ninth is code for the Earth as an organic planetary body distinct from the inorganic planetary system, called the Hebdomad or the Seventh. In many mythologies throughout the world nine is the number of the Goddess. Three times three is the preeminent signature of feminine divinity. Graves says, "The Triple Muse is woman in her divine character: the poet's enchantress, the only theme of his songs."[181]

Considered cosmologically, the Eighth is the sphere of the fixed stars, the Zodiac. The Apocalypse of Adam (NHC V, 5) contains a long poetic passage describing thirteen constellations in which the Illuminator (*phoster*) "will pass in great glory . . . leaving the living fruits of gnosis." The text asserts that "those who reflect upon the knowledge of the Eternal One in their hearts" will receive enlightenment directly from the zodiacal realms. This may well have been the realm to which Gnostic seers looked in order to construct the cosmic scenario of the Sophia mythos. A passage in *On the Origin of the World* attributes the creation of the zodiac to the goddess: "And she put them [the stars] in the sky to shine upon earth and render temporal signs and seasons and years and months and days and nights and moments. In this way the entire region around the sky was adorned" (II, 4, 112:28).

The telestai wrote and talked extensively as part of their educational work but they also reserved some teachings for oral-only transmission: "For they will be known up to the cosmic region of the Aeons because the language they guard concerning the Originator of the Aeons was not committed to books, nor was it written" (Apocalypse of Adam, 85.5). The Nag Hammadi writings allude to special instruction preserved for "mind-mandate transmission" like the *termas* or wisdom treasures of Nyingma Buddhism.[182] One type of Gnostic *terma*, comparable to the Buddhist "Earth Terma" written in symbolic scripts on scrolls, has survived in the non–Nag Hammadi text titled the Two Books of Jeu (Bruce Codex). The Tibetan tradition of discovering *termas* hidden in rocks is echoed in the Gnostic text: "For they [these teachings] will be on a high mountain, upon a rock of truth" (85.10). Another parallel occurs in Allogenes (NHC XI,3: 68.5–25) where the *mystes* is instructed to "write down the things that I shall tell you and of which I shall remind you for the sake of those who are worthy, who are to come after you. And you will leave this book upon a mountain and you will abjure the guardian, 'Come Dreadful One.'" This recalls the Nyingma tradition of hidden books guarded by fierce demons until the right person comes along to discover them. Buddhist scholar Tulku Thondup notes that a type of *terma* called "Pure Vision teachings" is not exclusive to the Nyingma sect, which may allow the possibility of such phenomena outside Tibetan tradition.

The company of the Eighth, also a code name for the inner core of the Mystery cell, would have been particularly disposed to read and conceal certain teachings in the zodiacal realm. *Termas* have a time-release property: They remain in the place of concealment until the appropriate time comes centuries later for them to be discovered.[183] For the telestai the realm of the starry zodiac was a cosmic clockface inscribed with immense, animated images, the constellations, each corresponding to a world age. Not only could they read the prevalent lessons to be learned by humanity in each age, encompassing vast periods of time, but they also had methods of decoding the fine print of the zodiac. In each of the thirteen images they saw a coded language that records human potential, rather in the way that the genetic language records—and writes—the full potentiality of organic life.

Such a capacity to read nature at the cosmic level is typical of shamanic cultures where stargazing and divinations were common practices. The indigenous pre-Buddhist religion of Tibet, Bön Po, was an ancient form of shamanism whose adepts specialized in skywatching and astral divination. The widespread evidence of astronomically aligned megaliths and sacred sites all over Europe proves beyond doubt that indigenous Europan shamanism was also star-oriented. In his *Jewish Antiquities* (1.68–72), the historian Josephus stated that the Sons of Seth were regarded by the ancient Hebrews as celestial seers who "discovered the sciences of the heavenly bodies and their patterns." This wisdom was thought to have come down from antediluvian times, before the Flood, and preserved on two tablets or standing pillars in a mythological site called Seiris. The Mountain of Seir was a holy site for the Children of Seth, as some Gnostics called themselves.[184] Jacques Lacarriere also considers sky lore to be the original matrix of the knowledge system of the Gnostic schools.[185] Such knowledge is certainly the source of the cinematic cosmic perspective we encounter in the Sophia mythos.

THE DENDERA ZODIAC

On the west bank of the Nile just a stone's throw from Nag Hammadi is Dendera, the site of a magnificent Ptolemaic temple dedicated to Hathor, the Egyptian Eve. A bas-relief on the roof of a small chapel there preserves the single intact zodiac surviving from antiquity. Axes in the infrastructure of the model show that its designers understood the entire 26,000-year cycle of zodiacal precession. The proximity of this astronomical treasure to the caves of Nag Hammadi has been overlooked by scholars, yet it is more than likely that the Egyptian codices originated from the official library of the Dendera temple, or what was left of it.

Just across the river from Dendera are the ruins of an early Coptic monastery, Tabennisi. At the time the codices were hidden in a cave around 345 c.e., the founder of the monastery, the cenobitic monk Pachomius, had just died. A generation later, the monastery came under the control of Shenoute of Athribis (348–466), the leading figure in the Coptic Christian church and a close ally of Cyril of Alexandria, the man who probably orchestrated the murder of Hypatia. To his dismay, Shenoute discovered that a small remnant of persecuted Gnostics had taken refuge in the Temple of Hathor. He wrote to Cyril that the heretics possessed "books full of abominations" that must surely be destroyed. Shenoute commanded the Gnostics to renounce their perverted beliefs and accept Cyril as their spiritual master. When the heretics resisted, Shenoute warned them in no uncertain terms: "I shall make you acknowledge the archbishop Cyril, or else the sword will wipe out most of you, and moreover those of you who are spared will go into exile." If anyone wonders what happened to the thousands of teachers and students of the Mystery Schools of antiquity, here is the answer in one line. Cyril replied with a clear endorsement of the genocidal imperative, stressing how it demonstrates the efficacy of the One True Faith:

> A good many of those who formally practiced magic collected their books and burnt them publicly, and when the total value was reckoned up it came to fifty thousand pieces of silver. In such ways the word of the Lord showed its power, spreading more and more widely and effectively.[186]

These lines were written about thirty miles from where the Nag Hammadi codices were hidden. Whoever concealed the codices did so under the menacing shadow of Shenoute, who "dreamed of freeing the world from demonic powers by searching temples and private homes for idols to smash," and, no doubt, books to burn.[187] The "violent and destructive behavior" of this Egyptian abbot was enforced by the people under his rule at the White Monastery, as many as two thousand monks and eighteen hundred nuns. Those who practiced the cenobitic way of life also had a duty to exterminate the Gnostic tradition, root and branch. One historian described Shenoute's monks as the "shock troops" of the new Christian movement in that ancient stronghold of the Mysteries, Egypt.[188]

The diehard Mystery adepts at Dendera across the river were certainly aware that their sacred legacy of teachings was going to be annihilated.

At the same time they would have known that the star temple where they took their last stand would endure. It would stand as proof of their ageless astronomical wisdom and their faith in *terma*-like transmission by use of the cosmic code, the zodiac.

DREAMTIME PHYSICS

The sacred story of Sophia begins at one moment in endless, measureless time, but not the first moment of the creation of the Universe. This term *Universe*, capitalized, refers to the totality of galaxies in the immeasurable matrix of space-time. The Universe already exists when Sophia's story begins, and it has never not been there. There is no moment when it arose, nor will there ever be a moment when it ceases to be. There is no big bang in the Gnostic cosmology, nor in its Hindu, Tantric, and Buddhist counterparts where *emanation* and *mirroring* are the dynamic principles that operate throughout the cosmos and within the human psyche: emanation, not creation; mirroring, not cause and effect. Eternity is immutable but the Universe is inherently unstable, perpetually in flux, its contents ever changing, morphing, cycling. Life is a mystery of ceaseless, seamless becoming, a living dream that constantly shifts from one scene to another, every event pivoting on the timeless moment, Now.

What changes in the Universe is not the power at its source, but the conditions for the manifestation of that mysterious sourcing power. "Eternity is in love with the productions of time," said the mystic poet William Blake. Every moment holds the exciting possibility that a *singularity* will emerge from the depths of the Eternal Now. Novelty will appear and ripple through the manifest worlds. Each galaxy (Pleroma) is a wellspring of singularities.

The Universe arises as a material apparition from a hidden power source, a *foundation awareness* that never discloses itself directly: the Originator. In Dzogchen the foundation awareness is called *rigpa*, in Hindu Tantra, *parasamvit*, in the Gnostic materials, *pronoia*. (I cite these parallels, not to display my dubious erudition, but to stress that Gnostic thought is not a freak, isolated phenomenon, as most religious scholars

take it to be.) Tantric metaphysical teachings tell us that the innate incli-
nation of the sourcing power is to veil itself so that it can appear as other
than what it is. Its self-veiling power is called *maya*. Wrongly considered to mean illusion, *maya* is in reality the power by which the foundation awareness, which stands beyond time, space, and matter, appears
through manifold activities in time and space, assuming material form.
Paradoxically, it hides in order to be revealed. The foundation awareness
does not confine itself *in* the acts and appearances it manifests but operates *through* them. The material apparitions it produces, including stars,
planets, human beings, and microbes, are real and alive, not illusory.
Gnostics did not teach that the material world is an illusion, but, as we
shall see, they warned that there is an illusionary factor working in the
cosmos and in the human mind, correlatively, that causes us to misperceive the world order and lose our place in it. This is the Archontic factor
that emerges in episode 4 of the sacred story.

GAIA EMERGENT

"There is a dream dreaming us," say the Bushmen of the Kalahari. The
Universe is a living dream. The mysterious source of all that happens
plays out its self-veiling, self-mirroring game in billions of stars in
billions of galaxies. The source of the world-process never discloses
itself, and, paradoxically, it seems to be powerless: it does not even do
anything to make the worlds emerge. Instead, it selflessly confers its
boundless power on a vast company of generative forces, called Aeons
in Gnostic cosmology. *Aeon* means "god," "cycle," "emanation," "generating power." There is one supreme Aeon and countless tributary
Aeons, one Godhead and many gods. The One God, the Originator,
gives its power to the other Aeons, or generators, as the Greek term
might be translated. The Originator—in conventional terms, God,
or the Godhead, not to be conceived, however, as a paternal creator
deity—does not create directly, the way a potter creates a pot. The One
God transfers potentiality to the generators in an act of selfless outpouring. It offers pure, unconditional singularity so that chance and change
can occur in the cosmos.

The generators then follow the example of the Originator: they receive the singularity and selflessly allow it to unfold all by itself. They create indirectly by a process comparable to dreaming, rather than by hands-on, artifactual production of worlds. They do not create at all, they emanate. They transmute the formless singularity into the germ of a formative intent, a discrete emanation. In Hindu Tantra emanation is called *parinama*, an exact parallel to the Greek word *aporria*, used in the Second Treatise of the Great Seth: "a single emanation (*aporria*) from the Eternal Ones, the unknowable Aeons, immeasurable and without definition" (54.18). Each such emanation is *monogenes*, uniquely generated. Restoring the mythos, I find it apt to translate Gnostic cosmological language by a term from modern astrophysics: *monogenes = singularity*.

Emanation theory is the descriptive norm in Gnostic cosmology, Asian metaphysical systems, and native-mind scenarios. It seems to be the way of describing the cosmos that is most natural to the human species, by contrast to biblical creationism, which is an entirely different kind of metaphor, with vastly different implications. Gnostic "creation myth" should not be so named, because the Sophia mythos presents a dramatic alternative to nonemanationist scenarios of creation such as the biblical Genesis story and big bang theory. The sacred narrative of the Mysteries is *emergence myth*, not creation myth.

Among the Australian Aborigines the source of all material appearances is called the Dreamtime. This is not a remote time in the past, an origin-point in linear time, but the *intensive* dimension of the Eternal Now. Every sentient being in the world, including inorganic forms such as rocks and features of the landscape such as mountains, is an animation of the Dreamtime—a perpetual, ongoing animation. The Dreamtime is an event that persists eternally without beginning or end and supports the constant play of phenomena. When the Dreamtime comes to expression in particular knowledge and behavior, the Aborigines refer to the *dreaming* of the creature who embodies that knowledge and exhibits that behavior. For instance, the "kangaroo dreaming" is the summation of the innate knowledge and instinctual behavior of all kangaroos going back to the Dreamtime ancestors.

Odd as it might seem, I venture to suggest that the Aboriginal concept of dreaming verges closely on what science calls instinctual drive, the informing force that runs the genomic program of a species. Psychology since Freud and Jung asserts that drives (German, *de Triebe*) compel and orchestrate all functions of the psyche. Dreaming operates through the full narrative of the genome sequence, so it has to be expressed in long stories, complex plots, mythopoetic sequences, songlines. To the natural mind dreaming presents a rhythmic form and narrative structure, and it operates through the interplay of polarities. In the shamanism of the Shaivite cults of southern India, which present close parallels to Gnostic "snake-worship," dreaming is "the *linga sharira*, the sexual body (considered as the plan or model of a species), which preexists the physical development of its carrier. It emigrates and evolves. . . . It is characterized by a Dharma, a goal to be accomplished."[189] Dreaming, capitalized, can also be used for the creative emanation of the Gnostic Aeons such as Sophia. Both the Sanskrit *parinama* and the Greek *aporria* describe the act of Dreaming. The essence of this cosmological idea is not evolution, but emergence. This is also the leading edge of the young genre of complexity theory, which applies vividly to both biology and astronomy.

Emanation theory, or Dreamtime physics, as it might be called, assumes the trendy notion of autopoesis, the self-ordering or self-organization evident all through terrestrial nature as well as in the cosmos at large. Lynn Margulis asserted that Gaian life-processes exhibit autopoesis in its most beauteous and complex form. The concept of autopoesis is central to the new science of complexity, or complexity theory, formerly called chaos theory, or stochastics. The term currently coming into use for this paradigm is *emergence*: the development of life and consciousness within a shared matrix in which new elements optimize the integral properties of the whole.[190] Fractals that display self-similar patterns in interesting scales present a way to comprehend the emergent identity or "deep structure" common to cell, organism, and superorganism. Gnostic seers detected in the kaleidoscopic fractal currents of the galactic core—the sublime choreography of dancing gods—the deep structure of all life and consciousness in the biosphere. Emergent identity implies the nonlocality of source and manifestation. "What is here, is there. What is not here is nowhere," says the Vishvasara Tantra.

The billions of galaxies in the Universe emerge from a primal ground that manifests through them, revealing, not itself, but the endless novelty of which it is capable. In all that emerges there is self-ordering and self-bounding, the two signatures of autopoesis. Each thing that lives is fractally internested with all that lives. The planet Earth exhibits these two features, autopoesis and emergent identity, in great and glorious profusion.

We might well ask, How did Gaia get to be autopoetic in the first place?

In episode 1, the FGS describes how *novelty* periodically and unpredictably emerges in the eternal cosmos. A singularity (*monogenes*) arises from the One that does not arise from anything. (Zen and Dzogchen teach that our every passing thought arises in the same manner, from the same source.) Eternal Becoming is constantly stirred by emergent singularities, allowing something new to happen in the tightly patterned, repetitive activities of the myriad worlds. Sophia's story is about such a singularity. It describes how humanity is implicated in the Goddess's effort to realize novelty and integrate it into the timeless cosmic order.

The spiral galaxy we inhabit is not the Universe entire, it is our local universe. To tell the story of our universe we need to understand conditions *specific to the home galaxy*, not cosmic conditions in a general and abstract sense. This understanding is precisely what Gnostic cosmology gives us. Jacques Lacarriere says that Gnostic seers "presaged and divined . . . what modern astronomy calls nebulae, spirals, and extragalactic clusters."[191] With their trained application of imagination, Gnostic seers were able to discern the properties and conditions unique to our world system. To my knowledge, no other metaphysical system presents this information in just this way. There is, however, a considerable body of indigenous material that corroborates one or another aspect of the Mystery cosmology found in the Sophia mythos.

This is how one Gnostic text from Nag Hammadi sets up the background of Sophia's story, the planetary biography:

> All the emanations of the Originator are Pleromas, and the root of all these emanations is the One that causes them to emerge from itself, and assigns them their destinies. Each Pleroma is then manifest autonomously, in order to realize originality in its own way (The Gospel of Truth, 41.15–20).

Current science supports the many-world hypothesis of the Gnostics. The Hubble photos provide spectacular evidence of the diversity and dynamics of the myriad galaxies scattered through space-time like glittering seeds. In some mysterious manner, a single unitary presence pervades all the galaxies, but within each galaxy are individual Aeons, gods, divinities. These are not entities as such, but vast currents. The German word *Geist*, "spirit," comes from the Indo-Iranian root *ghei*, "to move powerfully."[192] The supreme cosmic beings move powerfully: they are not entities but immense, living currents. The currents surge and circulate, merge, divide, subside, and surge again. The gods dance.

The Aeons are not distinct entities but currents distinguished by *intensities*, the discrete signatures of their flow-force, one could say.[193] The cosmic gods are coherent units of force, but not point-entities. The tonal and melodic composition of Rimsky-Korsakoff's symphony *Scheherezade* is a single orchestrated movement, yet the symphony, when played, is anything but a simple, singular unit. Likewise for the Aeons, which have acoustic and luminal signatures, phenomena that initiates learned to recognize in repeated sessions of instruction by the Light. Accomplished adepts identified an Aeon by its signature, a chord or vein of sound heard clairaudiently, just as a musician or conductor who knows *Scheherezade* can recognize the entire symphony from a single bar. Gnostics attributed to the Aeon Sophia a particular signature, alerting them to the richness and acuity of her intelligence. Wisdom is her name, her intensity, her flow-signature. Gnostics described the generators in the Pleroma—in astronomical terms, the galactic core—from firsthand experience of cosmic phenomena in paranormal states.

The goddess Sarasvati of Hindu myth presents a classic type of Sophianic intelligence. The attributes of Sarasvati contain some clues to the flow-signature of Sophia. "As Wisdom and Learning, She is the Mother of Veda, that is, all knowledge touching Brahman and the Universe."[194] "Wisdom" comes from the Indo-European root *weid-*, source of *vidya*, *veda*, *wit*, related to the Arabic *hikm* and the Hebrew *chockmah*. The corruption of the Hebrew term gives the *Achamoth*, a name applied to the fallen goddess: Sophia Achamoth, the goddess who fell to Earth.

Before the Aeon Sophia falls, she participates in a sublime ritual with the other Aeons in the Pleroma.

THE ANTHROPOS TEMPLATE

Most versions of the fall of the Wisdom Goddess link Sophia intimately to the activity of another Aeon, Christos, also named for its flow-signature, "anointing power." In cosmic terms anointing is the capacity of an Aeon to morph from a porous, foamlike state into a fluidic, dewlike state. Foam is not dew, but imagine foam turning to dew. That is anointing in the Pleromic domain. The product of anointing, *chrism*, is the love sweat of the gods. In the ecstasy of their dancing the Aeons break into a fragrant sweat, a bright, dewy eruption. This is anointing at the cosmic level.

Astrophysicists now accept the presence of "molecular dew" in the galactic arms though not yet at the galactic core, and they are reticent to assume it can have biological properties. Theorists of steady-state plasma cosmology may be approaching a recognition of the foamlike, high-density, low-mass porosity of Aeonic currents. Plasma cosmology is currently the best alternative to the big bang fantasia.[195]

The conjugation of Sophia and another Aeon, Thelete, in the core of our galaxy signals the opening event of the Sophia mythos. Between them these two generators configure the singularity offered by the Originator. The Greek word *anthropos* means "humanity" in the generic sense, distinct from other words for man and woman. It is gender-inclusive, unlike *andros*, "male," and *gyne*, "female." Anthropos is the Gnostic name for the cosmic matrix of the human species, the preterrestrial human genome. The Sophia mythos assumes a version of "directed panspermia," the theory introduced by Nobel Prize–winning Swedish chemist Svante Arrhenius around 1900 and accepted, in various forms, by astronomer Fred Hoyle, Nobel biologist Francis Crick (codiscoverer with James Watson of the structure of DNA), Lynn Margulis, and many other leading minds of our time.[196]

Coming together to encode or configure the Anthropos, Sophia and Thelete act in a manner consistent with cosmic law, "for it is the will of the Originator not to allow anything to happen in the Pleroma apart from a syzygy" (*A Valentinian Exposition* 36.25–30). *Syzygy* is an odd Greek word used by astronomers to denote the conjunction of celestial bodies. The Originator wills that all activity in the Pleroma be accomplished by paired Aeons, coupled gods, but this is not a rigid rule, and it is not enforced. In the case of the Sophia-Thelete syzygy that encodes the Anthropos, the will of the Originator is observed. Once it has been configured by the ritual dance of the coupled Aeons, the singularity is ready to be projected into manifestation in the cosmos at large.

What next occurs in the Pleroma is a collective act, the collaboration of all the Aeons, not just Sophia and Thelete acting as a distinct pair. In episode 3, the entire company of Pleromic gods unites in a choral dance to project the encoded singularity into manifestation. They seed it in the outer cosmos, the galactic limbs turning like a vast carousel around the Pleromic hub. The singularity nests in a nebular cloud. Although the language here is mythic, or mythopoetic, the description can be read as applying to the inner dynamics of the Galaxy. The myth clearly suggests astrophysical processes yet unknown to science, but perhaps beginning to be glimpsed in plasma physics, complexity theory, and the new paradigm of emergence.

Pleroma means "fullness," "plenum," "plenitude." The galactic vortices are all variations of a chalice form, a flattened torus with a central core (the galactic bulge) and a surrounding disc (the spiral arms). The hub of a galaxy, its Pleroma, is counterbalanced by the flat carousel structure, the spinning armature, called the Kenoma, "deficiency," "inferior realm." The Pleroma is a fullness, infinite potential that outpours itself into the realm of "deficiency," finite potential. In the Pleroma all possibility is complete, all is fulfilled, evolved to its fullest potential. Pleromic gods like Sophia *can only give of themselves*, selflessly, without affecting what they emanate or imposing themselves upon the conditions they set up in the Kenoma. The selfless outpouring of the Pleromic gods is a key theme of Sophianic cosmology. It is also the model of human generosity.

The Kenoma, the carousel armature of a galaxy, is the realm of chaos where finite, bounded potential develops. It is composed of dark elementary matter arrays (*dema*), atomic and subatomic fields, including proto-organic elements, residue of past worlds. Suns are born in the galactic arms and planetary systems emerge there. On some of the planets organic life unfolds, but the origin of life cannot, it seems, be located on the planet where it arises. Nobel laureate Francis Crick, one of the discoverers of the structure of DNA, argues that, owing to its overwhelming complexity, life on Earth must have been seeded from elsewhere in the cosmos. Lynn Margulis, coauthor of the Gaia hypothesis, also accepts the possibility that microscopic life-forms (propagules) can migrate freely through interstellar space. The universe is a dusty place, and some of the dust is organic residue. That emergent life on planets in the carousel arms of a galaxy originates in the center of the galaxy, as described in episode 3, is not yet recognized by science. This theory will be unacceptable as long as scientists cannot imagine that the core of a galaxy is a vortex of superorganic forces, alive, aware, and sensorially endowed, but this is how the Gnostics regarded the Pleromas.

In Tantric cosmology, the composition of the Kenoma is called *adrista*, "residue." It is, as science tells us, stardust that remains from previous cycles of evolution, cycles without beginning or end.

> Now the Eternity (which is absolute Truth) has no shadow outside it, for it is a limitless light where all is within and nothing is without. But at its exterior is shadow, which has been called darkness. From the darkness arises a force without form. This is the shadow realm of limitless chaos. From this realm, every kind of divine emanation emerges, including the world we inhabit, for whatever happens in chaos is previously implanted there by what produces it (On the Origin of the World 98.20–30).

Here the language of the Mystery experience plays into the cosmological scenario. The galactic core is a spinning vortex of Organic Light, a radiant substance that might be compared to soft, luminous nougat. It casts no shadow. Darkness belongs to the exterior regions of the galactic mill wheel, the Kenoma. The residue of previous worlds is continually recycled and reprocessed in the colossal armature of the spinning carousel. Whatever develops in the Kenoma was implanted there by Pleromic emanation—including humanity itself, or various strains of humanity, and other species.

A striking parallel to the stalk of light in the Gnostic narrative occurs in the Japanese myth of creation where paired sky gods, or Kami, project a "Jewel-Sky-Spear" from the cosmic center into the waters of primordial chaos.[197] The image of cosmic fertilization in the galactic limbs occurs in Egyptian mythology where the sky goddess Nut, curved into an oval, carries the constellations of the zodiac encoded on her body.[198] Cosmic embryonic imagery occurs in almost all high-culture cosmologies and universally in indigenous or "primitive" lore.

The text called On the Origin of the World (NHC II, 5) describes the boundary of the Pleromic core, called *menix*, hymen, *stauros*, or *horos*. Remaining in the core, Aeons can emanate into the arms, the realm of formless chaos, but they do not pass over into those regions. The opalescent stalk of light projected by the collectivity of Aeons may be compared to a klieg light shining through the wall of a white canvas tent. The beam of light passes through the walls, but the source of the beam remains inside the tent. Gnostic texts explain that these two primary conditions, Aeonic pairing and bounded emanation, are set by the Originator. They are cosmic laws but they are not enforced, so exceptions are possible.

Sophia is one of those exceptions.

Divine Desire

Astrophysicists now recognize that our galactic core has a central "yolk" and a distinct bounding region like the porous wall of a living cell. The worlds that emerge beyond the bounding membrane have autopoetic or self-ordering properties because they have been emanated by the Aeons, but they are neither created nor managed by them. Life in the living cosmos is autonomously self-ordering, and so too is our home planet. The self-ordering properties imparted to matter by the Pleromic divinities are usually left to run their own course. This applies for many worlds, but there are exceptions.

Episode 4 of the sacred story contains a pivotal event. It describes how Sophia cannot detach from involvement in the fate of the Anthropos. The power of divine desire is called *enthymesis* in the Gnostic texts. This word is related to *thymus*, the organ at the center of the chest. The ancient Greeks did not picture the soul as a butterfly (*psyche*) in a childish way, or merely by metaphoric trope. The actors in Homeric legend, both men and women, felt emotions with raw physical intensity. Even thinking was a corporeal sensation. The agitation of the thymus recorded in many passages of the

Iliad may indicate the actual shudder of the pericardium, the membrane enclosing the heart.[199] The Greek *thumon* probably derives from the root *thuein*, "to burn," "to smoke," "to sacrifice." Sophia's *enthymesis* is a burning desire that engulfs her like smoke and separates her from the rest of the Aeons. The compulsion to assist seizes the Goddess and spontaneously evokes the complex energetic response typical of an Aeon, the surge of sublime, superanimating power—Aeonic Dreaming.

—————— 12 ——————

THE INSANE GOD

A spectacular surge of desire compels the Aeon Sophia to plunge from the galactic core. Her unilateral act of dreaming earns her the name *Prunikos*, "outrageous, audacious, daring." The word connotes the behavior of a whore, hence the strange appellation, the Whore of Wisdom. The Valentinian school assigned a different motive to this event: "Valentinus taught that the last of the thirty Aeons is androgyne and this is Sophia. She wanted to see the highest god and was repelled by his Splendor; hence, she fell out of the Pleroma." According to this version, the true prototype of Lucifer is Sophia.[200] In either version, Valentinian or Sethian, there follows the most bizarre event in the sci-fi cosmology of the Gnostics: the emergence of an alien species, the Archons.

To be compelled by solitary passion and fall out of the Pleroma—such is the unique fate of the goddess Sophia. In episode 4, the Gnostic myth recalls the many accounts in myth and folklore of a female deity who falls from heaven or becomes embodied in the Earth. For instance, the Thompson Indians of the American Northwest recount this story:

> At first Kujum-Chantu, the earth, was like a human being, a woman with a head, and arms and legs, and an enormous belly. The original humans lived on the surface of her belly. [The legend recounts how the Old One] transformed the sky woman into the present earth. Her hair became the trees and grass; her flesh, the clay; her bones, the rocks; and her blood, the springs of water.[201]

Such parallels (a few others could be cited) show that Gnostic cosmology is deeply rooted in indigenous wisdom and reflects a sophisticated version of the native sense for life on Earth. The Sophia mythos describes the preexistence of Sophia in the Pleroma and her role in projecting the Anthropos.

It also describes in great detail the aberrant side effect of her plunge and its enduring implications for humanity. To my knowledge these elements of the Gnostic emanationist narrative are unique and exceptional.

In episode 4 of the sacred story Sophia undergoes the act of separation that will lead to her morphing into the very world previsioned in her Dreaming. Yet before that world, our blue-and-white marbled planet, emerged into material form, a momentous and unanticipated event took place in the galactic arms. In the region of the *dema*, the dense elementary matter arrays, Sophia's plunge produced what might be called a splatter effect. In a way she could not foresee in her Dreaming, she induced a cosmic anomaly, a freak event that sets up bizarre conditions for the later emergence of the Earth.

DEMENTED DEITY

Sophia exceeds the normal limits of Pleromic emanation when *enthymesis* causes her to fix her dreaming powers on a world to come, a world that did not exist when she envisioned it. And then she herself becomes that very world! What a tremendous reach of imagination the Mystery seers must have had, matched to the compassion they felt for the plight of the fallen goddess. It must have taken generations of disciplined paranormal investigation and creative collaboration to work out the Sophia mythos. To picture what she saw, the Gnostic visionaries had to recognize the dreaming power of the Aeons—as we, likewise, might do. Imagine the Anthropos template as a splotch of molecular dew deposited in the *dema*, like a patch of colored breath on an obsidian mirror. Such splotches exist, called galactic nebulae. The most prominent example in our galaxy is the Great Nebula in Orion, M42, visible to the naked eye. Such nebulae are known to be cradles of starbirth where suns are born over countless eons of time. The possibility that nebulae could also harbor weblike membranes of organic compounds, i.e., templates for life, is now regarded as plausible by some astrophysicists, as we have noted.

Once she plunges, Sophia descends into the region of the galactic nebula where the Anthropos template is deposited, but not into the nebula itself. The interstellar space of the galactic arms is a field of elementary matter.

Normally a Pleromic current of plasmic luminosity with its properties of high porosity, zero mass, and superanimating force, does not surge directly into the *dema*. When Sophia hits that region, her impact produces an extraordinary effect. It creates an impact zone of bizarre properties. What happens then is the weirdest event in Gnostic cosmology, perhaps in any cosmology so far produced by human imagination. The "high strangeness" of the Sophia mythos has warranted scholars like Richard Smith to compare Gnostic materials to "that most visionary of our modern literary genres, science fiction."[202] Indeed, Gnostic cosmology is a kind of theological science fiction.

When the Aeon Sophia pours into the *dema*, her spectacular plume of Organic Light produces a splatter effect. The *dema* is chaotic, not organized into coherent forms or organic worlds, but under the impact of the autopoetic, animating force of the Aeon, it becomes instantaneously organized. Aeonic Dreaming, the source of cosmic order, affects matter so that it becomes self-ordering. This is precisely what happens with the *dema*, but in an anomalous, premature manner, because Sophia's plunge does not follow the usual order of cosmic process. The text called the Hypostasis of the Archons describes this bizarre situation (II, 4: 93.30 ff., my glosses in brackets).

> A veil exists between the world above [in the galactic core], and the realms that are below [exterior, in the galactic limbs]; and shadow came into being beneath the veil. Some of the shadow [dark mass] became [atomic] matter, and was projected apart [partially formed into elementary arrays, the *dema*]. And what Sophia created [by her impact] became a product in the matter, [a neonate form] *like an aborted fetus*. And [once formed] it assumed a shape molded out of shadow, and became an arrogant beast resembling a lion. It was androgynous, because it was from [neutral, inorganic] matter that it derived.

The Aeon Sophia is a living, self-aware current of immense magnitude. By contrast, the matter in the *dema* is relatively inert, not inherently alive or awake, yet it has the potential for a kind of pseudolife, a simulacrum of biological existence. Episode 5 challenges us to imagine that the super-animating power of Sophia's Dreaming causes a spectral life-form to spring up in the outer chaos of the galactic arms.

Gnostics taught that the Archons are an imitation life-form, a mimic species. *Archon* is from Greek *archai*, "in the beginning," "prior to anything else." I have explained this terminology already, but it is worth repeating in order to emphasize that the Archons arise prematurely—hence the analogy to an abortion or miscarriage in the Nag Hammadi texts. This anomalous species comes into existence prior to the time when the Earth emerges by direct transformation of Sophia's own divine substance. Archons are Sophia's offspring, in a sense, but in an entirely different way than humanity and other organic species are. They do not emerge from her divine substance, Organic Light, but from its impact upon particulate matter in the *dema*. They are a freak species of inorganic composition, but they are alive and conscious in their own way.

At first the Archons have no habitat. They swarm around like an insect colony blown savagely across interstellar space, sucked toward Sophia's currents and repulsed again. Since they were not initially projected from the Pleroma, they lack autopoetic encoding. They have no innate intentionality, *ennoia*. Archons present an extra-Pleromic phenomenon, a cosmic aberration, *anomia*. Their emergence from the field of primal matter is premature, so they are compared to an aborted fetus. The body form of the Archon resembles a premature fetus. This is perhaps the most bizarre, arresting image in the Gnostic materials. The Archon legion of embryonic insectoid forms attaches itself to Sophia like an infestation of swarming lice. The cosmic miscarriage of the Goddess will have extenuating consequences for humanity.

In Episode 5 the high strangeness continues. From the Archon legion emerges a second form, a mutation called the *drakonic* type in the NHC. The Apocryphon of John says that Sophia herself caused a leader or master entity to emerge among the Archons.

> And Sophia desired to cause the thing that had no innate spirit of its own to be formed into a likeness and rule over primal matter and over all the forces she had precipitated. So there appeared for the first time a ruler out of chaos, lion-like in appearance, androgynous, having an exaggerated sense of power within him, and ignorant of whence he came to be. (NHC II, 5: 100.1–10)

This entity, called the Demiurge, is a weird, frightening mutation, "having a lion-like body with the head of a *drakona*, a reptile" (Berlin Codex 37.2–25). Two types of Archons, a neonate or embryonic type, and the draconic type, are not elaborately described in the surviving materials. They are indicated with the utmost brevity, but clearly enough to give the idea that something very bizarre is happening. The leonine-reptilian Archon, who is also called Yaldabaoth, is dominant and aggressive compared to the more passive Archons whose form resembles a prematurely born fetus. Although the "chief Archon"is androgynous, it rapidly assumes a markedly male, macho posture. *He* now takes charge of the extraordinary situation produced by Sophia's plunge, or at least he tries. At the conclusion of episode 5, the Demiurge proceeds to create a habitat for himself in the vastness of the galactic arms.

Virtual Heaven

Gnostics taught that the Demiurge cannot create anything because he lacks the power of intention proceeding from the Pleroma and ultimately based in the Originator. Archons cannot originate anything, but they can imitate, copy, duplicate. Their mimetic capacity is called *phantasia* to distinguish it from the real-life, animating power of the Aeons, called *ennoia*. Yaldabaoth is called the *antimimon pneuma*, "the counterfeiting spirit" in the Apocryphon of John and other cosmological texts. The celestial mansions he contrives are called *stereoma*, a stereometric projection like the holograph of a living thing. The holographic image is not alive but it can replicate something that is. Using the Coptic word HAL, "simulation," Gnostic cosmological texts explain that the many-mansioned heaven of the Demiurge is a virtual cosmos, a virtual reality (VR) world.* Although he sees the superanimated patterns of the Pleroma only as static, fossil-like forms, not fluid, alive, dancing forms, the Demiurge borrows enough sense of order to model his world, a habitat for the drone Archons.

---

* The Coptic language is written in Greek letters using exclusively capitals. In the rare instances where Coptic words are cited, I will follow the convention of putting them in capital letters to approximate how they appear in the surviving Gnostic texts.

> The Lord Archon organized everything in his world according
> to the model of the primary Aeons, given for him to see that he
> might recreate them. Not because he had seen the imperishable
> Aeons [by his own power], but by the power in him taken
> from his Mother, that allowed him to produce by likeness
> (Apocryphon of John II 32.30–33.5).

The cosmos of the Archons is not a viable human habitat, and cannot be. It is not the possible world Sophia anticipated in the unilateral Dreaming that precipitated her plunge. So the myth teaches us, and the myth is true in physical terms. We do not inhabit the planetary system as a whole, we inhabit the Earth exclusively. The Archons who inhabit the planetary system are aliens in our realm. Yaldaboath's world is merely a simulation (Coptic HAL) of the dancing, scintillating mandalas in the Pleroma, not a genuine *emergent* world like ours, pervaded with potential for novelty, beauty, innovation, chance, and change. The clockwork cosmos of the planets simulates "the model of the primary Aeons." The planetary system is organized by geometric and cyclic laws that reflect divine life, but the system itself is not alive, not organic. By contrast, on Earth the living, animating qualities of the Pleroma inform all things.

The spontaneous generation of the Archons is certainly one of the more difficult features of Gnostic cosmology to take seriously. The eruption of an inorganic species in interstellar space is truly bizarre and may look highly implausible. How can any organism arise without a habitat from which to arise? How could spontaneous generation of this kind occur? Those who balk at this episode would be advised to investigate the abiogenesis of Acari insects demonstrated by Andrew Crosse in 1837. His experiment showed the precipitation of nanobot-like insects by agitation of an electromagnetic medium.

The *stereoma* of the Demiurge is the planetary system exclusive of the Sun, Moon, and Earth. These three bodies make up an independent cosmos. Earth, Sun, and Moon form a symbiotic system enclosed on itself and dynamically distinct from the clockwork mechanism of the other planets. Outrageous as this notion may appear, it is not inconsistent with scientific thought. Physicist Jim Yorke, who coined the term "chaos," observes: "We tend to think that science has explained everything when it has explained how the moon goes around the Earth. But the idea of a clocklike universe has nothing to do with the real world."[203]

An obscure cosmological text from Nag Hammadi is titled Trimorphic Protennoia, "three-formed original intention." This is arcane jargon for the three-body system previsioned in Sophia's Dreaming before her plunge. If the Archons had not arisen when the Aeon crashed into the *dema*, we might be living in a planetary system consisting only of mother star, Earth, and moon. The *trimorphic protennoia* is consistent with Gaia theory, if we assume that the sun and moon are intimately engaged in the operations of life within the terrestrial biosphere. They are "off-planet" but integral parts of the Gaian ecosystem.

We on Earth inhabit a three-body cosmos.[204] Sophia is essentially the matriarch of a single-parent family—a single-planet goddess, if you will. But she relies on the support of the surrogate bodies, sun and moon, to manage her terrestrial brood. In terms of current astrophysical knowledge of the existence of many Earthlike planets, and the many variations of planetary systems known to be out there in our galaxy, such a three-body world is totally feasible.

Our imaginative powers may be severely tried by some aspects of the Sophia mythos, especially in episode 5, but it would be a shame to be put off from continuing to contemplate this sublime scenario. Gnosis is a way of knowing in which the knower is intimately engaged with the matters known. To contemplate the sacred story is to become implicated in it. If we have difficulty with the cosmology of the Archons, it may be precisely because we are implicated in it in ways we have yet to understand. Such, at least, is how a Gnostic teacher would perhaps have addressed our difficulties at this point.

COSMIC MISTAKE

The Archontic heaven is the setting for an act of cosmic madness:

> Now when the outer heavens had been consolidated along with their forces and all their administration, the Demiurge became insolent. And he was honored by an army of angels who gave

blessing and honor to him. And for his part he was delighted and boasted to them, "Lo, I have no need of anyone else, no other gods." He said, "It is I who am god, and no others exist apart from me." (On the Origin of the World, 103.1–15)

Arrogant and blind, the Demiurge deems himself to be at the center of creation, lord of all he beholds. Gnostic texts state plainly that Yaldabaoth is insane, a demented god, or imposter deity. The Demiurge is indeed a sort of god, a cosmic entity in his own right, but he is not a Pleromic Aeon. He is a self-deified inorganic phantom deluded about his own identity. This is not meant as a figure of speech or a mythological trope. Not by a long shot, for the Gnostic materials clearly show that the adepts of the Mysteries perceived Yaldabaoth and the Archons as real, physically existent inhabitants of our planetary system. They are aliens who wrongly attempt to penetrate the biosphere, and they are something else as well.

God exists, but he is insane. And he works against humanity. Such is the heretical message proclaimed by the Sophianic adepts of the Mysteries when they came out publicly to refute Christian ideologues. Gnostics warned that humans coexist in a planetary system with a demented entity who can access our world through our minds. Sophia's "son" is a problem child, to say the least. The threats that the Demiurge poses to life on Earth have barely begun to be realized.

The Archontic heaven is said to be *anomou*, "anomalous," because it results from Aeonic action outside the Pleroma. Let's recall the variant of this term, *anomia*, applied to the discussion of the Palestinian redeemer myth in part 1. The anomaly in the outer cosmos that has caused the organic Earth to be captured in the inorganic planetary system has definite effects in the human psyche as well. Gnostics taught that the strategy of the Archons is *apaton*, "ruse," "deception." The Apocryphon of John says that the delight of the Archons is to deceive, to have us perceive their world as other than it is, and to misperceive our own world. The Coptic word SOREM, "error," "deviation," defines the Gnostic motif for the Archons whose emergence in the cosmic order is called "the generation of error." The corresponding Greek word, *plane*, means "error," "going astray."

Gnostics warned of the paramount danger posed by the side effect of Sophia's plunge: humanity may be deviated from its proper course of development. It will miss its chance for novelty and fail to define its unique evolutionary niche in the Gaian ecosystem. It is as if the presence of the Archons in the planetary system sets up a deviant field that distorts human thinking. "The world system we inhabit came about due to a mistake," says the Gospel of Philip from Nag Hammadi. This may be one of the strangest notions ever proposed.

It may also be one of the most essential truths we need to master, both in physical and psychological terms, to ensure our survival as a species and secure a sane and happy future for this troubled world.

13

THE PASSION OF SOPHIA

The presence of the Archons in the cosmos at large and their effect upon the human mind were paramount concerns for the Gnostic seers. The Levantine *gnostikoi* were specialists in the detection of extrahuman, deviant forces. In a word, they were parapsychologists; or, to put it otherwise, psychic detectives. At the same time, they were accomplished cosmologists. Nothing they saw in the cosmos, none of the wonders they observed in heightened perception—or hyperception, as it might be called—were remote and removed from the human dimension. In all their theorizing and researches they observed a supreme guiding principle: As without, so within.

To see in cosmic events the actional mirroring of psychological processes—such is the *psychocosmic parallelism* typical of the Gnostic mind and method. I use the neologism *actional* to indicate that the mirroring is a real action, both enacted and interactive, not merely a matter of passive or static reflection. The Gnostics' deep insight into the parallelism of psyche and cosmos was not a game of Jungian correspondences, a mere play of analogies or symbolic transpositions. The practice of Gnosis was a way of apprehending directly the existential reality of the cosmos and participating in how the cosmos *acts* within the human psyche. The Sophia mythos can be a frame for deep ecological learning, extending even to the extraterrestrial realm, if we are willing to accept that we are actionally implicated in everything the narrative describes.

Humanity is part of the solution to Sophia's plight, but not only that. As the mythos unfolds it becomes ever more obvious that we as a species are also part of the explanation for her plight. The way we describe Sophia's dilemma may ultimately determine the way we can describe our own role in the symbiotic weave of life.

THE REPENTANT SUN

When the Archons emerge from the chaos of the galactic limbs, the Anthropos is still incubating in the nearby nebula (episode 5). Sophia has not yet morphed into the planet where humanity will emerge. Yet the future experience of our species, the Earthbound strain of the Anthropos, has already been affected by our alien cousins. Archontic deception, focused in the dementia of the Demiurge, will eventually infect human consciousness and attempt to deviate the life-process on Earth. But even as this threat arises, other events in the cosmos are unfolding that will determine how humanity can face and overcome the menace of the Archons.

Episode 6 of the sacred story describes how, even while the scaffolding of planetary systems takes form, a newborn star emerges from the nebular cloud where the Anthropos is embedded. The star is not produced by Sophia's agitation of the *dema*, but through other processes that unfold independently, and continually, in the galactic limbs. Due to the superior mass of the stellar body, the celestial mansions of the Demiurge (the proto-planetary disk, in astronomical terms) rapidly gravitate to the newborn star and assume circular paths around it, rather in the way that iron filings form a symmetrical pattern when sprinkled on a sheet of paper placed over a magnet. Now the emergent planets move in fixed orbits, but without the Earth, for this planet does not yet exist. The arrogant Demiurge declares himself to be the sole god in the cosmos, lord and master of all he surveys.

To reprimand the Archons, Sophia invokes the radiant image of the Anthropos template nested in the Orion Nebula: "that luminous child" (NHC II,5:103). The rough Coptic transliteration is OYRHOME NATHANA TOS PPMOYOIEN, "the deathless human of light." She declares that the Anthropos is superior to the Archons, and predicts that humanity, when it emerges into organic form, will defeat the works of the Demiurge. Witnessing this declaration, Sabaoth, the newborn star at the center of the Archontic world, undergoes a conversion and consecrates her mighty forces to Sophia. In effect, the mother star revolts against the rule of the inorganic planetary forces and aligns with the dynamics of organic life, anticipating Sophia's complete metamorphosis into the Earth. The fallen Goddess recognizes this choice and produces from herself a divine emanation in her own likeness, the life force Zoe. In this way, the goddess joins her Aeonic force with the sun, the mother star of the planetary system.

All of which is quite a lot to handle, needless to say. This is one of the great cinematographic moments in the Sophia mythos. The drama of the repentant sun is a rich, elaborate episode, but perhaps not as mythologically obscure as it might first appear to be. Granted, the "high strangeness" of Gnostic myth really gets rolling with these events. After the astonishing assertion that Earth does not belong to the planetary system, but is merely captured in it, here comes another mind-boggling proposition: the Sun, the central star of our solar system, is a conscious being that aligns to life and stands against the inorganic planets in the system.[205] Sabaoth "repents" and sides with the Aeon Sophia, who is gradually undergoing a profound metamorphosis of her own as these cosmic events transpire.

Is there any way to make sense of the "conversion" of Sabaoth? Outrageous, you say? Unbelievable? Sheer mythological nonsense? Perhaps, but doesn't this episode come in some ways quite close to what Gaia theory is telling us?

By now, after some thirty years, the story of how the Gaia hypothesis originated has almost passed into planetary folklore. Working at NASA's Jet Propulsion Laboratory in the 1970s, James Lovelock was given the task of determining if life could exist on Mars. To do so he compared the atmospheric composition of Mars and other planets with that of Earth. The hypothesis emerged in the course of Lovelock's conversations with colleague Dian Hitchcock, leading them to understand how the terrestrial atmosphere is anomalous relative to the rest of the planetary system. Here is an assertion from the Sophia mythos, restated and transposed into modern coslomogical theory.

The differences between Earth and the rest of the planetary system are huge and make life on our home planet possible. The primary "anomalies" involved here are three: the state of atmospheric disequilibrium that keeps oxygen at around 21 percent, the constancy of salinity in the sea at around 3 to 5 percent, and the close temperature range of the biosphere despite a huge 30 percent increase in the heat of the sun since the Earth was formed 4.32 billion years ago. A Gnostic would say that these anomalies are precisely due to the Earth being an organic world autopoetically maintained by its indwelling divinity, the Aeon Sophia. Earth is everything that the other planets are not.

Of the three distinctive anomalies, the third is of course the most relevant to the drama of the repentant sun. The central star of our system is thought to be like a huge blast furnace bursting with hydrogen and metallic elements in a fantastic fiery meld. It discharges immense waves of heat and radiation, yet when the solar emanations reach Earth they are so carefully measured that they hold steady within the small range that permits life in the biosphere to emerge and flourish. A tiny fluctuation of solar input during the millions of years when the sun's temperature rose by 30 percent could have easily burned up the Earth many times over.

The mother star, called Saboath, is indeed benevolently disposed toward our home planet.

Two-Source Hologram

In the perspective of the Sophia mythos, "anomaly" is a double entendre. In one sense, it refers to the home planet standing apart from the rest of the planetary system, but it also means that the planetary system *in its entirety* is an anomaly. "The world we inhabit came about through a mistake," says the famous one-liner from The Gospel of Philip (NHC II, 3:75.5). The mistake is not our world per se, not the planet Earth, but the inorganic scaffolding of the planetary system where Earth is captured. The ornate expression *trimorphic protennoia* encodes Sophia's ideal anticipation of the environment suited to her designer species. The three-body system would be the right cosmic setting for the Anthropos to emerge and demonstrate its singularity. But due to the *unanticipated* consequences of Sophia's plunge, that is not how the prospect played out. It is entirely conceivable, however, that a planetary system could consist of one sun, the central star, and one planet with a moon.

On Earth we live in two systems at once: the terrestrial and the planetary, or extraterrestrial. This fact of science is clearly prefigured in the sacred cosmology, but for Gnostic perception it is not only a fact of science. Consistent with psychocosmic parallelism, this situation has *actional* effects within human experience. It affects how we live and think in an intimate manner. The planetary system exclusive of the Sun, Earth, and Moon (which is Earth's satellite, not actually a planet) is the realm of the Archons, an extraterrestrial species whose corporeal and mental makeup depend on inorganic chemistry. The Archons are really out there, residing in the planetary clockworks, *and* they also exist in our minds, as part of the way we think and perceive. (For further reflections on the troubling issue of the Archons, see chapter 21.)

In the brilliant metaphor of science fiction writer Philip K. Dick, who was deeply influenced by Gnostic ideas, human reality is *a two-source hologram*. It is as if one hologram of a setting, such as a prison, were superimposed over another hologram of a different setting, say, an elaborate tree house, and we live in the merge. The three-body system of Sophia's original Dreaming does exist after all: Her Dreaming persists even as she herself is deeply immersed in it, embodied in the Earth. And the Earth is not a hologram. But at the same time we live in the setting of the planetary system, the clockwork cosmos of blind mechanics. Gnostics taught that the planetary setting is *a deviant field that distorts our perception of Gaian dynamics*. Granted, this is not a notion we can easily grasp, or even accept for reflection. It is truly arcane, a steep challenge to analysis and imagination.

The narrative at this point challenges us to comprehend how the Archontic can merge into our own. How can we detect subliminal effects that disguise themselves in the routine operations of mind and imagination? If Gnostics were indeed experts in the cognitive and noetic sciences and adepts at parapsychology, as I believe they were, they would have cultivated such detection to a fine art. We can and perhaps must learn to do the same, for the cosmic situation forces the task upon us.

Gnostic cosmology is dualistic, but not in the same way as the cosmology of Zoroaster—Persian duality, discussed above in connection with the rise of Jewish theocracy. Let's recall that the religious doctrine of Persian duality, absorbed by the Hebrews during the Babylonian Captivity, posits the opposition of Good (Ahura Mazda) versus Evil (Ahriman) at the cosmic level. This is *absolute* duality. It assumes a split in the Godhead, in the divine realm, at the *one* source of all that exists. Hence it may be called *split-source duality*. It may also be called *single-source duality* because it assumes that good and evil have the same origin, due to a split at the source, in the Godhead—an idea flatly refuted by Gnostics. In their protest against Christianity, Gnostics opposed Christian theology and dualist ethics based on the Jewish notion of a wrathful, punishing father god who was also, believe it or not, the source of divine love.[206]

Split-source duality is *not* what the Sophia mythos presents, however. It is of the utmost importance to distinguish Persian split-source duality from the two-source duality of Gnostic teachings. In the Gnostic view there is *no split in the Pleroma* and consequently there is *no absolute opposition of Good and Evil*. In fact, Gnostics did not characterize the problem posed by the Archons in terms of evil at all. They framed it in terms of *error*. They taught that we come to understand how evil arises in the world by tracing the working of error, the Archontic factor. The appearance of the Archons in the cosmic scenario of terrestrial formation is called "the generation of error."

Two-source duality has profound ethical and psychological implications, utterly different from those of split-source duality. The *Clementine Recognitions*, a fourth-century collection of anecdotes that illustrate theological arguments, describes how Christian converts who argued with the Gnostic Simon Magus were outraged by his insistence that good and evil do not come from the same source, as they believed. This issue was a flashpoint of Gnostic heresy. It drew enormous hostility toward Mystery initiates who denied that evil in the human world could have a divine origin. Instead, they pointed to an alien exobiological origin. This argument infuriated early Christians who followed the theological doctrines of the Jews, who, in turn, had assimilated Persian single-source duality. The Qumranic materials state over and over again that the Lord God sends evil into the world, as well as good. If the same omnipotent parental deity is the source of good and evil, there must be a split at the source, Gnostics argued. God must be, at best, an unstable schizophrenic. At worst, a murderous psychopath.

Christians and Jews alike deeply resented the Mystery adepts for pointing out that a deity of infinite goodness would not introduce evil into the world. Gnostics not only demonstrated the logical absurdity of the Persian view, they had an explanation of evil to offer in place of it. But to Christians and Jews alike all this arcane business about the Archons was weird, convoluted, and difficult to follow. Beyond that, it was anathema, a dangerous doctrine to be condemned and attacked. It revealed the off-planet father god to be a demented alien who hates humanity. Christians and Jews alike took this shocking disclosure as the supreme insult to their faith. (And still do, to this day.) Initiates who came forth from the Mystery sanctuaries to deliver that particular message to the world at large paid heavily for this exposé.

Two-world duality does not just occur in the planetary system, it inheres in the very nature of material existence. *Abiogenesis* is the name geologists give to "the development of living organisms from non-living matter; as in the supposed origin of life on Earth" (*Oxford Dictionary of Earth Sciences*, 2003 edition). The reality of life is that organic forms seem to be seated upon an inorganic infrastructure. Paradoxically, life seems to have both an inorganic and an organic origin. Reduce proteins and polypeptide chains to their elemental components and you get into the realm of inorganic chemistry, Archon territory. Gaia theory often dances right on the fine, rubbery ridge between organic and inorganic chemistry. How can organic life arise from the inorganic? (As one anonymous wit has noted, "Hydrogen is a light, odorless gas, which, given enough time, turns into people.") Gnostic seers who detected this anomaly applied their highest powers of reasoning to interpret it. For them the two-world setup was not an incidental or irrelevant matter, but an utterly real situation that profoundly affects human experience.

THE ORION NEBULA

Abiogenesis figures into Sophia's metamorphosis into the Earth, which, let's recall, has been ongoing from the moment of her plunge. Organic Light, the substance of Sophia's body, is alive like blood is alive, or like slime mold (a surprisingly agile and intelligent entity) is alive. Aeonic currents consist of a substance like nougat foam, extremely porous and mass free. The luminal currents that compose a Pleromic Aeon contain no inorganic elements, for such elements belong to the Kenoma, the realm of outer chaos, the elementary particle soup, *adrista*, cosmic residue. But as soon as Sophia plunges into that realm she begins to absorb elementary matter. It is as if the seething luminal foam sucks up masses of minute colored metallic filings.[207]

As the drama of the repentant sun unfolds, Sophia's metamorphosis into a planetary body escalates steadily. It seems that the Goddess may have been as perplexed as we are about the admixture of organic and inorganic life. The paraphrase of Irenaeus (*Against Heresies*, 5.4) says:

> At one moment, they [the heretics] affirm, she would weep and lament on account of being left alone in the midst of darkness and vacuity; while at another moment . . . she would be filled with joy, and laugh; then again, she would be struck with terror; or, at other moments, would sink into consternation and bewilderment.

The conversion of Sabaoth comes as a huge relief to the Goddess for it means that she is no longer alone in her plight. Now there is another cosmic entity who shares her difficulties. Not an Aeon from the Pleroma, but a lesser deity from the outer realm of chaos, the Kenoma. The Archontic realm of elementary matter provides the material for the planetary system, but the sun, the central body of that system, is not a planet. It is a star. The star called Sabaoth, the central body of our solar system, is not produced by Sophia's impact in the *dema*. It arises from a totally independent process.

While the Archontic world is forming, there is another development event in the Kenoma, the galactic arms where Sophia now finds herself. The spiral armature revolves constantly about the Pleromic hub, and as it does so, it churns the fields of elementary matter into radiant grains we call stars. Star making is a perpetual activity of the galactic limbs, according to modern astrophysics. Stars are not shot from the galactic core, they are ground like grains from elementary matter of the rotating limbs; or they arise as vortices in interstellar plasma. "The mills of the gods grind slow, but they grind exceeding fine," goes an old saying. This grinding activity produces specific formations that do not devolve from Aeonic emanation. At atomic and subatomic levels, the dynamics of the galactic armature are relatively independent of the core.

Astrophysicists believe that the mother star of our planetary system radiated from the Great Nebula in the constellation the Hunter,

Orion. In the myth, Sabaoth emerges to encounter interstellar activity already in progress. Sophia's presence has shaped events in the spiraling galactic arm. The glorious opalescent plume of Organic Light that surged from the Pleroma terminated at a node, exactly in the way growing things do: for instance, the leaves on the stem of a fern grow in reducing fractal patterns until the fern curves on itself and closes into a node, the endpoint of its organic formation. There is also a cosmic node where the newborn sun appears and defines a vortex in the field of interstellar plasma. The two nodes interlock when Sabaoth aligns with Sophia. The mythic details at this point refute the now waning theory of a "protoplanetary disk" with a central sun. An oval or ellipse is an egg-shaped form with two foci, whereas a circle has only one focus, its centerpoint.

Does the mythic image of Sophia-Sabaoth in a "structural coupling" (to borrow a term from Gaian theory) stand up against modern cosmology? The fact is, the orbits of the planets in our solar system are elliptical, not circular. Each planet, including the Earth, has two foci, the aphelion, more distant from the sun, and the perihelion, nearer to the sun. The sun is at the "center" of the orbits of the planets, but the orbital tracks actually have two centers. When Johannes Kepler determined the elliptical form of the planetary orbits in 1604, he declared that he had rediscovered the secret knowledge of the Egyptian Mysteries.

THE ABORTED FETUS

The triumph of the Anthropos over the Archons is the prominent theme pervading the sacred narrative of the Mysteries, the Fallen Goddess Scenario. The assertion that "humanity exists, and the offspring of humanity exists" is striking. Does it imply that the Gnostic seers detected in the Anthropos the genomic matrix of more than one strain of the human species? If so, the genetic template embedded in M42 would be the source of many human races, of which we on Earth are one strain. But an exceptional case, due to inhabiting the planet that uniquely embodies the Goddess who encoded the multi-strained Anthropos *ab origine*, from the beginning.

It strains the human mind to its limit to contemplate such a concept. What an extraordinary proposition of human origins. One must wonder, how could anyone have ever worked it out?

Surviving material on Gnostic anthropogenesis is scattered, corrupted, and inconsistent. The cosmologies in The Hypostasis of the Archons and On the Origin of the World present a jarring jumble of incidents, some repeated but with variations, others standing alone and seemingly extraneous. There is no uniform plotline for what transpired before Sophia morphed into the Earth. Among the rubble, baffling passages stand out like scenes in a badly edited movie, impossible to place in sequence. Yet these scenes often prove to be essential to the trajectory of the story arc.

For instance, On the Origin of the World describes a moment when "the heaven and his earth [KAZ] were destroyed by the troublemaker that was below them all. . . And the six heavens shook violently for the forces of chaos had destroyed it . . . and Sophia regarded the breakage and sent forth her power and cast him [Demiurge] down" (II,5:102). Reviewing and reworking the narrative to integrate such passages takes years, but the results can be quite stunning. Higher iterations of the FGS go well beyond the "legacy version" in chapter 10. The amplified narrative describes how the first Archontic world-system (stereoma) was so unstable that it collapsed. It came to be replaced by a second structure, which is the solar system as it exists today. These events happened before the Earth and its moon took form, but the sun was present and played a key role in establishing the second stereoma. In the first system—picture something like a badly engineered carousel—Saturn occupied the center. But Saturn is a planetary body with insufficient mass to hold the dwellpoint for such a platform. The sun is a solar body that can do that, so it took the central position in the second stereoma.

Anyone who finds this scenario far-fetched might consult the proponents of the Electric Universe / plasma cosmology model ("Thunderbolts Project"). Their efforts to develop a new paradigm for astrophysics run at times in close parallel to Sophianic cosmology. They argue for the existence of a previous version of the solar system with Saturn at the apex of a polar arrangement. Exactly what close restoration of the FGS tells us.

Eight out of nine episodes in the FGS cover events that transpire before Sophia turns into the Earth, and even then humanity has not arrived on the scene. Yet the conditions the human species will face when it finally emerges on the home planet are clearly prefigured in many passages of the preterrestrial story arc. Take the arrogance of the Demiurge, for instance: "It is I who am God, and there is no other apart from me." (The Reality of the Archons, NHC II, 4:94.20. The episode is repeated in several texts.) There is the primary dogma of monotheism, common to the three Abrahamic religions. The faithful take it as the supreme standard for their conception of the Creator. The Gnostic sees it as the deceit insinuated in the human mind by a monstrous alien, the demented pretender god who works against humanity and nature. Gnostics warned that the Archons are driven by envy (*phthonos*). They want to become like humans but they cannot, leaving four options: they can either deceive humanity into becoming like them, or flat out destroy it. Or, even worse, they can use tactics of deception to destroy humanity. Even worse again, *they can attempt to deceive it into destroying itself.*

Fast forward from the preterrestrial scenario of the FGS to 2020. Now something happens that has been a long, long time in the making. Sophia and Thelete did not design the human species to run on MS-DOS or Apple OS. The Anthropos runs on nous, a dose of divine intelligence. But the super-smart globalist overlords are implementing another plan. The manifesto of the Great Reset declares the intention to replace some people by machines and inoculate others with a nano-scale "operating system" that turns them into cyber-human hybrids. The vaccine contains fibroblasts derived from "lung tissue of a 14-week-old aborted Causasian male fetus" (MRC-5 product information). Ultimately, IT will run all transactions in the social order on technocratic-transhumanist gimmicks and "change what it means to be human."

In 2020 the entire world confronts the consummation of the work of the Archons. The assault is insane and inhumane, flagrant, punitive, and all-encompassing. Is there any way out of the nightmare? Can sanity be recovered? Can a true new world arise from the ruins of this horrific feat of deceit?

Unlike Old Testament prophets, Gnostics did not predict. But the sacred narrative does contain one passage that addresses the final defeat of the Archons. It describes Sophia's defiance of the Lord Archon, Yaldabaoth, who presumes to be the master of the universe:

> You are mistaken, blind one. There is an immortal Child of Light who came into this realm before you and who will appear among your spectral forms (*plasmata*). . . . He will trample you in scorn as potter's clay is pounded. And you will descend to your origin, the abyss, along with those who belong to you. For at the consummation of your works, the entire defect that has become revealed by the truth will be annihilated, and it will cease to be and will be as if it had never been. (On the Origin of the World, 103 passim)

Before turning into the Earth, Sophia is constantly in the presence of the Anthropos template, the cosmic matrix of the "immortal Child of Light," embedded in the Orion Nebula. This sight is there in the night sky, visible to the naked eye. But to perceive the cosmic locale of the origin of the human species is one thing, and to perceive humanity when it stands before you is another. The human psyche has a precise, innate setting for self-recognition, like a tri-focal lens that captures three overlaid plates. First comes recognition of yourself as a subject, the single-self identity. Next comes the perception of the humanity in you, signaling that you are a member of a species. (More precisely, a racial strain of the generic species.) And finally, there is the perception of the humanity in others. The IT takeover can only succeed by total annihilation of that threefold recognition and even the faculty that provides it. That is what it will take "to change what it means to be human," a stated goal of the Great Reset.

But what do we know about being human in the first place? Could the Archontic menace of technocratic control and transhumanist fantasy carry the impact it seemingly has, if the races of this Earth were grounded in a shared truth about human identity? If we really knew what we stand to lose, might we be more prepared to defend and preserve it, and finally defeat the machinations of the alien mind-set? A large issue, that one.

Fortunately, the Sophianic narrative contains an event charged with instructive insight on the identity and role of humankind in the natural world. It comes in episode 8 (9 in later revisions) with the description of a decisive event that happened after the Wisdom Goddess turned into the Earth.

14

THE COMING OF THE SYMBIONT

The first seven episodes of the Sophia mythos relate what happens to the Goddess up to the point when she morphs into the Earth and compromises her Aeonic form. In episode 8 there occurs another decisive event, quite different from what has preceded, because it transpires *after* life has begun to explode rampantly in the biosphere of the emergent planet.

Unfortunately, descriptive material on this key event is extremely scanty in the surviving materials. Crucial parts of the mythos are missing, like lost sections of a shattered mosaic. Sophia's metamorphosis into the Earth was certainly of paramount importance in the sacred narrative of the Mysteries, yet in order to trace and recover some essentials of that event, we are obliged to rely yet again on the writings of the Church Fathers against the Gnostics (also called the patristic literature, or simply the polemics). This is a dubious source of information, to say the least. Reading the "dossier for the prosecution," as it might be called, we must distinguish genuine elements of Gnostic knowledge from what has been unwittingly misconstrued or, more often, deliberately skewed and misrepresented. Disinformation is rife in the anti-Gnostic polemics. Half the time when it comes to Gnostic theology and philosophical argument, we can safely assume that the Fathers did not understand what they were refuting. Yet they would have had to represent some points clearly and accurately, if only to make their refutations more effective. With mythographic or trance-induced content, by contrast, it would have suited the patristic adversaries to present the material more or less accurately, so that its absurd and grotesque nature (to their minds) would be self-evident.

We may, then, expect to find the patristic writings rather more accurate in relating certain narrative details of the mythos than in representing intellectual notions held by the Gnostics.

FORMATTING PROBLEM

In episode 8 of the FGS, Sophia reaches the stage where her terrestrial body bursts with life. Fitted to the accepted geological timescale, this moment would correspond to the dawn of the Cambrian Age, about 585–550 million years ago, when the planet produced a profusion of shellfish and many organisms with skeletons. A bit later, in the Ordovician period, came the first fishes and land plants. With evolution running at warp speed, the varieties of fauna and flora were rampant and prodigious. The sheer profusion of biota overwhelmed Sophia. She was, after all, new to this state of cosmic motherhood! Fortunately, she could rely on the benefit of chrismation, the "anointing" of the Aeon Christos (episode 2). *Hermetic sealing* of all genomic plasms designed in the Pleroma insures morphogenetic identity upon their release into planetary laboratories. Thus, the myriad species erupting in the biosphere maintained their proper boundary settings, morphogenetically intact. But *interspecies* activity was another problem altogether. It was random, disorderly, and tending toward mass disruption. Sophia struggled to manage and coordinate the interactions between diverse multitudes of creatures and establish symbiotic harmony. But that specific task exceeded the range of her autopoetic powers. Her plight elicited a response from the Pleromic Aeons who had been witnessing the trajectory of her plunge from the outset.

Now Aeons united their attention to undertake a momentous project, an act of intervention. But how was it to be accomplished?

Ancient sources present an array of odd names for Aeons in the Pleroma: Mythical, Mingling, Ageless, Silence, Depth, Union, Self-grown, Pleasure, Immovable, and others. These names, which occur in Greek, do not translate in any meaningful way to our minds today unless they are taken to designate *discrete functions, actions specific to each Generator*. Like the words *electrician, drummer*, or *courier*. A courier is someone who delivers messages; the name connotes the function. Likewise for the baffling names of the Aeons who resemble biological agents, such as peptide, enzyme, and ketone. Such terms designate specific biological activities. Without comprehensive knowledge of the operations of the human body, they are meaningless.

As seen with chrismation, Aeonic functions are technically specific. Pleromic intercession for the specific problem facing Sophia could only have been accomplished by a divine agency that matched the task. It required an action to induce *symbiotic harmony* among the myriad species of fauna and flora. Species-specific evolution was insured by hermetic sealing, but full coordination of *interspecies* behavior had to come through a different solution. It required the Aeons to supply Sophia with an added capacity for assemblage of the multitudinous components of the planetary superorganism—technically, a force of aggregation. But is there a name among the Pleromic Aeons that fits that activity?

Restoration of the mythic narrative here raises a scripting issue that, I may safely presume, no conventional scholar would dare to attempt, or even consider. The challenge is daunting, but it cannot be ignored. The FGS is not merely a relic of ancient religion. It is also a current and ongoing project of imagination, like a movie being written as it is filmed. Fortunately, a name for the required function can be found: *Ekklesia*. Translated literally as "Church," it suggests an edifice for religious congregation in the Pleroma. Which is plainly absurd. Ekklesia derives from the Greek verb *kaleo*, "to call together." The technical function suited to Pleromic intercession would be exactly that, the power to congregate or aggregate. All through the natural world, different species commingle yet hold their proper boundaries. It is a miracle of life so common that it passes without notice, but try to imagine how nature would look if it were absent. That is what Sophia was facing.

The goal of the intercession was to congregate all forms of life and secure the paramount synergy of nature, symbiotic harmony among different species. The appropriate agency for this task was Ekklesia, Congregation, Aggregation. Specified as an agency, the Aggregator. Defined by its action to induce biospheric symbiosis, this Aeon might be called by a more user-friendly term, the Symbiont.

Only two ancient sources, *Against Heresies* (Book One, Ch. IV), attributed to Irenaeus, and the badly damaged treatise, *A Valentinian Exposition* (NHC XI,1), preserve traces of this momentous event, the coming of the Symbiont. Both versions follow the Christocentric doctrine of the Valentinian school, making Christos the agency of intercession. But the restoration of the Fallen Goddess Scenario in these pages follows the Sethian school. Hence, the scripting issue (signaled above) prompts an outrageous switch, the replacement of Christos with the Symbiont.* Accordingly modified, the paraphrase in Irenaeus reads:

> The Symbiont dwelling on high took pity on the sister Aeon, and having extended itself through and beyond the stauros [boundary of the Pleroma] it *imparted a figure* to Sophia, but merely as respected substance, not so as to impart intelligence... The Symbiont imparted to Sophia form *as respected intelligence*, and brought healing to her passions, separating them from her, but not so as to drive them out of her mind altogether. (*Against Heresies*, One, IV. Emphasis added)

This passage exhibits some subtle nuances, typical of Gnostic style, and unlikely to have been contrived by Irenaeus, who objected strongly to Pagan mythmaking (which would, in any case, have been beyond his capacities). If this passage is reliable, it clearly shows that the Gnostic seers who authored the Sophianic narrative had rather precise ideas about the rescue mission effectuated by the Pleromic gods. To venture a paraphrase: "The Symbiont *configured* events in the natural world, without altering the basic vital intelligence that nature draws from Sophia."

To "impart a figure" and to configure are the same action. In computer idiom, this is formatting. In the early stages of her Earthly metamorphosis, Sophia had a "formatting problem" with the multitudinous array of biota that sprang from her body. The intercession undertaken by the Symbiont was intended to solve this problem. How accurate is the suggested paraphrase in rendering the original language (Greek, surviving only in Latin) penned by Irenaeus around 180 c.e.? That is debatable, of course. The paraphrase is accurate, however, in the way it distinguishes activities of the planetary body autonomously commanded by Sophia from a specific aspect of coevolution provided by the Symbiont. The ramifications of that distinction are profound and far-reaching. Why? Because the intercession of the Symbiont happened before the

---

* On the long and hefty considerations for this switch, see the Author's Preface for this edition.

anthropine species emerged as the human animal living on the Earth. Which begs the question, What is the role of *that* animal in the vast symbiotic web of life?

A Divine Fragrance

Irenaeus, Bishop of Lyons, campaigned against heresies around 180 C.E., surfing the wave of anti-Gnostic outrage that broke over Pagan Europa in that century. He wrote in Greek, but only fragments of his work survive in that language, compared to numerous complete versions in Latin. Scholars unanimously claim that the NHC consists of translations into Coptic from Greek originals, which have never been found. However, there are residual clues.

The Egyptian desert has produced many treasures over the centuries. "P. Oxyrhynchus 405" is the title of four tattered fragments of papyrus found in a rubbish dump in northern Egypt around 1900. It contains around twenty words in Greek presumed to construct a sentence attributed to Irenaeus. The fragment has been dated to 200 C.E. With *Against Heresies* dated to 180 C.E., that is about as close to a "lost original" as it gets. The badly damaged tractate, *A Valentinian Exposition* (NHC XI, 2), offers a second source. It contains baffling, largely indecipherable passages that glitter off and on with fleeting allusions to Aeonic activity that only make sense—if they ever can—when fitted into a larger scenario: "from these places—the love (*agape*)—is emanated— the entire Pleroma—The persistence endures always, and—for also— the time—more [*that is*]—the proof of its great love" (XI,2, 18-30). The residual clue here is about persistence, that which endures: *hypomenein*. The passage asserts that the love of the Pleroma endures, persists. But how? What sense can be made of this statement? Where does it fit into a larger scenario?

A Valentinian Exposition presents a Christocentric version of Pleromic intercession. The Sethian revision draws upon ancient evidence from elsewhere. There are rare clues that support the outrageous switch. It happens that one of them comes from the same garbage heap where P. Oxy. 405 was found, and it goes like this: "The fowls of the heavens, and of the beasts, whatever is beneath the earth, or upon the earth, and the fishes of the sea, these are what draw you unto the Divine."[208]

One could not ask for a more explicit and succinct expression of Pagan animism. Scholars who do not themselves admit to animistic sensibilities designate this view of the world as pantheism, and panentheism: the Divine living in everything. Direct encounter with the Divine in the natural world is the default setting of the anthropine species. The Symbiont *preserves* the attraction of the Divine through the innate bond between humanity and the nonhuman world, including other animals. In animistic cultures, cross-species bonding came to be personified in certain figures who can be called liminal residents of the landscape. Significantly, both terms cited above begin with the suffix *pan-*, "all, inclusive, present everywhere." But Pan (considered closely in chapter 2, "Pagan Roots") is also the name for the ancient nature god of the Greek peoples. Was the human-goat hybrid a Pagan epiphany of the Symbiont? Perhaps so. Likewise perhaps for Kokopelli, the hunch-backed flute player of Native American legend. Passages in *A Valentinian Exposition* place Ekklesia close to Sophia in the intercession event: "And he wanted to [leave] the Thirtieth—being [*a syzygy*: coupling] of Man [RHOME] and Church, that is, Sophia—to surpass [Aeonic limit] and bring [down] the Pleroma." (XI,2: 31.36). The same text repeatedly uses the word *sperma*, "seed," in describing the activity of intercession.

The Latin *genius loci*, "guardian of a place," denotes an intermediary force that binds the human witness to the natural setting. Other figures identified in worldwide mythological lore may also stand for the haunting presence of the Symbiont after the feat of intercession was accomplished. "The persistence always endures—the proof of the great love of the Pleroma." The animistic premise that nature and the human psyche operate in union, dynamically linked, is fundamental to ecopsychology, as I have shown elsewhere in these pages. That being so, does the Symbiont persist within the depths of the psyche as well as it does throughout external nature? Might it be possible to detect something like an after-effect of the Symbiont, assuming the guise of an intrapsychic figure?

Exploration of that enticing question will be found in chapter 23, "The Species-Self Identity."

15

THE WAY OF THE REVEALERS

Sophia experienced many emotions in the process of turning into Gaia, the living Earth. If you want to know what they were, go out and walk in nature, in the wild. See what you feel—or better still, *see with your feelings*. Of course, not everything we may feel in the presence of nature corresponds to what the Goddess felt as she was morphing into the planet, or as she now lives, fully morphed. But we can learn to feel accurately what the planet feels. Humans can empathize with the passions of Sophia. We can make a discipline of awe and become transentient. Doing so, we might realize an altered sense of humanity.

If the Gnostics were right, we are a species emotionally equipped to grow into empathy with Sophia, and know how we fit into her story.

NATURAL WISDOM

The Gnostic revealers, who called themselves the Children of Seth, claimed a sacred lineage originating back into prehistoric times. There was great and enduring power in what they knew, yet the guardians of the Mysteries were not able to preserve their way of life after 400 C.E. Why not? One reason may be that the sacred, as it comes to expression in human experience, does not lend its power to aggression and domination. Consequently, it may also be difficult to protect. Not only the teachings and practices specific to the Mystery experience, but the very recognition of the Godhead of Nature, which is innate to the human species and essential to its survival, had to be suppressed for salvationist religion to prevail and the global program of patriarchy to be implemented. This momentous act of domination can best be understood by considering the mind-set of those who achieved it.

Sir John Woodroffe observed that "an ancient feature of the ancient Mysteries is the distinction it draws between the initiate whose Shakti is awake (*Prabuddha*) and the *Pasu*, the unillumined or 'material' man, as the Gnostics called him." To the initiates who were on intimate terms with Sophia, "material man" was the materialistically minded person who only sees in nature a depot of resources to be exploited for human purposes, or even for mere whims. "The Natural, which is the manifestation of the Mother of Nature, and the Spiritual or the Mother as She is in and by Herself, are one, but only the initiate truly recognizes this unity," Woodroffe wrote.[209] Paradoxically, materialistic people can be defined as those who do not recognize the true nature of the material world. This explains how a culture of rampant materialism can mindlessly destroy the natural resources of the planet we inhabit.

Yet even at the worst stage of full-scale societal immersion in blind destruction of the natural world, many people are still prone to recognize the sacred dimension of nature and react negatively to the predations of materialism. They are then forced by empathy with Gaia to adopt an adversarial posture of self-defense and nature defense. Aggressiveness is fundamental to materialism, but it can also play a role in defense of the sacred, including the sacredness of the Earth and nonhuman life. The difference between predatory and defensive aggression has been noted by Erich Fromm, who asserts that "man is phylogenetically a non-predatory animal, and hence his aggression, as far as its neurophysiological roots are concerned, is not of the predatory type."[210] It stands as a matter of choice if one believes this view or the opposing view, that humans are inherently predatory, prone to fight tooth and nail for "the survival of the fittest." In any case, common sense can tell the difference between aggression per se and aggression (the use of violent force) in the cause of self-defense. It remains to be seen how defensive aggression can be applied to challenge and defeat predatory aggression against the planet.

However clearly the Western initiates of Hypatia's time were able to see the perils of materialism—rooted as it is in the patriarchal agenda with its salvationist program of redemption as cover, which the initiates understood in great depth and with great psychological acumen, including the Archontic factor—they were not able to act with sufficient force of defensive aggression to protect the Mysteries. In a matter of a few centuries, the mounting wave of salvationist frenzy annihilated them.

HUMAN NOVELTY

The triumph of Christianity destroyed the tradition of the Mysteries and left the work of the Gnostic revealers in ruins. The sublime revelation of Gaia-Sophia was incomplete, but that was, in a sense, the way the telestai always conceived it. A Tantric scripture says, "Revelation (*Akasavani*) never ceases. When and wherever there is a true Rishi or Seer there is Revelation."[211] The tragedy was not that the Great Work of initiation was not completed, but that the millennial commitment to fostering human potential was brutally and ignorantly interrupted.

Yet the Great Work continues, and Sophia's story is ongoing. Episode 9 introduces the fascinating notion of Sophia's "correction" (*diorthosis*), as distinguished from her "conversion" (*epistrophe*), the process by which she turned into the Earth while still remaining essentially what she is, a massive yet mass-free torrent of Organic Light (episode 7). Both of these concepts are crucial to our engagement with the Goddess, the former because we are somehow implicated in her Correction, the latter because only through empathic communion with Sophia in the physical elements of the biosphere can we live into the role she dreamed for the Anthropos.

After the coming of the Symbiont, the Goddess was left to her own resources. Now totally identified with the life-processes of the planet she has become, Sophia finds herself in the world of her own Dreaming. Her isolation is, one could say, almost autistic. Gradually, a particular species called humanity emerges and joins the other species living in the Gaian habitat. The unfolding of human novelty, so eagerly anticipated by the Goddess, now begins. Considering the vast sweep of the sacred story, it is easy to leave ourselves out of the picture! But Sophia never does. To understand how we are implicated in her Dreaming, let's recapitulate the episodes:

After a singularity was released as a selfless offering from the Source (episode 1), Sophia and Thelete conjoined in a ritual dance to config-ure the Anthropos (episode 2), thus encoding the genome of our species with a specific endowment of traits and talents. Then the Pleroma as a whole projected the Anthropos into the *dema*, the fields of elementary or subatomic matter circulating in the galactic limbs (episode 3). When Sophia plunged from the Pleroma (episode 4), her fascination for human novelty directed her Dreaming toward an emergent world in the chaos below, but she had no idea that she herself would turn into that world! Her precipitant action caused the weird inorganic species of Archons to spring into being. Before the Earth was formed, they rapidly proceeded to construct their own world-system, overseen by the arrogant Demiurge who took himself for the only god in the cosmos (episode 5). To shame the Demiurge, Sophia invoked "the deathless Child of Light, the Anthropos," whose presence she beheld in the nebular glow of Orion.[212] The mother star Sabaoth, born from the nebula, was also composed of inorganic matter like the planetary world of the Archons. But Sabaoth was so impressed by the contrast between the Anthropos and the Archons that she "repented" and aligned herself with Sophia (episode 6). Then Sophia morphed into the Earth, which became captured in that system (episode 7). Finally, a concerted effort by the Pleromic Aeons affected a rescue mission to assist Sophia in the management of her vast and varied progeny—the coming of the Symbiont (episode 8).

The promise of human potential is the singularity that flickers in Sophia's Dreaming, *but with this novelty comes a certain risk of deviation.* Let's recall that Sophia herself deviated from the cosmic order, "moved by love or audacious yearning," Irenaeus says. Compelled by her own desire and acting without a consort, the Goddess is called *Prunikos*, "outrageous, exceeding the bounds of propriety." Her action can be compared to the shameless self-display of a prostitute. By the conversion of her divine currents into the sensory and material substance of the Earth, the "Whore of Wisdom" cavorted lasciviously with the elements.[213] Along with passion and pleasure on a cosmic scale, Sophia underwent immense convulsions of grief and confusion.

> This collection [of Sophia's passions] they [the heretics] declare was the substance of the matter from which this world was formed. For from [her desire of] returning [to him who gave her life], every soul belonging to this world, and that of the

Demiurge himself, derived its origin. All other things owed their beginning to her terror and sorrow. For from her tears all that is of a liquid nature was formed; from her smile all that is lucent; and from her grief and perplexity all the corporeal elements of the world. For at one time, as they affirm, she would weep and lament on account of being left alone in the midst of darkness and vacuity; while, at another time, reflecting on the light which had forsaken her, she would be filled with joy, and laugh; then, again, she would be struck with terror; or, at other times, would sink into consternation and bewilderment. (Irenaeus I, 4.2)

Empathy for the plight of the Goddess may be essential in seeing how to face our own plight on Earth. Like the Goddess, we are sensuously and physically enmeshed in the terrestrial world, and we are particularly prone to the extraterrestrial influence of the Archons who arose as an aberrant side effect of Sophia's fall. The realignment of the Goddess with the cosmic center—her Correction—depends on the one species most deeply implicated in her aberration. Gnostics did not precisely define how the human species contributes to Sophia's Correction, or if they did, the evidence does not survive. But the writings on hand make it clear that humankind faces a triple challenge: recognize its true cosmic origins in the Pleroma, find its evolutionary niche in the biosphere, and evolve its singular potential, thus achieving the *telos* or peak evolutionary aim for our species. Such is humanity's cosmic challenge, according to the Sophianic message of the Mysteries. But the seers of that ancient tradition warned that humanity cannot meet and master this challenge without overcoming the insidious deviance posed by our cosmic cousins, the Archons.

Error Theory

Self-knowledge is self-luminous and fundamental and the basis of all other knowledge. Owing to its transcendency it is beyond both prover and proof. It is self-realized (*Svanubhava*). But Shruti (Revelation) is the source from which this knowledge arises, as Shamkara says, by removing (as also to some extent reason may do) false notions concerning it. It reveals by removing the superincumbent mass of human error.[214]

Teachers in the Mystery Schools never posed an opposition between reason and revelation. Their method of education combined both, allowing one to enhance the other, but carefully preventing the rational, reductive side of reason from inhibiting our innate reception to Sacred Nature. Woodroffe shows Gnostic flair when he asserts that revelation removes "the superincumbent mass of human error." In their role as guardians of the ongoing revelation of Sophia, Gnostics were deeply concerned with human error, closely related to the Archontic factor in their worldview.

The Gnostic theory of error is one of the most sophisticated ideas ever conceived by the human mind in the mind's attempt to understand itself. It does not make Archons the source of human error but indicates their intrapsychic influence as a key factor that causes error to run wild, extrapolating beyond the scale of correction. The Anthropos is a learning animal. To learn we must be free to err, to make mistakes, for in correcting our mistakes we advance the process of learning in a way unique to our species. We evolve precisely because of the extraordinary scope of error we have been allowed. We evolve not just by learning, as all sentient creatures do, but especially by learning from our mistakes. The exceptionally wide latitude for error typifies human singularity. But if we allow our mistakes to go undetected and uncorrected, we demonstrate that singularity in a destructive way, a deviant way. Humanity alone is capable of such extensive deviance from the life-plan of Sophia that we threaten our own survival, and even seem to imperil the planet itself.

The *telestic* method of the revealers was fourfold: to preserve the ongoing revelation of the Divine Sophia in the Mystery experience (instruction by the Light); to cultivate human potential through the many facets of individual talent (the singularity of the Anthropos); to teach the theory of error (including the "high strangeness" of deviation by the Archons); and to develop noetic practices for fulfilling humanity's role in Sophia's Correction. Such was the agenda of the Mysteries, the Great Work of coevolution brutally interrupted by the assault of Christianity.

GNOSIS AND BUDDHISM

The passage from Sir John Woodroffe cited above highlights the parallel between Gnostic instruction and Asian teachings on the self-liberating nature of the foundation awareness. *Rigpa*, the name given to the foundation awareness in Dzogchen, is equivalent to the Gnostic *pronoia*, literally, "foreknowing," understood in the sense of a grounding awareness that exists before any knowing arises. Operating in the pre-thetic mode (Sartre's term for the mind acting before it posits a concept of its action), *pronoia* makes all intellection possible. Ch'an, Zen, and Dzogchen affirm that primordial awareness can never be defiled or obscured, although it seems to be. To realize enlightenment is to know directly how the foundation awareness clears and liberates itself, spontaneously, moment by moment. This transcendental insight would have been universally realized and applied by the revealers of Gnostic tradition. A revealer was a living Buddha, a teacher of enlightenment. So were the telestai, the teachers in the Mysteries, Buddhalike, yet they did not teach only enlightenment or the self-liberating nature of mind. They taught how to own and evolve the spark of creative genius inborn to our species. They inseminated culture, literature, and the sciences and arts.

The Western Mystery tradition differed from its Asian counterparts on two distinct points: its educational emphasis, just noted, and its dedication to the Magna Mater, Gaia-Sophia. Although there is ample evidence to equate, say, the Prajñaparamita of Mahayana Buddhism with the Aeon Sophia of the Gnostics, there are significant differences to be observed as well. Religious scholars such as Guiseppe Tucci and Edward Conze confirm the parallels—for instance, Tucci called the wisdom of the Hindu Tantras "the expression of Indian gnosis"—but tend to ignore the differences. A definitive essay by Conze, "Buddhism and Gnosis," published in 1979, outlines eight basic similarities and twenty-three close parallels between the two systems. In a key remark on the divergences, Conze wrote:

> [The tenor] of Gnostic Sophia literature is essentially different from that of the Buddhist wisdom books. Assuming that man has fallen into this world from a more perfect condition, the

Gnostics expended much ingenuity on trying to describe the
process which brought about this fall. Classical Buddhism shows
no interest in what may have preceded ignorance.[215]

Even though it misinterprets the Gnostic teaching on the Fall, this
remark is extremely pertinent in contrasting the revealers to their Asian
counterparts. Gnostics did not say that human beings have fallen into
this world from a more perfect condition. This is the most common
and insidious misperception about Gnostic teaching, repeated by many.
Gnostics asserted that *part of the Godhead* falls into an unusual engagement with material evolution. Sophia falls, not humanity. Yet this act is
not a split in the Godhead, as supposed in Persian duality (split-source
metaphysics). It is due to an overflow of divine generosity. Sophia fell
into her own Dreaming, but the Dreaming was anomalous because the
Goddess engaged in it unilaterally, without a Pleromic consort, and then
exceeded the Pleromic boundary. Her exceptional emanation became
our habitat.

The notion that humanity suffers from a fallen state is alien to genuine
Gnostic teaching and goes against the tellurian spirit of the Mysteries.
There is nothing in the Sophia mythos that says the Anthropos falls from
a more perfect condition, but there is a clear warning that our species
may fall under the deviant influence of the Archons, our cosmic cousins
out there in the planetary system. The warning of the mythos is that we
may betray our humanity by failing to realize and actualize its unique
status in the cosmic order. Needless to say, if we are ignorant that we
have a divine endowment in the first place, we are not likely to own and
develop it.

Conze rightly noted that Buddhism shows no interest in what gets
humanity into ignorance, but in the Mystery tradition knowing how this
happens was half the work. In its too often preclusive emphasis on the
"mind nature," Buddhism falls short of the nature-minded approach of
the Gnostics. The greatest difference between Buddhism and Gnosis is
that Gnosis provides a guiding narrative, a directive script for assisting
humanity to find its niche in the natural world, and Buddhism does not.

Let's recall that the Mystery adepts did not call themselves *gnostikoi*,
a name applied to them in an insulting way by their adversaries, the

Church Fathers, but telestai, "those who are aimed." The noun *telos* means "the aim," "the goal," "the ultimate that can be done," but it does not mean perfection. "The ultimate" is supremely attainable by developing a given potential to its optimal level, but perfection is unattainable. The standard of *zaddik* imposed by the Dead Sea sectarians implies a level of superhuman perfection that is unattainable, although humanity is measured by our efforts to attain it. The suprahuman ideal of *zaddik* defines salvationist religion and subjects its believers to an unliveable, inhumane standard. But telos implies *what can actually be attained*, and telestic method shows the way of attainment. The contrast between *zaddik* and *telos* is enormous and cannot be reconciled.

The Mysteries were teleological rites intended to enhance the full range of human faculties to the optimal level. Those who advanced to the higher ranks of the Mysteries assumed the sacred commitment to guide humanity by teaching self-direction. The telestic method both satisfied human needs and went beyond them, opening the way for each individual to realize transpersonal purpose. The guiding rule of the Revealers was: the transpersonal fullfils the personal, the personal cannot fulfill itself. The sacred commitment of the Mystery School guardians involved several initiatives that would have been common to all cells throughout the network in Europa, the Levant, and Egypt: instruction by the Light, participation in the revealer cycle, the consecration of the Anthropos, the disclosure of the inner guide, and development of the guiding story, the Sophia mythos. This is the legacy of the revealers, the deathless promise of Gnosis, ultimate wisdom, knowing as the gods know.

A SHEAF OF CUT WHEAT

The Latin orator Cicero, who is known to have been initiated at Eleusis, wrote: "In the Mysteries one learns more about nature than about the gods" (*On the Nature of the Gods*, 1.42). With the myth of the fallen Sophia at the center of their worldview, the Pagan initiates were consecrated to exploring the supernatural dimension of nature. To keep their communion with the Goddess alive and open-ended, they plunged repeatedly into deep sentient immersion with nature. The method they used to undergo the ultimate learning experience was conferred by the Goddess herself, as described in the Homeric hymn to Demeter:

> She taught them the ministry of her rites, And revealed to them her beautiful mysteries, Which are impossible to transgress, or pry into, or divulge, For so great is one's awe of the gods that it halts the tongue.

The hymn also hints at the sacrament partaken in the Goddess's rites: "the earth concealed the white barley, according to the plan of Demeter, she of the beautiful feet."[216]

THE ELEUSIS BAS-RELIEF

The heresy hunter Hippolytus (170–236 c.e.) reported a striking eyewitness detail from the Mysteries that has baffled scholars through the ages: at the moment the initiates emerged from their encounter with the Mystery Light, the hierophant who led the ceremony showed them "a sheaf of cut wheat." This action was considered to be "the great and marvelous mystery of the ultimate revelation" (*Refutation of All Heresies*, 5.28–31). Fragments from the ruins of Eleusis present three images that epitomize the organization, method, and supernatural source of Gnostic illumination, and make this arcane allusion comprehensible. The architrave frieze of the Lesser Propylaeum shows the sheaf of cut wheat, "white barley," the biological source of mystic illumination. Next to it is a sixteen-petalled rosette with interior and exterior petals. Next to this is the image of an upright urn or ringed pillar.[217]

The rosette was the symbol of the organization of the Mystery cells consisting of sixteen adepts, eight men and eight women as depicted in the Orphic bowl of the winged serpent and the Pietroasa bowl, two rare surviving artifacts of Mystery rituals.[218] In the Orphic bowl carved from greenish white alabaster, sixteen naked initiates, men and women alternating, lie on their backs with their feet touching. At the center of the bowl is the winged serpent of Kundalini, the occult source of supervitality, regeneration, and paranormal faculties.

Eight and eight doubled are universal signatures of Mystery cells. The Temple of Dendera displays high on its external façade a large eight-petalled rosette next to the head of a bull. This graphic code informs those who can read it that the Mystery cell operating from that temple dated its inception to the Age of the Bull that began in 4480 B.C.E. Although the Dendera temple is a late constructon of the Ptolemaic Period (332–30 B.C.E.), its zodiac attests to intimate knowledge of cosmic timing based on the complete precessional cycle of 25,920 years. Axes inscribed on the Dendera zodiac pinpoint specific dates in the Age of the Bull and even earlier, dates known to be associated with key moments in dynastic history. The members of the Denderic Mystery cell—possible source of the Nag Hammadi codices, as suggested above—would have been fully aware of preserving sacred knowledge going back thousands of years. The telestic method depended on initiates having a vast overview of human and planetary evolution, so that they could determine the lessons appropriate to humanity in each zodiacal age. In Mystery code "the Eighth" or Ogdoad indicated the realm of the zodiac, as well as the circle of adepts who divined in zodiacal patterns the guiding motifs of Gaian evolution.[219]

In Tibetan meditation ritual, the invocation of the White Tara involves the visualization of "a white eight-spoked wheel at the center of the heart chakra." The wheel emerges from a flood of white light seen when the practitioner unites with the image of the female Buddha. The divinity specific to this visualization is called Chintachakra Tara, "Wish-Fulfilling Wheel Tara."[220] It is probable that the Eightfold Wheel of the Law, symbol of the Buddha-dharma, is an Asian variant of the Mystery rosette. The cross-fertilization of Buddhist and Gnostic movements occurred in the Gandhara region of the Hindu Kush, the extreme point to which Alexander the Great penetrated into inner Asia.

The inner petals of the double rosette at Eleusis represent the initiates dedicated to retaining and developing the instructions received by repeated encounters with the Mystery Light, while the outer petals represent the eight initiates dedicated to interpreting, translating, and externally transmitting those instructions. These two roles were periodically rotated, allowing the adepts to concentrate on different tasks on different shifts. Equal and complementary efforts went into maintaining the secret operations (*orgia*, "workings") of the cell and maintaining the external, educational and training activities of the cell members. The roles changed seasonally and reflected the ages-old initiatory technique of guiding society by Goddess-centered rites of death and renewal. Temples were oriented to the seasonal points so that these rites could be enacted in situ.

Before the temples were built all this was enacted in open nature, in *nemeta* (sacred groves) and the majestic setting of megalithic circles, dolmens, and menhirs, under the circling stars.

All ancient testimony of the Mysteries attests to the sublime encounter with the Divine Light. This is a form of luminosity that does not appear to ordinary awareness, owing to the filters of human perception, including the egoic filter. The mental gloss of self-reflection is like light shining on a window pane that makes it impossible to see through the window. Once the ego melts away, the parameters of perception are shifted and the Light is there, a *substantial* presence in the world, soft, white, and shadowless. It is also sentient, animated and animating, aware of itself and what comes into contact with it. The illumined mystic in *The Sophia of Jesus Christ* praises the beauty of "the Light that shines without casting shadow, full of indescribable joy and ebullience" (Berlin Codex 115). The

Organic Light is everywhere and permeates all things. It does not shine *on* what is seen but *from* what is seen, emitting a soft white luminosity with the texture of marshmallow, in which matter floats.

Initiates encountered the living Light when their perception was altered by temporary ego death due to ingestion of the sacred brew, the *kykeon*. Once in its presence they were instructed by the Light itself. One of the most important lessons to come from this experience concerned the nature of perception. Normally we assume that our perception of the universe originates with us, the percipients. This point seems so self-evident that it hardly needs to be argued, or proven.

But what the ancient seers of the Mysteries learned about their perception of the world was immensely different from this assumption.

ANOTHER MIND

The cylindrical urn pictured in bas-relief on the Eleusis pediment represents the current of the Organic Light conceived as a cosmic downpour formed into round standing columns. The *telesterion* or inner sanctum where initiates encountered the Light was composed of many columns. The *mystes* in an altered state moved among them as if dancing through a slow Niagara of molten marble. In the motionless falls was immaculate stillness, as deep and dense as a bottomless pool of rolling thunder, the sound of silence, AUM. When the adepts concentrated on certain signals and signatures, the rolling silence broke into silence ringing with a rich orchestration of tones. Trained in clairaudience, the telestai listened with pitch-perfect discrimination, able to follow the cadence of specific tones as if they were tracing a vein of precious ore. The bas-relief on the pediment represents both an urn (hollow sound of the rolling silence) and a polished cylinder fitted with rings (high cadences of ringing silence). The undulant surges of the Organic Light were sound currents as well as visible waves of pale, lustrous radiance.[221]

Certain Mystery texts in the NHC compare the Mystery Light to a fountain overflowing with a soft rush of immense torrents. In the Discourse on the Eighth and the Ninth, the initiate exclaims,

I am Mind and yet I see another Mind, the one that animates my soul. I see the one that moves me to pure forgetfulness of myself. . . . I have found the origin of the power above all powers, that has no beginning. I see a fountain overflowing with life. (58 passim)

Those who can hold attention on the Organic Light enter "the assembly of the Eighth," a Mystery code term for members of the receiving cell (interior petals). The Apocryphon of John and The Sophia of Jesus Christ also describe torrents of mystic illumination. This "downloading" of the Mystery Light was depicted by the stylized pillar on the Eleusis pediment. The shadowless Organic Light is white and visible, manifesting everywhere, although it cannot be observed everywhere at once, in a single, encompassing gaze, because it literally overflows the human capacity of seeing.

To preserve the sacrosanct character of the Mysteries, the telestai set precise guidelines for initiation. They realized that the soft, mass-free porosity of the Organic Light cannot be detected in ordinary, ego-bound awareness. Yet they also understood the reluctance to dissolve the ego, and its tenacious tendency to reassert itself. Most of the time required for initiation involved preliminary training and counseling intended to bring the initiant to a level of impersonal transparency, such that when the ego was dissolved, its stubborn tendencies for reification would be minimal. Long before the moment they were initiated, participants would already have attained an extraordinary reduction of ego fixation. Preliminary preparation could take as long as twenty-one years, with the actual process of initiation accomplished in a matter of days.

The ancient rites celebrated at Eleusis and elsewhere required a sacrament to dissolve the ego and induce non-ordinary perception: the potion brewed from the white barley. This practice explains the third image on the Eleusis pediment: the sheaf of cut wheat. The sacramental intuition of nature has to be induced by the sacrament given by nature because the requisite surrender of ego cannot be achieved voluntarily, and for other reasons as well. The telestai used a brew of psychoactive plants to temporarily loosen and lift the cognitive filters that block direct perception of the Organic Light. Doing so, they followed the ages-old wisdom of indigenous people around the world. Andy Fisher observes in *Radical Ecopsychology*:

> Our life among others is one of "constant spiritual interchange," where through various kinds of contact-making the powers of meanings of nature are transmitted. Thus, a person may acquire the powers of a plant or animal by eating it.... A common Native American belief is that our "humanity remains incomplete and unhinged" until we have received such empowerment from other-than-human beings.[222]

Initiates in the Mysteries realized that the Goddess requires of those to whom she reveals herself the humility to admit that they cannot fully know what it means to be human without the inspired guidance of nonhuman beings, including plants.

Deeply concerned about schizophrenic side effects and egocentric control games typical of the Illuminati and their subjects, the telestai of the Pagan Mysteries relied on the plant world for guidance in the initiatory program. By contrast, the Illuminati program forbade experimentation with natural psychoactive plants, flowers, and fungi. In the biblical narrative, Yahweh (the chief Archon or Demiurge) forbids Adam and Eve from eating of the Tree of Knowledge, but Gnostic myth reverses the plot, making the Serpent an ally and the forbidden fruit a source of illumination. The purpose of the patriarchal taboo is to deny the primal religious experience that comes to humanity in communion with nature through the intermediary of sacred teacher-plants.* According to the thesis proposed by R. Gordon Wasson, the ritual ingestion of sacred plants was not only the core of shamanic practices going back to Paleolithic times, it is the origin of all genuine religious experience for the human species.[223]

Initiates at Eleusis ingested an entheogenic potion, the *kykeon*, to induce ego-free reception to interspecies communication.[224] In the ancient

---

* Sacred teacher plants comprise about 200 species known to modern pharmacology that exhibit a chemical composition able to produce psychomimetic effects. In the larger sense all plants are sacred, of course.

Mysteries as in the rites of shamanic psychopharmacology all around the world, sacred plants mediated between the human witness and the Organic Light, the primary substance body of Sophia. The consciousness that animates the nonhuman plant world keeps humanity humble and encourages us to observe and preserve the proper boundaries between culture and nature.

PERCEIVING GAIA

"The Perceptual Implications of Gaia," an article by David Abram written for *The Ecologist* (1985), is an outstanding statement on Gaia theory in terms of cognitive science and noetics. Although it makes no allusion to the Mysteries, this lucid essay touches the ultimate secret of initiation. Abram asserts that perception is "a reciprocal phenomenon organized as much by the surrounding world as by oneself." He suggests a two-way dynamic in perception, by contrast to the assumed one-way process of perceiving that does not affect the percipient, but merely offers a world to be observed. Writing a good decade before ecopsychology emerged, Abram says that "the psyche is a property of the ecosystem as a whole," and tacitly advises that we get beyond "the conviction that one's mind is anything other than the body itself."[225]

Abram's three points are intimately related to instruction by the Light, the supreme intiatory experience that culminated at Eleusis with that mysterious gesture by the hierophant. The sheaf of cut wheat displayed on the pediment there is more clearly seen in a cameo of the serpent-tailed Cecrops, guardian of the sanctuary at Eleusis.[226] Cecrops holds the sheaf to his chest and gestures with his finger to his lips.

Hippolytus, who was not initiated, reported that initiates were shown by the hierophant "a sheaf of wheat in silence reaped." This gesture revealed "the great, the marvelous, the most perfect secret for one initiated into the highest mystic truths" (*Refutation of all Heresies*, 5.3). This secret, which could only be learned directly from the Divine Light, reveals how our perception of the world is given externally, yet given in such a way that we are allowed to experience it as originating from us, internally.

Initiates who beheld the hierophantic gesture had been carefully prepared to realize several things at once. The stalk of wheat containing in its head the seed to reproduce itself mirrored their experience, even as they felt its biochemical effect. Standing there in a group, they realized that their minds were now fertile with seeds of wisdom to be transmitted to future generations. The grain in the head of the wheat held its reproductive power, but also, due to the fungus of ergot, its revelatory power. The *mystai* understood the two powers, biological and mystical, as a unity. They participated in body and mind in a higher type of generation, the epigenetic transmission of initiated wisdom.*

The sheaf of *cut* wheat revealed to the *mystai* the true nature of their own cognitive activity: the human mind is removed from nature, cut from the ground, its natural source. Mind appears to be independent, as if our perception of the world originated with us. The lesson of the hierophant's final gesture was heightened by the spectacle of the Rarian fields around Eleusis, full of grain rippling in the first light of day as the initiates emerged from the sanctuary. (The Greater Mysteries were celebrated in autumn, just before harvest.) They saw the cut sheaf in the hand of the hierophant and beyond it, the rippling fields of mature wheat sprouting from the earth. At that moment came the key illuminist insight, what they had come to know through instruction by the Light: as the wheat is given to us by Demeter, so is our cognition of the natural world, the place where it grows. The moment they emerged from absorption in the Organic Light the revelation intentionally given to the initiates was the certainty that our cognition of the external world is given externally through the power of the Earth goddess, Gaia, rather than internally, as we are wont to believe.

They realized where their cognition was actually grounded, now that they had Her Mind.

The certainty that our cerebral process of perceiving the world is given to us externally, and supported at every moment by the ambient field of the biosphere, is a sublime and rapturous experience, the signature

---

* Epigenetics, "above genetics," is a new paradigm in biological science. It allows for reprogramming of the DNA blueprint through a molecular mechanism, reverse transcriptase. The mRNA "operating system" for Covid-19 is an Archontic deviation of epigenesis.

of initiated awareness. This certainty informs Abram's seminal essay on the perceptual implications of Gaia. That perception is "a reciprocal phenomenon organized as much by the surrounding world as by oneself" was known directly in initiation. The *mystai* realized that perception is reciprocal, yes, but rather like the reciprocity in which a millionaire gives part of his fortune to someone who has nothing, and they lavishly spend it together. They realized that the entire cognitive field of human beings and of all sentient life is set up and supported by the external world, a projection of the living intelligence of the planet—in Abram's words, "a property of the ecosystem as a whole."

Receiving Her Mind, the *mystai* became instruments of Nature as selfless as the golden wheat waving in the fields around them. To them "the conviction that one's mind is anything other than the body itself" would not even have been a conviction, but a vivid, direct, irrefutable reality. Gnosis is full-body, psychosomatic illumination. You do not see the Organic Light in your head or in your mind, or even in your heart: you encounter it with your entire body, standing upright. The Mystery seers beheld the Organic Light while standing before it, without hallucinations or introspective distractions. Doing so, they received a download of Gaian intelligence, a direct influx from the Planetary Mind.

Perceiving Gaia as the Eleusinian initiates did was also an act of love, because the realization that our minds are not our own inspires immense affection for the Other. Humanity cannot survive without observing the interspecies bond. To love all that is not human, animals and plants, insects, the atmosphere, empowers us to be human. Loving Gaia is the highest calling of humanity. It is also the path of enlightenment that can lead us to coevolution in the most direct way, the safest and sanest way, because the spirituality of the Mystery experience grows directly from our biological endowment.

When the initiates emerged from the inner chamber at Eleusis into the clear autumnal light, and beheld the golden grain of the Rarian fields, and on the nearby hills, the outline of lithe poplars and cypress trees, they saw nature through the power of seeing given by nature, sacred and inviolable power.

PART THREE

HISTORY'S HARDEST LESSON

Demeter and Cecrops, Guardian of the Mysteries

THE END OF PATRIARCHY

M onotheism begins with a god who hates trees.

> Ye shall utterly destroy all the places wherein the nations which
> ye shall possess served their gods, upon the high mountains,
> and upon the hills, *and under every green tree*. And ye shall
> overthrow their altars, and break their pillars, and burn their
> idols with fire; and ye shall hew down the carved images of
> their gods, and destroy the names of them out of that place.
> (Deut. 12:2–3)

The Demiurge of the Old Testament is jealous, insisting that no other gods be honored before him. This demand of course implies that there are other gods, competing deities. They are Pagan divinities who pervade nature, manifesting in all manner of creatures, in clouds and rivers and trees, even in rocks. Monotheism will tolerate none of these sensuous immanent powers. It makes the Earth void of divinity, its inhabitants subject to an off-planet landlord.

By a strange twist the biblical deity who claims to have created the natural world forbids humanity to adore his handiwork. For an artist to insist on personal adoration for himself instead of, and in exclusion of, his work, is rather perverse considered in human terms, but with the supreme deity of the Hebrews it is perfectly normal. The wrathful, capricious temperament of Yahweh belies deep insecurity, for if Gnostic myth points to the truth, this god is a fraud, a violent and demented imposter. One Gnostic scholar describes him as a sullen, disgruntled bully, prone to fits of rage, who "propagates a gang of angelic henchmen, rulers ('archons') ... and goes about setting up his rule in the classic style of a petty tyrant."[227] The Demiurge and his legion of planetary drones are a parody of Jewish Scripture, but not just that. Like Philip K. Dick's metaphor of the Black Iron Prison, the Archons represent the metaphorical entrapment of the human spirit in self-contrived delusions.

"The message of an alien God and an evil Earth" was wrongly attributed to Gnostics by Christian ideologues who embraced the Jewish god and enforced the cult of monotheism.[228] To accuse the Pagan initiates of hating the flesh and rejecting the sensory world was plainly absurd, but the accusation served well to distract attention from the life-hating attitude of the accusers. To sustain the ruse, the divinity of the Earth, central to the Gnostic worldview, had to be utterly denied. But the Goddess was not so easily eliminated. In the Old Testament all traces of adoration for Jehovah's creation refer either directly or indirectly to Wisdom, the Divine Sophia, who is nature deified. This includes the so-called sapiential literature named after the Goddess: *sapientia* is Latin for wisdom. *Sapientia* is the distinctive trait of *Homo sapiens sapiens*. Gnostics taught that human sapience, the wisdom unique to our species, is corrupted by obedience to the imposter deity, the counterfeiting spirit, *antimimon pneuma*. The religion of the extraterrestrial father god ruptures humanity's empathic bond with the Earth, Sophia embodied, yet it is that same religion that has given humanity in the Western world its historical and spiritual identity.

ASHERAH AND MENORAH

The commandment of God in Deuteronomy was difficult to observe, and when observed, it produced some dire consequences. For one thing, it estranged the ancient Jews from their nature-worshiping neighbors in Canaan, and, indeed, from communion with the natural world itself. Discussing the antinature theology that Christianity inherited from Judaism, Paul Shepard observed that "the evangelical assertion of the new Word was not intended to make man fit into the world, but to verify his isolation. . . . Where traditional myths had been part of the great man-culture-nature-divine cybernetics, the new myth extolled the mystery of God's purpose, and the discontinuity of events."[229] From its inception, the "new myth" to be enacted historically on Earth worked against humanity's bond with the living planet, and denied human participation in the cyclic continuity of nature. "The mystery of God's purpose" necessitated the desecration of the holy sites of nature-loving people, trees and sacred objects in every green place. Denial of the sensual beauty of the natural world and the numinous power that flows from the Goddess into the human heart was the beginning of the fear of God. The need to destroy whatever arises from the Pagan sense for life is due to "a fear-instinct, and has been thorough, and has been really criminal, in the Christian world, from the first century until today," as D. H. Lawrence observed.[230]

The altars, pillars, and idols condemned by Yahweh were placed in groves of trees. The name of the Canaanite goddess Asteroth means "sacred tree," although this translation is redundant because all trees were sacred to the ancient people of the Near East and Europa. Trees were revered as divine before carved images of trees were set up to be worshiped. This shift was perhaps not due to psychic distancing, as we might suppose, but to environmental sensitivity in the region of Saharasia where verdant forests and rich grasslands were lost in a catastrophic climatic change after 4000 B.C.E.[231] Was Yahweh's condemnation symptomatic of reverse psychology? Did seeing fertile fields and sumptuous forests disappear in a few generations produce a sense of powerlessness that inverted itself into a vengeful lust for power over nature? "I will not stand by and watch nature destroy the woods and fields, so I will assert my own power to destroy, acting in nature's stead." This may be a plausible explanation for the "prior wounding" that led to the violent antinature fixation of patriarchal religion.

The Hebrew word *asherah* occurs over forty times in the first five books of the Bible, sometimes to indicate "the potent *cultic presence* of the female deity named *Asherah*," sometimes to indicate the carved wooden idols used to represent her.[232] Asteroth-Asterah-Astarte was native to the Near East and Palestine, but she belonged to a vast pantheon of tree goddesses found worldwide: the lovely hamadryads of Greek myth, such as Daphne the laurel; the Egyptian Isis who is often represented as a tree trunk sprouting bountiful leafy limbs; and the sensuous, sloe-eyed *apsaras* of Hindu mythology, including Queen Maya, the mother of the Buddha.[233] Yahweh's curse on the *asherah* was not his personal peeve, but

a pathological hatred that stuck to the deepest sources of human imagination where the psyche is rooted in nature. When the cults of the Goddess
were suppressed, her idols thrown down, her leafy groves laid bare, the
Jews invented the menorah to replace what their overlord commanded
them to destroy. The seven-branched candlestick is a schematic abstraction from nature, the spectral imitation of an *asherah*, a sacred tree.

In Gnostic terms the replication of nature in lifeless form exemplifies
HAL, Archontic simulation. In the shift from organic form to abstraction an entire range of values is lost and other values contrary to organic
life are adopted as if they were equal, or even superior to, the lost values.
This is the Archontic tactic of *antimimon*, countermimicking.* The
shift from *asherah* to menorah reveals how the Lie insinuates itself most
deeply in the human psyche. Jeffrey Burton Russell succinctly explains
the Zoroastrian notion of the Lie, *drugh*:

> The first human couple have free will, and initially they choose
> to love and serve Ohrmazd [Ahura Mazda, Absolute Good]. But
> Ahriman [Absolute Evil] tempts them to sin by using against
> them the essence of sin itself: the Lie. The lie is that Ahriman,
> not Ohrmazd, has created the world, and Mashye and Mashyana
> [the primal parents] believe it.[234]

For the ancient Hebrews who adopted this scenario, the lie Yahweh
tells them is that he, not Sophia, created the world. And they believed it.
This inceptive Archontic deceit about the creation of the world mutated
into a delusional narrative that uniquely possessed the Hebrews. Like
a crooked contract devised by an evil swindler, the Lie contains some
nefarious subclauses. The false creator-god confers on his devotees the
privileged status of an elect, the Chosen People. There is a real estate
provision to insure ultimate possession of the Earth. Their mandate

---

* Antimimon 2020: Measures to save lives ruin lives and incite suicide. An IT-linked
  vaccine to immunize against a virus attacks the natural immune system in which viruses
  (exosomes) act as benevolent agents of adaptation. Sanitization prescribed to protect
  health inflicts deleterious effects on health. Social distancing to save lives is a psychological
  torture technique used by three-letter agencies. Mask-wearing is like waterboarding but
  you choke on your own saliva. Carbon dioxide is toxic, but you have to rebreathe it to
  protect others.

requires adherence to a hateful ideology of race supremacy that eventually morphs, after centuries, into a full-blown psychosis: the elected race does not merely serve the off-planet deity, it becomes the presence of that deity in the world (the Sabbatean-Frankist heresy, 1666). This permutation is so pernicious that it operates like a biological imperative, as if the alien forces hacked into the neural circuitry of their proxies. The fate of the Hebrews delivered them into the torment of a god-complex fixated on domination of the world, all based on a lie about the creation of the world. This was the consummate setup for paranoid schizophrenia. And still is.

From its origins Jewish religion exhibited a marked tendency for Archontic substitution and the co-optation process that goes along with it, as seen in the menorah. When the germ of religious dementia in the Zaddikim went pandemic in Christianity, converts to the new faith co-opted Pagan images and ideas in a furious totalitarian spirit of righteousness, cleverly legitimated by ideologues such as Saint Augustine:

> When temples, idols, groves, etc., are thrown down by permission from the authorities, although our taking part in this work is a clear proof of our not honouring, but rather abhorring, these things, we must nevertheless forbear from appropriating them to our own personal and private use; so that it may be manifest that in overthrowing these we are influenced, not by greed, but by piety. When, however, the spoils of these places are applied to the benefit of the community and devoted to the service of God, they are dealt with in the same manner as the men themselves when they are turned from impiety and sacrilege to the true religion.[235]

The command of Yahweh from Deuteronomy drove Church political policy, and it still does, although the process disguises itself. It has often been observed that Christianity is rich in graphic imagery of the kind forbidden in Judaism. This is because salvationism in Europe and the European colonies enslaved the native imagination, co-opted the indigenous creativity, and coerced the populace to fabricate religious décor. Yet the converted peoples defiantly preserved their imaginative life, often making Christian art disguise their indigenous ways and tribal memories. Islam was a later mutation of the Zaddikite ideological virus, but in a more virulent form that attacked indigenous capacities even more strongly, exactly in the way viruses mutate to overcome immune defenses. Thus, Islamic religion reasserted the taboo on visual imagery (iconoclasm) and forced a return to abstraction from natural forms, the principal mark of Archontic mentality.

The Gnostic theory of error carefully traces the elision from error to evil, and does not equate them. *Drugh*, "the Lie," is an advanced form of error that readily blurs into evil. Deceit is evil, even when those who practice it do so in error and blindness, out of sheer ignorance. When she shamed the Demiurge, Sophia called him Samael, "the blind one." In Zoroastrian religion, *drugh* opposes the principle of truth and justice, *asha*. (And there is the root of *asherah*, by the way. The English word *truth* derives from the archaic root *dreu*, "tree," related to the Greek *dryad*, "tree nymph," and the Celtic word for shaman-priest, *druid*. Truth is about trees.) Once the Hebrew priesthood adopted split-source duality during the Babylonian Captivity, they formulated a homegrown version of Zoroastrianism, bizarrely twisted. Countermimicry is the single most essential factor in the weird deviance that unfolded in Jewish religion, setting up the male-god fixation.

It is also the hallmark of the technocratic imperative to run the world on AI. The assertion that intelligence can be artificial is yet another insane permutation of the Archontic Lie.

MODEL MORALITY

The father god who dictates rules for living is not a theological supposition. Rather, it is a mental fixation that arises automatically when organic reality is co-opted in a lifeless replica, or, to say the same thing otherwise, when a concept rooted in sensory experience is replaced by a denatured form of thinking conceived to exist in an abstract or transmundane setting, off-planet, rather than in the natural world. To repress the goddess Asteroth, living trees had to be destroyed and her sacred rites performed "in every green place," forbidden. The organic form of the tree was then replicated in the menorah, but the menorah does not *represent* the tree. The shift from organic form to replication insinuates a value contrary to the living reality so displaced. Barbara Walker notes that the menorah, which is often "decorated with yonic symbols," recalls the sacred tree of seven branches reaching into the night sky, and corresponding to the Seven Sisters, a constellation mentioned in the Bible (the Pleiades).[236] All this is far from what it symbolized in Jewish liturgy: the power of the monotheistic male deity who creates the world, and rests from his labor, in seven days. To the Gnostics seven was the number of the Archons. The Hebdomad was the domain of Yaldabaoth, the demented god who falsely claims to have created the natural world. The menorah replicates a tree but replaces the values of nature and the Divine Sophia, who is nature incarnate, with a contrary set of antinatural values. It is as if you mind-modeled nature and then imagined that the lifeless model in your mind itself produces nature.

The rise of Jewish monotheism was an immensely powerful event in human experience, but not because monotheism was ever true or good or right for humanity. The male-god fixation belies the preference for simulation over reality that is *the primary innate threat of deviation for the human species*, Gnostics warned. We incur this risk due to being exceptionally endowed with modeling and abstracting faculties. *Preference for replication will come to the fore in human cerebral activity, taking on a life of its own, if it is not detected and kept within limits.* It is this preference that erects and empowers the male creator god in human imagination. Yahweh-Yaldabaoth is the god-idea that conforms best to our mind-modeling propensities. We are created "in His image" because in the mono-deity we falsely see ourselves reflected at the height of our replicating powers.

Replication is reductive to an infinite degree because abstract modeling tends automatically to generate models of models of models, thus inducing the illusion that everything that exists can be rendered in a single master model, a supreme and all-inclusive idol-idea: monotheism. In the Sophia mythos, the planetary system of the Archons is a "scale model" of fractal patterns in the Pleroma, but the celestial clockwork is not alive, not sentient and aware, as the Pleroma is and as Earth is. The power of inorganic forms cannot be denied, however. All that is inorganic has immense structural and mimetic or duplicative force, as seen in crystal formations such as quartz and bone. The architecture of inorganic form can be magnificent, but it does not support sentient, animated experience.

Likewise, countermimicry that replaces living form by abstraction does not support living, self-conscious experience but drives humanity into blind, antihuman, zombielike behavior.

Jehovah is the arrogant god who models reality (Archons imitating the Pleroma) and imposes a model reality in place of life's organic unfoldment. The Archontic tactic is to replicate and dissimulate, so that the replica carries values contrary to what it copies. The treelike menorah commemorates a god who hates trees. The monotheistic male god is extremely rigorous with this tactic. In the Old Testament narrative Yahweh was not satisfied to drive the imaginative, picturing faculties of his people into abstraction—"Thou shalt not make unto thee any carved image"—so he goes further, much further. He inflicts the same imprecation upon another faculty crucial to morality and choice: our narrative, storytelling powers. He demands that history be a single plot of which He, who stands beyond the world, is the sole author and the executor. Rather than a story open to learning and discovery, enriched by constantly evolving interaction with the natural setting where human experience is reflected, the male deity imposes a totalitarian drama whose outcome depends on supernatural intervention. Archontic replication (the Coptic HAL, "simulation") is not mere imitation but a process that insinuates values working against life. Countermimicry of humanity's storytelling genius gives patriarchy its supreme advantage over the genuine and spontaneous evolution of our species.

How does Jewish sacred narrative in the Old Testament differ from other indigenous tribal narratives? It differs dramatically on two counts. First, the pattern of historical abuse set up in the Old Testament is elevated to a "Divine Plan," but not in the same sense, say, that quarrels among the gods in Greek myth are reflected in human conflict. Pagan myth always has a psychological value, and often an ambivalent one, pointing to *the clash of instincts within human nature*; yet the resolution of conflict has to come down to human capacity. The directive script of the ancient Hebrews, charged with the wrath of God and fear of the Lord, makes off-planet, extrahuman resolution the only possible solution for human conflict. Ultimately, historical violence is anchored in familial abuse.[237] Jehovah is the reification of a father complex that is not by any means unique to the culture that produced it. The tyrannical, tormenting father who also judges and rewards is the main agent of patriarchy in all cultures. The power of the father god in the human psyche is directly proportional to the power of the father figure in a family constellation. Jewish sacred narrative is unique in making the dysfunctionality of the human family the condition for the Creator's "final solution" of the historical drama: Judgment Day.

There is a second difference between Jewish sacred history and indigenous narratives: the biblical directive script is about psychic distancing from nature and alienation from generic humanness. This is contrary to the universal form of indigenous narrative that relates how "the people" emerge from nature, but remain grounded there, reflected in their habitat where they learn to live by observing organic laws and interacting with other species. The rules for living for the ancient Hebrews came from *outside the natural world* in the form of a model morality dictated by a distant superterrestrial deity. Such is the Archontic character of the Jewish moral code, widely taken as paradigmatic for humanity as a whole. The code comes packaged in a story that is itself a product of insidious counter-mimicry: salvation narrative is to the story of humanity's coevolution with nature (genuine indigenous narrative) what the menorah is to the *asherah*.

HUMANITY BETRAYED

Perhaps the hardest lesson of history is that biblical salvation narrative does not lead to the highest fulfillment of human potential, but to its betrayal. It could be said that in patriarchy, humanity has been betrayed by the deific father figure. The denial around this act of betrayal is so deep that a *fantasy solution* has to be contrived to avoid facing it. (Recall that both Erich Fromm and D. H. Lawrence observed the tendency in Judeo-Christian religion to concoct a fantasy solution for failure to live up to God's inhumane expectations.) In a pathological twist that takes many generations to devolve, the experience of being betrayed plays over into the act of self-betrayal. The grand scenario of religious experience in the West presents chapter after chapter of humanity's self-betrayal, disguised as a process of expiation to win the love of the absent father god.

The directive script of Judeo-Christian-Islamic monotheism impels our self-betrayal, because the script replicates indigenous narrative, the story of coevolution that we really *could* be developing and enacting, and deceptively insinuates antihuman and antinatural values in its place. Hebrew monotheism is often associated with ethical idealism, as if the model morality dictated by the father god guarantees the best possible behavior on Earth. But if humans possess an innate capacity for moral discernment, such a capacity cannot be commanded from without, nor imposed through rules and formulas from on high. At its worst, the power delegated to "authorities" and "rulers" subverts and eventually annihilates human conscience.

Understanding the dynamics of countermimicry is not easy, but without exposing how the process works, we will never disengage it. Even a mythologist and cultural historian as astute as William Irwin Thompson cannot see his way past the Archontic spin of salvation narrative. In *Transforming History*, where he outlines a home-schooling curriculum for the future, Thompson calls the Old Testament "a pivotal document in the cultural evolution of consciousness" and asserts that "history is the medium through which the mind moves to its destiny with god."[238] The claim that biblical history presents a model of moral education for humanity has profoundly shaped the course of human experience, no question about it, but has it done so for the betterment of humankind and the planet? If morality is something other than a modeling of behavior by predetermined rules, this claim is wrong, dangerously wrong. The ancient Hebrews did not discover conscience, the power to choose what is right. They merely introduced a set of rules purporting to dictate what is right.

Asserting the bioethics of deep ecology, Arne Naess wrote: "Just as we need no morals to make us breathe, you need no moral exhortation to show care."[239] Rooted in nature, humanity does not need preset behavioral rules to follow, but uprooted from nature we are compelled to replicate what we're missing. This is where the Archontic factor subverts human potential and "the mind moves to its destiny with god." Exposing and overcoming co-optive replication may be *the* spiritual challenge that decides the fate of humankind. A steep challenge it is, but look at the alternative. Behind the ages-old rhetoric about "the messianic destiny that awaits at the end of history" (Thompson again) looms the reality of the world as it is today:

The terror of history lies in the great destruction it has wrought on our planet and our people, and in the perversion of our natural religious sensitivities to place and the source of Life. We are left with the dull mentality of the competitive, acquisitive, contractual being whose essence is determined by the outcome of situations. Thought is consumed in the fearful expectancies of coming events, daily tedium, and sentimental recall of the past. As historical beings, we stand condemned by our history and are helpless in the face of it.[240]

The essential lessons of history are not easy to see, because they are lessons *about* history as much as lessons to be drawn from it. To penetrate "the dynamic of the pseudomyth, history," as Paul Shepard called it, requires a lot of close textual analysis, of course. More crucially, it necessitates a deep, dispassionate look into the human psyche to see how salvation history mirrors the hidden workings of humankind's most narcissistic, self-destructive impulses.

One of the more sobering lessons of this process is that history cannot teach us how to be human, but it can and does condition us to accept and enact inhumanity. This lesson touches the essence of the Gnostic protest against the Judeo-Christian salvation narrative, the directive script of Western civilization. The Levantine Gnostics tried to warn the people of their time and setting about the risk of humanity abandoning its divine birthright, surrendering its role in coevolution, and betraying its authentic identity, the Anthropos. In short, they had profound insight into the psychological sources of the dominator culture of the authorities. "Gnostics realized the true source of the constriction of patriarchal structures to lie in the Demiurge," as one scholar astutely noted.[241]

The god who hates trees is the founding father of toxic patriarchy.

Accessory to Evil

From its inception patriarchy has relied on salvation narrative to underwrite its program of genocide, ecocide, sexual repression, child abuse, social domination, and spiritual control. This script works beautifully for the dominator agenda because it was deliberately written for it. How can a story about love, forgiveness, and divine benevolence endorse the perpetration of evil? This seems impossible and against all reason, until we realize that the story is not what it appears to be. The salvation narrative of the Bible is *a story of perpetration*, conceived to support and legitimate the program of "the authorities," the Archons. In the New Testament the true intent of the narrative is disguised in banal adages about love, grace, forgiveness, charity, and other noble principles.

The great religious ideals of humanity expressed in salvation narrative are not the remedy to the pathological violence that engulfs us, they are complicit in it. The pathology originated with those ideals. They feed and legitimate it. They encourage and excuse it. This is perhaps the hardest, most bitter lesson that history can teach us.

Defenders of their faith often argue that crimes against humanity committed in the name of Jehovah or God or Allah are the deeds of "extremists" who do not represent the true principles of love, peace, and tolerance enshrined in the religious creeds they invoke. But the extremists maintain that *they* are the true believers, selflessly willing to act on divinely dictated principles. Where is the final truth here? Are perpetrators who invoke a divine sanction for their acts the true exemplars of their faith, as they claim, or are they violent aberrations from the norm, as the other, nonperpetrating members of the same faith would represent them?

History shows that the religious ideals attached to salvation narrative have consistently been used to legitimate violence, rape, genocide, and destruction of the natural world. Today, as I write these words, the world is wracked by an ecological crisis due to antinature theology, and consumed by violence and terrorism rooted in religious causes. In Iraq suicide bombers massacre their own people on a daily basis, either for colluding with the occupation forces, or for being on the wrong side of a medieval dispute over the succession from Muhammad. The commander-in-chief of the occupation forces has openly admitted that the Christian father god guides his political decisions, thus attributing to God's plan a fascist agenda that inflicts murder and oppression on countless people in the Near East and elsewhere in the world. The work of the perpetrators is double destruction: to take life and to ruin lives. If they are lucky enough not to be caught up in the mayhem, Muslims and their Christian and Jewish counterparts stand aside, watching what is done in the name of their cherished beliefs. In the final balance the people who commit and promote violence and murder in the expression of religious beliefs may be a minute fraction of the faithful, but they are the ones who determine the course of events, shape history, affect society, and threaten the biosphere.

How can an aberrant few who pervert the religious principles they claim to uphold have such preponderant power in the world?

One explanation would be unanimity of belief. Even when passively held and not enacted by most believers, religious beliefs can inspire and legitimate extreme actions done by a righteous few. For instance, belief in divine retribution is part of the creed shared by Jews, Christians, and Muslims alike. Many good and decent people do not act on this belief, however. They do not make themselves instruments of God's power to exact retribution. Some few do, and the entire world suffers the consequences. Religious extremists gain a disproportionate measure of power through the passive consent of those who share their belief system—and that would be billions of believers. Although many Christians object to the invocation of their beliefs in the cause of war and politics, they still identify with beliefs such as the mission of the righteous few to fulfill God's plan (second component of the redeemer complex) and a final day of reckoning when God makes all things right (fourth component). Unanimity of belief is a binding force that gives common identity to believers so that they do not have to face life's difficulties entirely on their own. Equally so, it fosters a blind force of collusion that implicates all believers in the actions taken by fellow believers, even if they are but a minute number of the faithful.

It might be objected that the *interpretation* of the beliefs that good, peace-loving people hold in common with extremists, sets them apart from the extremists. However, the fundamental force of religion does not inhere in its interpretations. In reality, interpretations count for little, although they do provide convenient cover to hide behind when blood runs in God's name. A twofold dynamic operates in unanimity: identification with *beliefs*, and participation in the *story* in which the beliefs are scripted or encoded. Nonextremist peace-loving people find their identity in beliefs, but they do not enact the destructive behavior that could be, and often is, attributed to the beliefs they hold. They also adhere to the story that enshrines their belief system, but they interiorize it, holding it as an article of personal faith, not to be imposed on others. Extremists who enact violence in the expression of their beliefs partic-ipate in the story of their faith in a very different way. Sectarian and fundamentalist violence relies less on acting on beliefs than from *enacting the story* in which the beliefs are encoded.

Narrative Spell

The power of the story is what turns believers into dangerous fanatics. This is a most dangerous situation, for the narrative spell of salvation history can drive the entire human race toward deviant and inhumane behavior. Human beings can act contrary to their own humanity if they are following a script about what it means to be human that is errone-ous, delusional, and loaded with false expectations. I submit that this is precisely the danger that Gnostics saw in the salvation narrative of the early Christians.

Perpetrators often cite passages of Scripture to justify actions such as suicide bombing or the invasion of Iraq, but they are compelled above all else by the dramatic force of the story they are living out. Today, various factions of society are competing to see who can act out the end-game narrative in the most violent, dramatic way. The power of unanimity favors the "extremists" because they follow a script attributed to superhuman authorship: nonextremist believers cannot challenge the script without going against superhuman authority, which they are, as believers, not inclined to do, or unable to do. Average, tolerant, peace-loving folk do not exteriorize the story of their faith in a violent manner, yet they are accessory to the violence inherent in the story. Tolerant believers ("moderates" in the jargon of the daily news) may have a deeply pious regard for the story in which their religious beliefs are encoded, or a merely sentimental attachment. In either case they are usually not compelled to act out the imperatives that inform the script. Nevertheless, the force of unanimity throws them into collusion with those who do. There is another hard and bitter lesson to be learned from history: how good people can be accessory to evil by sharing the belief system of the perpetrators. Belief implicates those who believe, and it implicates them absolutely.

To understand this alarming situation is to recognize how difficult it would be for things to be otherwise. Suppose that good, decent people were to assert the power of their convictions against the perversion of those convictions by fanatics. How could they do it? The force of unanimity sets up a situation in which the few dominate the many. Unless the moderates confront and oppose the rabid few in a direct and dramatic manner, almost on a one-to-one basis, there will be no change in the dynamic. Unless moderate, peace-loving people take responsibility to act decisively, perpetrators and perpetrating groups will always have the edge. They will gain an excess of power from the passive collusion of those who share their belief system. This explains how evil and wrongdoing can prevail in the world even though, at any given moment, there are countless more good and decent people acting with kindness and tolerance than there are perpetrators.

There is no totalitarian solution to violence. There are diverse causes and types of violence in the world, and not all perpetration of violence seen in history can be attributed to those who follow the salvation narrative. But the violence that has most profoundly shaped the entire world, exacted the greatest price in human suffering, caused untold harm to nonhuman creatures, and disastrously affected the environment—*that* violence *is* driven and indemnified by the redeemer complex. To undo just the violence arising from that source would already be an immense spiritual victory for the future.

Patriarchy, the primary historical instrument of domination, uses salvationist beliefs to secure unanimity but, as cultural anthropologist René Girard observed, "religion protects man only as long as its ultimate foundations are not revealed."[242] This is a startling remark, but it leaves us wondering: Protects man from what? It might be thought that lofty ideals such as charity, tolerance, and forgiveness, which are written into the salvation narrative, serve to protect us from violence. But Girard disagrees, and so do I. Religion protects humanity from seeing its complicity in the violence that infects religious beliefs. This is not the only kind of violence in the world, but it is by far the most insidious, lethal, and far-reaching.

To reiterate: Hard-core perpetrators differ from non-harm-doing believers by their fanatical enactment of the story in which their beliefs are scripted. Kind, decent, well-meaning people may honor the story, and do not need to live it aggressively, yet their lives are dominated by those who do. How can this collusive bond can be broken? By exposing and refuting the dementia of salvationist beliefs, as the Gnostics did. And even more crucially, by breaking the narrative spell of the dominators. The refusal to go along with the salvation narrative might be called spiritual disobedience, comparable to the civil disobedience of Thoreau and Gandhi.

The most effective way to defeat patriarchy is to defy and disown its self-legitimating narrative.

Many people of traditional religious faith could do this and still retain their faith in the principles of love, charity, peace, and tolerance. Is it possible to have faith in those principles in themselves, independent of a legitimating narrative? If it is not, the world may not be saved from salvationism. However, by disowning the story yet remaining true to their ideals, kindhearted people would prove that religion can be practiced without colluding with those who make it a pretext for domination. To dissociate from the salvation narrative would be the most effective way for decent and peace-loving people to end their complicity with authoritarian systems, whatever form they take. Breaking the narrative spell is the game-changer in the battle for human sanity.

THE DIVINE SCAPEGOAT

In considering why some Europeans committed genocide and mind-less destruction of nature in the New World—a historical pattern by no means over, but continuing furiously on a global scale with corpo-rate agendas implemented by IT now at the forefront of the assault—I initially proposed that the victim-perpetrator bond works in the course of history as it is known to work in dysfunctional families. The redeemer complex, the insidious core of salvationist belief, asserts the redemptive value of suffering in such a way that it legitimates and even sanctifies suffering. On top of all that, the victim-perpetrator bond makes suffering extremely contagious. The invaders of the New World were descendants of indigenous peoples whose way of life was destroyed by carriers of the Palestinian redeemer complex, as if by a biological plague. Infected by the same virus, they in turn destroyed the way of life of the indigenous people of the Americas. Like the Christians who converted their distant ancestors to the redeemer complex, some of the invaders believed in a god who could redeem sin, and this belief permitted them to commit sin, to inflict suffering in His cause and even to feel sanctimonious about it. Spanish mercenaries burned the natives of Central America by thirteens "in honor of Our Redeemer and the Twelve Apostles," Bartholomew de las Casas reported.[243]

The Sanctified Victim

The lethal insanity of the victim-perpetrator bond is staggering. The complicity of victims and perpetrators is a gruesome pact, but there is still a deeper dimension to this horror. Discussing the question of what "makes God accessory to the manifest sinfulness of the human world,"

Alan Watts observed: "Beyond this theological nightmare there is the fascination of supernal masochism."[244] The factor of "supernal masochism" comes to expression in what can be called *victim-perpetrator collusion*. The two parties are not merely complicit in their beliefs, they are intricately and intimately codependent in their actions. Victims and perpetrators need each other desperately and use each other both viciously and vicariously to keep their bond intact. This is not true of first-time, out-of-the-blue victims, of course, but of the addicted kind, those who come back for more, glorify in the victim role and blindly follow the same narrative as the perpetrators, convinced that it puts them on higher moral ground than those who harm them, or believing they are called to suffer for the sake of others.

But now a huge objection: If the redeemer complex is so utterly wrong, so contrary to the essential good nature of humanity, how can it be so powerful? If it is really so demented, how can the salvation narrative capture and convince so many people? If the answer to this question is lacking so far, it is because the breakdown of the four components of the redeemer complex and their permutations through history has not yet exposed the nucleus of the complex, the numinous source of its overwhelming power: the divine victim.

In his two main works, *Things Hidden from the Foundation of the World* and *Violence and the Sacred*, cultural anthropologist René Girard probed deeply into the redeemer complex. At many points his analysis comes close to the Gnostic understanding of redemption theology and the threat it poses to human society. Girard identifies what he calls (rightly so, I reckon) the "generative mechanism" of all religion. This is "the victimage mechanism" or "surrogate victim syndrome."[245] In plain English (Girard is a Catholic revisionist, postmodern deconstructionist, and cultural anthropologist with a lisp, and he's French), this mechanism is *scapegoating*. It manifests in social enmeshment as violence enacted through a ritual of victimization that simultaneously expiates and perpetuates the causes of violence.

The original scapegoat was the sacred king, a figure we encountered in tracing Jewish theocracy. In the time before male-only theocracy emerged around 4000 B.C.E., people living in pre-urban societies had to come to terms with wrongdoing in their midst. They realized that perpetration will happen, more often than not, with no way to discover who the perpetrator is. If the perpetrator cannot be found and punished, victims must accept living without compensation and closure. Most of the time, this is the way it goes in the world. There can be no absolute guarantee of justice in human society. Our ancestors were sensitive folk who found this situation cruel, even intolerable. But they were not so delusional as to concoct a way to avoid it, or disguise it, or pretend it was not so. In fact, they came up with a rather good solution to the problem of perpetration.

They decided to blame the male chief of the community for any and all wrongdoing in cases when the actual perpetrator could not be found. Let's recall that in prepatriarchal societies, the tribal chief or king was empowered by a priestess who represented the Goddess. The rite of *hieros gamos*, sacred mating, guaranteed that the king-to-be was courageous but tender, a noble and innocent man who could surrender to a woman in the most intimate act of human contact. By accepting blame even though innocent, the tribal king became the "surrogate victim" who would bear the sins of the community. To ancient sensibilities it seemed wrong to place a woman, the life giver of the species, in the dicey role of scapegoat, so the surrogate victim was always a man. Being a sacred king had its perks, but it carried the risk of being killed to expiate the unsolved crimes of the community. In ancient Greece, the sacrificial king was called the *pharmakon*. Girard explains that *pharmakon* means both malady and remedy. "The victim [selected for scapegoating] draws to itself all the violence infecting the original victim and through its own death transforms this baneful violence into beneficial violence."[246]

This system worked because it encouraged the king to model honesty and kindness, and assist or guide members of the community to do the same. Far more important than the role-modeling function, however, was the fact that scapegoating the king *purged the community of the need for retaliatory violence*. One of the most vicious forms of behavior in human experience, retaliatory violence is particularly gruesome when the perpetrator of the inciting act cannot be identified. Pagan society inherited the custom of prepatriarchal communities: to allow retaliation in cases where the wrongdoer was known and could be punished or killed by the kin of their victims. "An eye for an eye." That was considered fair enough. But when retaliatory violence has no certain target, and when it is sanctified by religious beliefs and driven by an inflamed sense of righteousness, it wreaks hell on Earth. It becomes an ecodical and genocidal tool, and beyond that, an apocalyptic weapon.

Sacrificial kingship was the original, uncorrupted form of Girard's "victimage mechanism." In the small-scale communities where it arose it worked rather well. But over time and with the increasing complexity of society in urban settings, victimage devolved into a complex pathological mechanism, and the drive for retaliatory violence—ever present in human nature—morphed into the redeemer complex.

In a bizarre twist, the divine victim merges into the numinous prototype of the redeemer.

"Lying Order"

Over time scapegoating devolved into a grand religious scheme for making everything right in the world, or defeating what was not right, rather than a modest and provisional custom for keeping the peace. Girard says that scapegoating in its later, degenerate form is "not simply an illusion and a mystification, but *the most formidable and influential illusion and mystification in human experience* [my italics]."[247] Scapegoating is the root of "religious delusion," but also what gives religion such vast social and political power. It only works, however, as long as the people in the religious system do not see how it works. "Religion protects man only as long as its ultimate foundations are not revealed."

Girard shows that those who benefit from scapegoating are—*or appear to be*—protected from the violence within themselves, while in fact they allow others to live it out for them. It permits them to disown any association with it. Victimage provides a sense of absolution, but covertly it allows both victims and perpetrators to participate deeply in the pathological transactions of violence. Girard's astonishing analysis reveals the victim-perpetrator bond in its *collusive* aspect: Victims deny they could ever do violence to others. Perpetrators deny the violence they do to others. *At its root this is one and the same denial.* Scapegoating, he asserts, is the hidden core of "all the forms of lying order inside which humanity lives."[248]

The most extreme and grandiose pathological mutation of scapegoating is the redeemer complex centered on the figure of the divine victim. Perpetrators can use Christianity to legitimate their actions because both they and their victims believe in the same solution to the problem of evil. Split-source duality implies that pain and suffering come from the one good god. But so does relief from those evils, and justice and vindication as well. It is a win-win situation. Salvationist faith is an open license to murder, torture, rape, lie, manipulate, and control, because whatever the perpetrators do, they are assured of the passive collusion of the victims—but only *the believing victims* who embrace the same creed and follow the same plan, the plot of salvation history. Salvationist faith offers those who suffer at the hands of others the right to claim the high moral ground. Many of the sayings of Jesus in the New Testament assert and indemnify that arrangement. Victims who accept the redemptive value of suffering and embrace the belief in a supernatural agent of retribution can be tortured and killed to the end of time, knowing they will come out on top, vindicated by the father god and miraculously revivified to join the company of the saved. At the same time those few who fanatically enact the dominator agenda can be assured that they are forcing the world to conform to God's plan. Victims and perpetrators collude in a game of "supernal sadomasochism," (to play on Alan Watts's tart observation).

Along with the lie about who created the world comes the lie about how victims and perpetrators will triumph over the world in the end-game scenario of victimage.

The divine victim presents another instance of countermimicry: this figure imitates the tribal scapegoat, the instrument of justice suited to the indigenous psyche, but invests it with a supernatural value that overwhelms and cancels the human sense for the right outcome. Gnostics saw the deception in divine redemption and tried to expose it. They must have been terrified to see how belief in superhuman redemption glorifies and mystifies suffering, and sanctions its adherents to inflict suffering, or be accessory to it, without admitting that they are, even (or especially) to themselves. And they must have been taken unawares when they found themselves targeted by the pathological violence that breeds like a lethal virus in victim-perpetrator collusion.

Victim-perpetrator collusion is vividly dramatized in both the Old and New Testaments, but the "Passion of Christ" is the ultimate enactment of the redeemer complex on the stage of history. At the center of this drama is the innocent lamb (read: scapegoat) who bears the sins of the world. The belief system attached to the divine victim offers a solution to evil. Girard skillfully shows how this solution is delusional. Yet it works.

But I would emphasize that the solution works only for people who are themselves delusional. In an insane world, insanity makes sense.

Another hard lesson of history is this: humanity cannot achieve coevolution with the planet as long as society follows the agenda of divine retribution. We cannot have a religion of nature, which René Dubos said was imperative for survival, as long as religion and politics keep their infernal deal struck long ago in Canaan and made official by Constantine. Roman Christianity is not the entire problem, all salvationist belief systems are, but it is the most triumphant of perpetration schemes. It has conjured hell on Earth, eradicated the Gnostics, destroyed the Mysteries, destroyed the learning of antiquity, torn out the Pagan heart of Europe, murdered midwifes and healers, colonialized the globe, burned and hung the tribal children of the Americas, bankrolled the despoliation of nature and the pernicious deception of Third World peoples, and to hide its crimes, it cast a spell of guilt and ignorance over sixty generations.

Break *that* spell and the black magic of redemptive theology will begin to dissolve, allowing the divine scapegoat to expire of its own unnatural causes.

A UNIQUE MESSAGE OF LOVE

The divine victim mirrors to humanity, not the solution to our suffering and a way to overcome it, but our total, consuming enslavement to it. Victimage works because it makes the force of suffering look stronger than the life force itself.

COMMANDED TO LOVE

If all this were not enough—and it is quite a lot, a vast abyss into which to gaze without dizziness—there is a final, fatal twist, like the barb on the hook that keeps it buried in the mouth. The immense power of scapegoating is due to victim-perpetrator collusion, but the divine victim of salvation history is not just a victim: He is also a God-sent emissary with a unique message of love. Jesus is *the* preeminent messenger of love, many people believe. When the Pharisees asked him "which is the first commandment of all," he replied:

> The first of all the commandments is, Hear, O Israel: The Lord our God is one Lord. And thou shalt love the Lord thy God with all thy heart, and with all thy soul, and with all thy mind, and with all thy strength: this is the greatest and first commandment. And the second is this: Thou shalt love thy neighbor as thyself. There is no other commandment greater than these. (Mark 12: 29–31)

All of which sounds wonderful until we ask the question: Who really needs to be commanded to love? Anyone who has loved anything in life, be it another person, an animal, a place in nature, a work of art—whatever—knows that love comes by its own power. It cannot and need not be commanded. Imagine that you are shown the Grand Canyon and commanded to love it. You might not love it, but if you do, you do not have to be commanded. We love spontaneously, through the power of love itself, which cannot be commanded. If this is the self-evident truth about love in human experience, why should love of God and love of one's neighbor be any different?

The command to love is the supreme manipulative ploy of the authoritarian lie, the deepest cut into the moral sovereignty of the human animal. (In a two-line poem "Retort to Jesus," D. H. Lawrence said that whoever forces himself to love engenders a murderer in his own breast.) But to be a little more generous, it could be called the central plea of divine paternalism, whose leading spokesman is Jesus Christ. Much of what Jesus said is patent nonsense that goes against human nature, like the above verses, but no one blinks an eye when these commandments are pronounced. Why not? Because the messenger of love is the divine victim in human guise, and to refute Jesus would dispel the absolving power of the scapegoat. We would be completely *on our own* with no rules to follow, forced to judge what is good and evil by reliance on human standards with no absolution for perpetrators and no vindication for victims. This is the unbearable existential truth of the human condition—but no, we only suppose it is unbearable. In fact, we have not tried it out, we have never lived it through to see how it really feels. There is so much religious and historical conditioning layered onto the human psyche that it impedes access to the naked veracity of our own experience. R. D. Laing asserted that the ultimate destruction that can be done to a human being is to destroy its capacity to have its own experience—and patriarchal monotheism has done this, using religion as its pretext. Speaking from the same perception, Gnostics warned that salvationism would defeat our divine endowment, nous, the human potential to learn and evolve. How can we know what humans are capable of doing *out of their own resources* if we rely on a superhuman agency to predecide the most elementary issues of life?

The message of love is the barb on the hook of victim-perpetrator collusion. And the bait on the hook is Jesus. (Somewhere in his works, Joseph Campbell presents a medieval woodcut depicting Jesus lowered from heaven on a huge hook—to show that he was "a fisher of men.")

The message of the "man of sorrows" is so contrary to the human condition that it has taken centuries of apologetic manipulation to make it look even halfway right. In *Beyond Theology* Alan Watts wrote:

> We are spiritually paralyzed by the fetish of Jesus. Even to atheists he is the supremely good man, the examplar and moral authority with whom no one may disagree. Whatever our opinions, we must perforce wangle the words of Jesus to agree with them. Poor Jesus! If he had known how great an authority was to be projected upon him, he would never have said a word.[249]

And the process goes on still. In an essay entitled "The Christian Paradox—How a Faithful Nation Gets Jesus Wrong," environmental writer Bill McKibben (*The End of Nature*) says of the verses from Mark 12 that command love: "Although its rhetorical power has been dimmed by recognition, that is a radical notion, perhaps the most radical notion possible."[250] If we assume this is true, we will be compelled to do anything and everything imaginable to get in line with "the teachings of Jesus," believing that following his advice will change the human condition. If we mere humans have difficulty putting his sublime message into practice, it has to be all our fault. If Jesus said things that were universally true and essential to living the way humans should live, and we get Jesus wrong, this is a grave problem, indeed.

But if Jesus himself was wrong, that is a problem far graver.

Look at history and consider all that has been said and done to show that Jesus was right, compared to what has been said and done to show that he was wrong. Of the latter argument there is almost nothing. If refutations of Jesus existed, they have most certainly been destroyed, as the writings of the Gnostics were destroyed. What does the near total absence of a counterargument tell you? In the theological library at the Catholic University of Leuven, where I sometimes do research on the Gnostic writings or the Dead Sea Scrolls, there are entire floors of long stacks of books that argue that Jesus was right. The surviving Gnostic argument against Christianity can be found in one book, *The Nag Hammadi Library in English*. It is like finding one edible flake of oatmeal in a reeking landfill the size of a football stadium.

The collected writings of the Church Fathers dedicated to refuting the Gnostics—the dossier of the prosecution—alone occupy several yards of shelf space. And the patristic literature is merely a sliver of the sum total of apologetic and defensive discourse that has been produced to prove that Jesus was right. We tend to believe that Jesus was right because there has been such a monumental effort to convince the world that this is so, but the extent of the argument is no proof of its veracity. In fact, it could be evidence of the contrary: a monumental effort to convert the human mind to the bad faith of betrayed humanity.

Why is it so difficult to refute Jesus? Well, apart from the staggering complexity of the redeemer complex and the murky pathology of victim-perpetrator collusion—both of which represent a formidable challenge to human understanding, requring an extraordinary exercise of patience—there are two other considerable obstacles in the way. The first is the problem posed by "the teachings of Jesus," and it has several knotty aspects.

Jesus himself wrote nothing down, so the words attributed to him were written by other people. To trust that we have a fair and accurate record of what the Lord said, we must trust those who recorded his words. But even if we trust Jesus, believing that he really lived and had a unique message for humankind, trusting those who wrote down that message is another matter. Let's consider that his message can be found exclusively in the words attributed to him, commonly printed in red in the New Testament. Extract all these passages and you have what Jesus is alleged to have said. But the teachings are not in these words alone. They are also in all that has been said and written *about* those words—namely, the exposition of the teachings. One can accept all this material as a valid part of "the teachings of Jesus." But with the exposition we face the same problem again: to trust those who produced it. We are always one step removed from Jesus, depending on the unknown people who wrote down the words attributed to him, and on the many known people who have provided a supporting commentary on those words. In short, we are in a position of having to trust what others say in order to know that Jesus said.

Now, there is a way to get around this problem. Let's assume that all that Jesus taught, the essence and scope of his message, can be found in the verbatim passages printed in red. This narrows down the task considerably. No matter what has been made of what Jesus said, if we cannot find the essential message in his own words, then we are really not getting to his message at all, are we? Even though we cannot be entirely sure that the verbatim record is a true account of his words, we can proceed as if it is. We can then look at the words themselves, the language, the expressions, and see what kind of teaching they present.

Without requiring too much scrutiny, this exercise easily reveals that there is little original content in the words attributed to Jesus. Note also that the commandment to "love thy neighbor" did not originate with the Galilean. It can be found in Leviticus 19:18: "Thou shalt not avenge, nor bear any grudge against the children of thy people, but thou shalt love thy neighbor as thyself. I *am* the Lord." In the way this commandment is stated, it clearly refers to conflict within the Jewish community to which it is addressed. Its intention is to restrain retaliatory violence within the limits of the tribe. The declaration, "I *am* the Lord," emphasizes that the command comes from a superhuman agency that must neither be questioned nor challenged. There is no teaching here, merely a command given to a particular tribal group to behave in a certain way. Commandments do not teach us anything. Jesus does not teach, either. He merely cites this commandment, but then, in another context, he modifies it:

> Ye have heard that it hath been said, Thou shalt love thy neighbor and hate thine enemy. But I say unto you, Love your enemies, bless them that curse you, do good to them that hate you, and pray for them who despitefully use and, and persecute you. (Matthew 6:43–44).

Now, it seems, these verses really show the original essence of Jesus' teachings. Jesus here refutes the Old Testament law of "an eye for an eye," considered in Pagan and indigenous societies to be a perfectly adequate solution when the perpetrator is known. It is often said that Christianity makes its greatest advance over Judaism by rejecting eye-for-eye morality for universal love. But considering what we have learned about scapegoating, it would be wise to listen closely to what the divine victim says about victimage in the verses cited. The great moral advance Jesus proposes is a straightforward endorsement of victim-perpetrator collusion: "do good to them that hurt you." When this commandment is combined with the assurance that abuse and persecution will earn the Redeemer's favor—"Blessed art thou when you are persecuted for my sake"—victims have a divine sanction to be abused, and even to invite abuse.

DOUBLE-BIND MORALS

The second most cited feature of Jesus' teachings that is said to be truly original is the golden rule: "Do unto others as you would have them do unto you." But again, this adage is far from original to the Galilean. Not only is the golden rule found in slight variations in all the cultures of the world, but among the Jews it was known to have been the central teaching of the rabbi Hillel (fl. 30 B.C.E.–10 C.E.), the outstanding spiritual and ethical leader of his generation. When asked the same question that was put to Jesus, "Which is the first commandment of all?" Hillel replied: "Do not do unto others that which is hateful unto thee." It is extremely important to observe, however, that in quoting Hillel, Jesus changes the syntax of the phrase from negative to positive. The switch of syntax completely undermines the original sense of this principle.

What is hateful to someone is pretty clear to that person. This aversion immediately tells the person what not to do to others. Thus stated, the Golden Rule is a viable deterrent that avoids the language of reward and punishment. Psychologically, this is a wise guideline. It is not utopian morality, something that sounds good but cannot be put into practice. It is honest and existential. It can be tested, and we can learn from experience it if works. But the positive syntax of Jesus' version has a double connotation that makes it utterly different. It is about what we want from others, not about what is hateful and cannot be tolerated. What we want from others is a huge, distorting consideration. It makes my behavior toward others dependent on what I can get, or imagine I can get, from them. These considerations completely distort the basic ethical relationship between people, which depends on detachment from using people for personal ends.

Then there is a second distortion. When Jesus says "do unto others" rather than "do not do unto others," he insinuates an obligatory note. The golden rule in his version could be paraphrased like this: "You are obliged to treat others in whatever way that you might want them to treat you." How does this principle work in practice? Well, imagine that I want my neighbor to offer me a free vacation in Tahiti. What I do then, consistent with the ethics of Jesus, is turn around and buy my neighbor an all-expenses-paid vacation in Tahiti.

It is not hard to make the golden rule in Jesus' version look ridiculous, but it is not necessary, either. The proposition is self-evidently ridiculous, even fatuous. By contrast, "Do not unto others what is hateful to you" is eminently sane. It is hard to make it look ridiculous. In the element of obligation it carries, Jesus' version of the golden rule belongs to what ethicists call *prudential morality*. This version is meant as a moral code that obliges us to do things for the betterment of our own souls. It is prudent to do good to others, for instance, because we will be rewarded for doing so. In *The Faith of a Heretic*, Walter Kaufmann argues that Judeo-Christian morality "does not know the value of a deed done for its own sake," without expectation of reward (or punishment). "The ethic of the Old Testament is an ethic of prudence and rewards, as if the point were that it pays to be good."[251] (The qualification of "as if" does not fit the case: Old Testament ethics are precisely so, *as is stated*, not as if. Born in Germany of distant Jewish parentage and raised as a Lutheran, Kaufmann converted to Judaism at age nine.) Jesus' version of the golden rule combines prudential morality with the fantasy element of arbitrary desire. "Think about what you would like others to do for you, then do it for them, not for their good, but for the reward it will bring you." This is an exact paraphrase of Jesus's teaching. Prudential morality is perverse behavior that has nothing to do with responsible regard for others.

Upon close inspection the teachings of Jesus amount to nothing more than some pithy suggestions for victimage counseling. It would take an entire book to go through the verbatim record and discover what's truly original in it, what is purely derivative, and what is just plain deranged. Two outstanding observations will have to suffice: the so-called teachings are not teachings are all, they are merely pronouncements of divine paternalism, and most of the language uses double-bind formulas that set up schizophrenic propositions, like the Beatitudes from the Sermon on the Mount. Whoever wrote the words printed in red was both extremely malicious and extremely clever. The teaching attributed to the divine victim is a diabolical ruse. The saccharine, schizoid ethics of Jesus make it look good for victims to collude with perpetrators. In so many instances the principles that Jesus expounds are wrong for the human condition and utterly impracticable in existential terms.

Jesus was wrong on a lot of counts but perhaps supremely so on one issue. Of all the dubious advice pronounced in the New Testament, one commandment is particularly harmful: the famous injunction to "resist not evil" and "turn the other cheek." If everyone did this what kind of society would result? Evildoers would easily triumph over pacifist cheek-turners. The advice is patently absurd and cancels itself out, but taken on faith it serves an unmistakable purpose: to give total liberty to the perpetrators.

It is difficult to tell what is more unfortunate: Jesus was really sincere in proposing this kind of behavior, or he was being intentionally perverse. In either case, the ethic of cheek turning is utterly wrong because it obliges people who are not inclined to harm others to *rely on those who do harm* to embrace the same practice of nondefense. But will people who are inclined to harm and abuse others change their behavior voluntarily, just because they are confronted with someone who does not resist them? In what instances in history or social life has this occurred? Examples, please! To propose a code of morality that relies on the good will of perpetrators to desist from their ways *without facing challenge or retaliation* is a real stroke of schizoid genius.

One may begin to wonder if such a code does not originate with the perpetrators in the first place.

The double-bind propositions that inform the "teachings of Jesus" would dazzle a talented schizophrenic and put the most ingenious cult guru to shame. The phrases from the Sermon on the Mount— such as "The meek shall inherit the Earth"—have effectively enforced victim-perpetrator collusion for seventy generations, the time elapsed since Jesus lived. "The way to a man's belief is through confusion and absurdity," Jacques Vallee observed. He was speaking about the "spiritual control system" of the ET/UFO phenomenon, but he may as well have been discussing Christian ethics. With commandments to do what comes naturally, how can you fail? But the formula of moral insanity ensures the outcome: because what is natural cannot be commanded, you will fail.

Here is another hard lesson of history: the twisted ethics of patriarchal religion stated in "the teachings of Jesus" were never conceived to better the human condition, or to guide people toward loving and responsible behavior. It was only made to look as if they do all that. There is real genius, true manipulative brilliance, in the sadomasochistic mysticism of redeemer ethics. The Gospels are worthless as a guide to personal morality, but they are extremely efficient tools of psychosocial control.

INHUMAN DIGNITY

Needless to say, it looks pretty bad to badmouth Jesus. This is a great part of the difficulty of refuting the manifest insanity of redeemer ethics. Somehow, by challenging or disrespecting Jesus, we seem to be slighting our own humanity. This is odd but it really does feel that way, and such a feeling makes an extremely strong deterrent.

Deep-seated resistance to refuting Jesus is a huge obstacle that stands in humanity's way of reclaiming its divine birthright. Why is this resistance so endemic and so persistent? It is that way because the image of the divine victim has been enshrined in human imagination as *a mirror of human dignity*. Any attack on Jesus is felt as a slight to human dignity. Anything said against Jesus is immediately suspect because the human figure of Jesus has been assigned with precious and unique importance. It has come to represent the innate self-valuation of the human species. Any attack on the person Jesus, or any critique of the message of love that comes to us through the divine redeemer, feels like a body blow to our shared sense of humanity.

But what if we have located our sense of humanity in the wrong place? In the wrong person?

The Demiurge of the Old Testament is an arrogant, demented pretender who claims that humans are "made in His image." These four words are the corporate motto of Abrahamic faith. Branded on the human soul, "Made in His Image" signifies the total enslavement of humanity to an alien, off-planet agenda. If Gnostics were right, the rise of salvationism was a unique mistake for our species, not a new moral revelation. Nothing serves the hidden controllers for cover better than a message of cosmic love. The fine print of the message carries a set of nested imperatives that are neither sane nor practicable: resist not evil, love your enemies, do good to those who harm you, turn the other cheek, accept abuse, forgive the perpetrator. These propositions are nested in the love message that encloses them with a sugary coating. The message of love is a ruse to endorse and foster the victim-perpetrator bond.

No matter how hard we try, we cannot derive a genuine message of love and goodness from divine paternalism. The source is just too corrupt. This is perhaps the hardest of all lessons that history can teach us.

Human beings have a deep unfaltering intuitive sense that tells us that love cannot be the basis of morality, although it is the central and directing factor in our total capacity for moral (i.e., conscious, responsible) *expression*. The basis of morality is our sense for life, our devotion to the life force.* This is what allows us—indeed, inspires us—to accept and follow the spontaneous force of love without having to force or command it. The same intuition gives us the confidence to *learn* how to love as the experience unfolds, and to learn through loving how to face situations where love does not apply. But that precious intuitive knowing is vulnerable to influences from outside, especially from the domain of religion. The brutal impact of salvationist conditioning destroyed the innate reverence for life in Europeans, and that is why they behaved as they did when then encountered their distant mirror in the indigenous tribes of the Americas. The Europeans *envied* what they saw, and destroyed what they could not really have, that is, could not reclaim as part of themselves, but only possess, steal, plunder. With their conversion to redeemer ethics, the entire world was disinherited from a legacy of

---

* The life and work of Wilhelm Reich present a courageous expression of this statement. Reich's exposition of the mystico-military temperament, character armoring, the patriarchal authoritarian syndrome, and "the emotional plague" goes deeply into the primal wound of human dignity and the perversions of divine paternalism. Reich's cure for social evil was self-regulation based on sexual integrity.

spiritual, Earth-based knowledge so rich and vast that we may never comprehend what was lost when the Mysteries were destroyed.

Stunted by the loss of that ancient legacy, some Europeans who invaded the Americas could not recognize the common humanity in the native peoples they encountered. (Columbus notes their contentment in his journal with an air of bafflement.) With their basic sense of humanity corrupted by the superhuman ideal, the deceit of Christ, they felt no need to act humanely.

We behold as we believe. What the conquistadors beheld was virginal nature to be violated and wealth untold to be stolen, because they had been violated and had their sacred birthright stolen. Spiritually and morally impoverished, they were ideally qualified to be perpetrators in conquest and conversion. Greed was an easy option, because the richness of what they beheld, the scope and depth of the native sense of life, was inaccessible to them: they could not claim back from outside what they had lost within.

Sophia declared to the Demiurge, "You are blind, Samael," and shamed him for not seeing the luminous image of true humanity, the Anthropos. The Gnostic teaching that Yaldabaoth and the Archons cannot comprehend humanity contains a strong warning against the belief that we are "made in God's image." Only a God who does not recognize and respect what humanity is would be arrogant enough to create it in His own image.

Indigenous wisdom teaches that each species is made in the image of its habitat, the bioregion where it lives, and we are no exception to that principle. Gnostics looked forward to Sophia's Correction, yet nothing is known about how they conceived it. As a beneficiary of their sacred lineage, I presume to conceive it on their behalf. And not only I, but growing numbers in the world today, Gnostics or otherwise, share a momentous realization: our generic self-image as a species, which grounds our sense of humanity, must be liberated from the image of divine victim upon which it has become fixated. The redeemer complex is a nefarious ruse that frontally destroys the power to see ourselves mirrored in the Anthropos. Instead, we see the god-man crucified on the cross. We get resurrection but we lose the living Earth where our divine birthright is held for us. Accepting the divine scapegoat as the image of humanity, we cannot access true humanity. Christianity dehumanizes us, and does so in the spirit prepared by the *zaddik*, the Hebrew ideal of righteousness and transhumanist supremacy.

LOVING LIFE

The Divine Redeemer whose human reflection is the person of Jesus carries the sacred image of human dignity, but at the same time it undermines human sanity. The Redeemer is declared to be God's unique agent sent into the world to save it. He, the Only-Begotten Son of God, is the Divine Victim and, at the same time, the model of perfect humanity, the best person who ever lived, the salvation narrative says. The psychospiritual impact of this story is far different from what those who embrace the story and enact the beliefs it encodes claim it to be. "We are spiritually paralyzed by the fetish of Jesus" (Alan Watts, cited above). The promised salvific medicine is really a toxin that eats into the human spirit like acid. The image in which our common dignity is invested inflicts a mortal wound on that dignity.

What wounds human dignity most profoundly and permanently? Alienation from the Earth due to placing its self-image in a transhuman, superearthly figure. This displacement breaks the reflecting link to Gaia and the life of all species. It is also a lie. We are created, not in His image, but in the evolutionary "fit" to our setting, our habitat. We are created in the image of the natural world we behold, according to how we behold it. This is what the Mysteries taught by their unfailing dedication to the Great Mother.

We had dignity even before we had souls to save. At death's door we seek our modest, mortal dignity, no matter what our ego may be looking for on the other side. It is high time to claim back human dignity from the guardians of divine paternalism who promote and enforce the three Abrahamic religions.

The Divine Victim is to the Anthropos as the menorah is to the *asherah*. It is the pathetic, misplaced focus of human self-worth. Instead of a reflection of vital, joyous humanity, there is the agonized man nailed to a cross. The countermimicry in effect here substitutes morbidity for the life force and narcissistic agony for self-love. Jesus commands you to love your neighbor as yourself but tells you nothing about how to love yourself in the first place, so the advice is utterly useless. Self-love is the natural side effect of loving life. Jesus does not say, "You shall love your own life in the same way you love another person, freely and sponta-neously, asking nothing in return. And so doing, loving life in this way, you shall find the strength to bear what human love brings to you, both in its gains and its losses. And you shall accept to be loved in the same free, spontaneous way, making no claim on what you so receive." The words attributed to Jesus do not say anything like this, ever, because the message of love printed in red is not what it is put up to be. The message of love that comes from ultimate model of victim-perpetrator bonding cannot reach human suffering and touch the core of what transcends it. Nor can it even begin to reveal the genuine mystery of human love. The truth that is consistent with our genuine capacity to love our own kind and, heeding the presence of the Symbiont, nonhuman species as well, will not be found in the "good news" of the New Testament. Never. But the expectation to find it there makes it almost impossible to discern the inhumanity of Jesus Christ.

In *Where the Wasteland Ends*, Theodore Roszak observed that the domi-nation of Judeo-Christian salvation history has deeply wounded human imagination, preventing our species from evolving its narrative, myth-making faculties. "Christ belongs to history; his rivals were mere myths. Clearly, there occurred with the advent of Christianity a deep shift of consciousness which severely damaged the mythopoeic powers—far more so than was the case even in Judaism."[252]

Gnostics protested both the ethics and ideology of salvationism because they saw how it decimates our imaginative power and leaves us without proper guidance, uncertain of our boundaries, vulnerable to alien forces, to all manner of deviance, narcissism, and self-obsession. Two thousand years ago the guardians of the Mysteries realized that redeemer theol-ogy centered on the divine victim would entirely undermine their conse-crated task of fostering human potential and teaching self-direction. The crucifix is a fetish to conjure zombification. With countermimicry, what you see is definitely not what you get. It is not Jesus Christ who is crucified on the cross, it is human imagination, the inborn visionary power of our species. And this precious faculty will not be resurrected through reconciliation with the perpetrators who nailed it there, and who, at the same time and in the same twisted tale, declare the Divine Victim to be the Light of the World.

BEYOND RELIGION

R oman Emperor and Eleusinian initiate Marcus Aurelius (121–180 c.e.) concisely stated the essence of Pagan ethics: "Nature has constituted rational beings for their own mutual benefit, each to help his fellows according to their worth, and in no wise to do them harm."[253] His *Meditations* is a diary of philosophical reflections written while Marcus lived in remote encampments on the Danubian borderlands, protecting the Empire against invasion. It demonstrates the value scale of Pagan ethics more than any single document from antiquity. Marcus put into simple, direct language the code of honor and kindness of Pagan society, including slaves and emperors alike.

If Christianity prevailed because it was democratic (as has often been argued), then Pagan morality must have declined because it was merely egalitarian. In an egalitarian society, the same values apply for all people, regardless of how they suffer in life, or triumph over suffering. Everyone is equal before the power of fate. Salvationist ethics assumes that fate can be altered by special conditions given only to the faithful. It sets out a totalitarian agenda based on the redemptive value attributed to suffering that may be inflicted by God (the issue is unsettled), but that certainly God alone can alleviate. The advantage of the salvationist solution depends first on its democratic appeal—anyone who embraces the creed receives special attention from the savior god—and then on the strength of nonverifiable beliefs, which, patently ridiculous as they are, cannot be refuted by reason. Finally, salvationism imbues suffering with a universal value and confers upon it a magical, redemptive character. There was no antidote in Pagan culture to such grotesque mystification.

The Pagan principle of tolerance resonates through the *Meditations*. Gnosticism, which was body-based mysticism, and Stoicism, which was nature-oriented humanism, here converge. The beauty and finesse of the *Meditations* is counterpointed by their gravitas. This is not an ethic of obligation, a code that we attempt to live up to and fail, feeling better about ourselves for having tried. It is not prudential morality that promises to reward the soul (with God's favor in worldly success while living, or with resurrection in the afterlife) for every good thought and deed. It is not off-planet metaphysics with an end-game scenario of resurrection and divine retribution. It is a sober existential ethic of commitment to humane standards, a pact with what can really be achieved through human potential. If *then* we fail, the weight of sadness is immense, because the standard set for us was fully and truly within our scope.

A saturnine spirit weighs down Marcus's reflections, but three pages of his diary provide more moral edification than the New Testament in its entirety.

Gaian Morality

Social order is found throughout nature—long before the age of books and legal codes. It is inherently part of what we are, and its patterns follow the same foldings, checks and balances, as flesh or stone. What we call social organization and order in government have been appropriated by the calculating mind from the operating principles in nature.[254]

By now it ought to be clear that the Gnostic protest against the redeemer complex was more than a debate over abstruse theological issues. It was a frontal response to the mass-scale dementia that burst upon the world at the dawn of the Piscean Age. It was a valiant attempt to confront the evil that works against humanity's very will to survive, against the life force itself.

By contrast to salvationism, the Mystery religions, as scholars call them, were dedicated to continual rebonding with the ecstatic life force, Eros, and grounding in the life source, Gaia. The telestai who founded and led those ancient institutions believed that morality for human beings must be rooted in our relation to nonhuman nature.

This is also the conviction of many people today who advocate indig-enous wisdom and propose a shift away from redeemer ethics toward what might be called Gaian ethics. "We are human only in contact, and conviviality, with what is not human," writes David Abram in *The Spell of the Sensuous*.[255] The eight-point platform of deep ecol-ogy proposed by Arne Naess and George Sessions assumes the innate goodness of the human species—an assumption that holds, I would add, only *if* we as a species keep faith with the natural world. If the human species' bond to nature is intact, human nature will sponta-neously tend to do good, without having to be commanded. This is the first condition of Gaian ethics.

In an essay entitled "Self-realization: An Ecological Approach to Being in the World," Arne Naess wrote:

> We need not morals to make us breathe. . . . If your "self" in the wide sense embraces another being, you need no moral exhortation to show care. . . . You care for yourself without feeling any moral pressure to do it—provided you have not succumbed to a neurosis of some kind, developing self-destructive tendencies, or hating yourself.[256]

Kindness that comes naturally, not dictated by divine decree or under-written by a superhuman scheme of reward and punishment, may be inconceivable to many people at this late date in history. Why? Because dominator culture so degrades the human spirit that people under its spell cannot believe in any morality not dictated and enforced by "authorities." *The deception of the authorities (Archons) must first corrupt those whom the redeemer religion would convert.* The natives of Europa were not easily corrupted, so the campaign to impose the Judeo-Christian program of redemption had to be reinforced, time and time again, often by resorting to extremely brutal measures. Redemption is like "protection" offered by the Mafia. The system that offers atonement from sin must make sure that people will be in desparate need of its services.

Genuine morality cannot be commanded, but morality by remote control, as it might be called, is the norm in a society subordinated to a dominant elite who care nothing for humanity or nature. Remote-control morality is the path of social adaptation for countless millions whose essential goodness has been fundamentally corrupted by religion. The transhumanist standard of *zaddik* subverts and perverts all that is good, natural, beautiful, and spontaneous in the human animal. No wonder the technocratic masterminds of the Great Reset want to remotely control all human behavior by a subdermal "operating system," or "software for living," as Moderna calls it. The pharma giant does not even bother to call the mRNA agent a vaccine. Which, of course, it isn't. At least that's honest. But to date neither governments nor medical authorities are truthfully informing the public about the ingredients of the vaccines coming out in increasing varieties. In 1966, J. P. Jacobs and a team working for the Medical Research Council in the UK produced MRC-5, a cell strain developed from the lung tissue of a 14-week-old aborted Caucasian male fetus.[257] It does not appear that this cell strain features in Covid-19 vaccines, but it could. If not, where and how is it applied? A eucharist that contains matter derived from an aborted fetus would be conclusive evidence that the Archons have reached "the consummation of their works," as the Gnostics warned (NHC II, 5:103,25-27). The bizarre trope of the aborted fetus in Gnostic cosmology now reveals itself in the biophobic trickery of transhumanist genomics. The coronavirus hoax is certainly the greatest act of Archontic deceit ever perpetrated on the world.

I have proposed that Gnosis in practice is not *an* alternative religion, but an alternative *to all* religions. Fine, but can the Sophianic view of life also offer an alternative to the morality based in religion? Morality free of religious dogma is possible where religious experience is still grounded in the divine life force, rather than directed to (and by) an off-planet divinity. To move beyond salvationist ethics is not an option for everyone, however. Ever since the mixed message of love *and* retribution was delivered almost two thousand years ago, the Redeemer works mysteriously in our midst, the Prince of Peace oversees the increasingly troubled and divided world, and true believers keep faith in the Father's power to make all things right even if, mysteriously, people continue to treat each other in the most atrocious ways, and virtual gimmicks drive the population toward oblivion. As Helen Keller observed, most people do not want to be free. They merely want to be safe. Even the illusion of safety is better than nothing at all. It may well be possible to go beyond religion through belief-change—the single, most effective form of dissent in human society—but to get beyond the violence and coercion that redemptive religion uses to enforce itself, requires more than dissent. Religion has always claimed to bring peace and make the world safe—and lately, authorities who enforce anti-Covid-19 measures do the same—but the right future for humanity may depend on making the world safe from religion.

The value system of Pagan ethics is indigenous to humankind and needs no divine mandate, no stamp of superhuman approval. Gary Snyder asserts that "social order is found throughout nature. . . . It is inherently part of what we are," and the same could be said of moral order. The natural and instinctual processes that produced the human species also endowed it with the capacity to know itself and act morally—call this the Gaia-Sophia principle. The notion is not unique to this author. It is widely argued by deep ecologists, ecopsychologists, cultural historians, and many other alternative voices in the world today. That we evolve both our ethical values and our survival capacities from one and the same supernatural endowment, nous, was a primary Mystery teaching. Indeed, this is the moral essence of initiated wisdom.

It can be objected that natural morality is insuffient because it does not provide answers to the perennial questions posed by death, evil, and injustice, or the abiding mystery of what we're all doing here in the first place. Why does the world exist, rather than nothing at all? Heidegger asked. Salvationism does provide answers to such questions, but if they are wrong answers? Is safety all that matters, even when it is a sham? It seems that for billions of people in the past and today, wrong answers taken on faith are better than no answers at all.

But what if we really do not need faith to face the great questions of life? What if, to be fully human, we only need to embrace the specific situations in which these perennial riddles arise, when they arise? Meet death with full attention, nakedly aware, rather than with a preconceived belief about what comes after it? Face loss as it comes, rather than bargain with God over how it can be avoided or compensated? Can we live bravely and generously knowing that not everything in life works out, and not all situations can be made right? Can we take the hard part of life to heart and not resort to buffering lies to make it all acceptable? Perhaps through natural morality, we can. In Dzogchen, the highest level of Tibetan Buddhism, natural goodness (Tibetan *kadak*) is viewed as the *basis* of all genuine action, not a prescribed code of action. "Basic goodness manifests itself in every instant of pure presence." Chögyam Trungpa, the most radical proponent of Buddhism in the West, observed that religion enforces the tendency to punish ourselves (and, I would add, reward ourselves). "People still tend to take original sin seriously. They should let go of that. Maybe basic goodness will replace original sin!," he proposed. *Kadak* is spontaneous, not driven by moral imperatives of any kind. "Before any judgment, before any doctrine, it is possible to make contact with our own intelligence, as we can with true reality, and discover the resources it contains."[258]

Gnostics, too, affirmed that the infinite goodness of the Pleroma resides in human nature. We do not reach natural goodness by behaving in a certain way, following a set of rules. We act *from it* whenever we are fully alive in the authenticity of being Anthropos.

The Tolerance Trap

Christianity is a creed embraced by billions, but rarely chosen by anyone. The same is true of Islam, whose followers now make up about one-fifth of the world's population of six billion people. Jews are racially born into their religion. Or perhaps better said, they make their racial identity into a religion. Either way, they choose to be the chosen. Today we have utterly forgotten that heresy derives from the Greek *heraisthai*, "to choose." To be heretical means to have choices and not be forced or obligated to believe what one is told to believe. A heretic is free to choose what to believe, or not to believe.

A strong obstacle to going beyond religion is the widespread assumption that the three redemptive religions promote tolerance. One must read the sacred scriptures with a blind eye, already expecting what to find in them, to come away with any such message. Many people do not read the sacred writings of the faith they embrace, or they read them only in a selective way—choosing lofty lines about faith, hope, and charity from the letters of Paul, for instance—so that they do not endanger their faith. The beliefs stated in "revealed scripture" are less important than the beliefs held about it. To believe that the Bible advocates toler-ance, one must turn a blind eye to what it actually says *on the whole*, rather than in selected snippets. The history of Western religion clearly demonstrates how intolerance is endemic to the Abrahamic traditions. Gnostics knew this firsthand. They were frontline casualties in the war against humanity perpetrated in the name of religious ideals.

Many Christians find in the biblical history of the ancient Jews a para-digmatic tale for humanity as a whole. But fundamentalists who insist that the Bible is paradigmatic, and so contains the solution to all human issues, need to take a look at the Dead Sea Scrolls for a better idea of the sources of the Christian myth, and the solution toward which salvation-ism leads the world. The War Scroll, for instance, consists of eighteen columns describing the military attire, armaments, and battle divisions of the Sons of Light. It praises the "God of loving-kindness" who guards the Qumranic covenant and will ultimately save his people, or some of them, anyway: "He has gathered a congregation of nations for annihila-tion without remnant in order to raise up in judgment he whose heart has melted, to open a mouth for the dumb to sing God's praises, and to teach feeble hands warfare."[259] On page after page, the scrolls mix glow-ing praise for the Lord with harsh, violent imprecations and threats. Christian evangelism inherited the spirit of triumphalism that pervades the Qumranic writings, and immortalized it in the anthem, "Onward, Christian Soldiers."

The War Scroll contains the Zaddikite hit list, with the worst enemy at the top of the list. Column 11 names the foes of the Zaddikim whom the Lord commands to be annihilated "without remnant." The text here repeats the Star and Scepter prophecy, also called the prophecy of Balaam, found in Numbers 24:17. "There shall come a star out of Jacob, and a scepter shall rise out of Israel, and shall smite the corners of Moab, and destroy all the children of Seth." This line is from the Masoretic Bible, the standard Hebrew version of the Old Testament preserved from the eleventh century c.e., but the scrolls' equivalent is almost a thousand years older. It presents an expanded version of the biblical passage:

> There shall come forth a Star out of Jacob, and a scepter shall
> rise out of Israel, and shall crush the forehead of Moab, and tear

down all the sons of Seth, and he shall descend from Jacob and
shall destroy the remnant from the city; and the enemy shall be
a possession, and Israel shall do valiantly.[260]

The Star and Scepter prophecy was the national anthem to the Zaddikite
liberation movement. The enemy named in direct association with
this theme would have been considered the supreme opponent of the
Qumranic sect. Who is it? "The children of Seth," the self-designation of
Gnostics in the Mysteries. Moab was the upland region east of the Dead
Sea (now Jordan), the domain of the Nabataean kingdom where Gnostic
groups flourished openly for many centuries. There is a double identification in column 11, citing the enemy by their self-designated name and by
their locale. This is a potent indication of how badly the Zaddikim wanted
to eliminate Gnostics, but it is not yet the full story. There is even a *third*
explicit identification of the Zaddikite's archenemy in the same text.

The seventh line of column 11 in the War Scroll is damaged by a water
spot that blurs the writing, making one letter impossible to determine.
Most scholars translate the questionable phrase "the remnant from the
city," as in the Wise-Abegg-Cook translation, cited here. But other scholars allow that the blurred letter may be a *shin*, giving "the remnant of
Seir."[261] Seir is the name of the sacred mountain and original homeland
of the Levantine Gnostics. It is a code term that would only have been
used by Gnostics in their self-definition, or by an enemy on intimate
terms with them. To target the remnant of Seir was to attack the very
root and origin of the Gnostic movement.

The War Scroll delivers a triple threat to Gnostics: by name, location,
and origin. No other passage in the scrolls exhibits such a vehement and
redundant emphasis. This is not the only place in the DSS materials
where the guardians of the Mysteries are targeted, however. In his *Jewish
Antiquities* (1.70), the historian Josephus mentioned a sect of Sethians,
accomplished stargazers, who are known to have engraved secret teachings on stone tablets. The fragmentary text 4Q417–418, called The
Secret of the Way Things Are, picks up this allusion. Here the Lord
God of Israel reveals "the enigmas of his purpose." In triumphal hype
typical of the Qumranic writings, 4Q417–418 declares to the righteous
few: "You are the one who understands. Your poverty is your reward

in the remembrance of time, for the decree is engraved, and inscribed is every time of punishment, for that which is decreed is engraved in stone before God, over all [. . .] the children of Seth."²⁶² Despite the lacuna it is clear that God has specific designs to crush the children of Seth. DSS scholar and expert on Jewish apocalypticism, John J. Collins, fills in the blank and renders this line, "ordained by God against all the iniquities of the children of Seth."²⁶³

The Dead Sea Scrolls contain specific and numerous references to the Gnostics of the Egyptian codices, linking these two immensely important textual discoveries. But the connection between Zaddikim and Gnostics do not stop with textual references. In *The Gnostic Scriptures*, a partial translation of the Nag Hammadi library, Bentley Layton provides a map entitled "The Gnostic Sect and Its Opponents." It shows thirty archaeological sites associated with Gnostic teachings, teachers, or incidents. Location 16, dated to 350 C.E., is an encampment of Gnostics calling themselves Archontics. It is located on the western shore of the Dead Sea just south of Qumran, no more than a stone's throw from the main Zaddikite outpost.²⁶⁴

Did Gnostics encamp in the Judean wilderness near Jerusalem deliberately to spy on the Zaddikim? The archaeological evidence would seem to indicate so. The name Archontic is telling. Sects in the Mystery network were defined by region, such as Samothracian, or by the primary Pagan divinity of the sect, such as Dionysian and Orphean, but also by a special practice or expertise; for example, Ophites were adepts of the Serpent Power, Ophis (Kundalini). "Archontic" would have defined a group whose special mission was to observe the Archons—a counterintelligence unit, as it were.

The archaeological evidence cited by Layton points to the presence of Gnostics deep in Zaddikite territory, but what about textual evidence of the Zaddikim in the Nag Hammadi writings? Coptic Gnostic materials do not identify the Jewish sect by name, but unmistakably signal it in other ways. The NHC contain three documents that feature James the Just, head of the Zaddikim movement at the Jerusalem temple: The Apocryphon of James (I, 2), and the First and Second Apocalypses of James (V, 3 and V, 4). The two Apocalypses are potent statements of the Gnostic argument against both Jewish and Christian theology. In the First Apocalypses of James, a Gnostic revealer instructs James, the senior figure of the Zaddikim according to the encoded scroll identities, on the Archontic delusions of Jewish religion! The revealer warns James that "Jerusalem is the dwelling-place of many Archons" (V, 3, 25.18). As explained above, Gnostics viewed the Archons as an alien intrapsychic species, the source of a subliminal intrusion that deviates humankind from its proper course of evolution. Archontic interception of humanity was initiated in the meeting of Abraham and Melchizedek, the premier moment of Jewish salvation history. Needless to say, this is a sensational notion that comes close to looking like gross anti-Semitism. Let's take a moment to consider this sensitive issue.

The Coptic materials do contain a large amount of "anti-Jewish" elements, but Gnostic opposition to Judaism was ideological rather than racial. They protested against the redeemer complex, the pathological core of salvationist creed. The First Apocalypse of James asserts that "Jews are exonerated in respect to the Passion of Jesus, although Jerusalem is said to be the residence of many archons."[265] Gnostic scholar K. W. Troger (cited here) estimates that one-third of the Coptic corpus is anti-Judaic. Add to this the anti-Christian elements—consistent with the critique of Judaism, because Christianity absorbed and universalized the redeemer complex with its glorification of suffering as the mark of divine election, as we have seen—and it comes to well over half. In some texts, such as The Second Treatise of the Great Seth, the Gnostic critique of Jewish-Christian faith is lacerating and loaded with contempt and sarcasm.

But Gnostics were not religious bigots. G. R. S. Mead pointed out their enemies, the Church Fathers, tell us nothing about the "ethical and general teachings" of the Gnostics.[266] Why not? Because (so I reckon) these teachings were benign, even exemplary, and could neither be faulted nor caricatured. Gnostics did not protest the genuine ethical aspects (such as they are) of Jewish and Christian tradition, but the primary ideological positions. The initiates of the Mysteries were Pagans who demonstrated enormous tolerance for religious options. Able to see so deeply into the origin of human belief systems, they were ruthless in exposing what they perceived to be deviant and delusional in such systems.

The Gnostic teacher warns James the Just that the people of Jerusalem are "a type of the Archons," i.e., mentally and behaviorally deviated by the ideological virus of redemptive theology. Thus, the author of the First Apocalypse freely adapts James to the Gnostic argument against Judeo-Christian salvationism. The unnamed Pagan initiate encourages the man known at Qumran as the paramount model of a *zaddik* to seek the sobriety of Gnosis and reject the Law of the Torah (32.5–10). Here and elsewhere, the polemics of the NHC demonstrate intolerance for antihumane doctrines and delusional ideas. The *gnostikoi* were Pagan intellectuals like Hypatia, and Pagans were essentially tolerant of diverse religious views and practices. It took an exceptional situation to bring some Mystery initiates out into the public eye and compel them to voice strong objections to an ideology. For that to happen, they must have perceived in it a serious threat to human sanity.

Unfortunately, Pagan tolerance proved to be a trap. As H. L. Mencken observed, tolerance is fine, a noble and necessary thing in human society, except when it tolerates intolerance. In that case it will destroy itself, and even give advantage to its own destruction, because intolerance will certainly prevail if it is not resisted. The Gnostic protest against salvationism involved a battle of words, an impassioned intellectual dispute, but it provided neither the means nor the rationale for Gnostics to protect themselves against actual violence. Christianity inherited the militant mission left undone by the Zaddikim: to destroy the remnant of Seth. The intellectual and spiritual tolerance of the Pagan world contributed hugely to its downfall.

Spiritual Warfare

In the foreword to *Dharma Gaia*, a collection of writings on Buddhism and ecology, the Dalai Lama says, "The Earth, our Mother, is telling us to behave." It could be added that the Earth can also teach us *how* to behave. "It is important that we forgive the destruction of the past and recognize that it was produced by ignorance," the Dalai Lama advises.[267] Perhaps, but forgiveness of past perpetration against nature and nature-oriented ways of life cannot be confused with turning a blind eye to the perpetrators, discounting their legacy, and tolerating their ongoing agenda. The plea to reconcile with wrongdoers always carries the risk that redeemer ethics will again prevail, giving the wrongdoers an advantage over those they harm. Tolerance for beliefs is one thing, tolerance for the social enactment of beliefs is another. Pagan tolerance failed in the second case.

The "biospirituality" and "cosmic morality" proposed in *Dharma Gaia* will need to be defended by "warrior-lovers" dedicated to planetary welfare, as Gary Synder calls them. Chögyam Trungpa also invoked the "path of the warrior" as the modern enlightened way "to recognize, again and again, [in] each moment of our singular experience . . . the unconditional possibility of trusting our own hearts . . . and the manifestations of basic goodness in the living present."[268] The institution of the Mysteries lacked a warrior class comparable, say, to the Shao Lin tradition of Chinese Buddhism. It seems that the telestai taught many arts, but not the martial arts. Consequently, Pagan initiates were unable to defend themselves and their tradition from violence. They were powerful in what they knew, but their privileged knowledge did not protect their lives or the institutions of learning they founded. They fell under the assault of faith-driven people willing to use outright violence to impose their convictions.

Gaian ethics is not a call to faith in God, but faith in the human species. Faith can be evil when it is invested in beliefs that blind humanity to nature, and impede the genius innate to our species. If it denies the divinity of the Earth, faith can be lethal to human survival. It can be the long-suffering servant of violence. Humanity has a sacred birthright rooted in Gaia-Sophia, a birthright that carries a responsibility to protect life, including nonhuman life, and to make the world safe for *what life knows*. Religious ideology has been the central driving force in humanity's long campaign of violence against the biosphere, the very habitat provided for our survival. No one so far has confronted this problem as bravely or brilliantly as the Gnostics did.

Due to its strong antireligious tone, the core message of Gnosis meets with considerable resistance. The moment it is said that Gnosticism was "anti-Jewish" and "anti-Christian," red lights flash and the steel-plated barriers of two thousand years of negative conditioning come slamming down. How can the Gnostic message contain anything good if it was directed against the best message the world has ever heard? For most dedicated believers, from instructed theologians down to everyday churchgoers who barely know what they believe, to be anti-Christian is tantamount to being antihuman. Furthermore, the accusation of being anti-Jewish compounds the charge of inhumanity with anti-Semitism. All this contributes to the negative image of Gnosticism and Gnostics.

Nevertheless, the brutal truth must stand clear and transparent: the Gnostic message to humanity *is* sacrilege, blasphemy, and anathema.

Gnostics perceived the paramount danger of religious madness coming from the extremist fringe of Jewish religion, the Zaddikim, but it infected basic Jewish identity as well. Hence, the entire community of Jews was caught up in the drama of spiritual warfare glorified in the War Scroll. Following the Zoroastrian formula of cosmic duality, the Zaddikim identified themselves as the Sons of Light in conflict with the Sons of Darkness. They adhered to a secret doctrine based in the supernatural authority of Melchizedek, the power behind Christ. Although their belief system was turbocharged with hatred and vindictive, genocidal rage, it became the germ for the universal message of God's love preached in Christianity.

To be more exact, a spurious message of divine love concealed and transmitted the genodical germ.

In epidemiological terms, Christianity was the pandemic *vector* for the ideological virus of the Zaddikim. The ultra-righteous priesthood who inspired the Scrolls regarded themselves as a master race, even a different species. The vector of the Elohim (read: Archontic parasites) had to be introduced somewhere, sometime, in some cultural setting. It needed a racial host. Gnostics detected that the *anomia* arose in the early religious experience of the Hebrews, following the weird sequence of events described in part 1. Over centuries, the *anomia* generated the four components of the redeemer complex. The sulfurous, pathological core of that complex is *terror*, terror before the father god who creates the world and commands its fate; terror for those who follow the Lord's plan and those who do not; terror for the innocent victim tormented and dominated by the perpetrator; terror for the perpetrators who will be caught out and punished by God; terror imposed by the perpetrators who triumphantly manage to prevail in God's name;

terror for the entire world plunged against all human resistance into a Zoroastrian war between Light and Darkness; terror that drives human society to a final solution, the lethal madness of a species hell-bent on its own destruction.

The belief that the world can be saved by destroying it exemplifies *annihilation theology* (a term proposed in chapter 3). Written into the apocalyptic agenda of the Zaddikim, this belief was enshrined in Christian doctrine by the Book of Revelation of Saint John the Divine. John's rabid call to planetary holocaust concludes the New Testament, the good news of God's redemption achieved through His Son, who blithely tells everyone to "love thy neighbor." The Book of Revelation is quite a disturbing conclusion to the message of divine love. In his stunning monograph on the Book of Revelation D. H. Lawrence captured the power-hungry spirit of salvationism:

> The will of the community of Christians was anti-social, almost anti-human, revealing from the start a frenzied desire for the end of the world, the destruction of humanity altogether; and then, when this did not come, a grim determination to destroy all mastery, all lordship, and all human splendour out of the world, leaving the community of saints as the final negation of power, and the final power.[269]

Gnostics and Mystery initiates lived peacefully in Jerusalem and the Levant for many centuries. Of all people in that time and setting, they would have been best qualified to detect the dangers of the rising tide of Jewish apocalypticism. Skilled in theology and dialectical argument, they were able to refute fanatical beliefs, but unable to protect themselves against the violence driven by those beliefs. And they had no recourse to the establishment powers, either. Not only were *gnostikoi* like Hypatia apolitical, they deliberately refrained from involvement in politics and dissociated themselves from pseudo-initiates and Gnostic wannabes who often advised the theocratic regents of the era.

Hypatia may have made a rash move by commenting on a minor political issue in Alexandria, thereby targeting herself for a Christian mob unleashed by Cyril, bishop of the city. All around the classical world the teachers in the Mysteries had great authority because of their learning, their commitment to artistic and cultural life, and their management of the artisan guilds, but their special prestige also depended upon them standing above and beyond politics. They were powerless against the very same evils that religion forces upon the world today: terrorism, sectarian violence, jihad, apocalypse, divine punishment, annihilation theology, enacted in fanatical acts by the few who are willing to take their beliefs to the extreme, supported by the blind collusion of the many decent but passive people who share those same beliefs.

The Good Shepherd

Gnostics were not anti-Christian in the sense of being against love, altruism, kindness to others, charity, compassion for the poor and underprivileged, reverence for the Divine, and other so-called Christian virtues. But it must be asked, Are these values really unique to Christianity or the other Abrahamic religions? They are commonly claimed to be the signature attributes of the People of the Book, but this claim is transparently false. It ignores the historical evidence to the contrary, overlooks the transcendent humanism of the East, dismisses the sense of humanity *already* expressed in many other traditions, especially among native and indigenous peoples, and discounts the magnificent testament of spirituality found in Gnostic writings, which were almost totally destroyed by Christian fanatics.

Gnostics were accused of arrogance because they claimed direct access to Divinity by cultivating the faculty of nous, divine intelligence. But can this arrogance, if such it was, have been worse than the righteous attitude of the Christian fanatics who assaulted them with vindictive and murderous fury? The Anthropos doctrine (as scholars call it) was central to the Gnostic message. Their self-designation, "the standing race," suggests that they stood tall as representatives of authentic *humanitas*, but not of *zaddik*, the false ideal of human perfection.[270] In Asia the Anthropos doctrine may have been reflected in the figure of the Bodhisattva that emerged in Mahayana Buddhism around 150 c.e., at the same moment Gnostics came out publicly to oppose the first Christian ideologues.

At the dawn of the Piscean Age, Pagan initiates in the Near East faced an unprecedented challenge: how to present the Anthropos in a public or popular manner, in order to counter the growing popularity of the Christian Redeemer, the god-man Jesus Christ. As the new religion of divine redemption expanded its power base, the guardians of the Mysteries pondered how to mainstream the arcane concept of the Anthropos. Thinking along mythological lines, Syrian Gnostics from Antioch decided that a much-loved figure from ancient Middle Eastern mythology, Tammuz, would be an appropriate stand-in for the Anthropos, PTELIOS RHOME in Coptic. Tammuz was the divine shepherd, a lover of the Great Goddess, Ishtar, equivalent to the Greek Aphrodite. His legend was well-known throughout the Near East. As already noted, it is the source of the "child in the manger" cameo in the New Testament. Roman and Jewish authors who concocted the Gospels substituted the "Christ child" for the beloved shepherd who often slept in the stable. The suppression of Goddess religion in the Levant caused the legend of Tammuz to decline in the popular imagination. The Antioch cell considered how to reintroduce him in the guise of "the good shepherd," renamed Hermas.

Some representations of Hermas survive. They show a strong but gentle child, smiling broadly, standing upright with a lamb across his or her shoulders. This image was not original with the Antioch cell.[271] Its prototype can be seen in Hermes Kriophoros, the ram bearer, an ancient divinity of the Pelasgians, the indigenous pre-Hellenic people of the Peloponnesus.[272] But the initiates altered the original figure by replacing the ram with a lamb. This gentle, animal-friendly figure was to be the icon to represent humanity in the Piscean Age.[273] The poster child of the Wisdom Goddess, no less.

The Gnostic figure of Hermas considered by the Antioch cell never emerged, because it was co-opted by a proto-Christian group in the same city. Yet again, Archontic countermimicry came into play. Around 150 c.e. the Antioch congregation, the first group known to call themselves Christians (Acts 11:26), produced a book entitled the *Shepherd of Hermas*, attributed to the brother of Pius, then bishop of Rome. This early Christian document was included in the Muratori canon, a list of canonical books from the third century. It is also found in some copies of the New Testament, such as the Sinaitic Codex.

The Shepherd of Hermas is a loose allegory loaded with sententious advice alien to the Gnostic style and values. Scholars note that the doctrine it contains is peculiar because it does not match the Christology of the New Testament. Oddly, it identifies the figure of Hermas with the Holy Spirit, but the Holy Spirit in that early stage of Christian ideology carried strong allusions to the Divine Sophia. Although Hermas is a perverted co-optation, the figure was consistent with the intention to portray the shepherd, and by extension, humanity, as the progeny of the Aeonic Mother. But the iconic figure so intended was completely misrepresented in a manual of pious platitudes attributed to the Roman bishop. The Gospel of Philip records the Gnostic protest against this ploy:

> Many who oppose the truth and are messengers of error will set up their error against the pure thoughts of the Revealers. . . . They create an imitation remnant in the name of a dead man, calling it Hermas, the first-born of unrighteousness, in order that the existential Light may not be recognized by petty minds. (NHC II, 3, 77–78)

The initiates must have greatly despaired over this act of co-optation, knowing that anyone who could not see the error in the figure of Jesus Christ, the Archontic substitute for the Anthropos, surely would not see the intentional deceit in Hermas.

In the end, the icon that came to mirror humanity and transmit the message of divine love was an instrument of torture.

PART FOUR

RECLAIMING
the
SOPHIANIC VISION

Eleusis Pediment with Sheaf of Cut Wheat

21

UNMASKING EVIL

I n their case against redemptive religion, Gnostics made an astonishing revelation about its origin, the transmundane source of salvation.
Adherents to the three Abrahamic faiths all believe that their religion
comes from God the Father through a line of male emissaries: Abraham,
Moses, Jesus, Paul, Muhammad. As we have seen, Gnostics had some
rather strange things to say about this claim. The scenario of the Archons
and the threat of alien intrusion certainly present a steep challenge to
many people today and may well provide cause to dismiss the Gnostic
worldview as superstitious nonsense, if not sheer dementia.

Who is willing to consider that salvationist religion is an ideological
virus insinuated in the human psyche by an alien species? For the seers
of the Mysteries of Egypt and the Levant, this was not a belief to be
accepted or rejected. For them it was, I would argue, the direct result of
paranormal perception.

The Extraterrestrial Messiah

People are often offended by the knowledge they need
most. We resist our deepest education. . . . While we seek
agreement, protection, and security, our best path may be
toward discomfort.[274]

Gnostics allowed the transmundane origin of redemptive religion—
"Yaldabaoth himself chose a certain man named Abraham, and made a
covenant with him" (cited in full in chapter 7)—but proposed a different
way to view it. Yaldabaoth is the Demiurge, a.k.a. Yahweh-Jehovah, a

demented pseudodeity who works against humanity. This is the "Lord Archon," head of the legion of cyborg-like parasites who inhabit the solar system exclusive of the Earth, Sun, and Moon. Although they cannot originate anything, because they lack the divine factor of *ennoia* (intentionality), Archons can imitate and do so with a vengeance. Their expertise is simulation (HAL, virtual reality). The Demiurge fashions a heaven world copied from the fractal patterns of the eternal Aeons, the Pleromic gods who reside in the galactic center (see the Sophia mythos, episode 5). His construction is celestial kitsch, like the fake Italianate villa of a Mafia don complete with militant angels to guard every portal. The Demiurge has a master plan for humanity, copied from the guiding program of the Revealers, but grotesquely distorted. Salvation by super-human powers, rather than through the divine spark of intelligence innate to humanity and aligned with Sophia, is the hallmark of extra-terrestrial religion.

The Dead Sea Scrolls present graphic evidence that the Qumranic sect looked for rescue to come from the skies beyond the Earth. At the moment of the apocalyptic showdown, they expected the intervention of the Kedoshim, radiant warrior angels who would appear in shining round chariots. The celestial host would be commanded by a supreme overlord, whom scholars identify with the eerie, clonelike figure, Melchizedek. Numerous passages in the Dead Sea Scrolls describe the flight of the celestial rescue squad. In the fragmentary columns of 4Q405, The Songs of the Sacrifice of the Sabbath, an observer of the Kedoshim gives this eyewitness account:

> They do not sit still, the glorious chariots, the shining ophanim ... spirits of gods ... purity ... holy. The works of [its] corners ... of kingship, the glorious seats of the chariots ... wonderful power. . . . When they move [they do] not turn aside to any ... they go straight up. . . . When they rise the murmuring sound of gods [is heard], and there is an uproar of exaltation when they lift their wings, the [murmur]ing sound of gods. . . . And when the ophanim move forward, the holy angels return; [they emerge from between] its glorious [wh]eels with the likeness of fire, the spirits of the holy of holies. Around them is the likeness

of streams of fire like electrum, and a [lum]inous substance,
gloriously multi-colored, multi-colored, [purely] blended. . . .
And there is a murmuring voice of blessing in the uproar of
their motion, and they praise the holy one on returning to their
paths. When they rise up, they rise wonderfully; when they
settle, they [sta]nd still.[275]

This passage hardly requires comment. Anyone who has read even
lightly into the voluminous eyewitness testimony of UFO sightings will
recognize the frequently reported details: erratic and mysterious movement including fast glides and sudden stops, the play of colored lights,
rushing and murmuring sounds. The description of how the Kedoshim
chariots pause and float, then slide away, in total defiance of known grav-
itational laws, is particularly striking, and accords perfectly with countless modern reports of UFO activity.*

In addition to evidence of extraterrestrial hardware, the Dead Sea
Scrolls describe firsthand contact with alien-type beings, "close encounters of the fourth kind." 4Q545, The Vision of Amran, relates how two
figures argue over the fate of man who stands by, paralyzed in "the vision
of the dream." This encounter happens in a dream or dreamlike state,
comparable to modern cases of alien abduction. The terrified witness
asks, "How it is that [you have authority over me?" They said, "We] rule
and have authority over all the human race."[276] This exchange recalls
a passage in the Nag Hammadi Codex (III, 5), The Dialogue of the
Savior. "Judas said, Behold, the Archons dwell above us, so it is they who
will rule over us! The Lord said, It is you who will rule over them!"[277]
Another Gnostic text, The First Apocalypse of James, presents a detailed
account of alien abduction:

> The Master said: James, behold, I shall reveal to you the path of
> your redemption. Whenever you are seized and you undergo
> death-pangs (mortal fear), a multitude of Archons may turn on

---

* Extensive research into this genre led me to conclude that a few rare instances of UFO
sightings may be due to "alien craft" invading planetary airspace. The vast majority,
however, point to covert military technology for which the UFO narrative provides
convenient cover.

you, thinking they can capture you. And in particular, three of them will seize you, those who pose as toll collectors. Not only do they demand toll, but they take away souls by theft.[278]

The Gnostic master instructs James to repel the Archons by recalling how they originated and whence he, James, himself originates: "You are to say to him, 'To the place when I came, the Source, there shall I return.' And if you respond in this manner, you will escape their attacks." The Source is the Pleroma. The teacher reminds James of the Mystery teaching that humanity originates from a singularity in the Pleroma. The human species is a projection of divine imagination. But the Archons arise *outside* the Pleroma due to the anomalous impact of Sophia's plunge into the chaos below. They are alien, yet they are also akin to the Anthropos:

> You are to say to him [the alien intruder]: "They are not entirely alien, for they are from the Fallen Sophia (Achamoth), the female divinity who produced them when she brought the human race down from the Source, the realm of the Pre-Existent One (Originator). So they are not entirely alien, but they are our kin. They are indeed so because she who is their matrix, Sophia Achamoth, is from the Source. At the same time they are alien because Sophia did not combine with her like in the Source (her divine male counterpart), when she produced them."[279]

Gnostic instruction is precise on the matter of the Archons. It both exposes and refutes parallel material in the Dead Sea Scrolls. In 4Q544 Amran sees two supernatural beings, one dark and glittering (the "reptilian type" of ET?), and the other "pleasant in his appearance, and his face was laughing and he was covered in white." This is consistent with the Qumranic teaching on the two spirits, one of Light and one of Darkness, who watch over all human beings and occasion the choice between right and wrong. The translators comment: "Apparently Amram chooses to follow the angel of light and begins to question him about the meaning of his vision. The angel of darkness is Malki-Resha and the angel of light, we may presume, is called Melchizedek, ruler of righteousness. Melzhizedek as an angelic figure also appears in text 130,

The Coming of Melchizedek."[280] In short, the situation of the contactee in the scrolls illustrates a Zoroastrian dilemma, the choice between two absolutely opposing *extra-human* forces. This places our species in the crossfire between two alien influences, a good spirit and a bad spirit. The only salvation is to give oneself into the care of the Angel of Light, Melchizedek, the ET Messiah.

The Nag Hammadi account of alien contact presents quite a different perspective. James instructs the contactee to assert humankind's link to the Pleroma and the goddess Sophia, and put the aliens in their place, yet without fully disowning them. We ourselves will prevail over the alien legion, whether they appear in black or white tenure. This assertion gives some idea of the high sophistication of Gnostic instruction on the dicey topic of alien intrusion.

THE NOETIC PRINCIPLE

Gnostics saw in the Palestinian redeemer complex both the evidence and the instrument of extrahuman intrusion upon the human mind. They must have had a vast, transhistorical view of the psychic life of the human species, but they had, equally, a clear perception of what was happening in their time and setting. Hence the clear warning: "Jerusalem is the dwelling place of many Archons." Extrahuman influences upon humanity were a central concern in the Levantine and Egyptian Mysteries. As parapsychologists and experimental mystics, the telestai were highly accomplished in telepathy, clairvoyance, remote viewing, and lucid dreaming. They were certainly able to detect predatory entities and distinguish them from a wide range of neutral or benevolent forces in the cosmos. The real possibility of foreign entities invading or influencing the human psyche was a deep concern to them.

Yet the Mystery adepts did not blame human problems on the Archons. They were clear on the difference between error and evil. In the Dialogue of the Savior, Judas asks, "Tell me, Lord, what is the beginning of the path?" The response is: "Love and goodness. For if just one of these existed among the Archons, evil would never have come into existence."[281] The illumined teacher does not say Archons are evil, but that they lack love and goodness (attributes considered to be innate to humanity, as we have seen in considering Pagan ethics), so their influence on humankind is bound to be deviant. This again attests to the finely nuanced teaching of the Gnostic revealers. Evil arises in human behavior when we do not detect and correct our mistakes, thus allowing the Archons to put an evil antihuman spin on our behavior.

Not all that operates in the human psyche originates there. This is a primary noetic principle taught in the Egyptian and Levantine Mysteries, and the basic insight of Gnostic parapsychology. It is an uncomfortable idea, but it may also be an indispensable one. It is an idea we resist even though it is essential for "our deepest education."

No matter what one thinks of the Gnostic theory of error and the ET-Archon connection, it is startling to find a full and coherent account of alien intrusion in ancient documents dating from 400 c.e., a textual legacy of knowledge derived from far older origins. It is worth noting that the first great UFO wave of the twentieth century occurred in the summer and fall of 1947 when Jean Doresse was in Cairo examining the Nag Hammadi Codices, at the very moment the first Dead Sea Scrolls were found. The famous sighting by aviator Kenneth Arnold over Mount Rainier, and the alleged Roswell crash, happened in that same summer. This was also the year that the CIA was founded, with the dual intention (according to UFO conspiracy buffs) to co-opt alien technology and cut a deal with the aliens, allowing them to experiment covertly on human subjects. Three-letter acronyms—NHC, DSS, UFO, CIA—seem to proliferate like larvae when the Archons come into the picture. In fact, a CIA agent named Miles Copeland was dispatched to Damascus to examine and photograph some of the first scroll fragments to be unearthed. Apparently, Copeland microfilmed some fragments of the Book of Daniel, a foundation text of Jewish apocalypticism, material that has yet to be made public by Qumranic scholars.[282]

About one-fifth of all Coptic Gnostic materials concern the origin, motive, and methods of the Archons, including instructions on how to detect and overcome their influence. This material is both lucid and original, yet it has not been factored into the current debate over ETs and UFOs. The current literature abounds with reports of ETs, cyborgs, reptilians, close encounters, and tales of the cross-breeding of human and nonhuman entities, going all the way back to the Sumerian cuneiform story of the Annunaki. Such weird, sensational matters are not usually associated with religion and theology, yet Gnostic teachings connect these phenomena in a careful and intimate manner. Religious historians and Gnostic scholars are disinclined to interpret the Archons in terms of the current ET/UFO debate, or even to interpret them at all, but common sense invites the connection. When DSS scholar Hugh Schonfield observed that the Piscean Age dawned in an atmosphere of "messianic science fiction," he may hardly have imagined how right he was. Bizarre as it may seem, heretical writings almost two thousand years old elucidate a solution to the most baffling enigma of our time. In the matter of the ET/UFO enigma, the Gnostics were ahead of everyone today. Way ahead.

Messengers of Deception

The top investigators of the ET/UFO phenomenon, Jacques Vallee, Keith Thompson, and John Keel, have emphasized its religious aspect, but without allusion to Gnostic materials. Keel asserts, "The same manifestations that created our religious beliefs, created our UFO beliefs. A serious look at the Phenomenon would cause a revision in our way of looking at religion."[283] Keel's remark is eminently sober. Most ET/UFO speculation toggles erratically between two impassioned opinions: either aliens show us the way to our salvation, or they are out to destroy us.

Gnostics explicitly warned that the Archons work through salvationist religion to deviate us from our proper course of evolution, our share in Sophia's Correction. They do this, Gnostics claimed, because they *envy* us. Archons lack both *ennoia* (singular intentionality) and *epinoia* (moral-creative imagination), and they want to have this specific endowment of ours, to assimilate or steal it. This diagnosis of Archontic intrusion conforms in many respects to reports of people who have encountered alien entities, especially the Grays and the Reptilians.

Veteran investigator Jacques Vallee sees in the ET phenomenon a broad mutation of the religious experience of humankind. His warning that the ET/UFO enigma hides a "spiritual control system" comes very close to the Gnostic analysis. After initially assuming benevolence,

Vallee concluded that alien intrusion is sinister and predatory. This is also the Gnostic view. In *Angels and Aliens*, Keith Thompson emphasizes the collective or archetypal interpretation of ETs, based on Jungian psychology. In this view, the Archons would be trickster-type entities whose effect on us depends on how we "play" them. John Keel has also stressed the trickster-like aspect of aliens: the way "the Phenomenon" (as Keel calls it) shape-shifts, momentarily conforming to our beliefs about it and then, quite suddenly, contradicting what we believe.

In the end, Archontic activity eludes all belief. The Second Treatise of the Great Seth says that it is "pure senselessness." But, as Vallee astutely noted in *Messengers of Deception*, "The way to a man's belief is through confusion and absurdity."[284]

Many people will balk at the ET/Archon hypothesis, as I propose to call it. This may pose an obstacle to mainstream appreciation of Gnostic ideas. Then again, it may be the key to their wider acceptance. Scholars reject the Archon material out of hand, not even bothering to discount it as superstitious nonsense. Doing so, they conveniently absolve themselves from addressing the radical argument against salvationism, the ideology intimately associated with malevolent paranormal influence. Those who cannot think their way into this theory with an open, investigative attitude are missing a momentous insight into the human condition. To see how the Archons operate is to see into the elusive workings of our own minds. Knowing how we are deviated is certainly crucial to our survival. As George P. Hansen noted in *The Trickster and the Paranormal*, "When the supernatural and the irrational are banished from consciousness, they are not destroyed, rather, they become exceedingly dangerous."[285]

The FGS describes how the Archons emerge due to Sophia's plunge into elemental matter, the *dema* of the galactic arms. Gnostic seers called this unforeseen event "the generation of error." It induces a subliminal effect in the human mind, exaggerating our natural tendency to err and shifting it beyond the scale of correction. The presence of the Archons in the solar system *dangerously widens the margin of human error*, thus impacting the way we learn and evolve. At the very least, the Archons can be taken for a brilliant parapsychological metaphor that explains how humans can think and act out of scale, inhumanely. The self-betrayal of humanity through the redeemer complex happens, in part, at least, because we can think ourselves right out of our own minds and into an alien mind-set.

No matter what one makes of the Archons in a literal sense, the Gnostic theory of error is certainly one of the supreme achievements of human reasoning. The Gnostic seers insisted that Archons cannot control or manipulate us unless we give them power to do so. This happens when we do not optimize nous, our endowment of divine intelligence. Our omission is *their* salvation. Gnostic error theory states three simple, interlocking truths: (1) humans are creatures who learn by making mistakes; (2) to learn from our mistakes we must detect and correct them (hence our collaborative role in Gaian evolution and Sophia's Correction); and (3) when we fail to detect and correct our mistakes they can extrapolate wildly and drive us beyond human limits. The Archons intrude at just that point where we let our errors go uncorrected and lend their deviant force to what is already going off course. Without our cosmic cousins in the picture we would still commit errors, but we would always be able to stand back and correct our course before we got too far out of alignment with Gaia and our innate mental powers.

If the Gnostics were right, Archons really do exist in their own realm as inorganic, extraterrestrial forms, *and* as programs in our minds. Salvationism is an ideological virus spread by an alien species and enacted by humans who fall under their subterfuge. Such is the bizarre warning contained in the sci-fi theology of the Gnostics.

The Mother of Evil

Apply these concepts to the global situation of humanity today, and it will be self-evident that the Gnostic theory of error has something fundamental to teach us. Something that could well be crucial to our long-term survival.

If evil arises from error when error runs beyond the scale of correction, deepening our awareness of error enables us to nip evil in the bud. The Gospel of Philip says, "Ignorance is the mother of all evil." In a lucid passage on error theory, the Gnostic master says:

> So long as the root of wickedness is hidden, it is strong. But when
> it is recognized, it is dissolved. When it is revealed, it perishes. . . .
> As for ourselves, let us each dig down after the root of evil which
> is within each of us, and produces its fruit in our hearts. It masters
> us. We are its slaves. It takes us captive, to make us do what we
> do not want, and what we do want, we do not do. It is powerful
> because we have not recognized it. (II, 3, 83.5–30)

The Dialogue of the Savior says, "Anyone who does not know how fire
came into existence will be burned by it, because he does not know the
root of it." With typical Gnostic flair, the revealer adds, "Whoever does
not know the root of evil is no stranger to it" (II, 5, 134.5–20). Zoroastrian
single-source duality asserts an autonomous force of evil in the cosmos,
but Gnostics refuted this view. The root of evil is human error, the mind
mistaking itself. To defeat evil, we must unmask it by seeing its origin in
the erring operations of our own minds.

The ET/Archon phenomenon appears to be a riddle that compels a
solution which no one has so far worked out. But this riddle may actually turn out to be the answer to another riddle: the problem of evil.
Jacques Vallee calls ETs "messengers of deception," closely echoing
the Gnostic warning against "messengers of error [who] will induce
mistakes, working against the pure thoughts of the Revealers" (The
Gospel of Philip, 77–78). Deception is not exactly error, however, and
the difference warrants close examination. Gnostic materials give
several words for error: *plane* and *apaton* in Greek, SOREM in Coptic.
They also use the Coptic KROG specifically for deceit, by contrast
to error. KROG may be related to the ancient Iranian term *drugh*,
"deceit." This is a key term in Zoroastrian religion where the principle
of truth, *asha*, is opposed by "the Lie," *drugh*, a parallel to the cosmic
polarity of Ahura Mazda and Ahriman. This dichotomy exemplifies
single-source duality, as already explained. Gnostics did not find a split
in the Godhead, the tell-tale sign of two opposing cosmic principles,
so their interpretation of deception differed from that of the Hebrews
who inherited Zoroastrian duality.

You can mistake a coiled rope for a snake. This is an error. If I trick
you into taking a coiled rope for a snake, that is out-and-out deceit.

Gnostic thought agrees with Buddhism that the world is not an illusion in the sense of being unreal, but in the sense of being erroneously perceived. Buddhist scholar H. V. Guenther specifies: "Illusion does not mean the illusion of perception, but the false conclusion we base on perception."[286] In Buddhist and Gnostic traditions alike, the purpose of illuminist discipline is to "get behind the veil to find reality and become free. Going behind the veil has no spatial connotation. The phenomenal is the absolute and vice versa."[287] Gnosis, the counterpart to Buddhist *prajña*, is the preeminent human tool for ultimate discernment of reality. Error theory is original to the Gnostic schools, as far as I know, but Indo-Tibetan Buddhism offers some complementary insight on how error arises and operates. H. V. Guenther aptly summarizes the key insight of Asian psycho-phenomonology: "All the entities of the world of appearance are but the motion of original awareness. But although they remain in the creative play of the co-emergence of bliss and nothingness, internally this awareness, defined by its own obscurating power, becomes co-emergent ignorance."[288]

To see the Real for what it is requires being able to discern error, which is the unintentional mistaking of the Real, as well as deception, which is the intentional use of error, deliberate deceit. Error imposed by intention becomes *drugh*, the Lie. These nuances, excruciating as they may be, are essential to a sound grasp of the Gnostic theory of error, and bear directly on the issue of alien intrusion in the human mind. In short, there is a web of deception around the essential error that enmeshes us in "co-emergent ignorance" with the Archons.

With the textual evidence of Gnostic teachings in such a deplorable state, it may be instructive to draw on Buddhist parallels regarding the phenomenology of error. The Nyingma sage Long Chen Pa (1308–63) used the term *'khrul-pa*, "mistakenness," "going astray," to describe how the human mind slips into an erroneous perception of the Real. Because *'khrul-pa* is "a process of self-deception *intrinsic* to experiencing, one cannot appeal to any causal principles operating on the process from without."[289] The same applies for the Archons in Gnostic theory: our capacity to err is intrinsic to the process by which we learn and evolve. That being so, *it cannot be attributed to external causes such as aliens preying on our minds*. Nevertheless, if such entities exist, we are obliged to perceive how they might be implicated in, and take advantage of, our tendency to err.

The Tibetan term *kun-rdzob* "specious," "totally spurious" matches the Coptic KROG, "deception." Tibetan seers apply this phantasmal status to *tulpas*, solid, lifelike phantoms produced by lamas. In *Magic and Mystery in Tibet*, Alexandra David-Neel described a jovial *tulpa* she conjured up with the aid of her meditation teacher. It followed her around for weeks until she learned how to dissipate it. She explained that *tulpas* are "imaginary forms which are a sort of robot which they [lamas] control as they wish, but which, sometimes, manage to acquire some kind of autonomous personality."[290] Could it be that the Archons are tulpas produced, not by a feat of human attention, but by the stressed, hypervigilant attention of the Aeon Sophia, due to the shock of finding herself stranded in chaos, outside the Pleroma?

The sole writer on the ET/UFO enigma to equate the Gnostic Archons with contemporary ETs is Nigel Kerner. In *The Song of the Greys*, he suggests that the Archons arose due to the breakaway of a gigantic remote-sensing device protruded from the Pleroma. This image is arresting, to be sure, but Kerner has not done his homework. Nothing in Gnostic writings indicates that the Pleromic gods need to use Archonlike *tulpas* to perceive events in the extra-Pleromic worlds. It is more likely that the *tulpas* appear in the human realm as a result of two-world duality, the coexistence of planetary and terrestrial physics. They belong to the solar system, yet they intrude upon the Earth. They are messengers of deception because they do not inform us of their true nature. Nothing any ET has ever said has added one iota to the sum of human knowledge or offered one single insight that human beings could not produce out of their own resources. To the knowledge of this writer, there is no record of any ET encounter in which the aliens confess to the contactee that they are nothing but solid-seeming phantoms. (Don't hold your breath, folks.)

Archons lie by omission, never coming out to reveal what they truly are. The proof of their malevolence is their refusal to explain themselves in clear and honest terms. They take advantage of human credulity by appearing to be enigmatic. We cannot see through this deception (KROG) until we have first confronted the perceptual error in our own minds. If I do not first know how a rope can be mistaken for a snake, I will not be able to understand how someone can deceive me by disguising a rope as a snake.

Contrary to Nature

The ET/Archon hypothesis is pretty arcane stuff, I admit. This is high strangeness, indeed. But with the Gnostic theory of alien intrusion, the stranger it gets, the more sense it makes. The Sophia mythos does not have to be taken on belief and should not be. Nor should it be rejected for its seeming weirdness, or its often daunting complexity. It is probably the most lucid and imaginatively comprehensive scenario ever conceived to explain what has been called "the topic of topics"—namely, predation.[291] It is also the best guiding story for full actualization of our divine potential, including the power of imagination, called *epinoia* in Gnostic writings. The Divine Sophia expressly gave this power to humankind to detect and resist Archontic subversion. In a sense, the Archons are present in the cosmos to test us so that we are certain to make optimal use of our divine endowment. Mastery of that endowment requires facing our inhumanity (our Archontic side) and disempowering it, but not disowning it.

Gnostic heresy is a thing of the past, a dead issue, but the battle for truth persists in our minds. Humanity cannot find its way to alignment with Gaia-Sophia without mastering the problem of extrahuman predation. As suggested above, the Archon phenomenon may prove to be less a problem than the solution to the question, Whence comes evil? But this question may be inseparable from another one: Are we alone? If humans cannot fathom their relation to our cousin species, who are so deeply implicated in the scenario of terrestrial evolution, how can we possibly realize our membership in the cosmic community at large? Could admitting "the reality of the Archons" (title of an NHC text) be the first step to a wider view of how the cosmos is populated with all kinds of entities, benevolent and malevolent? Might not the capacity to recognize *one* predatory species provide the foundation for a cosmic perspective on our relation to all species? Could recognition of the Archons be the key to embracing our singularity in the cosmic order? We are still a long way from working through these issues.

Fortunately, there is rare testimony from late antiquity on the precise nature of Archontic intrusion. It presents an elegant explanation of the paranormal effect of nonhuman entities. This testimony comes from the church historian, Socrates Scholasticus (b. ca. 380 c.e.), who left an account of the murder of Hypatia. Scholasticus was not a Gnostic, but an apologetic Church historian. But he seems to have been in contact with genuine Gnostics, including a man named Macarius, an Alexandrian Gnostic who may well have been an elder colleague of Hypatia's. (In *Ancient Mystery Cults*, the best single book on the Mysteries, Walter Burkert explains that *makarismos* was the title given in "praise of the blessed status of those who have 'seen' the mysteries."[292] In other words, it was the honorific title of those who had beheld the Organic Light. This did not happen to all participants in the Mysteries, whose numbers ran into the tens of thousands over many generations, but only to a privileged few.)

In chapter 23 of his *Ecclesiastical History of the Church*, Scholasticus records an exchange between Marcarius and a disciple called Evagrius, known to have composed valuable works such as "The Gnostic, or, To Him Who Is Deemed Worthy of Knowledge," "To the Virgin," and "Six Hundred Prognostic Problems." The dialogue between teacher and student contains a succinct observation on intrapsychic intrusion:

> That chosen vessel, the aged Egyptian Macarius, asked me, why we impair the strength of the retentive faculty of the soul by cherishing the remembrance of an injury received from men; while by remembering those done us by devils we remain uninjured? And when I hesitated, scarcely knowing what answer to make, and begged him to account for it, he replied, "Because the former is an affection contrary to nature, and the latter is conformable to the nature of the mind."[293]

While his student stands and waffles, befuddled and unable to answer, the Egyptian looks sideways at his own question: "Why does the remembrance of injury done by devils leave us uninjured?" In his tacit response Macarius wastes no words, knowing the subject is grave, the nuance fateful.

Injury received from our fellow men is "contrary to nature," because our innate disposition is to be kind to each other, and show spontaneous affection, as Marcus Aurelius asserted. But the alien offspring of Sophia lack the love and goodness inborn to humankind. The difference between them and us determines the subterfuge they can affect on us. It gives them an insidious edge. Archontic deviation of the human species relies on conspiration by default, the surrender of our innate powers to an alien mind-set, and the betrayal of our discriminating skills. But it all happens so easily, without effort, as if there is no conspiracy at all, no collusion on our part. The intrusion of the Archons goes unnoticed, Macarius warns, because the alien effect we need to detect and resist is *disguised in the way we think*, "conformable to the nature of the mind."

SOPHIA'S CORRECTION

If the Mysteries are the ancient tap root of deep ecology, as I am proposing, it may now be possible to appreciate how deep that root goes. It is both deep in time and deep in the psyche, anchored in the psychic structure of humankind. In *Sacred Pleasure*, Riane Eisler wrote, "To realize that which cannot be lost, it is necessary to understand what really has been lost." The paradox fits Gnosis in a precise and poignant manner. The root that runs so deep, the wisdom anchored so profoundly in the soul-life of the human species, cannot have been eradicated. The effort exerted to destroy it has produced the longest, most violent drama of pain, deceit, and cruelty humanity has ever known, yet the very magnitude of the effort attests to the strength and depth of the inborn wisdom.

It is truly a miracle that our species has survived the religious campaign to eliminate the Goddess and her Mysteries. I suspect that without indigenous peoples all around the world preserving the native wisdom in their ways of life, we might never have seen it through to the day when I can write these words. The destructive power of authoritarian domination is immense, but those who now protest it (read: 2020 anti-reset activism) have only begun to understand *why* it has been so powerful. Archontic deceit makes those who are dominated by authorities accessory to their own abuse and enslavement. At any given moment there are vastly more good and decent people in the world than evildoers, yet those who intend evil gain a disproportionate advantage because they rely on the passive consent of the believers (read: 2020 Covid-19 compliance). This is the dark, dirty secret of victim-perpetrator collusion.

Patriarchy has birthed a world dominated by terror, but terror is merely error spelt with a *T*. The T is the cross, the Roman torture instrument, catholic symbol of divine love (more lately, a fashion accessory—which in no respect diminishes its nefarious effect). Terror begins with the false doctrine of salvation, the specious message of love. Terror consummates in the transhumanist dystopia where humans are zombies remote-controlled by AI. This is where the Zaddikim are hell bent to take the world, all the way to the last act of the psychodrama and into total auto-destruction, if there is no way to pull out of the prescripted plot. We behave as we believe.

How can the historical course of terror be averted? It helps immensely to see what the Gnostics saw, for they discerned the root of the dominator pathology now operating in full view through the technocratic agenda of the Great Reset. To dissociate oneself individually from fixation on the divine victim, the icon of universal humanity, is to act for the liberation of all races. (On the condition that you serve and save your own race first.) To face this challenge, the Gnostic unmasking of evil can be of paramount service. Gnostic teachings from the Mystery School network preserved the essence of Goddess-oriented shamanism typical of Europan cultures before Christianization, comparable to indigenous cultures worldwide. At the same time, these teachings presented a worldview of Iranian origins, outside Europa proper. The first *gnostikoi* were Egyptians, Levantines, Syrians, and Persians. Yet they protected Europe, or at least they tried. Owing to their cultural and historical background, they had an intimate perception of the evil that would spread into Europa where there was no immunity to it in the psychic makeup of the native peoples. The Gnostics in the Near East were the front line of defense against the dual menace of salvationism and theocracy. When that line of defense broke, something truly evil, an alien force working against life, poured into Europa. Exactly like a biological pestilence, it decimated the indigenous peoples from the inside out.

THEOCRACY REBRANDED

Jeffery Burton Russell, religious historian and author of a series of books on Satan, Lucifer, and the Devil, remarked that "The problem of evil transcends religion."[294] He might well have added that it also contaminates it. Gnostics enraged and outraged the early Christians on many points, but most especially because they claimed to know the solution to the problem of evil. The heretics from the Mysteries denied that good and evil can come from the same source. To the early Christians this was anathema, a frontal negation of the omnipotence of their father god. It blew the divine plan right off its foundations. Believers in the plan, both then and today, "ascribe the purpose of the terrible suffering of the world to God's purpose in leading us to the good through 'soul-making and mystery,'" but Gnostics refuted this interpretation and insisted that it is as ludicrous as it is dangerous.[295] In the Gnostic paradigm of two-source duality, the source of evil is not in the Godhead, but in the human realm exclusively.

To paraphrase René Girard (cited in chapter 18), religion conceals its source so that it can perpetuate suffering yet pretend to alleviate it. Either way, religion sanctifies suffering. Here the perennial mechanism of human evil comes fully into view: it prevails by making the force *and enforcement* of suffering look more powerful than the life force itself (as I observed at the opening of chapter 19). All religion in its core structure is a variant of theocracy. It may appear that humankind in the twenty-first century has advanced beyond the age-old strictures of blind faith. Far from it. While countless millions still cling to their religious indoctrination as if it were a life-saving medicine, the globalist technocrats are implementing the religion of the future, complete with their own version of the eucharist, the Covid-19 vaccination. The rise of theocracy described in part 1 does not merely recount obscure events in the distant past. It anticipates the future unfolding now. Communism is theocracy without the need for gods to legitimate it. The transhumanist technocratic agenda of the Great Reset is theocracy rebranded. This time around, self-entitled billionaires and wind-bag political ideologues play god. And they are playing for keeps.

In the course of human affairs, every truth capable of making life better requires a countermanding tactic, a way to implement that truth. Better said, a way to weaponize it so that it can destroy the machinations of evil. The Apocryphon of John that survives in four versions in the NHC says explicitly of the forces working against life, "their delight is bitter and their beauty is in depravity (*anomon*), their delight is in deception" (BG 56). To which may be added fear. Deception drives fear and fear supports deception. Since 9/11, the entire world has faced the assault of a triple wave of fear: of terrorism, of climate change, of coronavirus. Against this assault stands something the Gnostics foresaw even though they may not have been able to articulate it: Sophia's Correction. That is the countermanding tactic against the globalist takeover.

Correction (*diorthosis*) shows up only four times in the entire NHC. However, a comprehensive view of Gnostic teaching on the divine endowment of the Anthropos indicates how it might be accomplished. Clearly, it must be a collaboration between the Wisdom Goddess and her designer species, the Anthropos. The role humanity plays, the measure of participation we give to correction, depends on owning and cultivating the unique set of faculties that distinguish humans from other animals. This noetic skill set, as it might be called, comprises a set of faculties implanted in the Anthropic spore complex. The operative skills of the human genome are all variations of *nous*, the germ of divine intelligence. There are seven permutations in total, but the principal ones are *ennoia*, *epinoia*, *metanoia*, and *dianoia*.

Ennoia is intentionality. This component is dynamically close to the divine creative intent of the Aeons and mirrors it. The *ennoia* of Sophia and Thelete generates the Anthropos template, of which the human species living today is one discrete strain. We manifest *ennoia* in creative acts of all kinds, but its optimal expression requires the cooperation of *epinoia*, imagination. However, not just any fluke of imagination will do. Self-indulgent fantasy and narcissistic pretending, rampant in the current Piscean Age, are dead-end entertainments. Correction does not support those apps. (A crude Archontic analogy, but it works.) Such activities have to be corrected for optimal use of our noetic skill set. Gnostics taught the difference between *epinoia* (true imagination) and *phantasia* (mere make-believe). The instruction survived late into European history in a cogent rule stated in *Artis Auriferae*, "The Art of Goldmaking," a seventeenth-century compilation of alchemical lore:

> In all thine operations, let the Work be guided by nature, according to the slow progression of metals in the bowels of the earth. And in thine efforts be guided in all ways by the true and not the fantastic imagination.[296]

The Great Work is human coevolution with the living intelligence of nature. The teachers of the Mysteries blazed that trail and set the parameters for coevolution by establishing the telestic method, instruction by the Organic Light. As I have explained, ego death and surrender to the life force were the hallmarks of initiation. *Not* self-aggrandizement and deification. Ecstatic immersion in the awesome telluric force of the Earth induced the psychosomatic regeneration (*palingenesis*) of the Mysteries. In Gnostic cosmology, the figure of Zoe, the flame-born daughter of Sophia, represents the deathless regenerative power of the Anthropos (On the Origin of the World, 104.26-31). Mythologist Karl Kerényi explains that in Greek animistic religion, *Zoe* is the Dionysian factor of "indestructible life," contrasted to *Bios*, the limited biological life-process.[297] The intent (*ennoia*) to couple imagination (*epinoia*) with the powers of nature depends ultimately on surrender to those deathless powers in an ecstatic state of pure beholding.

Complementary to their method, the telestai propagated the sacred narrative, the Fallen Goddess Scenario. It is not merely a story, it is *the unique narrative tool* that can frame and guide human coevolution in the correct way, a sane and sustainable way. The preterrestrial events recounted in the nine episodes of the Home Story (as I now call it) may seem remote, but systematic practice with the narrative proves otherwise. The privilege to know the Aeonic Mother intimately comes with a responsibility: to learn her story and love it as you love the story of your own life.

For Gnostics, every event in the preterrestrial adventure of Sophia resonates and replays in some manner within the human psyche. Not symbolically, but *actionally*. In chapter 11, "Dreamtime Physics," I showed that "psychocosmic parallelism" (to give it a fancy name) is consistent with indigenous cultures around the world, and especially so with the hardiest survivors on the planet, the Australian Aborigines. The Dreamtime of the FGS is the *organic* dimension of the Eternal Now. Everything it describes in cosmic and mythical terms also occurs in the psyche and in surrounding nature, continually. The sacred narrative of the Earth is the gateway to "biology revisioned."[298]

The sacred narrative about Sophia invites us to participate in her Correction. It also places in our hands the paramount weapon for the overthrow of theocracy. Mythic imagination is our innate power to see how the cosmos works, and how the gods play, and even to play with them, but it is not a license to play god. We can safely leave that undertaking to our benevolent handlers, who clearly cannot resist the temptation.

THE DIVINITY OF REASON

Practice with the guiding narrative of the Mysteries brings another noetic faculty into play, *metanoia*. All paradigms invented by the human mind are merely framing devices. The trick, the key noetic skill here, is moving through the frames. *Metanoia* is the capacity not merely to construct a conceptual frame but to go beyond it. In the New Testament fable of Jesus, John the Baptist announced the coming of the messiah with the watchword *Metanoeite*. Scholars routinely translate this declarative expression in Greek into a call for remorse and penitence: "Repent!" Spun to a Gnostic application, it is the imperative to "go beyond, think beyond." *Metanoia* enables us to think beyond any given framework of perception or any limiting belief that may provisionally be useful. Ideas, even great ideas, are merely tools for learning, not permanent idols to be worshiped. Intelligence evolves as we devise and discard frames of learning, as we shift paradigms. Due to the high complexity of human intention (*ennoia*), we need to frame the learning process within limits so that we can optimize certain possibilities and perspectives that come into definition within the limits so defined. Having done so, we can then eventually outgrow those limits and reframe the knowledge acquired in another paradigm. Ideally, paradigms ought to regulate our creative intent (*ennoia*) but not rule it, and especially not overrule it. All too often, models invented by the human mind drive it into dead ends and against blindspots that cannot be detected because the paradigms in use conceal their own preclusive features.

The third permutation of nous is *dianoia*, "reason." In an important but badly damaged passage, The Dialogue of the Savior says that "reasoning power" allows us to hold the place of truth and stand against the tyrannical forces of error epitomized in "the guardian of the threshold"—Mystery jargon for the Archons. Technically, that threshold is the interface between the biosphere and the planetary system in which the Earth is captured. Hence, in their proper role the Archons are interdimensional demons, described as trolls and gatekeepers in Gnostic writings. "For the threshold is fearful, looming before you. But with a single mind you pass by it!" (III, 5:124. Note how this trope is endlessly repeated in IT simulation games.) The single mind is the calm and lucid mind, capable of reasoning in a clear, detached, methodical way. The Teachings of Silvanus advises:

> Listen, children, to this advice. Do not be arrogant in opposition of every good opinion, but take for yourself the side of the divinity of reason. Observe the sacred instructions of the Revealer, and you will live regally in every place on Earth and be honored by the angelic messengers, and even by the archangels who send them. Then you will acquire them for friends and allies, and you will access all places in the heavenly realms. (NHC VII, 4:91–92)

Reason is divine because it derives from nous. *Dianoia* includes critical thinking, but not in a rational, reductive sense. Applied in a genuine and correct way, this skill is not Cartesian reductionism and certainly not "critical theory." With *dianoia*, critical thinking is simply the cutting edge of common sense. It hones and enhances, rather than precludes, the faculty of creative imagination. For Gnostics who developed their *dianoia* to a genius level, there was no contradiction between reason and revelation. Their work in the Mystery Schools required them to translate what they learned through instruction by the Light, the supreme revelatory experience. Their mastery of *dianoia* made them into eloquent writers and speakers who could easily compete with the sharpest dialecticians of Athens or Alexandria.

The Beauty to Come

New Age guru and Mystery School revivalist Jean Houston (whom I do not endorse) says about the role of myth in human experience:

Myths serve as source patterns originating in the ground of our being. While they appear to exist solely in the transpersonal realm, they are the key to our personal and historical existence, the DNA of the human psyche.[299]

If our biological makeup carries the imaginal power of *epinoia*, as Gnostics taught, then myth is not just figuratively "the DNA of the human psyche." It is an actual, actional deposit in the DNA of the species. That being so, myth can be regarded as an agency driving and directing human behavior at the biological level. Does the noetic skill set of the Anthropos provide a specific faculty to detect and operate that agency? Indeed, it does. *Epinoia* gives access to the supernatural basis of the natural world. Its scope extends from the infrastructure of living matter outward to "all places in the heavenly realms," including the living script of the starry constellations.

Epigenesis is a young science founded on the work of two molecular biologists, Howard Tenin and David Baltimore. In 1970 they isolated an exotic enzyme from an RNA virus: reverse transcriptase. This discovery opened the path to investigate how RNA reprograms DNA. Doing so, it overturned the Darwinian paradigm that places the sovereign power of evolution in the nuclear DNA of cells. Reverse transcriptase, the specific biomolecular agent that enables "messenger RNA" (mRNA) to rewrite DNA, comes factory installed in the human genome. It is a precious gift in the divine endowment of Sophia and Thelete.

It so happens that the rescripting action of messenger RNA figures centrally into the current master plan of the technocratic overlords. The "m" in the acronym mRNA denotes the messenger, the rescripting enzyme. Astute observers of big pharma propaganda have noted that the companies peddling the Archontic eucharist do not actually call it a vaccine. Which, in fact, it isn't. It is a biochemical agent for reprogramming the human immune system and, if transhumanists have it their way, the entire ensemble of anthropine genomic traits. In the product literature required by law, Moderna calls it an "operating system" rather than a vaccine. When the authorities have to resort to being that honest, something deeply insidious must be in the works. The Archontic Lie that humanity is made "in His image" has failed in religious terms, but the dementia behind it persists. The Great Reset is the Archons' last stand, "the consummation of their works" signaled in that outstanding incident when Sophia confronts the Demiurge. Has the moment come when "the entire deficiency of truth will be revealed and dissolved by that luminous child, and it will be as if it had never been?"

Does the Covid-19 plandemic, the greatest crime against humanity ever attempted, present the opportunity for humanity to achieve its final triumph over the Archontic intrusion?

That may well be the case, but the outcome cannot be expected due to some version of divine intervention independent of human effort. Growing numbers of Sophianic devotees around the world—words I could not have written in 2006—carefully observe this qualification: correction in the social order depends on a critical measure of human participation. With that measure added, there is a brave and beautiful new world to come, another way to live on this planet once the millennial program of ultra-righteous supremacy finally collapses. Imagine a world without billionaire philanthropists and their lackeys, including political and religious misleaders of all stripes and sizes. Imagine demise of the globalist overlords who know better than everyone else how to live and insist on implementing their nightmare for the collective good. Imagine that the media-driven campaign of fear-mongering stops in its tracks. Imagine a social order without Authorities, a planet composed of nations governed by the sovereign will of their members. It's all possible through acts of human resolution that complement and support the superhuman event of Correction.

A happy prospect, for sure. But what about those who know nothing of the living Gnosis, the Organic Light, and the sacred narrative of the Mysteries? Will they also find their way into the beauty to come and take part in constructing a future social order on the ruins of the transhumanist nightmare? The Covid-19 hoax leaves no doubt that the cure is worse than the disease. The narrative of the virus is the virus. The measures the authorities fraudulently impose to "prevent the spread of the virus" are decimating lives and livelihoods across the world. The scale and intensity of the suffering entailed are inconceivable. But it may take that degree of suffering to bring the population to its senses and snap them (enough of them, at least) out of the Archontic spell, the trust in Authorities. In these pages I have argued strongly against elevating the force of suffering above the life-force—the main ploy of salvationist religion. But in the final perspective, suffering may be the catalyst that brings humanity to its final triumph over Archontic dementia.

Correction is a *diorthosis*, literally, "a split or dual regulation." Those who are privileged in Gnosis and those who are ignorant of it, alike, are sure to come together in many courageous and inspired acts of resolution and reparation. But also, necessarily, in acts of revenge. There are three Rs of Correction. Gnostics taught that the foundation of the Universe is love and goodness. If there is no evil in the Supernatural, as I contend, its human sources must be confronted on wholly human terms. The shift toward a better life on Earth today involves something like a rite of passage, a breakaway to freedom by way of trials and desolation. What is happening in the Great Reset is not the fault of ordinary, decent, peaceful human beings, but it is their fault to have allowed it to happen. The courage to face that desolating insight is the first step in liberation from the Authorities, but it is not alone an assurance of success. It also requires the courage to hunt down and terminate the psychopaths and enemies of life who operate on fear and deceit, the fuel of the Archons. Human nature may be essentially good and loving, but it is not love that got humanity into this mess and love alone can't get it out. Pagan trust in human goodness did not preclude brutal force in the cause of goodness. It supplied a crucial counterbalance: the responsibity to hate whatever denies and subverts innate goodness and works cruelly against it, inflicting a thousand cuts of betrayal. In Correction, the cruelty inflicted on humanity can be turned back on its origins and leveraged to a higher purpose. But it is not the Aeonic Mother who determines that shift; it is solely the responsibility of her designer species.

An old adage (attributed to Mark Twain) says that it is easier to fool people than to convince them they have been fooled. So what happens when, finally, they are convinced?

The wisdom to be drawn from the current desolation is there to own, but it has been buried for ages under religious pleading for love. Ancient voices called it out. The Greek tragedies gave vivid expression to a life-saving truth: *If you have to suffer, at least learn from it.* In the Orestes trilogy, Aeschylus depicts the conversion of the Furies, who embody the infernal rage of Mother Earth, into the Eumenides, benevolent overseers of the social order. In the closing passage of Eumenides, the Greek moral genius that birthed the Western concept of conscience delivers an incomparable message, more pertinent today than it ever was in 2500 years:

> Return in joy what joy has given
> In the mutuality of love unriven,
> And learn to hate with a common mind
> For that is the cure of many an ill of humankind.

23

THE SPECIES-SELF IDENTITY

Let's return for a moment to a spectacular event in the Sophia mythos: when Sophia reaches the stage where the planetary body begins to sprout with life—that is, the point when the biosphere is formed—the emergent life-forms are so rampant and prodigious that she is unable to manage them (episode 8). The gods in the Pleroma observe that their sister is overwhelmed by the immense diversity of life she is producing. She cannot manage the commingling of her progeny and establish symbiosis. Self-regulation (homeostasis) is a defining feature of the Gaian super-organism, as defined by Lovelock and Margulis. But the specific type of self-regulation that would enable Sophia to oversee and sustain harmonious behavior *between different species* of fauna and flora proves to be beyond the range of her powers. Her plight elicits a response from the Pleroma, a rescue mission, the coming of the Symbiont. The paraphrase of Irenaeus that describes this momentous event has been cited and analyzed in chapter 14.

Irenaeus states that many of the life-forms swarming in the biosphere "had already taken root and acquired their own power, so as to be self-maintaining." It is remarkable to find in an obscure theological argument against the Gnostics a clear allusion to organic behavioral plans recognized today in the grand orchestration of the biosphere. Chrismation, the act of hermetic sealing, insures that different species acquire their own power and can be self-maintaining. Hence, the astonishing integrity—and beauty—of what in modern biology are called morphic fields. By interceding, the Symbiont assisted Sophia to aggregate the total range of biota into an orchestrated and harmonious ensemble. In nature, all creatures down to the microbial level behave consistently with the properties specific to their morphic fields. At the same time, they are able to coevolve with other species. Irenaeus's paraphrase describes how the intercession enabled Sophia "to give form to the animate substance that has proceeded from her own conversion," assisted by "the instructions of the Symbiont." All species of plant and animal life, as well as microbial life, are securely woven into the vast orchestration of symbiosis, the vibrant web of life.

All, yes, but for one outstanding exception: the human animal, the anthropine species.

THE INTERMEDIARY

Episode 8 of the FGS raises huge concerns about the role of humankind in planetary symbiosis, a leading issue of deep ecology. It is also an imperative issue of theology, for theology is not solely a discussion of the identity and agency of God. Equally, it concerns the identity of the human creature relative both to the creator god and the totality of "God's creation." The intercession described in episode 8 begs the question, If the action of the Symbiont transpired before our species emerged on the planet, how can it possibly affect humankind? If it even does?

That question is one of the more difficult I faced in restoring the Sophianic myth of the Mysteries. But over fifteen years, it came to resolution through close scrutiny of first-hand testimony of mystical experience. Certainly, conventional scholars will on no account concur with where the narrative goes now. But, as argued elsewhere in this book, scholars who have not undergone mystical experiences in altered states, never reached the cognitive ecstasy of Gnosis, and never applied clear and sober scrutiny to the widely attested record of paranormal and supernatural phenomena, are in no way qualified to interpret ancient texts derived from that realm of experience.

Chapter 14 concludes with the question of how the persistence of the Symbiont might make itself known, not solely through interspecies interactivity (coevolution) but also, somehow, within the human psyche. Recall the clue on the persistence of Pleromic love in *A Valentinian Exposition*. This is certainly enigmatic, and perhaps unverifiable. Fortunately, it does not stand alone, a puzzle piece with nowhere to fit. Raking through Irenaeus with a fine-toothed comb brings up an explicit line of corroboration: "Having effected this [feat of intercession], he withdrew his influence, and returned [to the Pleroma]—while, in the meantime, she [Sophia] possessed a kind of odor of immortality left in her by Christ and the Holy Spirit" (One, IV.1).

Working a jigsaw puzzle often entails a moment when two clusters of pieces lock together. The corner of the barn fits into the apple tree beside it. Just so with the clues on the Symbiont that might point to its intrapsychic aspect. It so happens that the residual clues in play here do lock into a larger cluster. Passages scattered through the NHC indicate a rare teaching from the Mysteries encoded in the concept of "the intermediary," Mesotes. Gnostics detected a mysterious agency operating in the inner life of humanity, comparable to a Jungian archetype. *Mesotes* comes from *meso-*, "middle, midway." Literally it signifies a mean, like the mean between two numbers. Figuratively, and more broadly in the mystical sense, it denotes an intermediary agent, a healing or reconciling force—but between what and what?

The Second Treatise of the Great Seth (66.3–8) says that humans "become complete in the inward ineffability by a living code, attaining undefiled union through the Mesotes, the medium of IS." The exact Coptic is MESOTES NTE IS, with "IS" routinely translated as "Jesus." The Church Fathers who attacked the Gnostics consistently attributed the identity of Jesus to the Mesotes. Fine, but did Sethian Gnostics and other schools follow this attribution? The Greek Coptic materials do not present the name of Jesus written in full, but encoded in the letters IC with a bar over them. (Lacking Coptic fonts, C in this transliteration represents the Coptic letter equivalent to S.) Scholars routinely fill in the blanks, making IC into I(eseo)S, the Greek form of the Hebrew name Yeshua. They do so with considerable poetic license, absent textual evidence that the Gnostic authors behind the NHC used IS to indicate a presumed historical person. Is IC a person or an archetype? The short answer is, IC is a scribal convention. The full word could as well be rendered I(asiu)S, "the healer," a title rather than a common name. But translators assume that IC:IS indicates Jesus of the New Testament. In short, scholars do not allow that IC might indicate anything else but a literal person whose identity they have predetermined.

XC and XRC, which appear countless times, pose the same issue. The letter X transliterates to CH. XC:CHS passes for Christ but could as well indicate C[hresto]S, The Good One.[300] Note that "Christos" is more consistent with the final S—but Christos is the Gnostic Aeon, not the Christian Savior. In the many passages where XC or XRC appear, translators casually write Jesus Christ into the script. They wrangle words such as [X]PHCTO[C] to squeeze Christ the Savior out of it. Even where the Greek spelling uses *eta*, H, which is the short e, rather than *iota*, I, they convert the code to Christ and disregard the more direct rendering, CHRESTOS, the benevolent one. In short, Judeo-Christian overwriting has corrupted the file on the Mesotes. XC and XRC do not categorically denote the hallowed entity of New Testament theology. Considering all the Gnostic material that argues against the Pauline-Johannine redeemer, this equation is dubious, to put it mildly.

Initiates in the Pagan Mysteries did not allow that the historical Jesus, or any historical person, could perform the action of this mysterious supernatural agency—the Intermediary, to call it by another name. The code for the Mesotes, IC ETONE, does not equate unambiguously with the Christian Savior. The Coptic ETONE connotes living in a manner that transcends a discrete, incarnated person: everlasting life. To read into IC ETONE any historical person who lived and died is a far stretch for the archetype, and Gnostically inadmissible. A close study of the occurrence of this term in the NHC suggests a presence that transcends discrete embodiment. The Intermediary IC ETONE was no incarnate identity, yet it can present itself to the human witness, like an apparition. Gnostic heretics who stood radically against the Judeo-Christian dogma of divine redemption could not have viewed the Mesotes as an agent of salvation. Rather, they detected it according to what the name they gave to it signifies: the action of mediation, operating midway between two things. But what does it actually mediate? In what way does the Mesotes match the Aeon Ekklesia, the Symbiont?

If proposing the Symbiont-Mesotes conflation puts the authority of my scholarship at risk, I don't mind. I write from experience, and not only my own. There is a lot more. The evidence I advance here comes from a long record of mystical encounters. Clearly, mystical revelations and supernatural encounters are not empirical facts, but the existence of a substantial record of such experiences extending over centuries is a very great fact. In that record, one instance of mystical revelation stands in a class of its own. Unfortunately, interpretations of meeting the Mesotes make it extremely difficult to see that encounter for what it is, contrasted to what it has been taken to be. Absent first-hand testimony of this encounter, there is no way to purge the corrupt files on the Intermediary.

A Luminous Phantom

The full kit of Gnostic paranormal skills included clairvoyance, clairaudience, and other *siddhis*, occult faculties. "The Light was full of hearing and language" (The Paraphrase of Shem, NHC VII, 1, 1.30). The Sophianic narrative comes down to us in the testimony of trained seers, or the research of experimental mystics, if you prefer. They saw and heard things by observing how luminosity behaves. Through their instruction by the Divine Light, the telestai learned about events that unfolded in the remote prehistory of our planet. Their shamanic train-ing—technically, phylogenetic recall—enabled them to replay these events imaginatively, over and over again.* As they reviewed the story of Sophia's fall, the details of the narrative grew richer and more precise. Beyond that, the ancient seers learned to see how remote events played ahead into the circumstances of human life, including events of the inner life, the ongoing drama of the psyche.

Irenaeus records that Sophia "possessed a kind of odor of immor-tality left in her" by the Pleromic intercession. Elsewhere in the NHC (Eugnostos, III,3-4 and V,1) a line hints at the fragrance of the Originator, the source of all the Aeons. What lingers like an odor? And how could such a supernatural effect arise in the human psyche? How would it reveal itself? What phenomenon in nature might explain the mysterious appearance of the Intermediary? The Greek word for odor, *myrodia*, also means tincture, something that can be seen. Scholars who translate the heresiologists have to toggle Greek and Latin words to approximate what the Gnostics might have intended here. Tackling the

---

* In esoteric jargon, this is called "reading the akashic record." I have not compared modern examples to telestic investigation because I do not find valid parallels among those who claim this talent, such as Edgar Cayce and Rudolf Steiner.

Panarion of Epiphanius, a long polemic which in many passages repeats the paraphrase of Irenaeus verbatim, one scholar renders it "a certain savor of immortality."[301]

So, what *is* the residual effect of the Intermediary? A lingering fragrance, a tincture, a flavor? If it persists in the atmosphere to this day, can it be detected? *Tincture* implies coloration, a sense impression with visual properties. Might the Mesotes appear through an optical effect?

It has to be seen before it is believed. Fine, well enough thus said. But once seen, it becomes interpreted and turns into a matter of belief. Which is extremely problematic. Not to say, tragic. To see the Mesotes, the lingering psychic afterimage of the Symbiont, is a genuine visionary experience, verifiable and consistent among different witnesses. It is neither an illusion nor a religious hallucination. And many, many people have seen it. As disciplined seers, Gnostics must have detected this optical effect and studied it closely. Although arising internally to the psyche, the afterimage persists *in the external field of perception*. It hovers before wide open eyes, as when you look at an object in bright light and then turn away, and the afterimage lingers. It is a material effect, an optical imprint, a tint in the light. But in this unique instance, the afterimage is *alive*. This is the psychic imprint of everlasting life, IC ETONE. Brainwashed religious devoteees take it as the "everlasting Jesus." Rudolf Steiner saw it, and being a good Catholic boy after all, called it the Etheric Christ. For Gnostics then and now, it is the afterimage of the Symbiont persisting in the biosphere eons after the intercession. (To think of all this in another way, the intercession happens in the Dreamtime of the Eternal NOW and is perpetually in progress.)

In early Christian theology, rumors about the Symbiont fostered the false notion of the *parousia*, the second coming of Jesus. An event that never materialized, needless to say. Christian fanatics, such as Jacob Boehme, Meister Eckhart, Saint Theresa, and Saint John the Divine, believed they had encountered "the mystical Christ." The encounter was always one thing, the interpretation of it, something else again. In New Age circles, witnesses take the Mesotes to be an inner guide, like a guardian angel. Encounters with the luminous phantom of the Mesotes happen spontaneously—one could even say, naturally. The experience is highly consistent across different epochs and cultures.[302] It would take an entire book to consider the reports from witnesses as different as Bill Wilson, founder of Alcoholics Anonymous, and C. G. Jung, who relates his death bed revelation of the Green Christ in his posthumous memoir, *Memories, Dreams, and Reflections*. In Jungian terms, the Mesotes is an archetypal image (*Urbild*) like those described in his experiments with "active imagination," figures like Philomen, his guide, and Salome, the reflection of his inner woman, the anima.

The luminous phantom *is* like a psychic archetype that can be produced by an effort of picturing, yes, but it is also different and distinct. It is a *liminal* figure that hovers on the boundary between psyche and nature. It exists and persists independently and does not depend on the witness to produce it. Beyond that distinction, it has properties that belong to the terrestrial atmosphere in which it lingers. Believe it or not.

TURBULENT MIRROR

Considered dynamically, the luminous phantom of the Symbiont is a labile aperture in an atmospheric cluster of Bénard cells. (Lability is the chemical property of being unstable, fluctuating.) Bénard cells are hexagonal formations that arise when certain liquids reach the threshold of turbulent instability, such as oil heated in a pan, or in convection currents spiraling in the atmosphere. As John Gribbin explains in *Deep Simplicity*, Bénard cells are a spontaneous feat of nature, magnificent evidence of order arising within chaos:

> The most interesting stable patterns [in nature] appear right at the edge of chaos. . . . The specific interesting pattern that appears is a honeycomb arrangement of hexagons. This is happening far from equilibrium, thanks to the energy flowing through an open system and being dissipated. This is the secret of the existence of order in the Universe, and specifically the secret of life.[303]

Bénard cells appear spontaneously in atmospheric convection vortices clearly visible in Antarctic icefields and the desert sands of the Sahara.

The phenomenon is so prevalent that scientists speak of an "atmospheric Bénard sea." In *Turbulent Mirror*, F. David Peat says that "scientists think that the spherical shell of the atmosphere, possibly the whole atmosphere, might be a sea of seething Bénard cells."[304] This is precisely so, and precisely what witnesses to the Mesotes may come to know. But lacking adequate force of attention, the witness cannot steady the perception which is always liminal and precarious. It becomes blurred and unstable. The apparition fades, and then comes interpretation.

Of course, anyone of sane mind must be compelled to wonder how anything as exotic as "a cluster of Bénard cells" can assume human form. The "everlasting medium" does not really assume human form, but only appears to do so. (In Gnostic teachings, this was called docetic manifestation, from the Greek *dokein*, "to appear.") The Symbiont does not have, or ever had, human form. In keeping with the supreme selflessness of the Pleromic divinities, *the Symbiont imparts its biopsychic effect in our image, not in its own*. Thus, the encounter with the luminous phantom arises in human form. It can happen at any moment, and it has happened countless times through history, and before history.

IS ETONE is a biopsychic imprint that actually lives in the atmosphere. Imagine that you gaze at an object in bright light—say, an apple tree bare of leaves, etched against the deep blue of the winter sky. Turning away, you see the perfect afterimage of the tree, whether your eyes are open or closed. Now imagine that the afterimage grows like a living tree. It buds, flowers, fruits, dies back, and does it all again. *The afterimage is as alive as the original object.*

Just so, "the everlasting medium" is not virtual or merely subjective. It does really exist in the atmosphere, externally, although perceived as an intrapsychic phantom. Witnesses assume they are seeing an image located somewhere in the mind or in the zone of imagined space, in inner space, wherever that is. In reality, they are seeing an actual animation in the biosphere. A liquescent lattice of Bénard cells frames the glowing figure. The exquisite hexagonally faceted aura of the phantom radiates crystal-clear light, but the facets are gilt-edged, flushing the light with soft honey-gold hues. Every single facet of the honeycomb reflects in perfect detail the entire scene around the witness. Welling up within the crystal-clear luminosity is the soft, creamy whiteness of the

Organic Light. Tinted with the golden hues of the honeycomb faceting, the whiteness induces a sensation of deep serenity inwardly charged with supervitality. The sweet, rapturous surge of vital force streaming from the Mesotes creates the impression of being immersed in seething milk with currents of golden honey flowing through it—indeed, flowing through the body of the witness, drenching every cell. The appearance of the luminous phantom may be accompanied by an exquisite ringing like the chiming and pealing of countless bells.

Those who see the Intermediary know they are also seen by it, as if someone snapped a photo. This action is truly mysterious, and it is also mysteriously true. Recall that the Mesotes operates like an aperture. Like a camera lens, it captures the image of the one beholding it, the human witness. But then it does something else. Call it a miraculous conversion. It converts the self-image of the witness into another format: as if someone took a snapshot of you and when you looked at it, you look like someone else. Through the power of the Mesotes, the image of the human witness it reflects shows the witness to be not a single personal self but the generic self, a conscious instrument of the species-self identity.

THE DECEIT OF CHRIST

What distinguishes human animals from other animals? Principally, it is the capacity for conceptual thought, productive of symbolic codes and systems expressed in images and words. But this capacity also fosters and fuels the worst attributes of self-identification. At the very least, each human animal knows himself or herself as a subjective entity: the single-self identity. *Who am I?*, asked the Indian mystic, Ramana Maharshi. He considered it to be the single and paramount question to ask. Everyone knows the immediate answer, *I am me*, a self-aware subject, this unique human person. Thus you self-identify *as you*. But how do you identify as a member of the human species?

Gnostics who encountered the Intermediary in their mystical practices knew—as only Gnostics can know—its origin: the intercession of the Symbiont. They were also able to determine its *function* in human terms, its precise psychosomatic effect. That effect is twofold. The Symbiont imparts an *image*, the optical effect, and it confers a *sense*. Not everyone has the privilege of beholding the image, although many have done so. But the sense is universally accessible. Indeed, it is as accessible as the very air we breathe.

It is deeply tragic for the human species that another image intercepts and precludes the Symbiont's presence, and by doing so, impedes and cripples that special sense. At the close of chapter 19, I noted that it is not Jesus Christ who is crucified on the cross, it is human imagination. For twenty centuries, sixty generations, humans have seen in the image of the crucified savior the icon of humanity itself. Christ, we are told to believe, is the perfect model of humanity, a human-divine hybrid who as the "Christ child" also stands for all that is pure and innocent in each of us. This proposition is a vicious and destructive deceit that cannot stand if human animals are ever to find their role and responsibility in the great web of life, Sophia's living dream of the biosphere.

"We are human only in contact, and conviviality, with all that is not human," David Abram says. By entering into kinship with all species, human animals overcome the fixations of self-identification, which always terminate in malignant narcissism. The sense of empathy with other animals is the gift of the Symbiont. No creature lives by itself. The human creature who does not realize the species-self identity suffers an illusion of separation yet remains woefully ignorant of that affliction. The sense of empathy with nonhuman animals, including reptiles, insects, and microbes, supports the species-self identity. It also exerts a guiding function. The Mesotes imparts a subtle, nonintrusive guiding effect. Laurens van der Post, who lived with the San Bushman of the Kalahari, captured the taste of this experience when he wrote (in *A Mantis Carol*): "We all know more than we allow ourselves to know because of a certain cowardice in the face of the inexpressible, and fear of accepting its effect on us as guide to the nature of its reality."

The icon of the crucified savior is a pernicious imprint that occludes the species-self identity. It is a masterful tool of traumatic imprinting. It reinforces the victim-perpetrator bond and makes the force of suffering look more powerful than the life-force itself. It sanctifies sadomasochistic pain. To overcome it, the human creature needs something to replace it. The replacement cannot be given externally as a doctrine, an article of faith. It must arise as a free production within imagination. What falsely separates humans from other animals, and separates us in single-self fixations, impedes a deep bonding power within the psyche. The presence of the Symbiont fosters that power and restores the bond. Whether or not it is seen, it can always be felt. But that presence has to be known for what it is, free and clear of the erroneous interpretions loaded onto it.

Instances of the Mesotes encounter are far too numerous to cite here, as noted. (Mayura in Hindu myth, the Peacock Angel of the Yezidis, the *Argos Panoptes* of Greek myth, come to mind.) But it would be an unacceptable omission not to cite the case of controversial cult figure Carlos Castaneda. When he met the luminous phantom, he was overwhelmed with joy and came away supercharged with enthusiasm for the preciousness of humanity. His teacher, the Yaqui shaman don Juan, proved to be a real killjoy when he wryly informed Carlos that he only felt that way due to inveterate self-infatuation. The luminous phantom, don Juan told him, is "the mold of man," a phenomenon well known to the ancient seers of Mexico. He warned that "to fall on our knees in the presence of the mold of man reeks of arrogance and human self-centeredness." Only trained seers have the sobriety to see the phantom for what it actually is, the old sorcerer insisted.[305]

The mysterious benediction of the Symbiont belongs to everyone who lives, and ever will live, on this planet. Realization of the species-self identity is an act of transpersonal liberation. It is also a sublime leap into anonymity, a flashdance of transcendence. It shows you really what it means to be human *and an animal*. Not made "in His image," but made to express the generic image of the Anthropos. Those who received instruction by the Light in the Mysteries learned that humanity is not made in the image of an off-planet father god, nor even in the image of the Pleromic gods. The infinite selflessness of the Aeons does not allow them to imprint or impose themselves on the creatures that live in the experiments they conduct aross the Universe. Gnostics taught that the human species is a free-form novelty, an experiment of divine imagination. Yes, the Anthropos is endowed with properties not present in other species, but that does not make it superior to other species. Exceptional, but not superior. We cannot know our place in the cosmos through anthropocentric fixations, but disregarding the unique status of the human species is not valid, either.

The guiding effect of the Symbiont is a profound internal asset of human exceptionality. It imposes nothing. Instead, it supports and fosters the self-guiding capacity within each of us. But it can only do so if we hold empathy with nonhuman life to the same standard of humanity we seek for ourselves. Without the subtle guidance of the luminous phantom, humans would be even more driven by insane egotism than they already are.

THE GODDESS MYSTIQUE

We are children of Judeo-Christian, Muslim, Neo-Darwinist, or some other kind of religion. These religions are absurdities in that not only are they muddled, but they are dangerous to our relationship to the Earth and our nonhuman planetmates. The cultural background in which we have been brought up precludes our learning about the Earth as a whole planet.[306]

James Lovelock formally introduced the Gaia hypothesis in 1972 in the journal *Atmospheric Environment*. To develop the hypothesis he collaborated with evolutionary biologist Lynn Margulis, independently known for the theory of serial endosymbiosis (SET theory), currently a strong contender with the Darwinian model of evolution. SET theory proposes that organisms in the biosphere live *through* (endo-) each other rather than by preying on each other. Symbiosis is a serial activity because it extends through an eons-long chain of interactions in which larger, more complex organisms evolve by incorporating smaller, more elementary ones—such as so-called viruses.

In 1979 Lovelock published *Gaia: A New Look at Life on Earth*, but debate over the new theory did not assume volume until a critical response from W. F. Doolittle, entitled "Is Nature Really Motherly?" appeared in *Coevolution Quarterly* in 1981. Since then Gaia material has been cranked out at a furious pace, much of it concerned with the mythical and mystical aspects of the theory. "Gaia is like the myth of God, a mystery answering a mystery," wrote Claudio Guillen, professor of comparative literature at Harvard and the University of Barcelona. "It is a romantic metaphor that answers our need for oneness."[307]

But does the "romantic metaphor" of Gaia theory, magnificent though it is, really answer that need? Or do Gaia theory and the Goddess mystique—by which I mean the ensemble of quasi-religious, animistic, and mystical notions that have gathered around the scientific theory—confront us with questions to explore, rather than answers to settle for?

GAIA AND GNOSIS

No matter what evidence is adduced to back it up, a scientific theory is always a narrative, a story with a beginning, middle, and end, informed by a plot and stating a moral or message. "Scientists have much to gain from the awareness that they are storytellers," comments paleoanthropologist Misia Landau. In *Narratives of Human Evolution* Landau argues that scientific theories are "determined as much by traditional narrative frameworks as by material evidence." She sees in Darwinian theory, for instance, a variation of the hero narrative found worldwide. The hero in Darwin's tale is the human species itself. (Truth be told, Darwin had precious little to say about the human species, but it becomes central in the theories derived from his work.) The story of evolution comprises "a sequence of motifs—expanding foreheads and retracting jaws, increasing intellects and diminishing instincts—which forward the plot and are bearers of meaning in themselves (for example, the expanding dominion of mind over matter)."[308] The narrative form, which Landau aptly calls "an altar housing a diversity of faiths," is unavoidable in any description of human experience. The Sophia mythos is a cosmological narrative, but also a mystical and metaphoric one. The sacred narrative closely mirrors the core assumptions of Gaia theory. It also presents a stark contrast to the dogmatic assumptions of Darwinian evolution.

All in all, the Sophia mythos exhibits three outstanding features that resemble Gaia theory: autopoesis, the biospheric anomalies, and abiogenesis. Additionally, there are two other features currently under debate, and three more that lie beyond the scope of the theory in its current form, but could advance and enrich it, were they eventually to be formulated in scientific terms.

Gnostic texts denote autopoesis by the Greek *autogenes*, "self-generating." The paraphrase of Irenaeus indicates that the mythic narrative of the Gnostics described the autopoetic powers of Sophia. This is perhaps the most striking correlation between Gaia theory and Gnosis. Self-generation is a property of the "noösphere"—that is, the biosphere considered as a medium of consciousness, a notion introduced by Teilhard de Chardin. Practice with the telestic method (instruction by the Light) confirms that the biosphere is a medium composed of processes that look more and more complex and conscious, the more *intensively* we observe them.[309] (I might add that they also look more and more beautiful. The Organic Light is the most beautiful sight conceivable to the human mind. *To Kalon* was the central topic in Greek philosophy. It signifies, not just beauty, but The Beauty. That being so, it may have been a codeword among intellectuals for the Mystery Light of which no one spoke openly, as I do now.)

Among the intensive observations of Gnosis is the unique case of the Mesotes described in chapter 23. This is an enigmatic apparition that refects the human presence in nature not as an isolated personal entity but transpersonally, as a member of the anthropine species: the anonymous witness. And it *acts upon the witness* by inducing a sense of empathy with the nonhuman world, including the four-legged creatures, insects, reptiles, fish, and fowl. This encounter is mystical proof and, as such, inadmissible to hard science, but it would be unscientific to exclude it for that reason. In the future, it may be the evidence of mystical experience that brings Gaia theory to full maturity, while still preserving its scientific integrity. Such evidence would not necessarily contradict scientific findings and could, in fact, complement and confirm them.

The second salient correlation concerns the anomalies of the biosphere noted in chapter 13, which now merit a closer look. Gaia theory emphasizes three salient points: the constancy of the temperature of the atmosphere despite a 30 percent increase in solar radiation, the stable salinity of the ocean, and the ratio of oxygen at the critical threshold of 20 percent. In the Sophia mythos, the role of the mother star Sabaoth points to the first factor. The story says that the sun forgoes ("repents") its primary connection to the inorganic forces in the cosmos so that it can stream vitality toward organic life on the Earth. Zoe, the flame-born daughter of Sophia, represents the solar life-support system. The heat radiating from the sun rises enormously over time, but the mother star is so aligned with the Earth that the temperature of the atmosphere remains at the level that optimally supports life.

As for the other two anomalies, not immediately evident in the mythological narrative as I have so far reconstructed it, they could perhaps be teased out of the Gnostic material, with supporting references from indigenous lore. For instance, in *Voices of the First Day* Robert Lawlor shows how the Rainbow Serpent of the Australian Aborigines is a metaphor for the electromagnetic spectrum. Similar correlations could be developed for the Sophia mythos, but doing so is a long and meticulous task. Bear in mind, also, that crucial parts of the story have been totally destroyed—the creation of the moon, for instance.* Missing parts hamper and handicap the reconstruction of the mythos.

The third salient correlation concerns abiogenesis, the seating of organic life in inorganic chemistry. This is a deeply controversial subject within modern biology. In the patristic paraphrases, the adjectives "material" and "animal" refer to inorganic and organic processes, respectively. This distinction is far from clear due to the jumbled incoherence of the surviving material, but the difference between Anthropos and Archons is always emphatic. The Authorities lack *ennoia*, intentionality, they can only imitate, they are deceptive and predatory, driven by envy, and so on. They violate boundaries: the chief Archon "did not obey the place from which he arose" (The Apocryphon of John, NHLE, p. 111.13). This is a warning to the human species about its own boundary problems. When the Archons contrive their planetary mansions, they copy the living fractal patterns in the Pleroma, but the result is a blind clockwork mechanism of "celestial mechanics." With photographic evidence from the Hubble telescope and other advanced data-gathering devices, astrophysicists now recognize that fluid, fractal organization prevails throughout the universe on the galactic scale. The planetary system we inhabit presents a simulacrum of living fractal order, like a "deep fake." The Gnostic narrative admits abiogenesis in the *nesting* of our organic world in the inorganic planetary system, rather than the construction of organic life from inorganic ingredients.

The Gnostic assertion that the Earth does not belong to the planetary system but is merely captured in it is a huge challenge to modern

---

* FGS 1.0, the upgrade of the legacy version of the FGS in chapter 10, does recount this event. See the Home Story on sophianicmyth.org.

thinking, but not inconsistent with Gaia theory. I have proposed that *trimorphic protennoia* is the "three-bodied original intention" of Sophia before she plunged from the Pleroma. That our world-system was intended at the cosmic level to be a three-body world consisting of one planet with a satellite and a central star is not so preposterous as it may seem. Ongoing studies in Gaian physiology and ecosystemic chemistry, such as *Gaia's Body* by Tyler Volk, tend to affirm that Earth, Sun, and Moon are a closed system, distinct from the rest of the planets. It will not be long, I suspect, before Gaia theory formally incorporates solar and lunar activities into its framework, leading to the view of Gaia as an integral three-body system.

HUMAN SINGULARITY

Two other salient elements of the Sophia mythos are closely related to undecided aspects of Gaia theory: panspermia and singularity. The emanation of the Anthropos is a mythopoetic trope for panspermia, the seeding of life through interstellar space. Lynn Margulis affirms that tiny shielded particles of organic life called propagules could spread through outer space, and material evidence supports this view. In *What is Life?* Margulis notes that bacterial spores driven by solar winds from star to star might explain the origin of life on Earth, "but such a view is less amenable to scientific investigation than the view that life originated right here on Earth." Even if it started in outer space, "Earth itself is suspended in space, so any way you look at it, life came from space."[310]

I doubt if Professor Margulis (whom I met) would be receptive to the idea that a plasma jet from the galactic core morphed into the Earth, as the FGS describes. Or that Earthbound humanity is one strain of a cosmic singularity designed in that core. These are mythico-mystical concepts, not easily reconciled with science. If at all. In *The Tao of Physics* (1975), Fritjof Capra developed extensive parallels between mysticism and physics—but do parallel lines ever meet? In *The Web of Life*, published twenty years later, Capra boldly stated that "physics has now lost its role as the science providing the most fundamental description of reality."[311] He points to deep ecology as the matrix of new thinking in natural science. Only a physicist who is also a mystic, or vice versa, can assess the value of mystical experience for science. To the knowledge of this writer, such an exotic hybrid has not so far appeared on the planet.

The second salient feature, singularity, is closely related to panspermia in the Gnostic narrative, of course. The Greek *monogenes* is theologically rendered as "only-begotten," but "singularity" is far closer to the spirit of the Gnostic seers. Gaia theory becomes stronger on autopoesis with each passing year, but the riddle of human singularity persists. Readers will have noted that I do not use "singularity" in the conventional sense: a point of infinite density and volume assumed by matter that collapses into a black hole, proposed by Roger Penrose, or the merge of human intelligence with AI, proposed by transhumanist Ray Kurzweil. In Gnostic terms, singularity is a trope for the cosmographic signature of the human species. In Gaian biophysics, it implies a unique human contribution to the ecosystem.

Initially, Lovelock viewed humanity as perhaps holding the privileged status of a self-conscious circuit in the nervous system of the planet. Over the years, he modified this rather generous view. In *Gaia: The Practical Science of Planetary Medicine*, he wonders if we may not be a plague on the face of the Earth, or a form of pollution. Lynn Margulis is also ruthless on this issue. She cites Nietzsche's acerbic remark: "The Earth is a beautiful place, but it has a pox called man." Both parents of Gaia theory strongly oppose New Age formulations of the Goddess mystique that place the human species at the apex of an ascending spiral of evolution. (Barbara Marx Hubbard's model of the "evolutionary spiral" in her book, *The Evolutionary Journey*, is a particularly egregious example of this hubris.) I stand with Lovelock and Margulis against the anthropocentric grandiosity of such schemes. I have explained at length that human self-deification was not the purpose of the Mysteries. Nor does it belong to the future that opens to humanity in Sophia's Correction.

Lovelock uses the term "emergent domain" for the self-organizing ecosystem we inhabit. This is "a system that has emerged from the reciprocal evolution of organisms and their environment over the eons of life on Earth."[312] Emergence is the new buzzword in the biological sciences, as already noted. As this concept develops, it looks more and more like the emanation theory common to Asian metaphysics and the Mysteries.

With emergence, science is shifting sharply toward the "Dreamtime physics" of native wisdom (see chapter 11). The singularity of our species might resemble "reciprocal evolution" more closely than teleological evolution, toward which Gaia theory tends to move. Currently, "strong Gaia theory" assumes a teleological or goal orientation for the ecosystem with human behavior somehow implicated. This concept is still immature but it is an indispensable *approach* to the singularity question. To put the issue on Gnostic terms, we do not know enough yet about Gaia's Correction to realize deliberate participation in it.* To date, suppositions about the purpose that humankind serves in the ecosystem have to be handled with extreme care. Nevertheless, the current discussion of emergent domain by Lovelock, Margulis, and others establishes a vector of investigation that may eventually intersect with the sacred narrative of the Mysteries.

Three remaining salient features of Sophianic cosmology stand outside the current scope of the Gaia theory, but could advance and enrich it, were they to be translated in scientific terms. These are: how Gaia reproduces, how she explicitly relies on the human mind (nous), and how she engages with human imagination (*epinoia*). The mythos says nothing about how Sophia reproduces, but it says a lot about nous and *epinoia*. Only by developing and expanding these faculties *through direct interaction with nature* can we reach verifiable knowledge of Gaian biophysics and align it correctly to the Sophianic science of life.

Our future as a species resides largely in the challenge to undertake that adventure.

THE SYMBIONT EQUATION

Many elements contribute to the Goddess mystique, but the Sophianic teachings of the Mysteries remain offside and overlooked—so far. It has to be said that Gnostic-ISM is long gone, and the living Gnosis today (as

---

* I wrote this in 2005. Elaboration of the human role in correction since 2011 would fill another book as long as this one. The logs of the Gaian Navigation Experiment run to eight illustrated volumes of 250 pages each.

I like to call it) is manifestly exotic and complex. The underdog of world religions, as I called it in *The Seeker's Handbook* (1991), still gets a lot of bad press. If it is mentioned at all, it is only to be "dissed." For its part, ecotheology fails miserably to deliver a Gaian scheme of coevolution that incorporates human purpose in planetary symbiosis. Leading voices such as Rosemary Radford Ruether flatly assert that there is "no ready-made ecological spirituality and ethic in past traditions" (cited above, chapter 7), thus entirely ignoring the Mysteries of the Great Mother. Still, Ruether is light-years beyond feckless apologists such as Lutheran pastor H. Paul Santmire, author of *The Travail of Nature*. Santmire admits that the ecological promise of Christianity is at best "ambiguous" and then attempts to detect ecocentric features in the exhausted motifs of Christian discourse. But Christ is the dankest meme on the planet. In renewal of the cosmic lordship of the father god and his only begotten son—variations of the redeemer complex—Santmire sees an opportunity to spiritualize nature within the frame of Christian belief. But he cannot see that nature is spiritual in the first place, regardless of what humans believe. He insists that "no biblically legitimate creation theology or cosmic Christology will prompt its adherents to forsake the mission of the people of God under the cross."[313] Strict adherence to God's plan forces ecocentrically minded people into an adversarial posture, whether they like it or not, know it or not. Lacking an open and uncompromising rejection of redemptive ideology, believers who still look to religion for meaning and direction in life will continue their wanderings in the barren waste of Sinai.

Genuine religious striving to know our divine mother drives the Goddess mystique. That being so, it begs the question of where the Symbiont comes into play in Sophia's Correction. Let's recall that the Symbiont—seen for what it actually is, undistorted by religious indoctrination—exerts a dual impact on the witness: it mirrors the species-self, and it intensifies the interspecies bond. It simultaneously presents an *image* and propagates a *sense*. These two factors converge and cooperate in a profoundly mysterious way, leaving the witness with an altered sense of self that must be lived out to be comprehended. Granted, the species-self identity is not a concept that can be easily or readily understood. It has to be felt in a wordless but lucid way, as animals feel who lack the gift of verbal expression. One beholds the Symbiont with the mute attendance of an animal that recognizes what it is.

In the Eighth Duino Elegy, Rainer Maria Rilke invoked "the Open (*Das Offene*), so deep in animals' faces." The poem argues that humans only really sense what is "out there" through "the animals' vast gaze." The witness to the Symbiont beholds itself with "the dog's imploring look" (Rilke). To come away believing that reflection is the image of Christ, or Christ in you, or the Higher Self, or any other variant of human glorification, is utter dementia.

In the psyche of each individual, the innate image of the human self carries the emotion of self-love. At least you better hope so. But how does this self-love translate to love for humanity? If it does? The elision of the two strains of love relies on what might be called the equation of the Symbiont, best expressed in the second person: *Your self-love is to your love for humanity as your love for humanity is to your empathy with other animals.*

It almost reads like a mathematical formula of reciprocity. Sure, it is nothing more than an ornate intellectual statement. But what it states cannot be realized intellectually. A unique feeling runs through it like a deep canyon river. The image conferred by the Symbiont hovers in that fractal maze of Bénard cells where porous white light erupts in golden hues. But even without that display, the slow rush of empathy perfuses the atmosphere like a fragrance. It comes with knowing what it is to be a human animal. All that lives abides in consecration. Among all species, the human animal alone is responsible to uphold the sacred, minding that its existence is no more or less sacred than anything else in nature. Only the human animal can desecrate the unity of life.

The Mystery seers taught that something like a fragrance secures humankind in symbiosis with nonhuman species. Encountering the Intermediary may be a delusional experience. If so, it is certainly a universal one. While subjective testimony as you find here cannot be equated with scientific evidence, the existence of such testimony (which is voluminous) is evidence of its own kind.

The Symbiont is the autopilot of deep ecology and the beating heart of the Goddess mystique.

THE PISCEAN FIX

The guardians of the Mysteries called themselves *telestai*, "those who are aimed." But the arrow does not aim itself. What aimed the Gnostics was dedication to the life-story of the Aeon Sophia. They, in turn, provided the spiritual guidance system of classical Paganism, using shamanic practices ("archaic techniques of ecstasy") inherited from prehistoric cults of the Great Mother. With the dawn of the Piscean Age around 120 B.C.E., an upsurge of narcissism threatened their mission. (Due to features in the composite stars of the constellation, the end-date of the Age is uncertain. Some fifty estimates have been proposed.) A change of worldview was in the air as the rumor spread that cosmic fate (*hiermarmene*) might be overcome. Messianic fever in Palestine infected the entire Empire. The Jewish messiah figure, once elevated to a divine status *and* enshrined as "the representative of humanity" (Rudolf Steiner's term), appeased the human ego in ways the Mysteries never could. Many factors contributed to the Piscean fixation of toxic narcissism that now pollutes the modern world. Religious glorification of pain and condemnation of pleasure contributed hugely to the overthrow of Pagan morals. Dissociation from body and senses due to super-earthly concerns (reiterated today in addiction to virtual reality) struck the final blow. The deceit of Christ anchored the Piscean fix, and narcissism went viral.

The dawn of the Piscean Age saw a wave of UFO sightings as well as natural catastrophes, including the total destruction of Pompeii in southern Italy.[314] The eruption of Vesuvius in 79 C.E. buried the ancient city of Herculaneum and, with it, spectacular frescoes depicting Dionysian rites. Thanks to the ash cover left by the eruption, the frescoes were preserved. They show the infant god Dionysus looking into a mirror the moment he is seized and dismembered by the Titans. This rare graphic evidence of initiatory experience carries a message about liberation from single-self identity, distinct from the self-sacrifice of Christianity. Dionysos must be dismembered so that he can be regenerated and live again, but his ordeal is ecstatic: he "goes to pieces" in sheer rapture, surrendered to the greater, all-consuming life force of the Earth. Dionysos will return as Iacchus, the divine child of the Mysteries. But first he dies—while looking in a mirror. The issue of "identification" or expanded-self awareness takes deep ecology into an impasse (as explained in chapter 8, regarding the God-self equation), because intimate communion with Gaia-Sophia occurs beyond identity:

> Although enlightenment does truly dwell within us, it has to appear to come to us from outside because of our attachment to ego. Ego cannot penetrate its own illusion, cannot dissolve itself.[315]

This is Francesca Fremantle interpreting Dzogchen teachings, but her words apply precisely to ego transcendence in Gnosis. Her observation that enlightenment appears to come from outside resonates closely with the ultimate secret of the Mysteries, the sheaf of cut wheat. Celebrants of the Mysteries mastered the art of conscious dying by letting go of self-reflection. At the meltpoint of voluntary ego death, they underwent the Dionysian rush of surrender and entered transentient rapport with nature.

Suppression of ecstasy and condemnation of pleasure by patriarchal religion have ravaged the human soul to the core. The pleasures people seek in the twenty-first century are superficial, venal, asinine, and increasingly obscene. This is deeply unfortunate, for it justifies the condemnation of pleasure that rotted out our hedonic capacities in the first place! Narcissism is rampant, having reached a truly global scale. It now appears to have entered the terminal phase known as "cocooning," the ultimate state of isolation. Dissociation from the natural world verges on complete disembodiment, represented in Archontic ploys such as cloning, virtual reality, and the uploading of human consciousness into cyberspace. The vacuous echo chamber of social media replaces vibrant social life. The computer or iPad is the altar where millions worship daily. If the technocrats prevail, AI (artificial intelligence) and AL (artificial life) will overrule the natural order of the planet.

Is a return to the nature-based Pagan culture of the Mysteries really possible? Lynn Margulis asserts that "the cultural background in which we have been brought up precludes our learning about the Earth as a whole planet" (cited at the head of the chapter). This is especially true of religious conditioning, she says. I totally concur, but the revival of the Mysteries can be undertaken without religion, i.e., dogma, ritual, institution, hierarchy, ideology. In the perspective of twenty centuries, we are perhaps ready to accept a key lesson of the Piscean Age: making the ego sacred, we lose the sense of how anything else can be. Deep rapport with nature is not accessible to the sanctified ego or the self-conscious mind, but only to the ego-free awareness of the body-mind.

"Both our present science and our present technology are so tinctured with orthodox Christian arrogance toward nature that no solution for our ecological crisis can be expected from them alone. Since the roots of our trouble are so largely religious, the remedy must also be essentially religious, whether we call it that or not." This observation was made by Lynn White, Jr., in his influential essay, "The Historical Roots of Our Ecological Crisis."[316] White was the first to attribute the ecological crisis to Judeo-Christian religion. Fortunately, Gnosticism is not an alternative religion, it is an alternative to religion, a path and practice that must be lived and expressed one person at a time. Gnosis is psychosomatic illumination, the full-body rush of cognitive ecstasy and direct sensorial reception of the vital intelligence of the Earth.

25

SACRED ECOLOGY

If there is any real prospect of recovering and reviving Gnosis today, it will require looking closely at some problems endemic to the Piscean Age that remained unresolved due to the destruction of the Mysteries. Deep ecology may well find the spiritual and mythic dimension it lacks in the Sophianic worldview—such, at least, is the premise of this book. I cannot predict how this will happen, or even *if* it will happen, but I can offer a rough sketch of the conditions required for it to happen.

Gnosis is not a religion, yet it could well be formulated in an alternative Holy Trinity: Gaia, other species, Anthropos. Each point of the trinity concerns the ultimate question of how we as human beings view life and behave toward each other, as well as toward other nonhuman animals. In other words, the trinity comprises three perspectives: our view of Gaia, the living planet; our view of all species apart from ourselves, including microbial and molecular entities; and our view of our own species. The issues left unresolved by the telestai cannot be approached correctly without a clear formulation of all three of these views.

A Sentient Planet

Consider first our view of Gaia, the living planet. This is, let's say, the apex of the trinity of sacred ecology. After many years of reflection, James Lovelock carefully qualified the theory he introduced to the world: "I am not thinking in an animistic way, of a planet with sentience," he says in *Gaia: The Practical Science of Planetary Medicine*.[317] Well, he may not be, but a great many others are. The central problem in our view of Gaia is how to look beyond what hard science supposes, but without going all fuzzy with mystical make-believe.

This is precisely where the Goddess mystique fails the day, of course. It brings into play a set of wooly animistic beliefs about the planet. Both James Lovelock and Lynn Margulis resist the animism inherent to the mystique, and for good reason. Both the confectionary haze of New Age mysticism and the soft gloss of Neopagan sentimentality obscure the Sophianic perspective. Animist beliefs will not meet the challenges left unresolved by the seers of the ancient Mysteries, but Gaia theory *will* become animistic, one way or the other. It is just a matter of *how*.

The Gaia hypothesis and deep ecology appeared in the world almost simultaneously. These two closely related propositions have so far not merged, nor have they become associated either in popular or specialist discourse. One reason may be that specious assumptions attached to Gaia theory, mainly by New Age visionaries who champion the idea of a sentient planet, block or misconstrue those facets of the theory that might complement the principles of deep ecology. The specious assumptions concern the questions, Is Gaia benevolent? (denied by Margulis); Is Gaia able to control the planet in a conscious, intentional way? (denied by both Margulis and Lovelock); and Does humanity have a special role to play in Gaian biophysics? (variously disputed by Margulis, Lovelock, and others). If the advocates of the Goddess mystique that has grown up around Gaia theory are to be believed, the answer to all the above questions is a resounding yes. This affirmation inspires and encourages many people who are deeply concerned about the fate of the planet—but is it true? Or is it just wishful thinking on a global scale? A case of baseless cosmic pretensions?

In the initiatory revelation of the Mysteries, participants came to know Gaia by direct contact with the Organic Light. But that was mysticism and not science, right? Lynn Margulis defines science as "a way of enhancing sensory experience with other living organisms and the environment generally." With a sharp glance in the direction of Goddess worshippers, she warns against "debilitating biomysticism" and the "deification of the Earth by nature nuts."[318] Well, this Gnostic would argue that her definition of science is a pretty good definition of biomysticism. It is not the least bit "debilitating" to enhance sensory experience by deepened rapport with nature. On the contrary, the practice of biomysticism restores the palingenesis of the ancient Mysteries: regeneration through rapturous surrender to the life force.

In this book, I have advocated animism and asserted that Gaia is sentient not as matters to be accepted on belief, or rejected because of their unscientific character. Rather, they are propositions to be tested. How would we verify the sentience of Gaia, anyway? How could it be tested scientifically? How can we know that the planet can feel and respond as an animal does? To put the question in another way, How might Gaia *communicate* her sentience to us? The first point of the trinity—our view of the living planet—raises the formidable issue of communication. Anthropologist Jeremy Narby stated the issue with elegance: "How could nature not be conscious if our own consciousness is produced by nature?"[319] Thinking logically, Narby assumes that the consciousness we have cannot have evolved from any less conscious state. But human consciousness is intimately bound up with language. If nature (Gaia) is really conscious, how can she let us know that she is, unless she has the language to do so?

Ah, there's the rub. Our view of Gaia will stall out in blind speculation unless we can allow that she *can* communicate with human beings in language as we know it. Unless this is possible, we will never be able to confirm that she is sentient in the same way animals are, and we ourselves are. Ratcheting Narby's question to another level, I would ask: How can nature, which produced a species gifted with language, not be capable of using the language of that species to communicate with it? The Peruvian shamans who initiated Narby into the trance induced by the psychoactive potion *ayahuasca* attested to such communication. They said that the sacred plants talk to them, teaching them many things, including how to use the plants correctly. That is, nature talks to them in the language she enabled them as humans to evolve. Is that not utterly logical?

But it can be objected that Gaia, Mother Nature, does not have a larynx, mouth, and tongue. She lacks the physical organs of speech. Yes, she does, but we also speak without using those organs. Thinking is a subvocal language that we hear as if it were audible. We do not need a tongue to communicate mentally. Granted, most of our mental communication consists of talking to ourselves "in our heads"—the internal monologue. If we cannot *yet* communicate telepathically, one to another, may it not be solely due to lacking the skill to deliberately receive and transmit the subvocal language of our thinking? But what if Gaia, who equipped us with our communicating faculties, can already exhibit telepathic abilities that we may only evolve in the future? That being so, she could talk to us in any language on Earth without needing a mouth and tongue. According to the testimony of native peoples who use psychoactive plants to access the Gaian mind, this is exactly what she does.

Sophianic Animism

> I believe that most of what was said of God was in reality said of that spirit whose body is the Earth.[320]

Gnostics taught that the sentience of the Earth is direct evidence of Sophia's superanimating power of Aeonic Dreaming. The Wisdom Goddess dreams us out of cosmic plenitude, from the heart of the Pleroma. The optimal future for humanity is to reciprocate and live *transcendentally* by consciously enacting self-elected roles in the living dream of the Earth. Today, fifteen years after the original publication of this book, aspiring Gnostics around the world are learning to regard the Sophianic narrative as the script of a movie in the making. The plot of the film develops as it is being shot. Actors who elect into the Dreamtime of the Wisdom Goddess script their own roles and enact their parts accordingly. This practice of orchestration coordinates divine and human purposes. Participants rely on ongoing intel derived from living in Gnosis today.

The life force of the planet is animated and animating, giving expression to creatures who sense they are alive. The *perception* that the world is alive, not the mere belief, is animism. Gaia theory in its scientific form forces the question of animism but cannot answer it. The revival of animism does not involve the mere assumption of the sentience of nature, but direct experience of it. We would already have this experience naturally and spontaneously, as part of our ecognostic capacities, if impeding beliefs were removed, including the belief in single-self identity. Science fiction writer Philip K. Dick said that Gnosis consists of "disinhibiting instructions" that allow us to access a vast store of innate, intuitive knowing. What I propose to call *silent knowing* is a state of rapturous attention to the presence of the Earth. There you enter the eloquent muteness of being awed. The testimony of people who have experienced a spontaneous upsurge of silent knowing reveals a lot about communication with Gaia. One such testimony comes from the Irish mystic, writer, and painter known as AE.

George William Russell (1867–1935), who wrote under the pen name AE, asserted that "the immortal in us has memory of all its wisdom." In a simple, yet far-reaching analysis of his own mystical experience, Russell connected the immortal wisdom-bearing memory with the faculty of imagination. "This memory of the spirit is the real basis of imagination, and when it speaks to us we feel truly inspired and a mightier creature than ourselves speaks *through* us." The emphasis on *through* signals what I have called *transentience*. Lynn Margulis's SET theory is about endosymbiosis, creatures living *through* each other. Animistic perception confirms that living-through is *the* primary dynamic of the ecosystem. The realization and enactment of this dynamic by human animals can be called Sophianic Animism.

Russell's eloquent memoir, *The Candle of Vision*, is one of the great classics of Western spirituality. As an adolescent walking through the fields of Armagh in Northern Ireland, Russell became convinced that "a myth incarnated in me, the story of an Aeon, one of the first starry emanations of Deity, one pre-eminent in the highest heavens." In a library in Dublin he came across a dictionary of religions with an entry on Gnostics, and his eyes fell on the word *Aeon*, the Gnostic term for a god or divinity. From this spontaneous clue he took his signature, AE. The starry emanation of Divinity that he intuited purely from the resources of his inner life was the Wisdom Goddess, Sophia.

Russell was a writer, painter, and social activist of some importance in Irish political life. He was the *éminence grise* behind the Celtic Revival, an Irish cultural movement that formed part of the European occult revival, lasting roughly from 1885 to 1915. He was a close friend of Nobel laureate William Butler Yeats and Lady Gregory, who led the Celtic Revival. AE, who coined the word "supernature," was a natural mystic who needed no theory to guide him into cognitive ecstasy. In spontaneous trance he experienced a series of vivid cinematic visions of pre-Christian Europa or possibly Atlantis. His understanding of these experiences was aided by reading about the Gnostics and the Sabians, a sect of stargazers of ancient Iran. AE claimed that his experiences arose because he was disposed to "vital contact" with the natural setting around him.

In *The Candle of Vision* AE identified the Celtic river god Manannan with the stream of "the divine imagination," the faculty that came to expression in his trances. (The root *man-* occurs widely in world mythology, always with the connotation of a human but supernatural guide: for instance, the Hindu *Manu* and the Native American *Manitou*, which are versions of the Mesotes.) Like that other natural mystic, Romantic poet William Blake, AE identified the power of imagination with Christ—that glitch again—whom he called "the magician of the Beautiful." Describing the sensuous allure of the nymphs and dryads he encountered, AE said that they had "a beauty which had never, it seemed, been broken by the act of individualized will which with us makes possible a choice between good and evil, and the marring of the mold of natural beauty." AE was an exceptional mystic in that his clairvoyant faculties did not operate by blind "channeling," as occurred, say, with the "sleeping prophet" Edgar Cayce, and Jayne Roberts, the medium who produced the Seth material. His observation that the strict dualism of good and evil locks human awareness into a cognitive setting that cannot accept beauty, or "go with the flow" of nature's perpetual revelation, is a genuine Gnostic insight, and merits deep reflection.

Russell's visions were entirely body-based, somatically grounded, and all that he saw was as alive as himself. "That Infinite we would enter is living," he testifies. At peak intensity of trance, he felt "a growing luminousness in my brain as if I had unsealed in the body a fountain of interior light." The invocation of a fountain of light occurs in several revelation discourses in the NHC, as we have seen. AE's candle is a humble metaphor for the soft glow of the Organic Light. The candle burns for us all. "In every mind exists the Supernal Light of the ineffable Mystery" (The Second Treatise of the Great Seth, 67.10).

Russell cites the late classical mystic Proclus on the Divine Mind: "It had not yet gone forth, but abode in the Eternal Depth, and in the adytum [inner sanctum] of god-nourished Silence."

Russell had no access to original Gnostic writings, virtually unknown in his time, and he does not appear to have known G. R. S. Mead, the resident Gnostic scholar of the Theosophical Society. *The Candle of Vision* contains no allusion to the Aeon Sophia or an "Earth goddess" of any kind, except for homage to Dana, the Celtic river goddess. Yet everything AE says about the memory of Nature applies beautifully to the Sophia of Gnostic teachings. His waking dreams were Sophianic reveries drawn from vital contact with the Earth. As such, they are excellent models of animistic perception of the Goddess for aspiring nature mystics today.

AE said of his visions that their creator is transcendent to the waking self and even to the self that dreams at night, and yet this power, "a mightier self of ours," makes itself "our slave for purposes of its own." This language comes close to the Gnostic intuition that the fallen Sophia relies in some sense on human collaboration to achieve her Correction. Russell's sublime little book does not answer all the questions that arise on the path to knowing Gaia, but it sets the mood to contemplate those questions. His invocation of *Sige*, "god-nourished Silence," is particularly apt. The self-conscious mind cannot reach silent knowing, but silent knowing can *reach into it* at rare moments when the internal talk ceases, allowing other things to be heard. Everyone has these moments, when the world turns quiet and an indefinable calm washes over us. To linger on such moments is quite natural. To induce and sustain them is a practice of Gnosis.

A GAIAN TRINITY

To admit that the Earth is alive and intelligent is one thing, and to understand how it is so, how to engage that intelligence and interact and communicate with it, is something else again. The challenge of knowing Gaia is unlike any other on Earth. Lynn Margulis has insisted that "nothing mystical is meant here [in Gaia theory]; we suggest no conscious, benevolent goddess or god."[321] The Mystery seers did attest that Sophia is conscious and benevolent (which, by the way, does not preclude her being capricious or even vindictive), but no one is bound to take their word on this. Gaia-Sophia does not demand our belief, but she most surely depends on our willingness to learn.

At the start of this chapter, I proposed the Holy Trinity of Sophianic animism: Gaia – Nature – Anthropos. This scheme is easy to visualize, and a brief elaboration can be instructive. G at the apex of the triangle is the Aeonic Mother embodied in the superorganism of the Earth, Gaia-Sophia. Her aura encompasses and grounds the entire triangle. The baseline runs from A, the Anthropos, to N, Nature, the whole Earth including the totality of biota and the biosphere itself. At the center stands H, the human animal, distinguished from the Anthropos, which is the extraterrestrial template of all human races. Finally, there is an S for the Symbiont as the agency that mediates both ways, toward the Anthropos and toward Nature. It descends from Sophia's origin, the Pleroma, to the baseline. The four permutations of H-G, H-A, H-N and H-S are categorically inclusive for our experience on the planetary scale. Nothing can be said about human behavior either individually or collectively that does not appear framed in this elementary set of relationships.

The line coming down vertically to the horizontal base represents the descent of the Symbiont. This detail recalls the Christian trope of the descent of the Holy Spirit, the Paraclete, widely celebrated in Evangelical sects. In fact, residual clues to the Pleromic intercession use that allusion: "They [Gnostics] call her Mother and Ogdoad, and Sophia, Earth, Jerusalem, Holy Spirit and, in the masculine, Lord. She inhabits the Intermediate Region and is above the Demiurge, but is below, or outside, the Pleroma until the consummation" (Epiphanius, *Panarion*, II, 198:12). The Paraclete-Symbiont goes to the baseline, balancing Anthropos and Nature. There is the total setting for the practice of sacred ecology. The Symbiont descends from the Pleroma as Sophia did. It resonates like an encompassing harmonic chord that bonds the Anthropos to Nature. Across the A-N baseline, that chord generates recognition of the species-self and induces empathy with the entire range of nonhuman life. The Paraclete is a prop of Christian faith, but the Intermediary equates widely with animistic spirits of nature: the Manitu, the Spirit of the Wilderness known in many guises to native peoples of the Americas, White Buffalo Calf Woman of the Lakota Sioux, Pan, Kokopelli, and many other theriomorphic figures.

In the sweat lodge ceremony of Native American peoples, you enter the lodge on hands and knees, often naked, and doing so, pronounce a simple formula of reverence: "All my relations." That is also the formula for the Sophianic Holy Trinity. It is easy enough to say, disarmingly easy. But the intention carried in those three words is extremely potent. Sophianic animism overthrows the ages-old conflict of human versus nature. In the natural paradise where Sophia places her designer species, reproduction, work, and death are non-negotiable conditions. They can be viewed as blessings of the Aeonic Mother, or perhaps better said, blessed opportunities. But the Hebrew creation story has the off-planet father god curse humanity precisely on those three measures of our mortal state. Yahweh is a hateful god who casts the triple curse on his own offspring, the animals made in His image. The Biblical malediction runs against all that is natural and necessary on this Earth. It extrapolates into the biophobic dementia of Deuteronomy, codified in hundreds of alimentary and hygienic taboos. And it gets worse. In 2020 the entire world suffered the postulant eruption of that biophobia in the pandemic scam that condemns breathing as a public crime and makes every living person into a walking bioweapon.

THE PETELIA AMULET

On the baseline of the Gaian Trinity, self-recognition as a species aligns with the view of nonhuman nature, especially the two- and four-legged creatures of other animal kingdoms. But this alignment is, so far, only a theoretical proposition. Or better said, a prospect, something to be developed, like a provisional arrangement for starting a business or undertaking a large project—constructing a bridge, for instance. In fact, the bottom line is like a bridge. It represents the interspecies link between humanity and all that is nonhuman. To live with nature and respect it on its own terms, independent of us, is the premise of deep ecology. This paradigm stands in strong contrast to mere ecological conservatism that situates the human species as the caretaker of the natural world, assigned (many would argue) to that role by the creator. The assumption here is, the terrestrial paradise is there for our use and survival. If we value it *only* because it supports us, caretaking is clearly an act of self-interest. Deep ecology protests this outlook and insists that we respect and even revere nature regardless of how we need it and benefit from it.

Throughout these pages I have repeatedly warned that taking Christ as the supreme representative of humanity, not to mention the mirror and model of human divinity, is a symptom of religious dementia. To untold millions, the crucified savior is the stand-in for species-self identity. Sacrificed by his own father, the Savior suffers vicariously for human sin. Abraham's (presumably forestalled) sacrifice of Isaac in the Old Testament morphs into the torture and death of the "Lamb of God" in the New. The ram that replaces Isaac reappears in the Paschal lamb, and finally Jesus takes the fall for human sin. The script is horribly consistent and always gets worse (rather like the progression of Hollywood movies over recent decades). Tribal sacrifice in the Old Testament escalates into a divine act of redemption in the New Testament. No way of getting around it—child sacrifice is the founding ritual of Judeo-Christianity. Islam celebrates its version of the rite with halal slaughter, expending righteous cruelty on chickens, sheep, and goats. Abrahamic faith founded on murdering and torturing the innocent dominates the collective psyche of billions who inhabit this precious Earth. What could go wrong?

For centuries salvationist religion used the *Imago Christi* to decimate and overwrite the animistic intuition of native Europans and other peoples around the world. Christian legends were contrived to repress the immanent presence of the Symbiont. The conversion of Saint Eustace is a good example. It was said to be inspired by seeing a male figure posed between the horns of a stag, as if crucified. Who could it be but Jesus Christ? The emperor Constantine built a chapel on the spot where the incident occurred, not to commemorate a flash of atavistic clairvoyance, but to assert authoritarian ideology.[322] In *The Grail Legend*, Emma Jung and Marie-Louise von Franz show the immense depth and complexity of the identification of Christ with a stag. Allegorical art of the late medieval period identifies the Savior with the unicorn. (An epiphany of the Organic Light, by the way: see Parzival, XII:613 where the damsel in distress, Orguleuse, calls her slain lover a "monoceros of fidelity" by allusion to a noble knight who has seen the Grail.) Some time in the early Middle Ages, Christian ideologues turned Pan, the randy nature god of Paganism, into the Devil. The perverted co-optations of doctrinal Christianity were so intensely enforced that it became impossible for anyone apart from trained mystics to know that Christ, the Divine Redeemer, has nothing to do with the numinous animal spirits of native legend.

The deceit of Christ simultaneously misdirects us from seeing our true place in nature and seeing *what* we actually are as human animals, beyond *who* we are as social personalities. The interspecies bond supported by the Symbiont (central on baseline A-N) has to be restored *first* by correcting the self-image of humanity. This challenge depends fundamentally on two factors: true knowledge of our origins, and the innate and sovereign faculty of conscience. Sophianic myth provides the first factor in the origin story that describes how two Aeons, Sophia and Thelete, design the human genome in the galactic center (FGS episode 2). A rare archeological find commemorates this event in a concise way that cannot be forgotten once you see it. Discovered in Calabria, southern Italy, in the 1830s, and dated to around 200 B.C.E., the Petelia amulet is a fragment of gold leaf, barely larger than a postage stamp. Believed to originate from an Orphic cult, it states the initiated recognition of human origins that was fostered in the Sophianic Mysteries:

> I am the child of earth and starry heaven,
> But my origins are in heaven alone.
> You yourselves know this.

The archaic script OIGENOSOYRANION can be literally translated as "my race (*genos*) is celestial (*uranian*)".[323] The Anthropos is the template of our species from which all races derive. *The Anthropos itself is imaginal, but the races are existential and biological.* At no time when you stand before another human animal do you see the embodiment of the genomic template. Across the entire range of the planet, no one actually sees a trace of generic humanity. Whenever you encounter another individual or a group of people, whether it be in a family circle, in a community, or in a mass gathering at an airport or on the street, you never see humanity embodied before your eyes. No single human animal ever has or ever will present that case of embodiment. The Gaian trinity is the platform for an argument against universality: all pleas to act in the cause of humanity enforce the subversive deceit of racial uniformity. Yes, the Anthropos is a unity, but it is imaginal, not incarnate. The origin of the genome in the galactic core is the first condition of human existence. Second comes the extra-Pleromic projection nested in M42, the Orion nebula (which can be seen with the naked eye). And third, there is the full range of human animals present on Earth, but only encountered in racial variations. Never generically.

That being so—if you can allow that it is so, noble reader—how obvious can it be that taking Jesus Christ or any other icon for the living image of all humanity is utterly delusional? Even Jesus comes from a particular ethnic strain. Arguments that he was not Jewish are spurious and not worth refuting. They miss the point entirely and misdirect attention from the Archontic ploy of the Incarnation, which Gnostics rigorously refuted. Considering the god-complex of the Hebrews, it is no wonder that we are asked to believe that the supreme model of our species would come from that ethnicity.

In the Book of Revelation that concludes the Bible, the Savior, now elevated to the "Son of Man," sits beside the father god to execute the ultimate authoritarian display of power, the Last Judgment. Who is the ultimate enemy of god's plan in that scenario? *To Mega Therion*, the Great Beast. In this scene, the biophobic mania of the ancient Hebrews comes to screaming consummation in antilife insanity loaded with an extra dose of theriophobia. Saint John the Divine, the putative author of Revelation, suffers a feverish hallucination that shows him a monster with seven heads and ten horns. Astride the Great Beast sits the Scarlet Woman. She is called "Mystery, the Great Whore," an expression that is never explained, although it uncannily echoes the "Whore of Wisdom," an epithet for Sophia. The Whore and the Great Beast in combination present a horror to be exterminated, for it threatens the final triumph of the father god. Can the divine will of Yahweh *actually* be defeated, or is this all merely a huge charade? Whatever the case, the heavenly response to the Great Beast is an attack from destroying angels who pour out bowls of wrath upon the Earth, as if dispensing a series of lethal vaccines. Saint John hallucinated the end of the world by a succession of plagues decanted from different vials. The script he wrote drives the behavior of many people, including those who do not overtly hold religious beliefs. Is it possible that history will unfold in the way the directive script of Revelation drives it? If there is no power to oppose and defeat it?

In the future, sacred ecology will incorporate reverence for animal powers including, perhaps, the Great Beast itself. The animal kingdoms are also productions of the dreaming power of the Great Mother: consider the Symbiont-Nature nexus of the trinity. Elsewhere ("Gnostic Sabotage in the Book of Revelation" on nemeta.org), I have argued that the Great Beast of the Apocalypse may encode the identity of the Aeon Sophia herself, the planetary animal mother. After all, isn't *that* beast the sole supernatural power that can pose a genuine threat to the plan of the father god and the redemption through his only-begotten son, the crucified savior? Due to an unfortunate trope, "the number of the Beast," 666, has come to signify the power of the Authorities, rather than what can defeat them. Using a vaccine-delivered bar code, the globalist overlords would control everyone's ability to buy and sell, but that interpretation of the final tyranny relies on a mistranslation. The correct rendering of AGORASAI H POLESAI is "gather and trade" (Revelation 14:17). Certainly, the authorities may control who buys and sells as long as people remain dependent upon fraudulent financial systems constructed without their agreement—global markets, for instance. But to control those who gather and trade locally by free and mutual consent is another matter altogether.

AGAINST UNIVERSALITY

However, it may prove instructive, the Gaian trinity always directs attention back to the human participant at center: the "H" in the triangle, to spin a trope. Let's recall that the equation of the Symbiont incorporates the factor of self-love. Self-love is to love for humanity as love for humanity is to empathy with nature at large, especially other nonhuman animals. For self-love to be more than narcissistic indulgence, it must support a special app: conscience. Love for oneself is a merited quality. It has to be learned, earned, and proven. The proof comes essentially in the act of assuming responsibility. Most people would agree that a "good person" acts on conscience. The claim to love yourself unconditionally, no matter how you act, is perverted and, in reality, impossible to uphold. That qualificaton does not imply never making mistakes, for mistakes can be admitted and sometimes corrected, or their consequences can be accepted and compensated. Self-correction is an inherent feature of Gnostic practice.

To lack conscience *and* not be ashamed of lacking it is the perfect signature of a psychopath. To be endowed with conscience and face another human animal who lacks it is a daunting test. The problem with having a conscience is that it is almost impossible to conceive of not having one. Yet absence of both conscience and shame is flagrantly manifest in those who assume authority over others. The Gaian trinity is a closed circuit that has to be secured and sustained, not only by love, but equally so by the courage to take responsibility for facing human evil and to protect what is loved. In many human animals, failure to confront the absence of conscience in others leads to failure to protect the circuit of life.

In 1928, German philologist Friedrich Zucker published a book based on extensive linguistic comparison, *Syneidesis-Consientia*, in which he concluded that the Semitic languages, Hebrew, Arabic, and Aramaic, contain no terms equivalent to conscience as understood in Western civilization.[324] It so happens that these languages have uniquely been the medium for the Archontic virus to spread through the world. (To be "anti-Semitic" thus means to oppose the authoritarian ideologies propagated through those languages.) Another scholar of that era, La Rue van Hook, warned explicitly: "In seeking to understand the nature of Greek religion, we must try to divest ourselves of modern religious conceptions which are largely Hebraic."[325] He references Greek religion because the concept of conscience now accepted in the modern sense originated in that genre. The word *syneidesis* first occurs in *Orestes* by Aeschylus, around 408 B.C.E. It may seem outrageous to infer that human conscience can be dated from that moment, or any specific historical moment. But the essence of conscience resides in how the human mind defines it as such, making it a self-attributed property of awareness that determines how one behaves. Previous to that moment it was not so defined and thus cannot be taken for conscience as understood today. Search as you will, you will find no equivalent to this exact characterization of conscience in the philosophies of India or China, either. Forms of social conscience, yes, but individual conscience, no.

A social order based on conscience and free consent does not need the rule of authorities to oversee and manage all aspects of human activity. In the beauty to come, the sovereign conscience of each individual underpins the entire range of social transactions, and there are no authorities to make the rules or inflict punishment for breaking them. Because there are no authorities (either of religion or the state) who set the rules in the first place. To succeed, defiance of authority has to be enforced by rejection of universality along with the toxic germ of liberalism that infests it. To paraphrase a notorious statesman of the twentieth century: "This approach to a genuinely humane world replaces the liberal idea of the individual and the Marxist concept of international brotherhood with the unified will of different peoples rooted in blood and soil. This may be a simple proposition, but the consequences of it are colossal."

A moral code compatible with sacred ecology would exclude punishment. But equally so, it would exclude forgiveness. Instead, it would apply a lethal imperative to actions that violate the sanctity of life such as rape, abuse of children and animals, and despoliation of nature. Recourse to lethal measures comes with the responsibility to protect what is loved. In Sophia's Correction, the social contract will have to be inspired by the choral song of the Eumenides, "Learn to hate with a common mind / For that is the cure of many an ill of humankind."

THE PAGAN SENSE OF LIFE

With the eradication of the Mysteries, humanity lost the most important spiritual resources of the Western world, and this loss has allowed the West to lead the entire planet toward excess and self-destruction. The process that began six thousand years ago, perhaps triggered by a vast climatic catastrophe in North Africa and the Near East, led to monotheistic religion with its suppression of the Goddess, and then, through the transference effectuated by Saint Paul, to the triumph of salvationism as the spiritual paradigm of the Western world. The history of Western civilization records the victory of patriarchy and legitimates its program. There is no more powerful ideology for oppression than redemptive religion.

The pandemic ideological virus is not incurable, however. Sophianic animism is the planetary medicine able to resist authoritarian rule and heal the primal wound from which it erupted.

If the veteran sages of the Pagan Mysteries were right, the highest religious ideals of humanity do not offer the remedy for evil but make us complicit in it. The salvation narrative that Gnostics exposed and resisted was embraced by people who murdered them, destroyed all their works, and then attempted to make it look as if they had never existed. But the Gnostic legacy still lives. It can be reclaimed and reinvented. Even the small flake of recorded teachings, flawed and incomplete as it is, contains enough primal wisdom to inspire a spiritual awakening and return us to our divine resources. The Sophia mythos does not belong in the past or to the past. It is *a once and future myth*, the timeless and insuperable alternative to the salvation narrative. It is a myth that nurtures and sustains those who embrace it, and fosters authenticity through direct experience of its subject matter: the passion of the Goddess. It does not ask, as the redemption story does, to be constantly legitimated, justified, reinstated. The redeemer complex is unredeemable. There is nothing in it that can be saved, nothing worth saving. But the lethal compulsion of the complex is formidable, using pain to reinforce guilt, and vice versa. Because the complex is so insidious, and the prior wounding runs so deep into the collective psyche, its power must be dispelled indirectly. To overcome the salvationist lie is possible by renouncing the story that makes the lie appealing. Break the patriarchal narrative and humanity can enter a future worth living, a future where optimal human promise is the everyday norm, just as it was in the Mysteries of the Great Goddess.

A CRUCIAL GENERATION

Today, many factors are converging that optimize the possibility of recovering the Sophianic animism of the Mysteries. Deep ecology, ecopsychology, shamanism and entheogenic practices, nature mysticism, ecospirituality, Neopaganism, and the Goddess mystique can all be tributary to that recovery. But these are only terms, trendy catchwords. What matters is the reality of experience behind these terms. Gnostically guided animism is the perfect complement to deep ecology, which, so far, has not incorporated the mythopoetic power of imagination. When it does, the course is set for alignment with Sophia's Correction. However one wishes to imagine this alignment, there can be no doubt that in just one generation of thirty years Western society has acquired a new spiritual dimension centered on the image of Gaia. Consider this sequence:

1972 James Lovelock published a one-page statement on the Gaia hypothesis in the journal *Atmospheric Environment*, followed by two brief papers coauthored with Lynn Margulis. The same year saw the publication of *Flesh of the Gods: The Ritual Use of Hallucinogens*, edited by Peter Furst, an important anthology that figured in the shamanic revival, and *Hallucinogens and Shamanism* by Michael Harner. Both books connect "archaic techniques of ecstasy" in ancient times with modern psychopharmacological knowledge.

1973 Arne Naess defined deep ecology in an article in the journal *Inquiry*. This year also saw the founding of the Institute of Noetic

Sciences with the aim to expand knowledge of the nature and potential of the mind and apply it to the health and well-being of humanity. Gnosis is the ancient prototype of the noetic sciences.

1974 *Goddesses and Gods of Old Europe* by Marija Gimbutas was published in English. Gimbutas presents solid archaeological evidence of human-scale Goddess-based societies millennia before the rise of urban civilization. *In Search of the Primitive* by anthropologist Stanley Diamond came out in the same year. Diamond proposes that "the search for the primitive is the attempt to define a primary human potential." This phrase resonates closely with the theme of "future primitive" developed by deep ecologist Dolores LaChapelle in her biography of D. H. Lawrence.

1975 Majorie M. Malvern published *Venus in Sackcloth*, the best book on Mary Madgalene, contributing an important human element of the Goddess mystique. That same year Czech psychiatrist Stanislov Grof published his first book, *Realms of the Human Unconscious*, a study of nonordinary states of consciousness that offers many insights on the mystical practices of Gnosis. Grof's groundbreaking work continued steadily for over thirty years. (We met at the World Psychedelic Forum in Basel in 2008.)

1976 *Where the Wasteland Ends* by Theodore Roszak presented a brilliant critique of Western pathology, including crucial insight into how the salvation narrative of Judeo-Christianity has wounded human imagination. Invoking the Romantics, especially William Blake, Roszak called for the revival of "the Old Gnosis" and the undertaking of "revolutionary mysticism." He warned against technological cocooning and the terminal narcissism of the Piscean Age, a couple of decades before the world fell totally under the spell of cybernetic mimicry. In the same year, *The Paradise Papers* (later published as *When God Was a Woman*) by Merlin Stone defined the leading edge of "Goddess reclamation." Her research confirms the role of women in the empowerment of kings and tribal chieftains prior to the rise of patriarchy.

1978 *The Nag Hammadi Library in English* was published, making Gnostic writings available to the English-speaking world for the first time. In the same year, *The Road to Eleusis* by R. Gordon Wasson, Albert Hofmann, and Carl Ruck proposed and proved the entheogenic basis of the Mysteries.

1979 James Lovelock published his first complete book on the new theory, *Gaia: A New Look at Life on Earth*. Simultaneously, there appeared the seemingly unrelated *Messengers of Deception* by Jacques Vallee and *The Dead Sea Scrolls and the Christian Myth* by John Allegro. The former is perhaps the best single book ever written on the ET/UFO enigma, and the latter is a deep plunge into the pathology of the Zaddikim, with many references to the Mysteries that were driven into oblivion with the rise of Christianity. Vallee's characterization of the ET/UFO phenomenon as a "spiritual control system" echoes with what Gnostics said about the Archontic nature of redemption theology. When he predicted that contactee cults may become the basis of future religions, he could hardly have imagined that the dominant world religions are themselves the outgrowth of such a cult. Thus, both Vallee and Allegro made vital contributions to the mythic and religious dimensions of the Sophia mythos at the very moment that Lovelock was elaborating its biosystemic dimension.

The list is highly selective and could easily be expanded threefold. But as it stands this brief inventory demonstrates how all the key factors that might contribute to restoring Gnosis in our time emerged, incredibly, within a seven-year period. The same period brought to light much essential knowledge regarding how and why the Pagan Mysteries were destroyed. We are now living just one generation on from the 1970s. Who knows what might be achieved in Gaia theory and Gnostic practice in the generation ahead? Perhaps the present generation will be the first to acknowledge the great, world-wrenching tragedy I have attempted to describe in this book: how and why the Western, Euro-American way of life has led the entire planet toward a nonsustainable future.

Renowned environmentalist René Dubos insisted that "our salvation depends on our ability to create a religion of nature."[326] I must assert that humans once had a religion of nature, millennial in duration, vast in scope, and profound in its insight into the very secrets of life, but it was destroyed by belief in off-planet salvation. The authoritarian doctrines of the Abrahamic religions crushed the indigenous wisdom of Europa and crippled the Pagan sense of natural human goodness. Following the Industrial Revolution, Euro-American society took the lead in world affairs, but the flagship nations were all sailing off course due to the "prior wounding." Is it a surprise, then, that "Western culture" cannot do anything but lead humanity even further astray from its true innate potential? The lack of moral and spiritual direction of the West is not a mysterious malaise arising out of nowhere. It is the result of a long-term and deliberate campaign of deceit and despoliation. Today, as in the remote past, the pernicious motivation that drives and directs the assault is rooted in the entitlement of the ultra-righteous, the Zaddikim.

The longing for Sophia stirs in many hearts today, but the spell of divine paternalism retains a strong hold. Those who belong to the tradition of the three Abrahamic religions, Judaism, Christianity, and Islam, tend to look toward their own religious roots for ways to recognize and recover Sophianic values. Particularly in the Christian fold there is an assumption that some kind of Gaia-centered "ecotheology" can be extracted or extrapolated from salvation narrative and the beliefs associated with it. Many intelligent, socially concerned people continue to think that we can get a viable ecotheology out of divine paternalism. The temptation to reconcile Sophianic principles with perpetrator religion is irresistible to all those whose cultural identity is stronger than their longing to surrender self and merge with the planetary life force, Eros. Every excuse made for the victim-perpetrator syndrome reinforces the ages-old repression of the Wisdom Goddess. Every reversion to redeemer theology and the ethics of Jesus undermines the quest for sacred ecology.

The most common argument for reconciliation invokes the caretaker clause: the father god created the natural world and gave it over to human caretaking. But this is patronizing cant. The Earth takes care of itself. Wilderness does fine on its own. The Garden of Eden is a misleading trope. The planet is a paradise even without gardens. Agriculture is not the sacred calling of the human species. We are not indispensable custodians of Gaia, who does fine on her own. The Goddess is not a feeble crone in need of geriatric services. The appeal to "save the planet," shouted from the rooftops by climate change activists, is yet another tiresome Archontic stunt of countermimicry: it turns an essential component of the atmosphere into an evil fume that must be reduced to "net zero carbon." The coronavirus hoax doubles down on this ploy and makes the very act of breathing a toxic threat. As critics of the Great Reset have observed, the globalist overlords find in the manufactured Covid-19 crisis a convenient excuse to enforce their plans to fight climate change. A Gnostic revival can play a decisive role in exposing and overthrowing these huge machinations of deceit.

UNFINISHED ANIMAL

Looking around the planet, it does seem that the immense majority of people are still firmly entrenched in patriarchal religion. Perhaps the weakest point in the ethical agenda of deep ecology is this: People are not easily convinced that human nature is essentially good and that we need no exhortation or off-planet moral commandments to make us care about each other and the Earth. But this view of the human condition is not really typical of *the human condition* per se; rather, it is the result of human condition*ing*. Those who embrace patriarchal religion as the sole source of morals must already have been corrupted by it. By offering a superhuman ideal to mirror our humanity, salvationism dehumanizes us. This is what the spurious message of love in the New Testament does. The double-bind ethic of Jesus is so demoralizing that without the entrapment of victim-perpetrator collusion working behind it, common sense would reject it as self-evidently absurd and dangerous to human sanity.

Patriarchy persists because it has produced generations of people whose wounded, undermined humanity compels them to execute its program, and enlist others to the cause. Those who really need to have their morals dictated by an off-planet god must have already betrayed their bond with the web of symbiosis that could teach them the morality of reciprocity, respect, and self-regulation. For a species created "in His Image," the creator is the source of all authority. The fate of that species is signed and sealed from the outset. But there are alternative views. Theodore Roszak proposed the term "unfinished animal" to describe humanity in the process of becoming, rather than a creature ready-made by an absent creator and ready to obey it mindlessly, acting on preformulated orders. The unfinished animal is a singularity in process, you could say. Cultural critic Neil Evernden strikes a similar note with his notion of "the natural alien." He points out that the human being is the one creature in nature that does not fit into a niche already provided by nature.

> Each organism has its world, and that enables it to function and
> persist. Each lives within that world to which it is made. The
> variability of the human world makes it very difficult to speak
> of humans having an environment, for the human surroundings
> vary with their world. It is this strange flexibility that makes
> it possible for us to believe in an abstract reality which pits us
> against, or more correctly separates us from, the earth that
> houses all organic worlds.[327]

We have to create our own niche, a "creative fit," and that is why we are
unfinished animals. But that is also why we are the outstanding expression of singularity among all species.

Throughout this book, I hope to have shown that the concordance
of Gaian biophysics with the Sophia mythos merits deep reflection.
Gnostics used the term *allogenes*, "someone from elsewhere," "a
stranger," to epitomize the human condition. The word carries two
meanings joined on a trenchant edge. On the one hand, it clearly
alludes to the preterrestrial origin of humanity: the human genome on
Earth was seeded from elsewhere. On the other hand, it points to the
way human beings can become alienated from their own reality by the
Archontic factor. It does *not* mean that we are strangers to the Earth
and don't really belong here. Rather, it warns about the tendency of
the human species, due to our designing and goal-directive capacities,
that causes us to misrepresent and misperceive the world, so that we
end up believing that we don't fit into it. So believing, we will tend
to look beyond the Earth to be rescued from our plight and released
into another, better life. Hence the promise of off-planet salvation
becomes credible: "For God so loved the world that he gave his Only-
Begotten Son that whosoever believeth in him should not perish but
have everlasting life," the Gospel of John assures us. But the Gnostics
had another credo:

> A great power was emanated to you, which the All-Originator,
> the Eternal, endowed in you before you came to this place, in
> order that those things that are difficult to distinguish you might
> distinguish, and those things that are unknown to the multitude

you might know, and that you might be released sane and whole to the One who is yours, in you, who was the first to save and who does not need to be saved. *Allogenes* (NHL XI, 3.50)

Salvation is not the crucial issue for humanity. Adaptation is. We *do* fit into the natural world, but not in any way that Gaia predetermines for us, as she does for other creatures. We are the novelty in *Her* nature. We are the singularity in Sophia's Dreaming, the exception upon which she relies in some way, if the seers in the Mysteries were right:

And the luminous epinoia was hidden in Adam, in order that the Archons might not reach that power, but that the epinoia might be a correction to the deficiency of Sophia. (Apocryphon of John, 20.25)

From time before reckoning indigenous people all around the world have observed the ways of nature and other species, and by doing so learned how to fit into their environment. By coercing us to "believe in an abstract reality which pits us against the Earth that houses all organic worlds," patriarchy and perpetrator religion have almost totally destroyed the precious legacy of native wisdom, and the natives along with it. There are still some threads of indigenous sanity to weave into a future worth living, but in the end it may not be native savvy alone that ensures the survival of the unfinished animal. Loving observation, empathy, and respect for nature and other species can teach us a lot about how to live, but to resolve the question of our niche something more is needed: imagination, the luminous *epinoia*.

Imagination is the genius of humanity, and in each people of each region of the world it manifests a particular creative and innovative spirit—the *genius loci*, the local genius, or spirit of place. The Sophia mythos tells us that the Goddess charged Zoe, the immortal life force, with the task of implanting *epinoia* in humanity. To put it another way, we carry divine imaginative force as a somatic capacity, evident in the phenomenon of bioluminescence, as already noted. Imagination and vitality are crucially wedded in the human psyche and mutually anchored in the body. No ideology can ever defeat or deracinate this union.

NATIVE RESURGENCE

The resilience of these two combined capacities is truly tremendous. History itself attests to its magnificent and insuperable strength— European history, in particular. It would be misleading to claim that the indigenous wisdom of the Europan peoples was in some distinct way superior to that of other peoples in the world (Australian Aborigines, or the Inuit of Greenland, for example), but nevertheless, the long-enduring legacy of that wisdom stands in a class by itself. What the Europans made of their native genius was nothing less than a primal social ecology—a way of life rooted in the experience of the sacred, including the entire nonhuman world, but also oriented toward culture, i.e., toward the primary needs of social continuity rather than social control, toward human potential rather than political hegemony.

This immense, deeply inspired enterprise of human spirituality flowered in the Pagan Mysteries. For millennia, the guardians of the Mysteries taught the arts of civilization, practical sciences, and ecological ethics. When the telestic tradition came under threat, its exponents did not defend themselves by force, but the inherent power of the indigenous spirit managed to survive. At key moments over the last two thousand years, the vital-imaginative genius of the European spirit has resurged with immense vigor and resisted the infection of redeemer theology.

Just three centuries after Hypatia's death the groundswell of native genius broke through in Spain, the very country that would later lead the genocidal assault on the New World. In the same century that saw the rise of Islam (dated to the Hejira in 622 C.E.), an infusion of Arabian mysticism into Europe produced a new literary and cultural genre: chivalry. Chivalric love, or courtly love, was a purely Pagan phenomenon that sprung from the life-soil of Europe at the darkest moment of the Middle Ages. It was a symptom of native immunity to the shaming, gender-alienating program of feudal Christianity and the sexual apartheid of Islam. The noble union of love and heroism was born in Andalucía under Moorish rule, proving that even in the Arabian peoples there was a strong natural immunity to the repression of the Abrahamic creeds, of which Islam is the third and most virulent mutation. The first troubador epic, *Antar*, was written there in the seventh century. For five hundred years the chivalric impulse grew and flourished, finally producing an extraordinary flowering of poetry, music, and literature in Provence and Aquitaine. The movement spread to Italy, Germany, the Netherlands, and England, encompassing all of Western Europe.

In the medieval cult of *amor courtois* the local genius of Europa asserted itself against the viral assault of salvationist religion. Romantic love turned the sexist strictures of patriarchy upside down, making the knight dependent upon his lady to dignify his exploits. In effect, the romantic movement of the Middle Ages reinstated the ancient rites of Goddess empowerment. It did more to humanize Western society than all the religious sermons preached from Augustine to Aquinas. The religion of personal love exemplified in such legendary figures as Tristan and Isolde presented a clear alternative to the creed of the perpetrators. "The cultivation of passionate love began in Europe as a reaction to Christianity (and in particular its doctrine of marriage) by people whose spirit, whether naturally or by inheritence, was still pagan," observed Denis de Rougemont in *Love in the Western World*.[328]

Those who embraced the resurgent Pagan ethos knew what they were up against. *AMOR versus ROMA* was a graffito of the time. Gottfried von Strassburg, author of *Tristan* (ca. 1210 C.E.) declared boldly that the carnal and personal passion of his lovers was a sacrament more powerful than Holy Mass. It is not surprising that Gottfried disappeared suddenly when the Vatican enforcers came to town. Yet his message lived to inspire millions who did not find the love to sustain their lives in the paternal promise of God's love.

It took a concerted genocidal campaign by the papacy under Innocent III to destroy Provençal culture and massacre the people who openly defied the authority of the Holy Roman Empire. At Béziers in 1209 C.E. thirty thousand unarmed people were murdered in one day, recalling the genocide at Bourges over a thousand years earlier. The latter was a purely secular act, but the former was sanctioned by the Church as a legitimate way to exterminate heresy. The Catholic Church adopted the genocidal imperative of Rome, not as a brutal perversion of the Faith but as the sovereign instrument for achieving its visionary plan. The destruction of the "love culture" of southern France shows that atrocities committed in the name of religion are not exceptions perpetrated by a few bad people, they are veracious expression of true believers who are enacting what their beliefs really require of them.

The second resurgence of the native Europan genius occurred in the Renaissance with the rediscovery of Pagan culture, literature, and manners by the intellectual class. As conquest under the sign of the Cross proceeded in the New World, the natives of the Old World attempted to reclaim what they had lost when their ancestors were decimated by the same program. This time the immune response of the native genius was weaker, however. Mere imitation of Pagan manners was an insufficient response to fifteen centuries of psychohistorical conditioning. Humanism was a failure, not only because its exponents did not have a viable concept of the Anthropos, but more so because Christianity had so infected the native imagination in fifteen centuries that it was impossible to recapture the true essence of the pre-Christian sense of life.

The third and most recent wave of resurgence happened with the rise of the Romantic movement, timed to the American Revolution. At the vortex of the movement a mere handful of men and women proclaimed a daring breakthrough for humanity, a reclamation of the divine endowment, imagination. One exemplar of the movement, British poet and mystic William Blake, equated the power of imagination with Jesus Christ in a way that suggests that Blake may have encountered the Mesotes, if, indeed, he did not take tea and biscuits with it on a regular basis.[329] The stated aim of the Romantics was to reclaim religious experience free of doctrines, rituals, and institutions. From 1775 to 1820 the movement flared white hot, and then slowly, painfully burned out. The grandiose proposals of Romantic renegades in Russia, Italy, France, Spain, Germany, and England were not fulfilled, and Romanticism went on the rocks, leaving more problems than it solved. Yet the inspiration it drew from the deep native roots of European soul-life continued to resonate well into the twentieth century.

The last heirs to the Romantic movement were post-Romantics such as the Irish mystic AE, German poet Rainer Maria Rilke, and British author, D. H. Lawrence. Often the Romantic diehards were of Celtic origin, racially or culturally. In pre-Christian times the role of Celtic culture was to unify Europa, and through the centuries the Celtic spirit played a leading role in resistance and creative resurgence. The Celtic literary renaissance led by modern initiate W. B. Yeats (who was also a key figure in the European occult revival) was the final breaking wave of Romanticism.

Post-Romantic novelist and poet D. H. Lawrence wrote *Apocalypse* (cited several times in this book) in the last three months of his life when he was dying of tuberculosis. Even as his own life was ebbing away, his final concern was focused on recovering the Pagan sense of life that had been lost for two thousand years. A recent biography says: "What he wanted to do was make this old, pagan vision something which modern man would have to concede was lacking in his own experience; Lawrence was writing a book offering his contemporaries a kind of psychic recovery of their connections with the old world."[330]

In *Future Primitive* Dolores LaChapelle, the doyenne of deep ecology, shows that Lawrence's life and work anticipated the new ecological awareness and prefigured the Gaian perspective. Publicly condemned as immoral and legally prosecuted for his last novel, *Lady Chatterly's Lover*, Lawrence was a man of profound moral sensibility who warned against the spirit of righteousness in its many guises, including "idol love" and "the dead vanity of knowing better."[331] Few of the Romantics could match Lawrence's trenchant insight into the toxic pathology of single-self identity, but his erotic sense for the natural world was widely shared by many of his predecessors. The nature mysticism of poets such as William Wordsworth is widely recognized as the forerunner of the ecology movement. Neil Evernden says of the Romantics that "they challenged not only conventional beliefs but the very process of formulating beliefs." The challenge has barely survived, however. One wonders if the native genius of Europe has enough innate vitality left to resist the conqueror virus and resurge yet again, perhaps one last time.

SILENT KNOWING

With regard to the deep-seated soul sickness of Western civilization, the bad news turns out to be the good news. Knowing how we are deviated could be the very truth—the deeper education we so resist—that leads us to participate in Sophia's Correction. It could be the knowledge that saves global society from its dominant pathological affliction, perpetrator religion. The legacy of divine paternalism is a hundred generations of bad parenting and abuse. That is a lot of dysfunctionality to overcome! But the enlightenment of the last thirty years looks extremely promising.

Still, the resurgence of the Mysteries is not a matter for magical thinking. It is neither a utopian dream nor a mystical fantasy, but a call to genuine, real-life consecration. The Dark Ages that began when Hypatia was murdered have never really ended. We live in the last days of Kali Yuga. This is a time, the old legends say, that affords exceptional gains along spiritual lines in some individual cases, but they occur against the background of extreme decay and degeneration for society at large. It remains to be seen who can and will respond directly to the voice of the Wisdom Goddess. Who will listen in the clairaudient rapture of silent knowing, taking instruction from the wellspring of the Organic Light? Who among us will be as attentive to the living Earth as the *mystes* who recorded the sublime, enigmatic disclosure of Thunder, Perfect Mind (NHC VI, 2)?

> I am the incomprehensible silence and the often-remembered thought
> I am the voice of many sounds and the expression of many designs
> I am the utterance of my own name
> For I am the Sophia of the Greeks
> And the Gnosis of the barbarians
> The one who has been hated everywhere, and loved everywhere
> I am godless and I am she whose godhood is multiple
> I am the one whom you have considered and whom you have scorned
> I am unlearned, and it is from me that you learn
> I am the gnosis of my seeking,
> and the finding of those who seek after me

-ACKNOWLEDGMENTS-

I am grateful to Chantal Valentine De Bock for offering me refuge in Europe and providing the safe and happy home I never had in childhood, apart from the sheltering embrace of Friendship Harbor. Without her incomparable care, patience, and devotion, this book could never have been written. *Merci infiniment, 'tit tresor*. Due to your kindness the first chapter in the true history of the European peoples has been written.

To others unnamed, those I know and many I do not and will never know, who made this book possible by the inspiration and support they offered, those who prepared the teacher so well by posing as students, who tolerated my arrogance and laughed at my jokes, who endured my adolescent caprices, and even those who stood in the way by withholding, missing or dismissing the beauty and abundance of the Sophianic vision—to these many and diverse individuals I confer the gratitude rendered upon me in March 1966, in Pokhara, Nepal, by the Mountain Mother of the Himalayas. Not merely a token acknowledgement, but the root cause upon which recognition of divine generosity can arise in the human mind. To them I confer the ultimate blessing of Zangza Ringtsun, the sky-bestowing look.

JOHN LAMB LASH
Bhairavi shift, Fall 2013
Andalucía

——— NOTES ———

PART 1: CONQUEST AND CONVERSION

CHAPTER 1: THE MURDER OF HYPATIA

1. Socrates Scholasticus, *History of the Church* (London: Henry G. Bohn, 1903), 348–49.
2. John, bishop of Nikui, *Chronicle* 84.87–103. In *Alexandria: A Journal of the Western Cosmological Traditions* 2, ed. David Fideler (Grand Rapids, MI: Phanes Press, 1993).
3. Manley Palmer Hall, *The Secret Teachings of All Ages* (Los Angeles: Philosophical Research Foundation, n.d.), 197, "The Mysteries and Their Emissaries."
4. Michael Wood, *In the Footsteps of Alexander the Great* (London: BBC Books, 2004), 74–75.
5. Werner Keller, *The Bible as History* (New York: William Morrow & Co, 1981), 322.
6. *Note*: Against the objection that the evidence of Pagan learning is not compatible with Gnostic thought, I would reply: There are plenty of Gnostic elements in Pagan literature—in Hesiod and Aeschylus, for instance—if one knows how to identify them. The prodigious writings of Plutarch, a known initiate, attest to the scope and diversity of the literary outpouring of the Mystery Schools. Usually, the more arcane elements of Gnostic teaching were reserved for intramural discussion in the Mystery cells and were not readily transposed into secular writing. However, when the moment came for the telestai to protest Christian doctrines, these elements found lavish expression both in print and oral discourse. The most complete and explicit text of initiatory instruction is *On the Mysteries* by Iamblichus, founder of the Neoplatonic school to which Hypatia was said to belong. It is firsthand and coherent, although expressed in a metaphysical idiom that is immensely difficult for the modern mind. The NHC presents an imbalanced, incomplete, and incoherent record of second- and third-hand versions of Gnostic teachings.
7. Thomas Dalton, *Eternal Strangers: Critical Views of Jews and Judaism through the Ages* (Uckfield, East Sussex : Castle Hill Publishers, 2020), 27ff. Citing Philo of Alexandria (*Against Flaccus*), Dalton recounts an incident in 38 C.E. when the populace revolted against what they regarded as the harmful and subversive influence of the Jews in their affairs.
8. Gilbert Highet, *The Classical Tradition* (New York: Oxford University Press, 1957), 3 and 566, note 1.
9. G. R. S. Mead, *The Gospels and the Gospel* (London and Benares: Theosophical Publishing House, 1902), 210.
10. Interview with Dan Burstein, in *Secrets of the Da Vinci Code* (New York: CDS Books, 2004), 100–105.

11. G. R. S. Mead, *Fragments of a Faith Forgotten* (New Hyde Park, NY: University Books, 1960), 46.

12. S. Angus, *The Mystery-religions* (New York: Dover Publications, 1975), 243.

13. Ibid. p 12.

14. Barbara Walker, *The Woman's Dictionary of Symbols and Sacred Objects* (San Francisco: HarperSanFrancisco, 1988).

15. Mead, *Fragments*, xiii.

16. In a thesis closely related to these views, Ralph Abraham has proposed that Buddhism derives from "Neolithic Orphism," one of the prehistoric Mystery cults of the Great Goddess. See the essay, "Orphism: The Ancient Roots of Green Buddhism," in *Dharma Gaia*, ed. Allan Hunt Badiner (Berkeley, CA: Parallax Press, 1990) and Abraham's *Chaos Gaia Eros* (San Francisco: HarperSanFrancisco, 1994).

17. Arne Naess first proposed the term "deep ecology" in an article, "The Shallow and the Deep, Long-range Ecology Movement," published in *Inquiry* 16 (1973).

18. Naess, "The Deep Ecological Movement," 26.

19. James Lovelock, "The Evolving Gaia Theory," a talk given in Tokyo, Japan, 25 September 1992.

20. Diorthosis: *The Coptic Gnostic Library*, paperback edition (Leiden: E. J. Brill, 2000), vol. 5, book 2, pp. 93ff. In the Valentinian school, Sophia's Correction depended on the intervention of the Christos, but other Gnostic schools emphasized the role of humanity over Christos. Much depends on how the Christic intervention (see chapter 14) is understood. How correction occurs cannot be determined from surviving materials and must be worked out experimentally.

21. René Girard, *Violence and the Sacred* (Baltimore: The Johns Hopkins University Press, 1989), 30–31.

22. Derrick Jensen, *Listening to the Land* (San Francisco: Sierra Club Books, 1995), 273–74. Emphasis added.

23. Girard, *Violence and the Sacred* 30–31.

24. Samuel D. Marble, *Before Columbus* (New York: A.S. Barnes & Co., 1980), 49.

CHAPTER 2: PAGAN ROOTS

25. *The Penguin Concise English Dictionary* (2002).

26. Dee Brown, *Bury My Heart at Wounded Knee* (London: Vintage/Random House, 1991), xvii.

27. Martin Bernal, *Black Athena*, 2 vols. (New Brunswick, NJ: Rutgers University Press, 1987), 1:106.

28. Ellen Ellerbe, *The Dark Side of Christian History* (Orlando, FL: Morningstar and Lark, 1998), 137.

29. Julian Jaynes, *The Origin of Consciousness in the Breakdown of the Bicameral Mind* (London: Penguin Books, 1990), 149, 154–55.

30. Garth Fowden, "Religious Communities," in *Late Antiquity*, ed. Bowerstock et al. (Cambridge, MA: The Belknap Press of Harvard University Press, 1999), 82–106.

31. LaChapelle, "Educating for Deep Ecology," www.talkingleaves.org, Spring/Summer 1998.

32. "The Sign of Socrates," 591d-e, in Robert Lamberton, *Plutarch* (New Haven and London: Yale University Press, 2001), 30.

33. Paul Shepard, *Nature and Madness* (Athens: University of Georgia Press, 1998), 62.

34. Apparently, some Europeans were able to recognize in Native American culture a counterpart to their own origins. In *Manitou* (Rochester, VT: Inner Traditions, 1989), James W. Mavor, Jr., and Byron E. Dix suggest that the similarity of megalithic sites in New England to those in the Old World must have been obvious to some colonialists: "The early seventeenth-century English settlers in America called the land New England because, among other reasons, it reminded them of home; they saw stone walls, standing stones and stone heaps like those of the English countryside" (1). Whatever the actual extent of such recognition, there remains precious little recorded evidence of it.

35. De las Casas, cited in James DeMeo, *Saharasia* (Greensprings, OR: Orgone Biophysical Research Lab, 1998), 384.

36. Partridge, 462.

37. Jane Ellen Harrison, *Themis* (Gloucester, MA: Peter Smith, 1974), 439.

38. Gordon Rattray Taylor, *The Sexual History of the Human Race*.

39. D. H. Lawrence, *Apocalypse* (London: Penguin Books, 1980), xv.

40. Ibid., 65, 43.

41. Plutarch, "On why the oracles came to fail," 419 B-E, cited by Giorgio de Santillana and Hertha von Dechend in *Hamlet's Mill* (Boston: David R. Godine, 1977), 275ff.

42. *The Oxford Dictionary of English Etymology*, 1982.

43. Marcus Aurelius, *Meditations* IX, 1, trans. C. B. Baines, modified by author (Cambridge, MA: Loeb Classical Library).

44. Pliny the Younger, letter to the Emperor Trajan (Pliny's *Letters*, 10.96), written in C.E. 110–111.

45. In Greek culture, tragedy did not befall ordinary people but only those exceptional few, men or women whom fate compelled to act in excess of the social norms that defined the limits of personal responsibility, and in defiance of the gods themselves. See my book, *The Hero* (London: Thames & Hudson, 1995), 21ff.

46. Jaynes, *The Origin of Consciousness*, 258.

47. Alexander Lowen, *The Betrayal of the Body* (New York: Collier Books, 1972), 179.

48. Gail Hawkes, *Sex and Pleasure in Western Culture* (Cambridge, MA: Polity Press, 2004), 31–32.

49. Arthur Koestler, *The Act of Creation* (New York: Dell, 1964), 260.

50. Attributed to Sextus the Pythagorean in sayings attached to the work of the Iamblichus, translated by Thomas Taylor. *Iamblichus on the Mysteries* (Kessenger Publishing), 373.

51. I first came across the notion that the human species underwent a decisive shift due to maturation of the forebrain circuits around 600 B.C.E. in the work of Rudolf Steiner. Curiously, the shift from empathic tribal participation to narcissistic self-concern has also been signaled by Carlos Castaneda (*The Active Side of Infinity*),

without reference to a date. I maintain that this sudden, modular increase in cerebral capacity, such as has been observed in clinical studies of the mental and sensory development of infants, was not due to any kind of extrahuman intrusion. However, extrahuman or supernatural interference (the Archontic factor, in Gnostic terms) may well have been hugely advantaged by this development.

52. Marjorie Malvern, *Venus in Sackcloth* (Carbondale and Edwardsville, IL: Southern Illinois University Press, 1975), 164, citing Huizinga, *Homo Ludens*.

CHAPTER 3: THE CONQUEST OF EUROPA

53. Jaroslav Pelikan, *Jesus Through the Centuries* (New York: Harper & Row, 1987), 69.
54. Rosemary Radford Ruether, *New Woman/New Earth*.
55. Andy Fisher, *Radical Ecopsychology* (Albany, NY: State University of New York Press, 2002), 19.
56. Riane Eisler, *The Chalice and the Blade* (London: Pandora, 1990), xvii. Eisler's invaluable model of partnership society can be complemented by the inclusion of the Wasson thesis on entheogenic religion (note 213) as a key element in our view of cultures that observe the sacredness of the Earth.
57. Dolores LaChapelle, *Future Primitive* (North Denton, TX: University of Texas Press, 1996), 49.
58. Jacques Lacarriere, *The Gnostics* (London: Peter Owen, 1978), 94.
59. Orphic Bowl: see Hans Leisegang, "The Mystery of the Serpent," in *The Mysteries*, Papers from the Eranos Yearbooks, Bollingen Series XXX, 2 (Princeton, NJ: Princeton University Press, 1978), 194–260. Also, the Pietroasa bowl, 245ff.
60. Terence McKenna, *The Archaic Revival* (San Francisco: HarperSanFrancisco, 1991), 149.
61. T. W. Rolleston, *Myths and Legends of the Celtic Race* (New York: Schocken Books, 1986), 19–20.
62. It might be objected that the Celts were Indo-European invaders of the "Kurgan" type, and so ought not be regarded as exemplary Europans. But some scholars locate the "Celtic hearth" at the source of the Danube, hence, in the heartland of Europe, not in the Caucasus where the Kurgan invaders originated. It would be digressive to cite sources and expand the argument involving Gimbutas, Eisler, et al., at length here. I am confident that my view of the Celts as the "guardian culture" of Europa will bear up against close examination.
63. *The Times Atlas of World History*, ed. Goeffrey Barraclough (Maplewood, NJ: Hammond Inc., 1978), 85.
64. Joseph Campbell, *Creative Mythology* (London: Penguin Books, 1982), 564.
65. Cited in Peter Berresford Ellis, *A Brief History of the Celts* (London: Robinson, 2003), 57.
66. Geoffrey Ashe, *Avalonian Quest* (London: Fontana, 1982) 172, 212.
67. Ibid., 213, citing Anne Ross in *Pagan Celtic Britain*, and 214, citing Stuart Piggot. The latter comment echoes the view of Kenneth Rexforth regarding the Neolithic

origins of the Mysteries. These references are among a dozen I could cite demonstrating how the definition of shamanism has been broadened, enriched, and clarified since Eliade's classic, *Shamanism: Archaic Techniques of Ecstasy* (French 1961, English 1964). At first narrowly associated with the Mongolian and Siberian cultural milieu, shamanism is now seen in a much wider perspective, but its connection with Gnosticism and the Mysteries still needs to be recognized.

68. Ellis (n. 62), 144.

69. Keith Critchlow makes cross-cultural comparisons based on the design of megalithic structures. In *Time Stands Still* (New York: St. Martin's Press, 1982), he proposes that "Asiatic shamanic cosmologies" share common ground with both Neolithic British (i.e., Druidic) and Native American ritual and cosmological systems.

70. Ellis, 174.

71. Ibid., 56.

72. Erich Fromm, *The Anatomy of Human Destructiveness* (London: Penguin Books, 1973), 143.

73. Peter Matyszak, *Chronicle of the Roman Republic* (London: Thames & Hudson, 2003), 206.

74. Mead, *Fragments*, 106.

75. Lloyd M. Graham, *Deceptions and Myths of the Bible* (Secaucus, NJ: Citadel Press, 1997), 444.

76. Eunapius cited in Karl Kerenyi, *Eleusis*, Bollingen Series LXV: 4 (Princeton, NJ: Princeton University Press, 1967), 17.

77. Procopius cited in C.W. King, *Gnostics and Their Remains* (London: David Nutt, 1887), 340.

78. James W. Mavor, Jr., and Byron E. Dix, *Manitou* (Rochester, VT: Inner Traditions 1989), 191.

79. Ibid., 193. The authors draw many parallels between indigenous European lore (particularly ritual architecture and megalith building) and Native American shamanism, as well as point out the genocidal behavior of Europeans toward Native Americans.

80. Pierre Chuvin, *A Chronicle of the Last Pagans* (Cambridge, MA: Harvard University Press, 1990), cited in Gregory Shaw, *Theurgy of the Soul* (University Park, PA: Pennsylvania State University, 1995), 1.

81. Eunapius of Sardis, *Lives of the Sophists*, 472; in Lamberton, *Plutarch*, 3.

Chapter 4: The Cult of Righteousness

82. Marija Gimbutas proposed the name Kurgan for the chariot-driving male warrior societies that emerged from the steppes of Asia around 4200 B.C.E. in several waves. Gimbutas traces the invasions in her books, starting with *The Goddesses and Gods of Old Europe*, first published in English in 1974. Although her theory remains controversial, it is widely regarded as the best model we have of the geographic and historical origins of patriarchy.

83. Mircea Eliade, *A History of Religious Ideas* (Chicago: University of Chicago Press, 1978), 1:335.

84. See Gershom Scholem, *Sabbatai Sevi: The Mystical Messiah, 1626-1676* (Bollingen Series XCII, Princeton University Press, 1973).

85. Geza Vermes, *The Changing Faces of Jesus* (London: Allen Lane, Penguin Press, 2000), 3.

86. Leo Deuel, *Testaments of Time* (New York: Alfred A. Knopf, 1966), 252–53.

87. Shepard, *Nature and Madness*, 62.

88. In Jewish tradition, various legends consider Melchizedek to be kin to Noah, hence an ancient, antediluvian figure. The fourth-century Church historian Eusebius recounts a tradition that the meeting of Abraham with Melchizedek took place near Mount Gerizim, close to a place called Salim, east of modern Nablus, one of the most troubled places in modern Palestine. See John Allegro, *The Dead Sea Scrolls and the Christian Myth* (London: Prometheus Books, 1992), 71ff.

89. W. N. Ewer, cited in John Allegro, *The Mystery of the Dead Sea Scrolls Revealed* (New York: Gramercy Publishing Company, 1981), 19–20.

90. Wilhelm Reich, *The Mass Psychology of Fascism* (New York: Farrar, Strauss & Giroux, 1980), 148 and passim.

91. Allegro, *The Mystery of the Dead Sea Scrolls Revealed*, 106.

CHAPTER 5: MESSIANIC MADNESS

92. Cited in Neil Asher Silberman, *The Hidden Scrolls* (London: Mandarin, 1995), 123.

93. Robert Eisenman and Michael Wise, *Dead Sea Scrolls Uncovered* (London: Penguin, 1992), 8–10. *Note*: This is not the consensus of scrolls experts. Great efforts continue to be made to distance Christianity from the Qumranic literature.

94. Nasi, "leader," "chief," "master," occurs in the Dead Sea Scrolls in fragment 4Q285 and the Community Rule when alluding to the successors of King David who will triumph and lead Israel to political autonomy. "Today the term is used to designate the President of the Jewish State." Eisenman and Wise, *Dead Sea Scrolls Uncovered*, 24ff. John J. Collins, the leading scholar on Jewish apocalypticism, notes that Melchizedek is never called the messiah. His role is eschatological prophet and supernatural judge—i.e., he is supernatural. See *Apocalypticism in the Dead Sea Scrolls* (London and New York: Routledge, 1997), 72.

95. Hugh Schonfield, *The Essene Odyssey* (Element Books, 1998), Ch. 1.

96. Josephus, *The Jewish Wars*.

97. Schonfield, *The Passover Plot* (Element Books, 1996), 30. (Emphasis added.)

98. Neil Asher Silberman, *The Hidden Scrolls* (London: Mandarin, 1995), 26.

99. See the *Cryptica Scriptura* in *Valis* (London: Orion Publishing Group, 1981), item 6. The parallel as I state it here is not exactly as Dick understood it, but close enough. He extensively develops the Gnostic myth of the fallen goddess in his trilogy: *Valis*, *The Divine Invasion*, and *The Transmigration of Timothy Archer*. Parts of the third book are set in Qumran where the Dead Sea Scrolls were found.

100. D. H. Lawrence, *Apocalypse*, 31.

101. Erich Fromm, *The Dogma of Christ* (Greenwich, CT: Fawcett Publications, 1973), 49.

102. Collins, *Apocalypticism in the Dead Sea Scrolls*, 56.

103. Ibid., 5.

104. Werner Keller, *The Bible as History* (New York: William Morrow and Company, 1981), 274.

CHAPTER 6: THE TRANSFERENCE

105. Baigent and Leigh, *The Dead Sea Scrolls Deception* (London: Corgi Books, 1991), 44.

106. On crucifixion, see Philip R. Davies, George J. Brooke, and Phillip R. Callaway, *The Complete Guide to the Dead Sea Scrolls* (London: Thames & Hudson, 2002), 96ff.

107. Shepard, *Nature and Madness*, 58.

108. Lawrence, *Apocalypse*, 31.

109. Schonfield, *The Passover Plot*, 224.

110. For a helpful synopsis of Eisenman's work, see Michael Baigent and Richard Leigh, *The Dead Sea Scrolls Deception* (New York: Simon & Schuster, 1991), chapters 12–16.

111. Ibid., 21.

112. Ibid., 239ff. Schonfield's work on Paul and the Damascus cell is exceptionally good.

113. Robert Eisenman, *James, the Brother of Jesus* (London: Penguin Books, 1997), 67.

114. Theodor H. Gaster, *The Scriptures of the Dead Sea Sect* (London: Secker & Warburg, 1957), 22.

115. Ian Wilson, *Jesus: The Evidence* (London and Sydney: Pan Books, 1985), 39.

116. Hershel Shanks, *The Mystery and Meaning of the Dead Sea Scrolls* (New York: Vintage Books, 1998), xvii, 64.

117. *Habbukak pesher*. A *pesher* (plural *peshera*) is a scholarly comment on a sacred text. The Pauline ideology of redemption by grace was hijacked from the Zaddikim. It is not an original religious proposition, but a cult formula.

PART 2: A STORY TO GUIDE THE SPECIES

CHAPTER 7: THE EGYPTIAN CACHE

118. Jean Doresse, *The Secret Books of the Egyptian Gnostics* (Rochester, VT: Inner Traditions International, 1986), 116–17.

119. Edwin M. Yamauchi, *Pre-Christian Gnosticism: A Survey of the Proposed Evidences* (Eugene, OR: Wipf and Stock, 1973), 181ff.

120. Karl-Wolfgang Troger, "The Attitude of the Gnostic Religion towards Judaism as Viewed in a Variety of Perspectives," *Colloque International sur Les Textes de Nag Hammadi*, October 1978, Québec. (Leuven: Editions Peeters, 1981, 86–120.)

121. *The Seeker's Handbook* (New York: Crown/Random House, 1991), 134.

122. Roger S. Gottlieb and Barnell, David Landis, eds, *Deep Ecology and World Religions* (Albany, NY: State University of New York Press, 2001), 17.

123. Ibid., 154.

124. Rosemary Radford Ruether, *Gaia and God* (New York: Harper Collins, 1994), 206.

CHAPTER 8: INSIDE THE MYSTERIES

125. Mead, *Fragments*, 46.

126. Mead, *Gospels*, 210.

127. At the time of writing the first edition of this book, I had not discovered *Pre-Christian Gnosticism* by Edwin M. Yamauchi (Eugene, OR: Wipf and Stock, 1973). It presents some tentative steps toward revisionist scholarship in Gnosticism, but there is still a long way to go.

128. Mircea Eliade, *Shamanism: Archaic Techniques of Ecstasy* (Princeton, NJ: Princeton University Press, 1974), 10, 77ff.

129. NHC II, 23. 20–28. On parallels between Gnostic teachings and the neo-shamanic lore of Carlos Castaneda, see http://www.metahistory.org/CCGnosis.php.

130. Introduction, *The Nag Hammadi Library in English* (San Francisco: HarperSanFrancisco, 1990), 6.

131. Aristides, cited in Angus, *The Mystery-religions*, 135.

132. Walter Burkert, *Ancient Mystery Cults* (Cambridge, MA, and London: Harvard University Press, 1987), 11.

133. Luther H. Martin, *Hellenistic Religions: An Introduction* (Oxford: Oxford University Press, 1987), 12.

134. *The Golden Ass*, translated by Robert Graves (New York: Farrar, Strauss & Giroux, 1983), 264.

135. *The Origin of Consciousness in the Breakdown of the Bicameral Mind* can be helpful in understanding the psychological setting of the Mysteries, but Jaynes attributes these "hallucinatory" effects to cerebral conditions, and denies that ancient telluric empathy could have enabled genuine contact with real, living, intelligent, godlike forces in the biosphere.

136. Heinrich Zimmer, "The Indian World Mother," in *The Mystic Vision*, Papers from the Eranos Notebooks, ed. Joseph Campbell, Bollingen Series XXX (Princeton, NJ: Princeton University Press, 1982), 79.

137. Glenn H. Mullin, *Female Buddhas* (Santa Fe, NM: Clear Light Publishers, 2003), 101.

138. Joan Halifax, *Shaman: The Wounded Healer* (London: Thames and Hudson, 1994), 21.

139. *The Zen Teaching of Huang Po*, translated by John Blofeld (New York: Grove Press, 1959), 93.

140. Widely cited. See Angus, *The Mystery-religions*, 96, and Burkert, *Ancient Mystery Cults*, 162. It appears that the actual source of this sentence is fragment 168 in the writings of Plutarch.

141. For an excellent account of luminosity in the after-death *bardos*, see Francesca Freemantle, *Luminous Emptiness* (Boston & London: Shambhala, 2001).

142. Angus, *The Mystery-religions*, 136ff. The word "dazzling" is inappropriate. The Organic Light does not dazzle.

143. Naess, cited in Warwick Fox, *Toward a Transpersonal Ecology* (Totnes, Devon: Resurgence Books, 1995), 230.

144. Ibid., 98.

145. In *Shamanic Wisdom in the Pyramid Texts*, (Rochester, VT: Inner Traditions, 2005), Jeremy Naydler makes a case for the shamanic nature of Egyptian initiation practices. Doing so, he supports my argument that Gnostic rites and ancient Mystery practices were sophisticated forms of shamanism. This rapprochement has been long overdue. However, Naydler overestimates the "out of the body" nature of such practices. Like Timothy Freke and Peter Gandy (*The Jesus Mysteries, Jesus and the Goddess*), he equates rites of kingship empowerment with genuine initiatory techniques. In my view, the telestai of the Mysteries did not empower tyrants and theocrats. Or those who did should be called Illuminati, not telestai.

146. John Myrdhin Reynolds, *The Golden Letters* (Ithaca, NY: Snow Lion, 1996), 144. On the perfection stage of Dzogchen practice, see Tulku Thondup, *The Practice of Dzogchen*.

147. Ibid., 98.

148. Richard Reitzenstein, *Hellenistic Mystery Religions*, 2:136–37. (Emphasis added.)

149. Clement of Alexandria, cited in Kurt Rudolf, *Gnosis* (New York: Harper & Row, 1997), 16.

150. *The Gospel of Thomas, Annotated and Explained*, Stevan Davies (Woodstock, VT: Skylight Paths Publishing, 2002), xiii–xvii.

151. Elaine Pagels, *The Origins of Satan* (New York: Vintage Books, 1996), 167–98.

152. Ibid., 67ff.

153. H. P. Blavatsky, *Occultism of the Secret Doctrine* (Kessenger Publishing, n.d.), 46.

154. Robert Turcan, *The Cults of the Roman Empire* (Oxford: Blackwell Publishers, 2000), 278.

CHAPTER 9: SCHOOLS FOR COEVOLUTION

155. Thomas Taylor, *The Eleusinian and Bacchic Mysteries* (San Diego: Wizards' Bookshelf, 1980), xi. Taylor cites an ancient source, perhaps Porphyry.

156. Commenting on Shakta teachings on the "Ocean of Nectar," Woodroffe offers some striking testimony on the Organic Light: "This is the pearl which those who have churned the ocean of Tantra discover. That pearl is there in an Indian shell. There is a beautiful nacre on the inner shell which is the Mother of Pearl. Outside, the shell is naturally rough and course, and bears the accretions of weed and parasite and of all things which exist, good or bad as we call them, in the ocean of existence (Samsara). The Scripture leads man to remove these accretions . . . Finally, it leads man to seek to see the Mother of Pearl and lastly the Pearl itself which, enclosed therein, shines with the *brilliant yet soft* light which is that of the Moon-Cit (Cicchandra) itself." (*Shakti and Shakta*, 215. Emphasis added.)

157. See *Temples and Sanctuaries of Ancient Greece*, ed. Evi Melas (London: Thames & Hudson, 1973) for several examples of the groundplans for such campuses, e.g., the temples at Olympia (111), Eleusis (85), and Delphi (69).

158. See Michael Allen Williams, *Rethinking "Gnosticism"* (Princeton, NJ: Princeton University Press, 1996), table 1, p. 34.

159. Edwin H. Yamauchi, *Pre-Christian Gnosticism* (Eugene, OR: Wipf and Stock, 1973): 166.

160. *Toward a Transpersonal Ecology* by Warwick Fox (Albany, NY: SUNY Press, 1995) is almost entirely devoted to the issue of identification. *Radical Ecopsychology* by Andy Fisher (Albany, NY: SUNY Press, 2002) also covers some important points in this debate.

161. *The Golden Ass* translated by Robert Graves.

162. Robert Graves, *The White Goddess* (New York: Farrar, Straus, and Giroux, 1983) 219. Graves argues that the Mystery rites at Eleusis and elsewhere were entheogenic. In fact, it was Graves who initially clued R. Gordon Wasson to the Mexican mushroom cult of Maria Sabina, thus kicking off the current entheogenic revival. The "kid in milk" motif is also found in ancient astronomical references to shooting stars seen to plunge into the Milky Way. The Jewish taboo against eating a kid boiled in its mother's milk reflects the patriarchal taboo against initiation, as do crucifixion (punishment for, and parody of, the tree-hung shaman), the "forbidden fruit" of Genesis, and numerous other biblical motifs.

163. Sir John Woodroffe, *The Garland of Letters* (Madras: Ganesh & Co., 1969), 41.

164. Sir John Woodroffe, *Shakti and Shakta* (Madras: Ganesh & Co., 1969), 87.

165. Woodroffe, *The Garland of Letters*, 111.

166. Ibid., 191. And following: "This primal power," 192; "An ancient feature," 88; "The natural, which is," 88. Emphasis added.

167. Woodroffe, *Shakti and Shakta*, 180.

168. For accounts of imprinting (psychological reprogramming) in ancient times, the main sources are self-styled occultists of the Rosicrucian and Theosophical schools. Both Manley Palmer Hall and Rudolf Steiner, for example, describe a "three-day temple sleep" in which the initiate underwent a trance-like suspension of consciousness in order to be reprogrammed.

169. Mary Settegast, *Plato Prehistorian* (Cambridge MA: The Rotenberg Press, 1987), 211.

170. Ibid., 215.

171. Morton Smith, "The History of the Term Gnostikos," in *Studies in the Cult of Yahweh*, ed. J. D. Cohen (Leiden: E. J. Brill, 1996), 2:34.

CHAPTER 10: THE FALLEN GODDESS

172. Bernal, *Black Athena* 1:69ff.

173. Ellis, *Celts*, 55ff.

174. Robert Graves, *The White Goddess* (New York: Noonday Press, 1969), 227ff.

175. On the nine *siddhis* of Hindu and Shaivite Tantra, see Alain Daniélou, *While the Gods Play*, trans. Barbara Bailey, Michael Baker, and Deborah Lawlor (Rochester, VT: Inner Traditions, 1987), 94ff.

176. Mircea Eliade, *Patañjali and Yoga* (New York: Schocken Books, 1979), 100.

177. Cited Taylor, *The Eleusinian and Bacchic Mysteries*, 3.

178. Heinrich Zimmer, "The Indian World Mother," in *The Mystic Vision*, Papers from the Eranos Yearbooks, ed. Joseph Campbell, Bollingen Series XXX-6, (Princeton, NJ: Princeton University Press, 1982), 70–102.

179. As of 2021, it must be noted that the name Sophia applied to a goddess does not occur in Greek mythology. Hesiod provides a meager clue on Gaia, the terrestrial goddess whom I conflate with Sophia of the Gnostics. Sophianic myth originated among the Aryan Caucasian racial stock in Persia. In Avestan, her name is Anahita. It does appear, however, that Greek myth may contain traces of Sophia in the attributes and actions of Pietho, goddess of persuasion.

180. My bracketing of [through the Christos] in this passage reflects the rescripting in chapters 14 and 23, consistent with Sethian Gnosticism and exclusive of the Valentinian spin, which unfortunately infects the sacred narrative with the salvationist virus and endorses the deceit of Christ.

181. Graves, *The White Goddess*, 388.

182. On *termas*, see Tulku Thondup, *Hidden Teachings of Tibet* (London: Wisdom Publications, 1986), 60ff.

183. Ibid., 69.

184. On the White Mountain of Seir and the children of Seth, see Jean Doresse, *The Secret Books of the Egyptian Gnostics*, Chapter VI, "The Sethians According to Their Writings." See also my article, "The Magian Order," on Metahistory.org.

185. Lacarriere, *The Gnostics*, 33.

186. Dan Russell, *Shamanism, Patriarchy and the Drug War* (Camden, NY: Kalyx.com, 1998), 296.

187. Beatrice Caseau, "Sacred Landscapes," in *Late Antiquity*, 21–59.

188. Ibid., 33.

CHAPTER 11: DREAMTIME PHYSICS

189. Daniélou, *While the Gods Play*, 80.

190. Emergence theory is still young, but its current formulations strongly recall the *pratitya samutpada* of Buddhist psychology. This term is variously translated as "interdependent origination," "conditioned genesis," and "mutual arising." See Lama Anagarika Govinda, *Foundations of Tibetan Myticism* (Newburyport, MA, and San Francisco: Weiser Books, 1969), Part V, Chapter 6, for a synopsis. Mutual arising is discussed in many Buddhist writings. A nod of thanks to my copy editor, Cannon Labrie, for signaling this important parallel.

191. Lacarriere, ibid., 18.

192. In *Sacred Land, Sacred Sex, Rapture of the Deep* (Durango, CO: Kivaki Press, 1988), Dolores LaChapelle, a leading exponent of deep ecology, stresses the need to think of nature in terms of processes, not entities.

193. LaChapelle cites Nietzsche (*Twilight of the Idols*) on the conditions for experiencing intensities: "Rapture as a state of being explodes the very subjectivity of the

subject" (*Future Primitive*, 331). Only such rapture yields the intensities by which Aeons are contacted. There is no better argument for going beyond identification than this single line from Nietzsche.

194. Danielou, ibid., 12.

195. On steady-state plasma cosmology, see Theodore Roszak, "Nature and Nature's God: Modern Cosmology and the Rebirth of Natural Cosmology," in *Alexandria* 5, ed. David Fideler (Grand Rapids, MI: Phanes Press, 2000), 103–138, where Roszak cites the work of Anthony L. Peratt, Paul Marmet, and Eric J. Lerner.

196. The term *panspermia* seems to have been introduced by the Abbe Lazzaro Spallanzani (1729–99), who wrote of germs distributed in the atmosphere. "Nowadays the term panspermia is taken to mean the cosmic distribution of microorganisms, whereas to begin with it meant germs distributed everywhere terrestrially." Fred Hoyle and Chandra Wickramasinghe, *Our Place in the Cosmos* (London: Phoenix, 1993), 64.

197. The seeding of the Anthropos by the Aeons looks like a remote and exotic item until it is compared to other scenarios. Gnostic scholars defer from drawing such parallels.) In a comparative study of creation myths, Jungian psychologist Marie-Louise von Franz notes that "primitive and semi-primitive civilizations" tend to have cosmogonies with many hypostases, "innumerable lists of divine and semi-divine beings" like the Pleromic Aeons. She recounts the Japanese myth in which the "Sky-Kami" (comparable to the Originator) presides over a vast company of divinities. Sky-Kami invited two of the lesser *Kami* (Aeons) to "make and consolidate the drifting earth." The lesser *Kamis*, He-Who-Invites and She-Who-Invites, take a stand "in the midst of the Sky-Mist" and lower to the world below the "Sky-Jewel-Spear whose staff was of coral." Von Franz observes that Gnostic material is close to primitive myth in general, and to this Japanese myth in particular. The "Sky-Jewel-Spear" of a coralline nature is like the immense stalk extruded from the Pleromic core by the Aeons. Von Franz cites the Valentinian version of the Sophia mythos, treating it as a clear parallel of the Japanese lore. See Marie-Louise von Franz, *Creation Myths* (Zurich: Spring Publications, 1978), 195ff.

198. This image occurs in a bas-relief in the Ptolemaic temple of Dendera, across the river from where the Nag Hammadi codices were discovered. Dendera was apparently one of the last refuges of Gnostics and Mystery School participants fleeing from persecution by Christians.

199. R. B. Onions, *The Origins of European Thought* (Cambridge University Press, 1951), 40 passim.

CHAPTER 12: THE INSANE GOD

200. Didymus the Blind (ca. 313–398), De Trinitate III, 42, cited in *From Poimandres to Jacob Boehme: Gnosis, Hermetism, and the Christian Tradition* (Amsterdam, In Der Pelikan, 2000), 81. I have written extensively on the theme "The True Lucifer is Sophia" on nemeta.org. The issue entails a major correction of spurious modern notions on the Lucifer-Satan complex.

201. Charles H. Long, *Alpha: Myths of Creation*, 36–37.

202. Richard Smith, afterword to NHLE, 1990.

203. Jim Yorke, cited in John Briggs, *Fractals: The Patterns of Chaos* (New York: Simon & Schuster, 1992), 12.

204. Three-body cosmos: Religious scholars and scientists alike will certainly reject as a personal extravagance my cosmological rendering of *trimorphic protennoia*. But the mythologem of Sophia's original Dreaming of a three-body system cannot be dismissed so easily. Some readers may find it intriguing that chaos theory (now called complexity theory or emergence theory) devolved from the failed attempt of nineteenth-century scientist Henri Poincaré to solve the "three-body problem." Years ago, I had the good fortune to consult with Dr. Miles Standish of the Jet Propulsion Laboratory in Pasadena, who brought this issue to my attention. Chaos, fractals, complexity, emergence—all the leading-edge concepts of modern cosmology derive from the investigations inspired by Poincaré's three-body problem. In Sophianic cosmology, the three-body cosmos, and not merely the Earth alone, is the matrix of organic life and awareness. Gaia theory continues to grow. As it does, I suspect that it will sooner or later incorporate the solar and lunar components.

Chapter 13: The Passion of Sophia

205. At the Electric Universe conference in Bath, England, in July 2018, biologist Rupert Sheldrake argued that the sun is a conscious entity. As I have noted throughout this book, EU/plasma physics is a close correlate to Sophianic cosmology. Close and growing closer. But the Thunderbolts gang have a way to go before they arrive at full-bore animistic illumination. Perhaps a dose or two of LSD would help.

206. The terminology is mine, but leading Gnostic scholars such as I. P. Culianu have meticulously dissected the problem of "the heresy of 'Two Powers in Heaven'". Yamauchi, *Pre-Christian Gnosticism*, 200.

207. *Note*: To avoid the spirit/matter dichotomy, I am not calling Sophia "pure spirit" and chaos "pure matter." In Asian emanation theory, consciousness, or spirit, if you will, and matter are coeval and coeternal in the cosmos. Consciousness does not create matter but configures it, shapes it, and dissolves it, while matter reflects or manifests what consciousness is doing. Spirit and matter operate *through* each other, remaining in some ways distinct, but also, in other ways, *converting into each other*. To know how they remain distinct and how they interconvert is to master the ultimate physics. This was the goal of some ancient yogic traditions and the *theurgia*, "god-working," of the Mysteries.

Chapter 14: The Coming of the Symbiont

208. P. Oxy. number undetermined

CHAPTER 15: THE WAY OF THE REVEALERS

209. Sir John Woodroffe, *Introduction to Tantra Shastra* (Madras: Ganesh & Co, 1997), 59ff.
210. Fromm, *The Anatomy of Human Destructiveness*, 143–44.
211. Cited in Woodroffe, *Shakti and Shakta*, 55.
212. Sophia evokes the Anthropos: Surviving Gnostic writings contain no full graphic description of Episodes 7 and 8 of the sacred story, although they do contain sparse references. By working from Irenaeus, it is possible to recover and reconstruct the mythic scenario. I am not inventing anything in the events described, except for one detail: I locate the nesting of the Anthropos, the luminous template for the human species, in the Great Nebula of Orion. My grounds for this addition to the story? A lifetime of skywatching supplemented by studies in ancient astronomy and sidereal mythology.
213. On the Whore of Wisdom, see "Prouneikos – A Colorful Expression to Designate Wisdom in Gnostic Texts" by Anne Pasquier, in *Images of the Feminine in Gnosticism*, ed. Karen King (Harrisburg, PA: Trinity International Press, 1998), 47–66.
214. Woodroffe, *Shakti and Shakta*, 51.
215. Edward Conze, "Buddhism and Gnosis," in *The Allure of Gnosticism*, ed. Robert A. Segal (Chicago and La Salle: Open Court, 1997), 172–89. The Tucci quote is from this essay. Buddhist scholar John Myrdhin Reynolds, who has extensively explored Buddhist-Gnostic parallels, describes a little-known Buddhist creation myth that reads like a paraphrase of the arrogance of the Demiurge. See *Self-Liberation through Seeing with Naked Awareness* (Ithaca, NY: Snow Lion, 2000), 96ff.

CHAPTER 16: A SHEAF OF CUT WHEAT

216. Homeric "Hymn to Demeter," trans. Charles Boer (Dallas, TX: Spring Publications, 1970), 130ff.
217. Eleusis pediment: plate 57, George E. Mylonas, *Eleusis and the Eleusinian Mysteries* (Princeton, NJ: Princeton University Press, 1969).
218. Orphic bowl and Pietroasa bowl. See *The Mysteries*, 245ff.
219. "The Dendera Revelation: Our Unique Moment in the Pattern of the Ages," unpublished manuscript by John Lash. For a summary of my work on the Dendera Zodiac, including my discovery of a fifth, hitherto undetected axis, see Colin Wilson, *The Atlantis Blueprint* (New York: Delta, 2002).
220. Mullin, *Female Buddhas*, 101.
221. The acoustic and visual effects I attribute to ecstatic cognition in the Mysteries recall reports of paranormal experience due to ingestion of *ayahuasca*. In these sessions, participants often hear high-pitched sounds, but the light seen is usually purple or iridescent blue, not white. However, Ralph Metzner's collection of testimonies, *Sacred Vine of Spirits: Ayahuasca* (Rochester, VT: Park Street Press, 2005), contains

at least one account of seeing something like the luminosity of the Organic Light. An early reader of this book also attests to having seen what may have been the Organic Light in an *ayahuasca* session. Without having taken *ayahuasca*, I cannot comment from firsthand experience.

222. Fisher, *Radical Ecopsychology*, 111. Citing Calvin Martin, *In the Spirit*.

223. Wasson Thesis: The enteogenic method of initation was rediscovered by R. Gordon Wasson in the 1950s when he went to Huautla de Jimenez in central Mexico to participate in a *veleda* (night vigil) with the Mazatec curandero Maria Sabina. Wasson (1898–1986), a financial advisor for J. P. Morgan, originally got interested in mushrooms through his Russian wife, Valentina. In 1952 British poet and mystic Robert Graves signaled him to an article by Harvard enthnobotanist Richard Evans Schultes on the survival of ancient mushroom cults in Mexico, leading Wasson to a lifelong friendship and collaboration. In 1968 Wasson privately published *Soma: The Divine Mushroom of Immortality*. The book had two objectives: first, to specifically prove that the soma of the Indian *Vedas* was the mushroom *Amanita muscaria* (fly agaric) known to be used in shamanic practices in Siberia and elsewhere, and second, to advance the general theory that *the religious experience of humankind originated from ritual ingestion of sacred plants*—the Wasson thesis. To understand the master idea Wasson proposed, it is necessary to distinguish religious experience from religion. The latter is a cultural creation of humans, but the former is what makes us human in the first place. Original religious experience was shamanic, but religion, considered as an institution and a body of doctrinal and moral codes, was a later construction that deviated from the primary experience.

Working closely with Wasson, R. E. Schultes and other enthnobotanists were able to identify about 200 plants that enhance neurochemical processes in the brain—hence they are *psychomimetic*, "mind-imitating." During the 1960s the word *psychedelic* ("mind-manifesting") came to be applied to LSD and other laboratory-made substances with the same properties as psychomimetic plants. In reaction to the negative social image acquired by the generation who used psychedelics, Wasson and his colleagues invented the word *entheogen* ("god generated within") as an alternative. The Wasson thesis is also called the entheogenic theory of religion.

R. Gordon Wasson drew upon the research by Marija Gimbutas, the Lithuanian archaeologist who, virtually single-handedly, recovered the lost Goddess-oriented societies of precivilization, and the reflections of Aldous Huxley whose book *The Doors of Perception* (1958) prefigured the Wasson thesis. Huxley warned that Plato had led the entire Western intellectual tradition down the wrong path by the emphasis on immaterial, off-planet Being rather than the sensorial miracle of Becoming. From his own experimentation with mescaline, Huxley asserted that mind-altering chemicals "induce for their users a sense of identification with a universal consciousness, or 'Mind-at Large,'" but he did so without specific reference to the planetary intelligence. The generation following Wasson and Huxley was led by Terence McKenna who brilliantly integrated enteogenic theory with the process philosophy of Alfred North Whitehead and the Gaia hypothesis. McKenna, who was known as the Gnostic astronaut, proposed that mushroom species such as *Stropharia cubensis* were distributed through space by a panspermic diffusion of spores. His notion that the sacred entheogenic plants have given us a psychic-cerebral boost and produced advanced language capacities in the human species is a novel extension of the Wasson thesis. For a comprehensive overview of the entheogenic revival, see the Introduction to Ralph Metzner's *Sacred Mushroom of Visions: Teonanacatl* (Rochester, VT: Park Street Press, 2005).

224. The Homeric hymn to Demeter describes how the Grain Goddess tells Queen Metanira to make a brew "of water with barley, and tender pennyroyal." Swiss chemist Albert Hofmann, who discovered LSD, showed that the *kykeon* of Eleusis was a psychedelic potion whose active properties derive from a fungal entheogen, ergot. See Albert Hofmann, with R. Gordon Wasson and Carl Ruck, *The Road to Eleusis: Unveiling the Secret of the Mysteries*, published in 1978.

225. David Abram, "The Perceptual Implications of Gaia," in *Dharma Gaia*, 75–92.

226. Cecrops with the sheaf of cut wheat. See Jane Allen Harrison, *Themis* (Gloucester, MA: Peter Smith, 1974), 263, fig. 63.

PART 3: HISTORY'S HARDEST LESSON

CHAPTER 17: THE END OF PATRIARCHY

227. Williams, *Rethinking "Gnosticism,"* 11. Excellent reference for deconstructing erroneous presumptions about what the Gnostics thought and taught.

228. H. Paul Santmire, *The Travail of Nature: The Ambiguous Ecological Promise of Christian Theology* (Minneapolis: Fortress Press, 1985), 22.

229. Shepard, *Nature and Madness*, 54–55.

230. Lawrence, *Apocalypse*, 42.

231. James de Meo uses the name Saharasia for the vast belt of land stretching from Algeria across North Africa and into the Middle East, including Saudi Arabia, and extending northward to the Caspian Sea. See *Saharasia* (Greensprings, OR: Orgone Biophysical Research Lab, 1998).

232. William G. Dever, *Did God Have a Wife?* (Cambridge, UK: William B. Eerdmans Publishing, 2005), 201, 211.

233. Representations of Queen Maya as a tree goddess are frequent in Buddhist iconography. See Joseph Campbell, *The Mythic Image* (Princeton, NJ: Princeton University Press, 1981).

234. Jeffrey Burton Russell, *The Prince of Darkness* (Ithaca, NY, and London: Cornell University Press, 1988), 22.

235. Letters of St. Augustine, no. 47, cited by Baigent and Lincoln in *The Elixir and the Stone*, 51.

236. Barbara Walker, *The Woman's Encyclopedia of Myths and Secrets* (San Francisco: HarperSanFrancisco, 1983), 634.

237. Here I follow the world's leading child advocate Alice Miller, author of *The Drama of the Gifted Child, For Your Own Good*, and other books. Her work on narcissistic deprivation and long-term psychological damage due to authoritarian parenting is vividly relevant both to the historical origins and the present-day observation of the Abrahamic religions. For a valuable study of parentally modeled religious abuse, see *A Violent God-Image*, an introduction to the work of Eugen Drewermann by Matthias Beier (New York and London: Continuum, 2004).

238. William Irwin Thompson, *Transforming History* (Great Barrington, MA: Lindisfarne Books, 2001), 44.

239. Cited in Fox *Toward a Transpersonal Ecology*, 216.

240. Ibid., 144, note 9.

241. John D. Turner, "A Response to 'Sophia and Christ'" in *Images of the Feminine in Gnosticism*, ed. Karen King (Harrisburg, PA: Trinity Press International, 2000), 186.

242. René Girard, *Violence and the Sacred* (Baltimore: Johns Hopkins University Press, 1981), 44.

CHAPTER 18: THE DIVINE SCAPEGOAT

243. Las Casas cited in James DeMeo, *Saharasia* (Greensprings, OR: Orgone Biophysical Research Lab, 1998), 383.

244. Alan Watts, *Beyond Theology* (New York: Vintage Books, 1964), 127–28.

245. René Girard, *Things Hidden from the Foundation of the World* (Stanford, CA: Stanford University Press, 1987), 104.

246. Girard, *Violence and the Sacred*, 95.

247. Ibid., 82, 135. Primitive rites of scapegoating were the main subject matter of Sir James Frazer's anthropological masterpiece, *The Golden Bough*, published at the dawn of the twentieth century. Girard's analysis of scapegoating pathology goes light-years beyond Frazer. Much can be learned from it that is helpful to restating the Gnostic critique of salvationism.

248. Girard, *Things Hidden from the Foundation of the World*, 162. *Note*: I believe only Girard has formulated, and systematically developed, this shattering diagnosis. Extracting it from his work is well worth the monstrous effort it demands. However, I would advise that reader take note that at the end of his brilliant exposé, Girard reverts to Catholic faith. He cites the example of Jesus Christ, who resisted not evil, as the best way to end the retaliatory violence that plagues human society. "Violence is the heart and soul of the sacred," Girard said, among many other brilliant, arresting things he said. Unfortunately, Girard suffers from the bad boy complex typical of French intellectuals. In his need to shock the bourgeoisie, he often misstates the crucial points of his excruciatingly nuanced analysis of religious violence. Victimage is the terrorist game that drives patriarchal religion, but it does not drive genuine religious experience—my distinction, not Girard's. Violence is "the heart and secret soul" of religious control, not of the sacred. Religion is merely a human social construct.

CHAPTER 19: A UNIQUE MESSAGE OF LOVE

249. Watts, *Beyond Theology*, 108.
250. Bill McKibben, in *Harper's* (August 2005): 31–37.
251. Walter Kaufmann, *The Faith of a Heretic* (New York: New American Library, 1978), 154.
252. Theodore Roszak, *Where the Wasteland Ends* (Berkeley, CA: Celestial Arts, 1989), 241.

CHAPTER 20: BEYOND RELIGION

253. *Meditations*, book 9.
254. Gary Snyder, *The Practice of the Wild* (Washington, DC: Shoemaker & Hoard, 1990), 19.
255. David Abram, *The Spell of the Sensuous* (New York: Vintage Books, 1997), ix.
256. Naess, cited in Fox, *Towards a Transpersonal Ecology*, 217. Originally given as a lecture at Murdoch University, western Australia, 12 March 1986.
257. Wikipedia, "MRC-5," (last updated March 2, 2021), https://en.wikipedia.org/wiki/MRC-5.
258. Fabrice Midal, *Chögyam Trunpga, His Life and Vision* (Boston: Shambhala Publications, 2004), 210ff.
259. 1Qm, Col. 14, in Wise et al., *The Dead Sea Scrolls: A New Translation* (San Francisco: HarperSanFrancisco, 1999), 163.
260. Ibid., 160.
261. Private conversation with Florentino Garcia Martinez at the Catholic University of Leuven, Belgium, August 2001. Translations of this passage differ widely, with some scholars rendering "the children of pride" rather than "the children of Seth," thus eliminating two out of three points of identification. See Theodor H. Gaster, *The Scriptures of the Dead Sea Sect* (London: Secker & Warburg, 1957), 274. Professor Garcia Martinez assured me that Seir is a valid translation, consistent with the Masoretic Bible where Numbers 24:18 says "Seir shall also be a possession for his enemies."
262. Wise, Abegg, Cook trans., *The Dead Sea Scrolls: A New Translation*, 381.
263. Collins, *Apocalypticism in the Dead Sea Scrolls*, 36.
264. Bentley Layton, *The Gnostic Scriptures* (London: SCM Press Limited, 1987), 6–7, map 1.
265. Troger, "The Attitude of the Gnostic Religion Towards Judaism as Viewed in a Variety of Perspectives."
266. Mead, *Fragments*, 159.
267. Dalai Lama in *Dharma Gaia*.
268. Fabrice Midal, *Chögyam Trunpga, His Life and Vision*, 212.
269. Lawrence, *Apocalypse*, 19.
270. On Gnostic arrogance: *Rethinking "Gnosticism."* Williams has also written a book, *The Immovable Race*, where he attributes the classical statuary poses of Pagan civilization to Gnostic influence.

271. One of the last holdouts of the Levantine Gnostics was the rich suburb of Daphne in Antioch, where tensions between Pagans and Christians ran especially high. See "Sacred Landscapes" by Beatrice Caseau, in *Late Antiquity*, ed. Bowersock, Brown, and Graber (Cambridge, MA: The Belknap Press of Harvard University, 1991), 21–59.

272. Hermes Kriophoros: see *The New Larousse Encyclopedia of Mythology* (Hamlyn, 1983), 88.

273. In the millennial vision of the Mystery seers, the Arien Age (1800–120 B.C.E.) would have been associated with the maturity of human brain circuits (imaged in the head and horns of the celestial ram), as well as with the dual danger posed by that immense modular leap in evolution: namely, hypertrophy of cerebral modeling capacities and imposition of authoritarian norms attributed to an off-planet deity. Facing the new conditions of the Piscean Age, including the rise of narcissism, they would have reflected closely on how to convert traditional methods of schooling to meet the needs of the time. They may have imagined that society in the future could be organized along educational lines, with social roles defined by how people fitted into "schools" (to risk a Piscean pun). I strongly believe that the telestai would have discussed how to mainstream the Mystery Schools and introduce a group dynamic favorable to self-direction, in a deliberate attempt to counter single-self obsessions such as "personal salvation." Due to violent resistance from converts to Christianity and Roman authorities allied with them, the Mystery guardians never had a chance to try out their plans.

PART 4: RECLAIMING THE SOPHIANIC VISION

CHAPTER 21: UNMASKING EVIL

274. John P. Conger, *Jung and Reich* (Berkeley, CA: North Atlantic Books, 1988), 3.

275. Florentino Garcia Martinez and Eibert J. C. Tigchelar, *The Dead Sea Scrolls Study Edition* (Leiden: Brill, 1991), 833–35 with interfacing Hebrew text. Brackets [ ] indicate where translators fill in missing words, or parts of words.

276. White, Abegg, Cook trans., *The Dead Sea Scrolls: A New Translation*, 435. See also Schonfield, *The Passover Plot*, 30.

277. NHLE, 251.

278. NHLE, 265.

279. NHLE, 265–66.

280. White et al., *The Dead Sea Scrolls: A New Translation*, 435.

281. NHLE, 251.

282. Baigent and Leigh, *The Dead Sea Scrolls Deception*, 35.

283. John Keel, *UFOs: Operation Trojan Horse* (London: Abacus Books, 1973), 181.

284. Jacques Vallee, *Messengers of Deception* (New York: Bantam Books, 1980), 110.

285. George P. Hansen, *The Trickster and the Paranormal* (Philadelphia: Xlibris Corporation, 2001), 32.

286. H. V. Guenther, *Yuganaddha* (Varanasi: Chowkhamba Sanskrit Series, 1969), 64.

287. Ibid., 20.

288. H. V. Guenther, *The Life and Teaching of Naropa* (Oxford: Oxford University Press, 1963), 79.

289. Long Chen Pa, "How Samsara Is Fabricated from the Ground of Being," in *Crystal Mirror*, vol. 5 (Emeryville, CA: Dharma Publishing, 1977), 345–64. Translation and notes by Kennard Lipman.

290. Alexandra David-Neel, *The Secret Oral Teachings in Tibetan Buddhist Sects* (San Francisco: City Lights, 1967), 114.

291. Carlos Castaneda, *The Active Side of Infinity* (London: Thorsons, 1998), in extenso. Whether or not he made it all up, what Castaneda says about the flyers is extremely pertinent to the Archons of Gnosticism. Note especially the words attributed to don Juan in *The Active Side of Infinity* (p. 22): "The *flyers* are an essential part of the universe, and they must be taken as what they really are: awesome, monstrous. They are the means by which the universe tests us."

292. Burkert, *Ancient Mystery Cults*, 93.

293. Socrates Scholasticus, *Ecclesiastical History of the Church in Seven Books* (London: Henry G. Bohn, 1853), 238.

CHAPTER 22: SOPHIA'S CORRECTION

294. Jeffrey Burton Russell, *Satan: The Early Christian Tradition* (Ithaca and London: Cornell University Press, 1981), 16. Burton is helpful for his deep research and often lucid insights on Zoroastrian duality and other theological dilemmas, but he holds the usual biased view of Gnostics: "What united the various Gnostics sects was the belief that the world was completely evil and cannot be redeemed" (64). In light of recent reassessment of patristic disinformation on the Gnostics, especially Michael Allen Williams' *Rethinking "Gnosticism,"* Russell's view (still staunchly maintained by the majority of Gnostic scholars and adopted by popular writers on Gnosticism) is completely untenable.

295. Russell, *Satan: The Early Christian Tradition*, 82, note 10.

296. *Artis Auriferae*, a seventeenth-century compilation of alchemical writings, cited by C. G. Jung in *Psychology and Alchemy* and elsewhere in his wonderfully befuddled writings on the Great Work.

297. Karl Kerényi, *Dionysos: Archetypal Image of Indestructible Life* (Princeton, NJ: Princeton University Press, 1996).

298. See Willis W. Harman and Elisabet Sahtouris, *Biology Revisioned* (Berkeley: North Atlantic Books, 1998), 201ff.

299. Jean Houston, *The Hero and the Goddess* (New York: Ballantine Books, 1992), 7. In her makeover of the Mysteries, Houston assumes the God-self equation.

CHAPTER 23: THE SPECIES-SELF IDENTITY

300. "After meticulous research, radical Biblical scholar Gerald Massey established that 'in Blockh's *Christian Inscriptions*, numbering 1,287 entries, there is not a single instance of an earlier date than the third century wherein the name is not written Chrest or Chreist.'" Lloyd M. Graham, *Deceptions and Myths of the Bible* (Carol Publishing Group, 1997), 411.

301. *The Panarion of Epiphanius of Salamis*, translated by Frank Williams (Leiden, The Netherlands: Koninklijke Brill, 2009), 184.

302. Writing on the visionary experience of Native Americans (specifically, devotees of the Peyote cult), Aldous Huxley observed: "they may see visions, which may be of Christ himself." *The Doors of Perception* (London: Vintage, 2004) 44. Indeed, Peyotists are known for adopting Jesus to their cultic practices, but that does not prove that the historical Jesus of the Gospels really existed, or that the Christ of Paul lives for eternity in our midst. It merely shows how the victims of genocidal aggression in the New World absorbed the psychic imagery of the European perpetrators. I contend that the genuine and essential content of the Mesotes encounter is consistent, a mystical fact attested in many times and cultures. Unfortunately, the corruption of that precious encounter owing to religious preconceptions and imposed beliefs is also consistent, and totally, sadly predictable.

303. John Gribbin, *Deep Simplicity* (London: Allen Lane, 2004), 41.

304. F. David Peat, *Turbulent Mirror* (New York: Harper & Row, 1990), 137, figures 3A, 3B, 3C. "An aerial photograph of the Sahara desert shows prints left by this atmospheric Bénard sea. These prints of the atmosphere's convection vortices also show up in snowfields and icebergs."

305. The entire chapter is worth reading for the sobering comments of don Juan, which I consider to be highly applicable to the Mesotes encounter. Castaneda wrote: "He [don Juan] said that the new seers are the only ones who have the sobriety to *see* the mold of man and understand what it is. What they have come to realize is that the mold of man is not a creator, but the pattern of every human attribute we can think of and some we cannot even conceive. The mold is our God because we are what it stamps us with and not because it has created us from nothing and made us in its image and likeness. Don Juan said that in his opinion to fall on our knees in the presence of the mold of man reeks of arrogance and human self-centeredness." *The Fire from Within* (London: Black Swan, 1984), 281. Upon reflection, and with close consideration of some passages in the NHC and the patristic writings, I would suggest that even some Mystery adepts did not see the mold of man clearly (I have in mind the Valentinian school), and tended to imagine that it possesses a range of magical and psychophysical powers.

CHAPTER 24: THE GODDESS MYSTIQUE

306. Lynn Margulis, *Slanted Truths* (New York: Springer-Verlag, 1997), 249.

307. Cited in Lawrence E. Joseph, *Gaia: The Growth of an Idea* (London: Arkana, 1990), 56.

308. Misia Landau, *Narratives of Human Evolution* (New Haven and London: Yale University Press, 1991), x, 12; citation, xi.

309. In *Goethe's Theory of Perception*, Henri Bortoft explains how Goethe considered that, normally, the faculties of sense perception do not show us the entirety of phenomena, but when nature is observed intensively, they can. See "Suggested Reading."

310. Lynn Margulis and Dorian Saga, *What is Life?* (Berkeley, CA: University of California Press, 1995), 59–60.

311. Fritjof Capra, *The Web of Life* (London: Flamingo, 1997), 13.

312. James Lovelock, *Gaia: The Practical Science of Planetary Medicine* (Oxford: Oxford University Press, 2000), 11.

313. Santmire, *The Travail of Nature*, 209.

314. On UFO sightings in ancient times, see *Extra-Terrestrials Among Us* by George C. Andrews (Woodbury, MN: Llewellyn Publications, 2002), *Passport to Magonia* by Jacques Vallee (McGraw Hill/Contemporary, reprint edition, 1993), *Flying Saucers on the Attack* by Harold Wilkins (Citadel Press, 1954), and *The Gods Have Landed*, edited by James R. Lewis (Albany, NY: SUNY Press, 1995). Ancient chronicles state that Alexander the Great saw a UFO ("a large silver shield") over the city of Tyre when he besieged it in 332 B.C.E. Most researchers agree that the earliest clear report is found in an Egyptian papyrus dating to 1350 B.C.E.

315. Francesca Fremantle, *Luminous Emptiness* (Boston: Shambhala, 2001), 49.

316. I can locate no printed source for this article. It is easily available on the Internet.

Chapter 25: Sacred Ecology

317. Lovelock, *Gaia: The Practical Science of Planetary Medicine*, 31.

318. Margulis and Sagan, *Slanted Truths*, 63.

319. Jeremy Narby, *The Cosmic Serpent* (New York: Jeremy P. Tarcher/Putnam, 1998), 138.

320. AE, *The Candle of Vision* (Wheaton, IL: The Theosophical Publishing House, 1965).

321. Margulis and Sagan, *Slanted Truths*, 63.

322. Joscelyn Godwin, *Athanasius Kirchner* (London: Thames & Hudson, 1779), 14.

323. British Museum registration 1843,0724.3. Several websites dedicate close attention to this artifact, including Emma Bergen, "Words of Gold," *Sophia's Mirror*, June 17, 2018, http://sophiasmirror.blogspot.com/2018/06/words-of-gold.html; and Ted Jenner, "The Gold Leaf of Petelia," *Ka Mate Ka Ora: A New Zealand Journal of Poetry and Poetics*, no. 11 (March 2012) http://www.nzepc.auckland.ac.nz/kmko/11/ka_mate11_jenner.pdf.

324. Cited in Friedrich Hiebel, *The Gospel of Hellas* (New York: Anthroposophic Press, 1949), 28.

325. Ibid. 33.

CHAPTER 26: THE PAGAN SENSE OF LIFE

326. Joseph, *Gaia*, 234.
327. Neil Evernden, *The Natural Alien* (Toronto: University of Toronto Press, 1999), 103.
328. Denis de Rougemont, *Love in the Western World* (Princeton: Princeton University Press, 1983), 74.
329. See Kathleen Raine, *Blake and Antiquity* and *Golgonooza, City of Imagination* on Blake and Jesus. Raine incorporates a fair amount of Mystery lore into her literary studies, but in treating this rich esoteric material she follows the allegorical method of late antiquity, revived in the works of the Cambridge Platonist, Thomas Taylor (1758–1835). This method assumes that the directive myths of the Pagan Mysteries, such as the myth of Demeter and Persephone, are metaphorical constructions that stand for something other than what they state. My view, by contrast, is that the ancient myths actually describe events that transpired in the long-term history (phylogenesis) of the human species. With allegory, we are constantly directed away from such realities toward metaphoric and symbolic codes that are assumed to indicate subjective phenomena in human soul-life, the psyche's way of reckoning its own processes, etc. Plutarch, one of the last known initiates, condemned allegory and insisted that the myths were descriptions of real events: "Whoever applieth these allegories to the blessed Divine Nature, deserves to be treated with contempt. We must not however believe that they were mere fables without any meaning, like those of the Poets. They represent to us things that really happened" (*Isis and Osiris*).
330. John Worthen, *D. H. Lawrence: The Life of an Outsider* (London: Allen Lane, 2005), 406.
331. "Kissing and Horrid Strife," in *The Complete Poems of D. H. Lawrence*, ed. David Ellis (Wordsworth Poetry Library, 2001), 596.

GLOSSARY

Abrahamic religions: Judaism, Christianity, and Islam considered as variations of a common belief system characterized by monotheism, patriarchal values, a linear time scheme for history, a divinely prescribed moral code, redeemer ideology, sexual apartheid, and the dominator agenda, including domination of nature and the assumption of human superiority over all other species.

Aeon: (*AY-on*) (Greek, "god," "divinity," "process," "emanation," "time cycle") Gnostic term for a cosmically pervasive process, aware, animated and animating. Aeons manifest sensory worlds by **dreaming**, rather than by the artisanlike act of creation attributed to the biblical father god. Adj., *Aeonic*.

actional: Proposed term for the inherence of cosmic processes in human experience and psychological processes. Asserts that the mirroring of mind and cosmos is a real action, enacted and interactive, not a passive or static reflection, and not merely a metaphor or symbolic "correspondence."

adept: Someone accomplished in heightened perception and the use of paranormal faculties. Identical to **siddha.**

annihilation theology: The notion that humanity can be destroyed in order save it. Implies the destruction of the natural world and the relocation of the saved ones in "a new heaven and a new Earth," with the damned exiled in a hell-world. Requires an agent of divine retribution.

Annunaki script: Ancient narrative written on Sumerian cuneiform tablets from 1600 B.C.E., describing a race of godlike extraterrestrials who descend to Earth, alter the human genome, interbreed with humans, and teach the arts of civilization. Charter myth of **theocracy.**

anomia: (Greek, "anomaly," "aberration") Gnostic term for the deviance that signals the moral and psychological effect of the **Archons.**

Anthropos: (Greek, "humanity," "human species") In Mystery idiom, the human genome or species template considered as a complex spore emanated into interstellar space by the Aeons of the galactic center (**Pleroma**). Generative matrix of the **human animal.** Adj., *Anthropine*.

anticosmic: Adjective applied to a worldview or practice that rejects the body and condemns matter as evil. Often applied (wrongly) to Gnosticism.

apaton: (Greek, "deception") Gnostic term for the main activity of the **Archons.**

apocalypse: (Greek, "lifting of the seal") One-time-only end-of-the-world scenario, typical of Persian **split-source** cosmology found in the Dead Sea Scrolls, but absent in the Pagan Mysteries, which celebrated perpetual renewal of the life force and cyclic existence.

Archons: (from Greek for "first," "from the beginning") Inorganic species produced by the impact of Sophia upon elementary matter *before* Sophia turned into the Earth. Cyborgs inhabiting the solar system at large who excel in the psychotechnology of virtual reality, intrude upon humanity by psychic stealth, and propagate the ideological virus of redemptive religion. Intrapsychic forces that exaggerate human error beyond the scale of correction. "Messengers of deception" (Jacques Vallee). Adj., *Archontic.*

Asherah: Canaanite tree goddess, or the ritual wooden object erected in reverence to her in sacred groves and leafy places condemned by the father god. Co-opted into the Jewish menorah, a seven-branched candlestick.

autogenes: (Greek, "self-generating") Gnostic term for *autopoiesis*, the self-organizing and self-regulating action of the cosmos and the natural world. *See also* **emergence.**

avatar: (Sanskrit, "one who descends") In Hindu myth, a god who comes to Earth to assist humanity in times of crisis, as in the ten avatars of Vishnu. Loosely, an incarnated divinity. Adj., *avataric.*

Bénard cells: Aggregates of hexagonal cells spontaneously formed in turbulent fluids and in the biosphere, a phenomenon connected to the **Mesotes.**

biomysticism: Exploration of the life force and the intimate processes of nature by experimental techniques including **Kundalini** yoga, trance and dance, sacred sexuality, and the ingestion of **entheogens.**

bodhisattva: (Sanskrit, "harmonious awakening") Ethical ideal in Mahayana Buddhism, defined around 200 c.e., possibly linked to the Gnostic **revealer.** An enlightened person who does not turn away from the ordinary world but forgoes self-liberation to release all sentient beings from delusion ("the Bodhisattva vow").

chaos, chaos theory: *See* emergence.

Christ: (from *christos*, "anointed one," Greek translation of the Hebrew *mashiash*, "messiah") In Christian theology, the "only-begotten Son of God" who assumes human form to enter history and redeem humanity from sin. Central figure in the redeemer complex. Said to have been incarnated uniquely in the historical person called Jesus of Nazareth; hence, the human/divine hybrid, Jesus/Christ. Regarded by the faithful as the ultimate model of humanity, and the locus of human dignity. The divine scapegoat.

Christos: (Greek, "anointed one") In Mystery idiom, a divinity in the galactic matrix (Pleroma) who performs chrismation, the hermetic sealing of the singularity configured by Sophia and Thelete. In the Valentinian version of the myth, this Aeon also intercedes to assist Sophia in the organization of animal life in the biosphere: the Christic intercession. But in the Sethian version, the divine agency that intervenes is Ekklesia, Aggregator. See also Symbiont.

Church Fathers: Early Christian ideologues who wrote elaborate, often ill-conceived arguments (polemics) against the Gnostics and the Mysteries.

coevolution: Evolving together in a complementary and symbiotic manner.

complexity, complexity theory: Current term for chaos theory. See emergence.

Coptic: A stenographic language invented by Egyptian scribes around 100 c.e., using the Greek alphabet (capital letters only) plus six letters from the demotic or popular form of Egyptian writing. Surviving Gnostic materials are translations from presumed Greek originals into Coptic.

consecration: The highest aim of initiation in the Pagan Mysteries, allowing initiates to devote their lives to the dual work of coevolution with Gaia and fostering human potential. Literally, "powered with." Contrast with deification.

correction: (in Greek, *diorthosis*) Gnostic term for the realignment of life on Earth with the cosmic center, the source from which Sophia (the autopoetic planetary intelligence) emerged. Distinct from off-planet redemption promised by the salvationist creed.

counterfeiting god: Gnostic term for the **Demiurge,** a.k.a. Jehovah.

countermimicry: (in Greek, *antimimon*) Gnostic term for co-optation that denies, perverts, or reverses the value of what is co-opted. In other words, substitution of something genuine by a phony version that distorts or reverses its original value.

cross theology: Scholarly slang for the ideology of redemptive religion.

Dead Sea Scrolls: Literary testament of an extremist Jewish cult, the **Zaddikim,** whose beliefs present in larval form the doctrines of Christian **salvationism.** Written in Hebrew and Aramaic on sheepskin. Dated from 268 B.C.E. to 68 C.E. when the main Zaddikite outpost on the Dead Sea, thirty miles southeast of Jerusalem, was destroyed by the Romans.

deep ecology: Social-ethical philosophy asserting that nature has intrinsic value, independent of its use to human beings, or even of the existence of human beings. Formulated in an eight-point program by Arne Naess and George Sessions in the 1970s. In contrast to shallow ecology, which views nature as worth conserving in order to serve and satisfy human needs.

deification: Elevation to the status of a god, a side effect of psychosomatic illumination, wrongly presumed to have been the aim of initiation in the Pagan Mysteries. *See also* **identification.**

dema: Stands for "dense elementary matter arrays." Proposed term for the fields of inorganic elementary particles circulating in the galactic limbs, distinguished from the organic substance of the core. Perhaps comparable to the "quantum foam" of Dirac.

Demeter: (Greco-Latin, *"dea-mater,"* "god-mother") Europan goddess, guardian of the Eleusinian Mysteries, who imparted the secret of the sacred entheogenic brew. Her daughter is Kore, or Persephone.

Demiurge: (literally, "half-working," "half-powered," so called because he can originate nothing but must imitate what already exists) The leader of the **Archons,** also called Saklas ("fool"), Samael ("blind"), and **Yaldabaoth.** A pseudodeity who claims to be the creator of the material world and demands slavish obedience from his creatures. Identical with the biblical father god, Yahweh-Jehovah.

dianoia: (Greek, "through the mind") A modality of **nous,** divine intelligence. The reasoning faculty *considered as an instrument of nature's* *own consciousness*, rather than an exclusively human capacity used to distance and analyze nature. The capacity to see nature "through the mind," and to interact and *dia*logue with what is thus seen.

directive script: Proposed term for a story encoded with beliefs that drive the behavior of those who adopt it.

dominator culture: Term proposed by Riane Eisler, Terence McKenna, and others, for the social and cultural rule of patriarchy, including authoritarian rule, centralist organization, sexual hierarchy, conquest of nature, and the imposition and implementation of redemptive religion (my addition).

dreaming: Anthropological term for the experience of aboriginal cultures who participate empathically and imaginatively in the Eternal Now, the Dreamtime. The timeless act of emanation in which the formative forces of the cosmos pervade and shape the processes of the natural world the human psyche. Current equivalent in physics, mathematics, and biology: **emergence.**

ecofeminism: Term coined in 1974 by French sociologist Francoise D'Eaubonne, asserting that domination of nature goes along with domination of women.

ecology: (from Greek, "science of the household," or "habitat") The interrelationship of living organisms and their environment, or the study of it.

ecosophy: (literally, "wisdom of the environment") Term proposed by Arne Naess for the wisdom to live harmoniously with nature without assuming that we, the human species, have a superior status or a dominant and directing role. Adj., *ecosophical.*

ego death: Method of initiation in the Pagan Mysteries, achieved by temporary melting or dissolution of focal self-consciousness and loss of **single-self identity**, allowing the initiate to be selflessly, ecstatically immersed in nature.

Eight, the Eighth: (in Greek, Ogdoad) Gnostic term for the realm of the zodiac. Also alludes to the eight members of a Mystery cell charged with interior work.

Ekklesia: (Greek "aggregator") The Aeon from the galactic core who intervenes to assist Sophia in management of the biosphere. It withdraws to the Pleroma but leaves a mysterious residual imprint, the **Symbiont.**

Eleusis: Sacred site west of Athens where the Eleusinian Mysteries dedicated to Demeter were celebrated for thousands of years prior to Christianity. The most historically famous and well-documented Mystery center in Europe—contrasted to Stonehenge, on which there exists almost no ancient textual commentary.

emanation theory: Asian metaphysical concept for the spontaneous process by which sensory and material worlds emerge from a nonmanifesting matrix of pure, overflowing awareness. *See also* **dreaming**.

emergence: Current term for development of life and consciousness within a shared matrix ("deep structure") in which new elements constantly arise to express and optimize the integral properties of the whole.

emergence myth: Proposed term for the Sophia mythos, contrasted both to biblical creation myth and Darwinian evolutionary myth.

ennoia: (Greek, "mental intent") In Mystery idiom, the intentional power applied by Aeons to produce sensory worlds and imbue those worlds with spontaneous, free-form creativity. In human terms, intentionality that produces spontaneous acts and guides goal-orientation; "free will."

entheogen: (literally, "generating divinity within") Term (now preferred over *psychedelic*) for psychoactive plants and fungi that open human consciousness to the divine presence within nature. Adj., *entheogenic*. On the entheogenic theory of religion or Wasson thesis, see note 213.

epinoia, the luminous epinoia: (literally, "hyper-intelligence") In Mystery idiom, the human faculty of imagination considered as a creative, coevolutional capacity and distinguished from mental fantasy and pretending.

error theory: Key Gnostic concept stating that humanity is distinguished from other species by its exceptional latitude for error, which requires that we evolve by making mistakes, but which also exposes us to the risk of deviation from our species-specific potential when our mistakes are not detected and corrected. Closely associated with the **Archons**, who drive human error beyond the scale of correction.

Etheric Christ: New Age term (introduced by Rudolf Steiner) for the **Mesotes**.

Europa: Proposed name for pre-Christian Europe, a region extending from the Shetland and Orkney islands to the tip of Iberia, from Brittany in France eastward to the Straits of the Bosphorus, and including the northern rim of the Mediterranean basin, Crete, Sicily, Corsica, Sardinia, Malta, Majorca, and the Greek isles.

Europans: The indigenous people of pre-Christian Europe.

evil: That which works against the capacity to live and thrive. Regarded in Gnostic teachings as an avoidable consequence of human error, but elevated in the **split-source duality** of Zoroastrian religion to an absolute cosmic power.

fractals: Self-similar patterns in different scales, generated by equations fed into a computer, the result of each equation being factored into the next equation (iteration). Believed to represent formative processes in nature (such as patterns on the branch of a fern that replicate the form of the entire plant), and to intimate the hidden deep structure of turbulent and emergent processes.

Gaia: (from Greek *ge*, "earth") Ancient name for the Earth found in the works of the Greek poet Hesiod. Adopted by James Lovelock on the suggestion of Nobel-winning novelist William Golding. Rejected by Dolores LaChapelle as a patriarchal contrivance and "just another abstraction." Written KAZ in Coptic.

Gaia theory: Formerly the Gaia hypothesis. Technically, the theory that the biotic and abiotic components of the Earth function as a single, self-regulating system in which the growth and activities of organisms respond to their environment, rather than passively inhabit it; thus regulating reactive gas composition, acid-alkaline balance, the salinity of the oceans, and temperature—in short, life makes Earth suitable for life. Loosely, the understanding that the Earth is a living, sentient superorganism regulated in concord with the life-forms that inhabit it.

Gaia-Sophia principle: Proposed term for the assertion that humanity receives both its instinctual survival skills and its moral sense in the same endowment. Implies the deep ecological notion that kindness and cooperation, rather than brutality and competition, are compatible with our deepest survival drives. Also assumes that genuine morality is impossible if humanity is not empathically rooted in nature and intimately allied to other species.

genocide: The deliberate murder of a racial or cultural group, or the process of eliminating an entire community or race, including the human race itself.

goddess mystique: The ensemble of animistic, mystical, mythological, and quasi-religious notions that have arisen around Gaia theory.

God-self equation: An idea initially proposed by Clement of Alexandria, who claimed that Gnostics were people who realized God "within," in their self-identity. Assumes that we are essentially divine, rather than instrumentally divine, as Gnostics taught. Widely adopted in New Age interpretations of Gnostic writings. *See also* **ego death** and **identification.**

Gnosis: (Greek, "knowing of things divine") The timeless method of cognitive ecstasy. Today, the best experimental basis for the noetic sciences.

Gnostic: (Greek *gnostikos*, plural, *gnostikoi*; "one who understands divine matters," "knowing as the gods know") Loosely, the Pagan intellectual class. Specifically, initiated teachers (telestai) in the Mystery Schools. Used by Plato for experts in statecraft and social control, or special advisors to the **theocrats**—a role rejected by Mystery initiates. Used by the Church Fathers as an insult meaning "smartass," "know-it-all."

HAL: (Coptic, "simulation") The highest power of the **Archons**, i.e., near-undetectable virtual reality.

Hebdomad: In Mystery idiom, the sevenfold planetary system exclusive of the Earth. Realm of the **Archons** and the **Demiurge**, Jehovah.

hieros gamos: *See* **sacred mating.**

Hellenistic era: The period from the death of Alexander the Great in 323 B.C.E. to 30 B.C.E., when Cleopatra, the last member of the Ptolemaic Dynasty who inherited the southwestern part of his empire, killed herself with the bite of an asp.

heresy: (from Greek *heraisthai*, "to choose") Any doctrine or belief acquired by choice after considering a range of options, by contrast to beliefs adopted or imposed to the exclusion of all options (orthodoxy). A *heretic* is someone who chooses what to believe.

Hermas: Folk name for the Sumerian shepherd Tammuz, pictured with a newborn lamb on his shoulders. Chosen by Gnostics for the icon of the **Piscean Age** but co-opted into a stock figure of Christian piety, without the lamb.

Hermetica: Writings attributed to Hermes (a title for the hierophant in the Egyptian Mysteries) that bear some resemblance to Gnostic teachings. Rediscovered by the Byzantine scholar Gemistos Plethon in the fifteenth century.

hierophant: (Greek, "one who shows sacred things") In the Mysteries, the initiate who led others to the **Organic Light.**

hyperception: Proposed term for the augmented or intensive perception acquired in the Mysteries. "Heightened perception" (Castaneda).

ideological virus: Proposed analogy for the salvationist belief system common to Judaism, Christianity, and Islam.

identification: Controversial issue in deep ecology, proposing that the way to increased empathy with nature is through expansion of self-awareness, rather than surrender of self as was required in the Mysteries. *See also* **ego death.**

Illuminati: Modern derogatory term for presumed Gnostics who in ancient times advised and handled theocratic rulers and directed the empowerment of sacred kings, a responsibility originally performed by priestesses of the Mother Goddess. Called *gnostikoi*, "special advisors," "experts," by Plato, who endorsed their method of "the noble lie."

illuminist path: Proposed term for body-based mysticism and shamanic techniques of ecstatic cognition practiced in the Pagan Mysteries.

infrasensory: Proposed term for altered perception that allows access to the inner workings of nature, such as molecular chemistry. What happens *within* the senses, contrasted to the content manifested externally *by* the senses. Hence, information the senses carry additional to what they normally show us. The "intensive dimension" of sense perception in Goethe's method.

initiate: A guardian of the Mysteries who taught the arts of civilization, the nature of the gods, the unseen worlds, cosmology, anthropology, and so on. Identical with **telestes.**

initiation: (from Latin *initiare*, "to begin," "to start"; an inversion of the Greek *telein*, "to end," "complete," "reach the goal") Ancient method of training for goal-orientation, the fostering of human potential, and coevolution with nature through intimate communication with the living intelligence of the Earth, Sophia.

Intermediary: The mysterious agency that mediates between human and nonhuman animals, comparable to the Manitu of indigenous peoples. *See also* **Symbiont.**

Jehovah: Father god of Judeo-Christian religion, identified by Gnostics with the demented Archon, **Yaldaboath**. Hebrew name for the **Demiurge**, Yaldabaoth.

Jesus: (from Hebrew *Yeshua*) A man alleged to have lived in the first century of the Common Era, variously viewed as a hippielike faith healer, a radical rabbi, an Essene teacher, a yogi from Kashmir, a pretender to the kingship of Israel, a Zaddikite terrorist, the expected messiah of the Jews, a magician, a false guru who usurped the role of John the Baptist, a Gnostic initiate, a Jewish mystic, an extraterrestrial from Venus, and the sole incarnation of divinity in human form. *See also* **living Jesus**.

Kedoshim: (Hebrew "radiant" or "sacred angels") In the Dead Sea Scrolls, supernatural entities who navigate in celestial chariots and fight on the side of the Sons of Light in their final battle against the Sons of Darkness.

koinonos: (Greek, "companion," "consort") A term applied to Mary Magdalene.

KROG: (Coptic, "deceit," "subterfuge") Gnostic term for the most insidious delusional effect of the **Archons**, diverting humanity from error into evil.

Kundalini: (Sanskrit, "coiled power," "the lesser" or "teeny-weeny Kunda") In Tantra and Asian yoga practices, the supervitalistic power compressed in the human organism, cause of the kinking and folding of DNA, which, when awakened, produces ecstasy, illumination, **hyperception**, and access to molecular memory. Considered to be the microcosmic aspect of Mahakunda, the serpentine power (vital-electromagnetic field) of the Earth.

kykeon: Greek name for the sacred brew drunk in the Eleusinian Mysteries, consisting of the psychoactive extract of fermented barley, or ergot (*Purpurea claviceps*), and the common herb pennyroyal, added to aid digestion.

living Jesus: (trans. of Coptic IS ETONE) Routine translation of the Coptic scribal code, more accurately rendered as "the everlasting healer." The mysterious plasmic imprint left in the biosphere by the intercession of the Aeon **Ekklesia**. A birthless psychic entity distinguished from a specific historical (i.e., mortal) person who lived and died in linear time.

luminous epinoia: *See* **epinoia** and **Zoe.**

Maccabean revolt: The Jewish resistance movement in Palestine, instigated in 168 B.C.E. with the murder by Jews of a Jewish priest. Lasted through the Hasmonean Period (165–63 B.C.E.). Later revived in the popular Jewish revolt that was crushed in 70 C.E. with the destruction of Jerusalem by Titus and the expulsion of all Jews from the city. The Jewish intifada.

Magian order (from *magi*, plural of *magus*, "one who contacts the higher realms," or "the macrocosmos") Prehistoric order of shaman-priests in Zoroastrian religion, the geographic and cultural origin of the Gnostic movement, originating around 6000 B.C.E. in northwestern Iran. They were the founders and guardians of the Mysteries, who consecrated themselves to coevolution with Gaia and education of humanity. Distinguished from the so-called **Illuminati,** who entered politics and engaged in social engineering.

Masoretic Bible: The oldest complete surviving text of the standard Bible in Hebrew, copied by scribes in 1008 C.E.

maya: (Sanskrit, "appearance," "apparition") Wrongly conceived as illusion. The real appearance assumed by something that is beyond conditional appearance, as a reflection in a mirror: you cannot enter the mirror, but you can appear to be in it. That is *maya.*

Melchizedek: (Hebrew, "prince of righteousness") Eerie figure without parentage or biological generation who confers the mission of the Chosen People on the biblical patriarch Abraham. Declared by Saint Paul to be the anointer of the anointed, the Christ; hence *the hidden power behind the Redeemer.* Supreme source of spiritual authority and agent of divine retribution for the **Zaddikim** of the Dead Sea. Also called the **Nasi.**

messiah: (Hebrew *mashiash,* "anointed king") Specific to Judaism, the warrior-king who would rule over an independent Jewish state in Palestine. Originally, this was the ancient name for a king, with no connotation of divinity. Anointing with fragrant oils was part of the rites of kingship empowerment under the rule patriarchy, but earlier the anointing was done through **sacred mating** of the royal candidate with a priestess of the Great Goddess. In Christianity, the only son of the father god, sent to save the world by blood sacrifice and deliver a message of divine love. In apocalyptic myth, the divine emissary and avenger expected to appear at the end the world. Adj., *messianic*.

Mesotes: (lit., "intermediary," "medium") Also called the Intermediary, a phantomlike presence in the atmosphere that mediates between humanity and other species. Supports and facilitates the **species-self connection.** Manifests in a cluster of Bénard cells, the biospheric after-image of the intercession of **Symbiont.**

metanoia: (Greek, "beyond intelligence") A modality of **nous,** demonstrated in the capacity to think beyond (*meta-*) what we know, beyond whatever belief or model or paradigm determines our mental focus or worldview.

monogenes: (Greek, "single-generating") Gnostic term for a cosmic **singularity** understood in terms of human potential, especially the uniqueness of our capacity to innovate and project goals, but also our excessive latitute for error.

monotheism: Assertion that only one god exists, contrasted to *henotheism*, which recognizes many gods but insists on the supremacy of one above all others. Strictly speaking, ancient Judaism was henotheistic, not monotheistic.

Mysteries: (from the Greek verb *muein*, "to be silent," "shut the mouth" or "speak in a murmur") Millennial rites of ecstatic communion with nature, the outgrowth of the indigenous, Goddess-oriented shamanism of pre-Christian Europe and the Near East. From 600 B.C.E. on, the Mysteries became the infrastructure for the educational institutions of the ancient world, i.e., centers of literacy and training in the sciences, arts and crafts (i.e., schools).

Mystery cell: A select group (Greek *thiasos*) of initiates who worked inwardly on certain projects related to human evolution, and outwardly transmitted what they knew through literature, education, and vocational training. Traditionally organized into sixteen members, eight men and eight women (as evidenced in the rosette on the pediment at Eleusis).

Mystery School: An educational center or campus attached to a temple belonging to the network of Pagan Mysteries, consisting of libraries, workshops, gymnasia, and agorae (open spaces for lectures and discussions).

mystes: Participants in both the Lesser and the Greater Mysteries. Plur., *mystai*.

mysticism: Direct, intuitive, suprarational experience of the divine element indwelling the world and the psyche, often characterized by an "oceanic feeling" of oneness with all things. *See also* **biomysticism**.

Nag Hammadi Library: Abbreviated NHL. Thirteen leather-bound packets, the earliest example of bound books, comprising fifty-two documents written in Coptic. Discovered in Upper Egypt in December, 1945. Widely assumed to be original writings that survive from various Gnostic sects existing in Egypt and the Near East between 150 and 350 C.E. Also called the Nag Hammadi Codices (NHC). Translated into English as *The Nag Hammadi Library in English* (NHLE). Scholars edition, the Coptic Gnostic Library (CGL).

narcissism: Pathological excess of concern for embodied identity (extending to specious notions of selfhood and "soul"), which both intensifies self-observation and detaches or dissociates the observing self from physical and sensuous reality. The dominant personal and social pathology of the **Piscean Age**.

Nasi: Zaddikite name for Melchizedek as the agent of divine retribution.

the Ninth: In Mystery idiom, the terrestrial realm where Sophia is embodied, and captured in the planetary system. "And she was taken up not into the Pleroma, but above the Demiurge, that she might be in the Ninth until she corrected her defect" (Apocryphon of John, 14.10)—an allusion consistent with widespread mythological lore on the ninefold nature of the Goddess (Robert Graves, Stone, Gimbutas, et al.)

nous: (Greek, "divine intelligence," "cosmic-creative mind," "intellect") In Mystery idiom, the divine potential endowed in humanity, enabling it to know its true species-specific identity (**Anthropos**), and to coevolve with **Sophia**, the Wisdom Goddess. Root of **metanoia, dianoia, pronoia, epinoia, ennoia**. Source of the term *noetic*.

Organic Light: Also called Divine Light, Supernal Light, White Light, Mystery Light. The primary substance body of **Sophia**, contrasted to her planetary body, the Earth. Source and medium of instruction (*mathesis*) in the Mysteries.

orgy: (literally, "work," "operation"; Greek plural, *orgia*) Festive rites of learning practiced by the Mystery cells, including entheogenic sessions, trance dance, sexual rites and romps, and snake-worshiping (**Kundalini**) ceremonies.

Pagan: Member of a society or culture whose primary orientation is to the natural world, the habitat. In the religious sense, panentheism, polytheism, and the animist worldview. In the Pagan sense of life, culture is organically situated in nature.

Paganism: Nature-based and Goddess-oriented religion of the indigenous peoples of Europa.

panspermia: The spreading of spores of life (**propagules**) through interstellar space.

palingenesis: (Greek, "regeneration") Rapturous invigoration by selfless immersion in nature, the psychosomatic effect of Pagan initiation in both the Lesser and Greater Mysteries.

pesher: A learned commentary on scripture found among the Dead Sea Scrolls. Plur., *peshara*.

phoster: *See* revealer.

Piscean Age: The period of time measured by **precession** in the zodiac that extends from 120 B.C.E. until about 2800 C.E., during which the spring equinox occurs in the constellation of Pisces, the Fishes (according to the true extent of the visible constellations). Characterized by excessive narcissism, the total decay of society, and degeneration of the human species as a whole, but offering exceptionally rapid spiritual realization for individuals consecrated to the species' true potential.

Pistis Sophia: (Greek, "the confidence of Sophia" or "wisdom confidence") Gnostic term for the confidence felt by the goddess Sophia for the divine potential of the human species. Also, the title of a long, non–Nag Hammadi text (Askew Codex) presenting a dialogue between a resurrected Gnostic master and Mary Magdalene.

plané: (Greek, "wandering," "erring," "going astray") Gnostic term for the human tendency to overlook its errors and, in doing so, stray from its true course of development. A primary mark of Archontic influence. Basis of the word *planet*.

Pleroma: (Greek, "fullness," "plenitude") In Mystery idiom, the central company or matrix of gods, or Aeons. In astronomical terms, the galactic center. Contrasted to the Kenoma ("deficienty," "privation"), the spiral arms of a galaxy into which the Aeons direct their **dreaming**.

The structure of core and encircling arms is consistent with a toroidal conception of cosmic formation.

peak experience: Term proposed by Abraham Maslow (1908–70) for optimal expression of human potential, including the awakening of paranormal faculties. Comparable to the telos or aim of the Mysteries.

polemics: Arguments of the Church Fathers against the Gnostics, the Mysteries, and Pagan philosophy. Also called patristic writings, and ante-Nicene writings (preceding the Nicene Council of 325 c.e.).

precession: Astronomical phenomenon caused by the slow wobbling of the polar axis of the Earth, producing the shift of the spring equinox against the background of the fixed stars (zodiac). Defines a cycle of 25,920 years consisting of various ages named for the constellations, e.g., Arien Age, **Piscean Age**, Aquarian Age. Used by ancient initiates as a master framework for guiding humanity and planning the cultural and spiritual education of the human species.

primal ecology: Proposed term for ecology rooted in the experience of the sacred, including the nonhuman world, but oriented toward culture and education, i.e., toward the primary needs of social continuity rather than social control.

pronoia: (Greek, "primal awareness," or "proto-knowing"; usually translated as "Providence") The omnipresent foundation of unconditioned awareness without subject or object that precedes and grounds all particular acts of knowing.

propagule: Microscopic spore capable of transporting life through interstellar space. *See* **panspermia.**

psychocosmic parallelism: Proposed concept for the **actional** mirroring of cosmic events in the human psyche, typical of the Gnostic mind and method.

psychohistory: The history of the human psyche, or history as a reflection of the operations of the psyche. Conversely, the ensemble of psychological patterns and leitmotifs determined by the events of history, often expressed as mythological themes, e.g., the fall, salvation, the apocalypse.

Qumran: Place-name for the caves southeast of Jerusalem where the Dead Sea Scrolls were discovered. Adj., Qumranic; hence, Qumranic literature.

redeemer complex: Proposed term for the ideological core of Judeo-Christian-Islamic religion, consisting of four components: creation of the world by a father god independent of a female counterpart; the trial and testing (conceived as a historical drama) of the righteous few or "Chosen People"; the mission of the creator god's son (the messiah) to save the world; and the final, apocalyptic judgment delivered by father and son upon humanity. Basis of **salvationist** beliefs.

redeemer ethics: The ethics of Jesus stated in the New Testament, calling for nonresistance to evil, forgiveness, reconciliation with the perpetrator, and identification of the victim with the righteous few who, no matter how oppressed they are, always hold the higher moral ground. In short, the ethical justification of the victim-perpetrator bond.

redemptive religion: The belief system based on the redeemer complex. Assumes that a superhuman power can make right all human injustice, and asserts that suffering pays off for those who are favored by the saving power.

revealer: (trans. of Greek *phoster*, from *phos*, "light," "illumination") Gnostic term for an illumined teacher, comparable to a buddha or **bodhisattva**. Also translated as "enlightener."

revealer cycle: The succession of teachers who appear in each zodiacal age to guide humanity through the lessons and problems specific to that age.

Romanticism: The sociocultural, philosophical, and artistic movement characterized by a return to nature (nature mysticism), idealization of human potential, humanist and egalitarian values, and the exaltation of emotion and passion, or direct intuition of reality, over reason and analysis. Lasted from 1775 to 1820 in Europe, with a long post-Romantic phase. Reflected in the Transcendentalist movement in America (Emerson, Thoreau, Melville, and others). Partially revived in the environmental movement.

Sabaoth: (*sah-BUY-ot*) In the Sophia mythos, the name of the mother star of our planetary system.

sacred kingship: The primary system of social authority in ancient cultures, centered on a male authority figure or **theocrat** identified with sacred or superhuman powers. The main political instrument of patriarchy.

sacred mating: In prepatriarchal societies, the ritual of empowerment of the sacred king or **theocrat**, who was authorized to assume authority by a priestess represented the Great Goddess, the original "power behind the throne." The ritual of sexual-spiritual anointing was called *hieros gamos*, "sacred marriage."

salvation history, salvation narrative: The story that explains how salvation will be attained, and why it needs to be attained. A divine plan for redemption reflected in the actual and factual events of history.

salvationism: The totalitarian belief system that asserts divine interces-sion in history, and imbues suffering with redemptive value. Includes Judaism, Christianity, and Islam, the three dominant mainstream reli-gions. Assumes superhuman rescue of humanity from its problems and off-planet, remote-control authority on morals, and divine retribution.

salvationist: A way of life that demands obedience, contrasted to the **illu-minist path**, which requires learning

samadhi: (Sanskrit, "perfect attending") Perfect, total, illuminated concen-tration of awareness conducive to cosmic consciousness of two kinds: with discrete, detailed content ("knowing nothing through knowing everything"), and devoid of all content ("knowing everything through knowing nothing").

sapiential literature: (from Latin *sapientia*, "wisdom") "Wisdom literature," such as the *Odes of Solomon*, which present (often in veiled form) mysti-cal poetry focused on suppressed figure of **Sophia**, the Wisdom Goddess. Includes some Psalms, the Wisdom of Sirach, and the Song of Solomon.

scapegoat: An innocent person or animal blamed for the offenses of a perpe-trator who cannot be identified or made accountable. *See* **victimage**.

serial endosymbiosis theory (SET): Alternative to the Darwinian theory of evolution proposed by Lynn Margulis, stating that larger animals evolve from microbial entities by a long-term process of symbiosis in which the smaller organisms live within the bodies of the larger ones, to the mutual benefit of both parties.

shakti: (Sanskrit, "sacred power") Generally, the supreme power that imbues both the sensory and material aspects of the cosmos. In Hindu Tantra, the goddess Shakti considered as a dynamic, world-emanating force distinct from the god Shiva, who represents the passive behold-ing of what is manifested.

shamanism: The practice of direct contact and communion with the sacred, supernatural beauty of nature, and access to the intelligence of nature. The ancient root of religious experience and the matrix of the Mysteries characterized by, or formalized in, "archaic techniques of ecstacy" (Eliade) that permit access to other worlds and to the **infrasensory** dimension of this world. The timeless spiritual calling of hunter, healer, diviner, dancer, and poet.

siddha: (Sanskrit, "accomplished") Someone trained in the use of paranormal powers (*siddhis*), such as clairaudience, remote viewing, lucid dreaming. Equivalent to **adept**.

Simon Magus: The earliest member of a Gnostic cell to be known by name, due to having broken anonymity and come out publicly to protest Christian beliefs.

simulation: The most advanced capacity of the **Archons**. Coptic **HAL**.

single-self identity: Proposed term for the fixation of human consciousness on the ego-self or literal and exclusional identity, disallowing a more permeable and playful sense of self, and inhibiting temporary dissolution of identity in selfless beholding of the world. *See also* **narcissism**.

single-source duality: *See* **split-source duality**.

singularity: In modern physics, a point of infinite density and volume assumed by matter that collapses into a black hole. In Mystery idiom, **monogenes**, the singularity of human potential with its exceptional latitude for error and its gift for novelty, innovation.

Sophia: (*so-FI-uh*) (Greek, "wisdom") The living intelligence of the Earth. Central figure in Gnostic cosmology and the Pagan Mysteries. The goddess Sophia from the **Pleroma**, who by the force of her **dreaming** came to be metamorphosed into a planetary body, the Earth. Her primary substance body is the **Organic Light**. Although the name is Greek, there is no mythological figure of that name in Greek myth. In the Avestan language of ancient Persia, she is called Anahita. Adj., Sophianic.

Sophia mythos: The sacred story of the Aeon Sophia in the **Pleroma**, and how she came to be metamorphosed into the Earth. Applied as a tool for guidance of the human species in the Mysteries. Leaves open the question of human participation in Sophia's **Correction**. May possibly serve as a guiding framework for developing the religious dimension of deep ecology.

SOREM: (Coptic, "error," "going astray") Gnostic term for the tendency of the human race to deviate from its proper course of experience, in part through its exceptional latitude for error, in part through the subliminal influence of the **Archons.**

species-self connection: Proposed term for way that human beings find their sense of self in identification with the human species, rather than in **single-self identity,** or modes of identity defined by language, family, culture, race, and religion. Requires the aid of a visionary model of genetic identity, such as the Anthropos. Engendered by the encounter with the **Mesotes,** when that experience is not overwritten by religious and cultural conditioning.

split-source duality: Moral and cosmological concept found in Zoroastrian religion and Zaddikite ideology, asserting that good and evil are absolute and autonomous principles that arise from the same source. Makes God or the Godhead the source of violently opposing tendencies. Also makes God responsible for making right the injustices that human beings suffer and cannot rectify. Contrast with **two-source duality.**

telestes: (from Greek *telos*, "aim," "end," "purpose," "the ultimate thing"; literally, "one who is aimed") What Gnostics would have called themselves. Self-designation of those who founded and maintained the **Mysteries.** An **initiate** endowed with special knowledge in divine matters, the will and work of the gods; hence, an expert on theological and cosmological issues. Plur., *telestai*; adj. *telestic.*

telestic method: The practice of accessing the Organic Light in a trance, unique to the genuine Gnostic teachers of the Mysteries. Also called *mathesis,* instruction by the Light.

Thelete: (Greek "the intended, what is willed, sovereign power") The mate and counterpart to the Aeon Sophia in the design of the human genome, the Anthropos.

terma: (Tibetan, "hidden treasure") In Tibetan Buddhism, a sacred teaching concealed in nature or in the human mind by an enlightened master, and left to be discovered at a later moment by a *terton*, or treasure finder, so that the teaching can be used to benefit humanity in the time and setting of its discovery.

theocracy: Government by the gods or descendents of the gods. The political paradigm of authority in ancient large-scale, agriculture-based, war-dependent societies.

theocrat: A sacred king, demigod, or human representative of the gods.

transentience: Proposed term for deep sentient immersion in all that lives: literally, "sensing through." Implies transcendence of **single-self identity** as the precondition of such immersion. "Beyond self and pouring through all that lives, so does it all live and pour through me."

transference: Proposed term for the process in which the Palestinian **redeemer complex,** originally confined to the cult of the **Zaddikim,** was converted into the totalitarian Christian ideology of salvation. Effectuated jointly by Saint Paul, Saint John the Divine, and the team of literary hacks and overfed Roman lawyers who wrote the Gospels.

two-source duality: Gnostic cosmological concept asserting that good and evil do not arise from the same source, but evil comes into play in human experience owing to the superposition of two different perceptual systems. Illustrated by the analogy of the two-source hologram in the writings of Philip K. Dick.

victimage: Term proposed by René Girard (*Violence and the Sacred*) for scapegoating as a tool of social order essential to protect society from its self-destructive impulses. Ritually expressed in the archaic rites of sacred kingship in which the power of the king depended on his willingness be sacrificed to expiate or rectify the moral failings and injustices of the community.

victim-perpetrator bond: The insidious tendency for those who are harmed and betrayed to become emotionally attached and morally identified with those who harm and betray them. Implies that some victims will become perpetrators in their own right. Primary cause of the European genocide of the Americas.

Wasson thesis: Also called the entheogenic theory of religion, stating that the original religious experience of humanity, as distinguished from religion as an institutional and doctrinal system, arose from the direct encounter with the sacred powers of nature through the ingestion of psychoactive plants and fungi. See note 213.

wisdom: (in Greek, *sophia*, Hebrew, *chokhmah*. The divine activity of sentient, autopoetic intelligence that informs nature and pervades human potential.

Yaldabaoth: (*YAL-dah-BUY-ot*) Gnostic name for the **Demiurge,** leader of the **Archons,** identical to the biblical father god, Yahweh or Jehovah. A demented pretender who works against humanity.

Zaddik: (Hebrew "righteous," "just") The superhuman and inhumane standard of perfection that informs the religion and ethics of radical Jewish apocalypticism. Inherited, but modified, by Christianity and Islam. Also spelled *tzaddik* and *tsedeq*.

Zaddikim: The ultra-extremist apocalyptic sect whose main outpost was located at **Qumran** in the caves above the Dead Sea from 200 B.C.E. to 68 C.E. Their genophobic ideology of salvation for the righteous few was the germinal (or viral) form of Christian redemptive theology. Adj., Zaddikite.

Zadok: Old Testament variation of **Zaddik**, referring to the secret priesthood ("Sons of Zadok") responsible for anointing the Jewish kings from the time of Solomon.

Zealots: Military wing of the **Zaddikim**. Political activists and terrorists committed to the liberation of Palestine from foreign occupation.

zodiac: The band of constellations or fixed star-patterns that lie on the apparent path of the sun (ecliptic), which is actually the orbital path of the Earth. The stellar or real-sky zodiac comprises thirteen visible star-patterns, uneven in size and extent, including the constellation of Ophiuchus, the Snaketamer. Not to be confused with the tropical or seasonal zodiac, consisting of twelve equal divisions of the ecliptic. The real-sky constellations give their names to the zodiacal ages (Arian, Piscean, Aquarian, etc.) measured by the long-term cycle of **precession**. We are currently living in the **Piscean Age**, which began between 150 and 120 B.C.E. when the spring equinox shifted into that constellation, coming from the direction of Aries, the Ram.

Zoe: In the **Sophia mythos**, the emanation of the goddess Sophia in pure, deathless vitality, distinguished from biological life which is mortal. Source of bioluminescence and **epinoia**.

Zoroastrian religion: The most obscure and problematic of ancient world religions, probably originating around 6000 B.C.E. in northern Persia (Iran), characterized by strict opposition of good and evil considered as absolute principles stemming from the same cosmic source (**split-source duality**). *See also* **Magian order**.

—— SUGGESTIONS ——
FOR READING AND
RESEARCH

My suggestions for reading and research on Gaia theory, deep ecology, the Pagan Mysteries, and the Sophianic message of the Gnostics fall into nine categories, with brief comments. Publishing details are given only if they are essential to finding the books. In most cases, current editions can by located via the Internet. With a couple of exceptions I have excluded scholarly works of primary value to insiders in favor of easier, more accessible reading. Categories 4 through 9 present contemporary non-Gnostic writings that I have found to be helpful in approaching the Mysteries and the theory and practice of Gnosis.

1. Primary Sources

Nag Hammadi Library (abbreviated NHL or NHC)
The standard edition, *The Nag Hammadi Library in English* (NHLE) edited by James Robinson, first appeared in 1977. Editions from several publishers are now in print. The NHLE is intended for mainstream readers, while scholars use the multivolume hardcover edition, *The Coptic Gnostic Library* (CGL), uniquely published by E. J. Brill, Leiden, The Netherlands. Brill also published a facsimile edition of the Codices in oversized folios with photographic reproductions of every page. The CGL presents the Coptic text on the left with facing line-by-line translations. It includes elaborate commentaries, glossaries, and meticulous scholarly detail work. The translations in the CGL differ in places from the NHLE.

The CGL also contains essential Coptic writings not found in the NHLE: the Pistis Sophia (Askew Codex), the Untitled Treatise, and the two Books of Jeu (Bruce Codex). A third non-NHL text, the Berlin Codex (BG), contains the Gospel of Mary, the Act of Peter, and drafts of two NHL codices, the Apocryphon of John and the Sophia of Jesus Christ. The first two documents are included at the end of the NHLE, and the drafts are merged into the corresponding NHL texts. Thus, you get the Berlin Codex in the NHLE, but you have to go to the CGL for the Askew and Bruce Codices. In 2000 Brill published a condensed five-volume paperback edition of the CGL with Coptic text (cost, around $550), but without the Bruce and Askew Codices. Pistis Sophia translated by G. R. S. Mead is an early version of the Askew Codex, not recognized by Gnostic scholars. But at least you can lay your hands on it. Outside the CGL, the Bruce Codex is more difficult to find, but there is a valuable translation by Charlotte Baynes, published at Oxford in 1939.

There are no other *complete* English translations of the Coptic Gnostic material apart from the NHLE and the CGL, but there are some partial alternative translations. *The Gnostic Scriptures* translated by Bentley Layton present some NHL material and other ancient writings of a Gnostic character. *The Other Bible* edited by Willis Barnstone is an excellent compilation of selected NHL passages and related materials.

Organization of the Codices

There are in all 52 documents in the NHL, ranging in length from a few lines to 40 pages. Scholars number the codices by Roman numerals, I through XIII, and the treatises in each codex by Arabic numbers, and by a title. For example, V, 4, the fourth treatise in codex V, is titled The Second Apocalypse of James. Some materials occur in more than one draft, notably the long cosmological treatise, the Apocryphon of John, found in codices II, III, IV, and the Berlin Codex. In the CGL the different drafts of this important treatise are printed side by side. In the NHLE they are all merged into one translation.

Scholars number the pages in each codex consecutively, straight through the packet from the first papyrus leaf to the last. For instance, codex VII contains five treatises (or tractates), a total of 127 pages counting each side of a papyrus leaf as a page. The Second Treatise of the Great Seth (VII, 2) runs from pages 49 through 69. The NHLE indicates these page numbers in bold. The pages of the codices average about 30 to 36 lines each, also numbered. Thus there is a four-level notation system: codex, treatise, page, line. NHC VII, 2, 54.10 indicates line 10 on page 54 of treatise 2 in codex VII, titled The Second Treatise of the Great Seth: "And the plan they devised about me, to release their Error and senselessness—I did not succumb to them as they had planned." This is a Gnostic master exposing the subterfuge of the Archons, and how he has foiled it. Scholars also use abbreviations for the titles: Treat Seth, for instance. Apoc Peter 83.1–5 is the same as VII, 3, 83.1–5, but the abbreviated title makes it easier to remember the text being cited. Apoc Peter 83.1–5 is a famous passage that describes "the laughing savior" on the cross: "He laughs at their lack of perception, knowing they are born blind." The crucified savior laughing scornfully at the ignorance of the mob below is one of the more sensational events in the Gnostic corpus. The four-level notation system allows us to pinpoint the location of particular and outstanding lines like this.

It is absurd to read any translation of the NHC straight from start to finish, as if it were an ordinary book. These documents have to be read selectively, approaching each one with some idea of what is to be found in it. The genuine, unadulterated message of Gnosis comes in specific glimmers or "bursts" such as the lines cited above, because the vast bulk of the surviving material is murky, dense, and incoherent. It is practically impossible to wring a clear, consistent paragraph out of many documents in the NHC. The entire opus is a terrible muddle of hand-me-down materials hurriedly rendered in a weird, conceptually impaired steno-graphic language, Coptic. For an in-depth guide to the reading the NHL, see the Gnostic Reading Plan at www.metahistory.org. To my knowledge, this is the only commentary that emphasizes the value of the Gnostic message as such, rather than treating it as an accessory to, or outtake from, Christian doctrines of salvation.

Non–Nag Hammadi Writings and Apocrypha

These include the Askew, Bruce, and Berlin Codices, as already noted. Apart from these documents, no other surviving *Coptic* materials can be identified as originating from Gnostic circles or the Mysteries, but there are diverse materials in Greek, Latin, Hebrew, Syriac, Ethiopic, and Aramaic. The primary source of Greek-language materials is the *New Testament Apocrypha* (NTA) compiled by Edgar Hennecke in 1904 (Philadelphia: Westminster Press, 2 volumes). It contains papyrus fragments, nonbiblical material on Jesus, Jewish-Christian gospels, unknown sayings of Jesus, discussions with disciples after the resurrection, acts of various apostles, and many gospels of a Gnostic and pseudo-Gnostic nature.

There is some stunning Gnostic material in the NTA, even though these works, which were excluded from the canon of the New Testament, are predominantly Christian in character. They provide glimpses of the Pagan-Jewish background of early Christian beliefs, and here and there they reveal the complex body of pre- and non-Christian literature that had to be pillaged to establish the Jesus narrative and the apostolic mission. The NTA is a mixed bag, with large a dose of evangelic cant, but some of its material is deeply engaging. The Acts of John describes a mystical dance performed by Jesus at the Last Supper, accompanied by a poem that contains lines such as "To the universe belongs the dancer. Who does not enter the dance, does not know what is happening." Pope Leo the Great (ca. 450) considered this document so scandalous that he condemned it as a "hotbed of manifold perversity," and ordered all copies be burned, mainly because it refutes the redemptive value of suffering and proposes ecstasy in its place. The Acts of John replaces the gruesome act of crucifixion by a mystical dance. This is the high point of the NTA.

There are also masses of *Old* Testament apocrypha, outtakes from the standard Old Testament, also called pseudoepigraphia. The most accessible of these works were compiled by Edgar Goodspeed in *The Lost Books of the Bible* and *The Forgotten Books of Eden*, including the *Book of the Maccabees* with historical background on the Gnostic-Qumran connection (category 3, below). The Books of Enoch and the Apocalypses of Ezra, Isaiah, and Baruch contain some clues to the Archon-Annunaki scenario ("the Watchers"), as well as other strange material that has now been incorporated into ET/UFO mythology. "Wisdom literature" or sapiential writings such as the *Odes of Solomon* present mystical poetry focused on Sophia, the Wisdom Goddess. (*Sapientia* is the Latin word for the Greek *sophia*, "wisdom.") *The Other Bible* edited by Willis Barnstone offers some tantalizing extracts from the *Odes*. A lot of this obscure material can easily be found on the Internet. For instance, www.gnosis.org.

Classical References

Among classical writings in Greek, Iamblichus' *On the Mysteries* presents the most complete and authentic testimony from an accomplished teacher of the Mysteries. Iamblichus (d. ca. 330 C.E.) was the head of the Syrian school of Neoplatonism to which Hypatia is thought to have belonged. Unfortunately, the sole existing English translation by the English Platonist Thomas Taylor is extremely tough going. (Taylor's own work, *The Eleusinian and Bacchic Mysteries*, is unreliable for a modern view of Gnosis because it presents an *allegorical* interpretation of Mystery teachings, inconsistent with firsthand instruction by the Light.) Iamblichus is rarely cited as a source of Gnostic ideas, whereas Plotinus, who confessed with exasperation that he could get no information out of the Gnostics, often is! Our grasp of the NHC would be hugely enhanced by reading known initiates such as Cicero and Plutarch, as well as other classical writers.

The NHL contains a fragment (VI, 5) from Plato's *Republic*, translated from Greek into Coptic. This means that at least one work in the cache dates from about 400 B.C.E., setting it apart from the other materials that are generally dated 200–350 C.E. Six to seven centuries is a huge separation in time, it would seem, but scholars do not consider the possibility that the "Greek originals" of other NHC texts could of an age comparable to Plato. So far there has been almost no comparison of NHC with classical Greek and Latin writings. Incredible as it seems, the Gnostic message has not so far been evaluated against the background of the Pagan intellectual tradition in which it stood!

The *Meditations* of Marcus Aurelius is the single and supreme testament of Pagan ethics consistent with the Gnostic view of life. Stoicism represents the mundane ethical profile of the *telestai*. I recommend the clear but somewhat overelegant translation by Maxwell Staniforth (Penguin Books).

Plato and Plotinus, the superstars of ancient philosophy in the West, are unreliable and misleading references when it comes to genuine Pagan Gnosis. They both emphasize otherworldly criteria and out-of-the-body mysticism (Plotinus even confessed embarrassment at the fact of having a body), totally contrary to the psychosomatic illuminism of the Mysteries.

Hermetica

Many scholars consider the Hermetic writings to be compatible, if not identical, with the Gnostic message, but (big surprise) I tend to disagree.

The *Hermetica*, a corpus of thirteen texts that surfaced in the Renaissance, is widely considered to be the remnant of original teachings from Egyptian Mystery Schools. These works are named after Hermes, Greek name for the Egyptian Thoth, god of wisdom, also called Trismegistus, "Thrice-Great," the formal title of a hierophant. The NHL contains a fragment of a Hermetic text, *Aesclepius* (VI, 8). Gnostic scholar G. R. S. Mead also wrote a major work on the *Hermetica*, *Thrice-Greatest Hermes* (three volumes, reprinted in a single volume by Samuel Weiser). To discuss how the *Hermetica* compares to the NHC would go beyond the limits of this book, but I will say that I find in Gnostic writings more evidence of firsthand, Gaia-oriented Mystery knowledge than in the pallid cogitations of the *Hermetica*. Be warned that the Hermetic writings fudge on the Gnostic Demiurge, making it a benevolent instrument of the gods rather than a malevolent and deceitful pseudogod.

Para-Gnostic Heresies

By this term I mean repressed spiritual movements in antiquity and afterwards that reflect some elements of Gnosis and the Mysteries. Principal among these are Mandeism, a first-century heresy that rejected Jesus in favor of John the Baptist as the true messiah, and Manichaeism, a third-century resurgence of Zoroastrian split-source duality. On the former, see *The Templar Revelation* by Clive Prince and Lynn Picknett; on the latter, see your local psychiatrist. Sufism, considered in certain aspects relating to the Divine Beloved, could be regarded as a para-Gnostic heresy. So could be the Jewish Kabbalah, and the Catharist heresy of the Middle Ages. I have ignored these and other para-Gnostic movements in this book: one life only gives you time for so much explanation.

The Polemics or Patristic Literature, Writings against the Gnostics

This is the record of the prosecution penned by the Church Fathers to condemn Gnostic heresy. It is a cluttered dossier that runs to dozens of thick volumes of stilted reasoning and outraged rhetoric. The standard edition is *The Writings of the Ante-Nicene Fathers* (Edinburgh: T & T Clark, 1904; Eerdmans reprint, 1996.) "Ante-Nicene" refers to the period before the first Nicene Council of 325 c.e. Not all patristic literature comes under this rubric because the defenders of Christian doctrine continued to write against Gnostic and Pagan religion for many centuries. Indeed, they continue to this day.

The main polemic writers were Justin Martyr, Tertullian, Epiphanius, Irenaeus, Hippolytus, Origen, and Saint Augustine, who was writing his *City of God* in the year Hypatia was murdered. *Irenaeus of Lyons* by Robert M. Grant gives a good account of the influential ideologue who established the canon of the four Gospels and condemned all alternatives to oblivion. Unfortunately, Grant's translation of *Against Heresies*, although highly readable, compresses the key passages on the fall of Sophia and the intercession of Ekklesia that produces the Symbiont. The scant material on these events is uniquely found in Irenaeus, so it is worth consulting the older, more complete translation of Book 1, Chapter 4, which can be found on gnosis.org.

The *Panarion* of Epiphanius, a Christian convert who entered a Gnostic cult to spy on it, contains a lurid account of an orgy in which participants consumed their sexual fluids as holy sacraments. Apart from such rare titillating items, reading the Church Fathers is not a pastime I would recommend to anyone, but the *Clementine Recognitions* provide some amusing anecdotal glimpses of encounters between Gnostics and early Christians. All these works can also be found on gnosis.org.

Mary Magdalene

This is the "woman who knew all," whom Jesus loved in a carnal and intimate way, if some stories are to be believed. Some scholars identify her as the author of the Gospel of Mary (Berlin Codex), appended to the NHLE. Medieval legend presents an alternative story of Mary Magdalene that has expanded into an item of modern folklore, lavishly embellished with esoteric speculation. The popular cult of MM began with *Holy Blood, Holy Grail* by Baigent, Lincoln, and Leigh, and peaks out (let's hope) in *The Da Vinci Code* by Dan Brown. With the unparalleled success of Brown's airport novel, books about MM have proliferated. Most of them are terrible and purely redundant. The best book on this important figure is the earliest, *Venus in Sackcloth* by Marjorie M. Malvern, which is out of print. *Mary Magdalene* by Lynn Picknett is not too bad. It summarizes the Magdalene-Cathar connection and suggests that we distinguish the message of Magdalene from teachings attributed to Jesus—without, however, telling how to do so. *The Goddess and the Gospels* by Margaret Starbird uses Magdalene as the vehicle for a critique of patriarchy and a symbol of ideal marriage, but otherwise remains strictly conventional. Metahistory.org contains a large section on MM, "The Magdalene Connection." For my heretical review of *The Gospel of Mary of Magdala* by orthodox Gnostic scholar Karen King, see www. metahistory.org/SheWhoAnoints.php.

2. SCHOLARS ON GNOSTICISM AND THE MYSTERIES

The Gnostic Gospels (1979) by Elaine Pagels is by far the most popular book on the Egyptian codices. It has made the subject of Gnosticism widely known, yet, paradoxically, Pagels' treatment of the material makes it difficult to know what Gnosis was really about. This is because she regards Gnosticism as alternative Christianity—as indicated by "Gospels" in the title—and completely ignores the Mystery connection. Her work will appeal to those who want to absorb Gnostic notions without any threat to what they already believe. In my view, using Gnostic writings to contrive a new, improved, pseudofeminist and quasi-mystical version of Christianity is a further co-option of Pagan Mystery wisdom, consistent with the ideological crimes of the Universal Church.

Modern scholars do not recognize *The Gnostics and Their Remains* (1887) by C. W. King (Kessinger Publishing reprint), yet it contains more valid and verifiable material on Gnostic/Mystery connections than Pagels and a busload of other experts combined. Citing patristic sources, King shows the vast extent of the Levantine Gnostic Mystery network, which survived in France and Spain into the Christian era: "Gnosticism was more than co-extensive than the empire of Rome, and long survived her fall" (337). Modern experts reject such statements as sheer nonsense.

The Gnostic Religion by Hans Jonas was originally written before much was known of the NHC, but it contains key insights not found in later, more well documented works. Jonas leans heavily on the standard "anti-cosmic" model widely (and wrongly) applied to the Gnostics: the soul entrapped in matter, denial of the body, creation of the material world by the Demiurge. He relies on the Valentinian version of the Sophia mythos in which Sophia is split into upper and lower parts, thus solving the problem of how the material world could be both the metamorphosis of her divine body and the creation of the "evil" Demiurge. This book contains a remarkable and much-discussed epilogue on Gnosticism and existentialism. Difficult but essential reading for a deeper grasp of Gnosis.

Two other scholarly works worth reading are *The Secret Books of the Egyptian Gnostics* by Jean Doresse, the French archaeologist who discovered the Egyptian codices in the Coptic Library in Cairo, and *Gnosis* by Kurt Rudolf. Both are rather dense but repay slow and careful reading. Digest these two books well, and there is little you will be missing. *Fragments of a Faith Forgotten* by G. R. S. Mead is a pre-NHL compilation of diverse materials, including polemics. It discusses the Askew Codex (Pistis Sophia) and the Bruce Codex. In *Gnosticism and the New Testament*, Pheme Perkins gives an unusually fair and charitable view of Gnostics seen from within the Christian fold. *The Allure of Gnosticism* edited by Robert A. Segal (Chicago and La Salle, IL: Open Court) contains writings on Gnosticism relative to Jungian psychology and contemporary culture, including the landmark essay by Buddhist scholar Edward Conze, comparing Buddhism and Gnosticism. It also contains some gross errors; for example, Murray Stein's assertion that the Demiurge (in Jungspeak, "the Yaldabaothian Ego") arises within the Pleroma and so represents a spark of divinity that has lost itself in matter!

Two difficult but essential books for those who want to go deeper into Gnostic studies are *Images of the Feminine in Gnosticism*, edited by Karen King, and *Rethinking "Gnosticism"* by Michael Allen Williams. The former is forbiddingly academic, yet it touches essential issues concerning the Sophia mythos and feminist aspects of Gnosis. The latter is a brilliant refutation of long-standing negative assumptions about the Gnostics, their methods and message. Williams totally refutes the anticosmic model and shows how patristic condemnation of the Gnostics backfires on itself.

There exists no history of the Gnostic movement. *The History of Gnosticism* by Giovanni Filoramo treats the Mysteries as a digression, and places the origins of the movement in the Christian era. Like many Gnostic scholars, including Doresse and Rudolf, Filoramo has a (veiled) dismissive and discounting attitude toward his subject. Important material on the pre-Christian and prehistorical origins of Gnosticism and the Magian order can be found in the extraordinary but little-known book, *Plato Prehistorian* by Mary Settegast (Cambridge, MA: The Rotenberg Press).

The two most accessible books on Gnosticism are both entitled *The Gnostics*. Jacques Lacarriere's slim book emphasizes the star-knowledge of the Gnostic sects. It contains a preface by Lawrence Durrell and a letter from Henry Miller, thus linking Gnostic ideas to key figures in twentieth-century literature. Tobias Churton's informative book offers three chapters on the Egyptian Gnostics, then traces the underground survival of Gnosis and the Mysteries (i.e., para-Gnostic movements) in Catharism, the troubadours, Renaissance humanism, Hermeticism and Rosicrucianism, ahead to William Blake and John Lennon. Although it is debatable whether or not genuine Gnostic teachings and methods were preserved in these later movements, they were certainly influenced by the lost tradition of the Mysteries.

Ancient Mystery Cults (1987) by Walter Burkert is the best single book on the Pagan Mysteries. It is clear, concise, and elegantly written. Burkert shows respect for his subject and distinguishes Pagan regeneration from Christian redemption (as does historian Robert Turcan in *The Cults of the Roman Empire*). The essential pre-NHL scholarly text on the Mysteries is *The Mystery-religions* (1925) by S. Angus. The subtitle *A Study of the Religious Background of Early Christianity* tells you immediately that Angus tends to view his subject as accessory to Christianity. The book is a mine of ancient references, but when it comes the concluding pages, such as chapter 7, "The Victory of Christianity," Angus argues that Christian religion is superior because it provides "a satisfying message" for the problem of suffering, which, he believes, the Mysteries did not. Angus does not delve into Gnosticism as such, and only connects Gnosis and the Mysteries in one paragraph of the book. All in all, Angus is rather schizoid in his treatment of the Mysteries. While he asserts that the figure of Jesus was modeled directly on the Pagan initiate and healer, Aesculapius, he accepts cross theology as a *personal* and *historical* message of salvation that appealed to the masses, was superior to the Mysteries, and rightfully superceded them.

For supplementary reading on the Mysteries, *Eleusis* by Karl Kerenyi and *Eleusis and the Eleusinian Mysteries* by George E. Mylonas are indispensable. *Hellenistic Religions* by Luther H. Martin presents a fair overview, but inferior to Burkert. Beware of books such as *The Mystery Teachings in World Religions* by Florence Tanner, and *The Gnosis*, an occult classic by William Kingsland. They belong to the genre of mystical speculation that goes back to Clement of Alexandria. Such books spread a smokescreen around the Mysteries. The God-self equation proposed by Clement finds its culmination in the "New Mysteries" of Jean Houston, author of *Godseed: The Journey of Christ*, a book that presents a psychodramatic technique for reaching the Divine Within. This exercise goes as far away from Gaian biomysticism as you can go without hitching a ride on the space shuttle.

3. THE DEAD SEA SCROLLS

Readers may observe that my book is the only one so far that links the Nag Hammadi Codices to the Dead Sea Scrolls, showing cross-references between these materials that no scholar (to my knowledge) has noted or investigated: for instance, the naming of the Children of Seth on top of the "hit list" in the War Scroll, and the location of the Archontic counterintelligence camp in the backyard of the Zaddikim. An early work by Millar Burrows, *The Dead Sea Scrolls* (1955), contains a chapter entitled "Beliefs" where the author compares Gnostic "salvation by knowledge" with the views of the Qumran sect. This rare instance of cross-textual study is instructive, but it merely grazes the contrast between *tzaddik*, the supermundane and inhumane standard of perfection of the Qumranic covenant, and *telos*, the Gnostic ideal of human potential realized in the Mysteries.

The most-cited firsthand account of the emergence of the redeemer complex in ancient Palestine is *The Jewish Wars* by Josephus. There are various editions, including the Loeb Classical Library. *The Dogma of Christ* by Erich Fromm gives a trenchant analysis of the social unrest of the Herodian period, with Freudian psychological commentary. On the scrolls and their history, there are many good books, including *The Hidden Scrolls* by Neil Asher Silberman, *The Dead Sea Scrolls* by John Allegro, *Deciphering the Dead Sea Scrolls* by Jonathan Campbell, and *The*

Mystery and Meaning of the Dead Sea Scrolls by Herschel Shanks. The last is especially helpful for its evaluation of the texts, but Shanks (a key figure in exposing the cover-up of the scrolls) remains ambivalent about the historical figure of Jesus as reflected in the Qumranic literature. On that thorny issue, I recommend *The Passover Plot* by Hugh Schonfield, a brilliant exploration of the Jesus persona. Also, *The Dead Sea Scrolls and the Christian Myth* by John Allegro is essential to deconstructing redemptive mythology. *Apocalypticism and the Dead Sea Scrolls* by John J. Collins is difficult but indispensable for understanding the odd permutations of the Jewish messiah complex.

For translations, *The Dead Sea Scrolls: A New Translation*, by Michael Wise, Martin Abegg, Jr., and Edward Cook is outstanding. Commentaries provided throughout the book make it possible to read the DSS coherently. Another good translation is *The Dead Sea Scrolls Uncovered* by Robert Eisenman and Michael Wise.

The Dead Sea Scrolls Deception by Michael Baigent and Richard Leigh is the best popular account of the Vatican's cover-up and disinformation campaign, intended to prevent the world from seeing the true origins of Christianity. Although it verges in places on sensationalistic journalism, *Deception* is intellectually mature, factually accurate, and founded on close and thorough research. *Apocalypse* by D. H. Lawrence, which I have cited throughout this book, is a stunning indictment of the inane and inhumane beliefs encoded in Judeo-Christian redemptive theology. It stands in a class by itself, a masterpiece of Gnostic deconstruction.

4. Gnosis Seen Through Non-Gnostic Writings

For orientation of the modern revival of Gnosis and the Mysteries, I would signal the reader to three key essays: "The Historical Roots of Our Ecological Crisis" (1966) by Lynn White, Jr., "The Perceptual Implications of Gaia" (1985) by David Abram, and "The Meaning of Gaia" (1990) by David Spangler. These three short pieces profile the essential ethical and methodological issues discussed in this book. White's article opened the debate over the anthropocentric and nature-dominating values of Christianity, leading directly to the ambiguous issue of "identification" that has stalled deep ecology in an impasse. I have critiqued the solution to this impasse proposed in *Toward a Transpersonal Psychology* by Warwick Fox, but there is still a lot to be clarified before deep ecology can acquire a genuine religious dimension free of dominator ideology and single-self narcissism.

The deep prehistorical background of Gnosticism can be glimpsed in the Goddess religions recovered by Marija Gimbutas in her breakthrough writings, including *The Goddesses and Gods of Old Europe* and *The Living Goddesses*. *The Myth of the Goddess* by Anne Baring and Jules Cashford and *When God Was a Woman* by Merlin Stone are essential reading in this vein. The former contains an illuminating chapter on Sophia and the repression of the Divine Feminine in Judaism. (*The Hebrew Goddess* by Raphael Patai is the standard reference text on this subject.) Robert Graves's *The White Goddess* is, of course, the unsurpassable, mystical-poetic celebration of Goddess lore. It glimmers with many reflections of the Divine Sophia. Ralph Metzner's *The Well of Remembrance* relies on Gimbutas to present a neoshamanic path compatible in many respects with Gaian biomysticism.

Writings on ecopsychology present helpful approaches to a contemporary Gaian Gnostic worldview, particularly *The Voice of the Earth* by Theodore Roszak, and the more difficult, insider-oriented *Radical Ecopsychology* by Andy Fisher. See also the anthology, *Ecopsychology: Restoring the Earth, Healing the Mind*, edited by Roszak, and *Green Psychology* by Ralph Metzner, currently the leading advocate of Gaian biomysticism and entheogenic practices. The anthology *Dharma Gaia*, edited by Allan Hunt Badiner, presents a rare ecological perspective on Buddhism. *The Way* by Edward Goldsmith is a foundation text of ecological ethics that allows us to imagine how Europans would have regarded the environment. Likewise for *The Practice of the Wild* by Gary Snyder, who advises that acquaintance with classical Pagan learning is essential to a saner view of nature. I have relied on *Nature and Madness* by Paul Shepard in framing the Gnostic protest against patriarchal religion. No other book complements and parallels my case against Christianity more closely that Shepard's.

Theodore Roszak's *Where the Wasteland Ends* is a powerful argument for the revival of the "Old Gnosis," taking William Blake and the

Romantics for its exemplars. (The best single work on Romanticism is *Natural Supernaturalism* by M. H. Abrams.) Cultural ecologist Neil Evernden highlights the role of the Romantics as precursors of the ecological movement. In *The Natural Alien*, he emphasizes the uniqueness of humanity, not in terms of its superiority over other species, but in terms of its need to find or construct its proper niche in nature, contrasted to other species for whom nature provides a niche. This argument is compatible with Lynn Margulis's call (see below) for the human species to find "a creative fit" with the natural world, or perish.

Finally, in the genre of ecofeminist theology that approaches, or wants to approximate, a Gaian-Gnostic worldview, *Gaia and God* by Rosemary Radford Ruether shows how problematic it is to reconcile Judeo-Christian theology with Sophianic deep ecology—impossible, really. But the effort, though futile, is instructive. The best route for ecofeminism to take into Gaia theory would be via shamanism, if its true origins would be explored. Even though shamanism is the taproot of the Pagan Mysteries, I can recommend no book on shamanism that does not falsely emphasize its male monopoly. Perhaps with Barbara Tedlock's testament to Goddess wisdom, *The Woman in a Shaman's Body*, it may be possible to relocate contemporary shamanic theory and practice in a Gaian perspective.

5. Deep Ecology and Gaia Theory

Some of the above works merge into this category. The foundation text of deep ecology is *Sacred Land, Sacred Sex, Rapture of the Deep*, by Dolores LaChapelle. *Future Primitive*, LaChapelle's critical biography of D. H. Lawrence, is a rich, resonant book that convincingly presents Lawrence as the primary forerunner of the deep ecological movement (see also category 6.) *Listening to the Land*, a collection of interviews conducted by Derrick Jensen, and *A Language Older than Words* by Jensen, are also essential deep ecological texts, as are the writings of Snyder and Goldsmith, cited in the previous category.

The best single work on the development of Gaia theory is *Gaia: The Growth of an Idea* by Lawrence D. Joseph. *Lovelock & Gaia* by Jon Turney is also helpful for an overview. *Gaia's Body* by Tyler Volk is more technically oriented toward the details of biospheric science. On the cultural and scientific implications of the theory, see *Gaia: A Way of Knowing* and *Gaia 2: Emergence—The New Science of Becoming*, edited by William Irwin Thompson.

Gaia: A New Look of Life on Earth (1979) by James Lovelock needs to be read back to back with his later work, *Gaia: The Practical Science of Planetary Medicine* (1991) for a full overview of where the theory began, and where it's heading. The essential books by Lynn Margulis, written with her son Dorion Sagan, are *Microcosmos*, and *Slanted Truths*, a collection of engaging essays on biology and evolution, including "Big Trouble in Biology" (a refutation of Darwinism), and "A Pox Called Man" (Margulis's views on the role of the human species in Gaian biophysics). Metahistory.org contains extensive writing on the parallels between Sophianic myth and Gaia theory.

Although not normally included in discussions of deep ecology or Gaia theory, Wilhelm Reich (1897–1957) was the one twentieth-century scientist whose work can contribute most crucially and centrally to experiential advances in both these fields. Thinking like a Gnostic, Reich investigated "the large outlines that shaped the errors of the human animal," and analyzed enslavement to ideological beliefs. Denial and suppression of the life force was his greatest concern, expressed in *The Murder of Christ*. *The Mass Psychology of Fascism* is a brilliant analysis of the "mystico-military" dementia of the Zaddikite sect, and a bold condemnation of Christian doctrines that elevate spirit over nature. In his later works, *Ether, God and Devil*, and *Cosmic Superimposition*, which he discussed with Albert Einstein, Reich proposed Gnostic criteria for science. He asserted that "sensation is the greatest mystery of natural science," and warned that the scientist "errs in proportion to the neglect of his own system of sensory perception and awareness." Reich's notion that genuine knowledge of nature must be grounded in sensory contact with nature is purely telestic, recalling the cognitive revelation at Eleusis.

Finally, I suggest that Goethean techniques of observation come close to Gnostic method, and may in some respects reproduce it. *Goethe on Science* by Jeremy Naydler presents an inventory of helpful citations. *Goethe the Scientist* by Rudolf Steiner is also useful. *The Wholeness of*

Nature by Henri Bortoft is a brilliant and thorough treatment of Goethe's theory of intensive perception. Quite simply, this theory asserts that the impressions of the world given to us by the senses are incomplete unless we look more carefully and intensively into what the senses actually present to us. Thus, nature has far more to reveal to us through our senses than we normally assume. Goethe insisted that intensive perception can go so deep into the dynamics of natural phenomena that it excels any theorization we might make apart from the phenomena. Bortoft's book is a primer of Gnostic natural science.

6. Contemporary Literature and Culture

Recent editions of the NHLE contain an afterword by Richard Smith describing the how Gnostic ideas have come to permeate many aspects of Western culture and literature. Smith cites Blake, Melville, Hesse, Doris Lessing, Lawrence Durrell, and the Beat Generation as literary heirs to Gnosticism. The list could easily be expanded three-fold, especially if we include science fiction writers such as Philip K. Dick and Roger Zelazny. In psychology, Smith cites C. G. Jung, the primary Gnostic revivalist, and in philosophy, Martin Heidegger, who is highly regarded by Dolores LaChapelle. Oddly, he does not cite D. H. Lawrence. Readers who want to get the feel of genuine Gnostic sensibility can look into Lawrence's last poems, which include many beautiful evocations of nature and animal life. In his polemic poems, Lawrence ruthlessly attacks single-self identity and narcissistic self-concern. His two-line "Retort to Jesus" says "And whoever forces himself to love anybody / begets a murderer in his own body." Which is pretty much what I tried to say in chapter 19.

Smith also discusses American cultural maven Harold Bloom, who wrote both fiction and nonfiction works of Gnostic derivation. In *Omens of Millennium* (1996), Bloom uncritically adopted the God-self equation, defining Gnosis as "direct acquaintance of God within the self," but in other respects he pleaded rather well for Gnostic values. Surprise, surprise, the book includes a brief, sober, nondiscounting passage on shamanism and entheogenic practices. It is difficult to say if Bloom's rather narcissistic style of armchair illuminism has had, or will have, any significant impact in religious or academic circles. I doubt it.

Films that come to mind in this category are *The Man Who Fell to Earth* by Nicholas Roeg (cited by Richard Smith), and the *Matrix* trilogy (reviewed on metahistory.org). In Arthur C. Clarke's *2001: A Space Odyssey*, the supercomputer who hijacks the mission is named HAL, Coptic for "simulation," "artificial intelligence." Clarke's book, *Childhood's End*, is one of many that explores the Gnostic theme of takeover by the Archons. Other sci-fi classics such as *Invasion of the Body Snatchers* also play on the threat of Archontic substitution. On Gnostic elements in the classic horror film, *Children of the Damned*, see www.Metahistory.org/damned.php.

7. Sophianic Cosmology, Including the ET/UFO Problem

In continuation of the preceding category, the science fiction writings of Philip K. Dick present a reworking of certain aspects of Sophianic cosmology. Dick's grasp of Gnostic–Mystery School instruction was selective, exhibiting some serious blindspots, but profound on those aspects that he did understand. His definition of Gnosis as "disinhibiting instructions" is superb, and his metaphor of the two-source hologram, likewise. Much of the pathos of his work lies in his staunch human resistance to HAL, Archontic simulation. Dick foresaw a world whose inhabitants would be unable to detect simulations, unable to tell a real cat from an electronic duplicate, or pearl from plastic. Much of what appears as futuristic in his novels has now become commonplace.

Although deeply concerned with Archontic substitution, or countermimicry, Philip K. Dick did not portray the Archons themselves. Rather, his best works depict people (usually children) who are living instruments of Sophia. His *Valis* trilogy merges Nag Hammadi material with concepts drawn from the Dead Sea Scrolls, producing a weird mix of Gnostic and Qumranic elements. In *The Divine Invasion*, second in the trilogy, two children are the incarnations of divine wisdom whose play is the universe. In *The Reincarnation of Timothy Archer*, third in the trilogy,

Dick adopts the heretical thesis of John Allegro that the sacrament of the Qumranic cult was *Amanita muscaria*, a psychoactive mushroom traditionally used by shamans. Dick's unpublished masterpiece, called "The Exegesis," contains long passages on Gnostic philosophy, Sophia, and the Demiurge. *Valis* is required reading for anyone interested in how Gnostic ideas can fertilize the literary imagination. See philipkdick.com.

Verging on science fiction, the multivolume writings of Zecharia Sitchin on the Annunaki scenario in Sumerian mythology nevertheless pass for serious work in the minds of many people. It is difficult to fault Sitchin on his scholarship—he reads ancient Hebrew, cuneiform, and half a dozen other ancient languages—but it is easy to see where he fabulates, or makes unfounded inferences. His "Earth Chronicles" take the Sumerian tablets on their word and accepts that the Annunaki-Archons are really our cosmic overlords. In *The Cosmic Code* (book 6), he asserts that the ancients had knowledge of molecular chemistry and the genetic code because the Annunaki brought it to them, not because they could have acquired it through faculties inherent to human potential (as I argue). Sitchin is smart enough, and quite entertaining to read. He remains atop the rapidly growing heap of books on the Annunaki-Archon scenario, not to mention a toxic spill of uneducated chatter on the Net. Since January, 2005, when my article "The Gnostic Theory of Alien Intrusion" appeared on metahistory.org, my ET/Archon theory seems to have entered the discourse. Nevertheless, there is still an almost total absence of metacritical analysis of the ET/UFO phenomena. So far, the Gnostic view that the Archons are cosmic pretenders, dupes trying to make us into their dupes, remains largely unknown.

Apart from myself, only two cultic writers, Nigel Kerner (*The Song of the Greys*) and William Henry (*Oracle of the Illuminati*), have directly equated the Archons with the Annunaki. *Flying Serpents and Dragons* by R. A. Boulay (Escondido, CA: The Book Tree) presents carefully researched material on ancient religion that suggests how the "reptilian agenda" of the Annunaki might have been insinuated into the Jehovistic cults of Palestine. Boulay is a notch or two above Sitchin. The best critique of the ET/UFO phenomena comes from Jacques Vallee in *Messengers of Deception* and his trilogy, *Dimensions, Confrontations, Revelations*. Vallee's analysis of the ET/UFO phenomenon as "a spiritual control system" is highly compatible with Gnostic teachings. *UFOs: Operation Trojan Horse* by John Keel is also excellent, lucid, and sobering. *Humanity's Extraterrestrial Origins* by A. D. Horn and *The Genius of the Few* by Christian O'Brien present convincing profiles of Jehovah as a vicious, tyrannical, reptilian Archon, the ultimate bad parent. See also the entry of "Biblical UFOlogy" in the Lexicon for metahistory.org.

Sophianic cosmology requires not only an imaginative approach to the Archons, those denizens of the planetary system exclusive of the Earth, but also a direct encounter with the wonders of the natural world. It is, one could say, a homegrown cosmology. In nonfiction, the best approaches to Sophianic cosmology can be found in recent writings on emergence (*Biology Revisioned* by Willis Harman and Elisabet Sahtouris), fractals (*Fractals: The Patterns of Chaos* by John Briggs, and *Turbulent Mirror* by John Briggs and F. David Peat), and plasma cosmology (*The Big Bang Never Happened* by Eric J. Lerner). All this is cutting-edge stuff, radical and controversial, but largely theoretical.

For a practical, firsthand approach to Sophianic cosmology, there is no better guide (next to Reich) than Goethe. As just noted, Goethean morphology, including the colloidal theory of light, is the scientific approach most compatible with the method of the Mysteries. Intensive observation, by which we enter more deeply into the self-evident contents of sense perception, is the best modern approach to initiatory knowledge of Gaia-Sophia.

8. Entheogenic Theory of Religion

Sacred Mushrooms of Vision by Ralph Metzner is the best single work on current entheogenic practice. Metzner's long essay, "Visionary Mushrooms of the Americas," covers the entheogenic movement from its origins with Huxley and Wasson down to Terence McKenna. *The Sacred Mushroom Seeker*, edited by Thomas J. Riedlinger, also presents an overview and evaluation of the movement that was born when R. Gordon Wasson met the mushroom shaman Maria Sabina (1894–1985) in Mexico in 1955. Wasson's book, *Soma: Divine Mushroom of Immortality*, is a literary treasure that can stand shoulder to shoulder with groundbreaking works such as *The Golden Bough* and *Black Athena*. *Persephone's Quest*, cowritten by Wasson with G. S. Kramrisch and Carl Ruck, is the definitive statement of the entheogenic theory, with extensive reference to Eleusis.

There are hundreds of text-heavy sites and heady forums dedicated to entheogenics on the Internet, but, unfortunately, they are all oriented toward recreational use of drugs and sacred plants, rather than sacramental use. The most sophisticated psychedelic site is deoxy.org. For research and guidelines on entheogenic practice, I recommend The Council for Spiritual Practices at csp.org.

9. Asian Mysticism (Tantra, Mahayana, Dzogchen)

Expositions of Asian mysticism and emanation theory that are helpful to understanding Gnosticism begin with the works of Sir John Woodroffe, all published by Ganesh & Co, Madras. *The Serpent Power, Shakti and Shakta*, and *The Garland of Letters* are indispensable. Here and there Woodroffe freely develops Gnostic-Tantric parallels. His work on Kundalini, the Serpent Power, is essential to understanding, and undergoing, the psychosomatic illuminism of the Pagan Mysteries. Woodroffe cites Tantric texts that describe in explicit language the epiphany of the Organic Light.

Among Buddhist scholars, John Myrdhin Reynolds (*The Golden Letters, Self-Liberation through Seeing with Naked Awareness*) makes the most pertinent Gnostic-Buddhist parallels. The writings of Herbert V. Guenther are also instructive, especially *The Life and Teachings of Naropa*, *Yuganaddha* (Vanarasi: Chowkhamba Sanskrit Series), and *Kindly Bent to Ease Us*, his trilogy of writings on Long Chen Pa, the preeminent Nyingma master. *Foundations of Tibetan Mysticism* (1960) by Lama Govinda is still the single most accessible text on Tibetan Buddhism. *The Science of Yoga* by I. K. Taimni (Wheaton, IL: Quest Books, The Theosophical Publishing House), a commentary on the *Yoga Sutras* of Patañjali, reads like a Nag Hammadi tractate would today, if the Coptic material had come down to us intact and uncorrupted. In *While the Gods Play* and *Shiva and Dionysos*, comparative mythologist Alain Daniélou relates Gnosis to the ancient shamanic methodologies of southern Asia.

Finally, I might point the reader to my other books as they relate to the subject matter and argument of this one. *The Seeker's Handbook* (Harmony/Random House, 1991) has a brief essay on Gnosticism and many references to Gnostic and Sophianic themes. *Twins and the Double* (London: Thames & Hudson, 1993) proposes that ancient shamanic techniques gave access to molecular and genetic processes, explains the scapegoating mechanism, and considers some occult phenomena that would have been routinely explored and studied in the Mysteries. *The Hero* (London: Thames & Hudson, 1995) describes the intimate connection between shamanism and Goddess religion, a connection in herent to the long prehistorical background of Gnosis and the Mysteries. This book also treats the Cult of Amor, a cultural phenomenon central to the medieval resurgence of the Pagan sense of life.

Finally, *Quest for the Zodiac* (Starhenge Books, 1999) explains the important distinction between the stellar or real-sky zodiac of thirteen constellations and the tropical zodiac of twelve signs. It also proposes a theory of phylogenetic transfer of the knowledge and skills acquired in peak experience. I suggest that this theory can point the way to the telestic method for high-end enhancement of human potential, formerly applied in the Mysteries.

JLL May 2006 Flanders

INDEX